T0385560

THE I TATTI
RENAISSANCE LIBRARY

James Hankins, General Editor

FILELFO

ON EXILE

ITRL 55

FRANCESCO FILELFO
♦ ♦ ♦
ON EXILE

EDITED BY

JEROEN DE KEYSER

TRANSLATED BY

W. SCOTT BLANCHARD

THE I TATTI RENAISSANCE LIBRARY
HARVARD UNIVERSITY PRESS
CAMBRIDGE, MASSACHUSETTS
LONDON, ENGLAND
2013

Series design by Dean Bornstein

Library of Congress Cataloging-in-Publication Data

Filelfo, Francesco, 1398–1481.
On exile / Francesco Filelfo ; edited by Jeroen De Keyser ;
translated by W. Scott Blanchard.
pages.   cm. — (The I Tatti Renaissance library ; 55)
English and Latin on facing pages.
Includes bibliographical references and index.
ISBN 978-0-674-06636-6 (alk. paper)
I. De Keyser, Jeroen, 1969–.   II. Blanchard, W. Scott, 1955–
III. Filelfo, Francesco, 1398–1481. Commentationes Florentinae de exilio.
Latin. 2013.   IV. Filelfo, Francesco, 1398–1481. Commentationes
Florentinae de exilio. English. 2013.   V. Title. VI. Series:
I Tatti Renaissance library ; 55.
PA8520.F5C6613 2013
878'.04 — dc23   2012035551

Contents

꿏꿏꿏

Introduction

꧁꧂

No text better illustrates the relationship of the Italian humanists to the literary and philosophical heritage of the classical world than Francesco Filelfo's *Commentationes Florentinae de exilio*. The work is, along with Leonardo Bruni's *Dialogi*, among the earliest examples of a humanist dialogue, and among its many purposes is to imitate the classical *consolatio*, a literary composition which promoted the therapeutic use of philosophical discussion to assuage the pain of experiences such as death or exile. Exile was a common misfortune for members of the political classes in Italian city-states of the Renaissance, and Filelfo's dialogue provides the richest source we have for contemporary reflection on that experience. Filelfo's dialogue is remarkable too for the knowledge it shows of ancient Greek literature, extraordinary for that period. But for modern readers perhaps its most interesting aspects lie in the historical circumstances that surrounded its creation. For the work's context derives from a major shift in Florentine political life that took place when Cosimo de' Medici and his followers seized virtual control of the government from the hands of its more traditional ruling class, the aristocrats or oligarchs whose regimes had dominated Florence for two centuries.

Filelfo's life (1398–1481) spanned a greater period of time than that of any other fifteenth-century Italian humanist, and he never spent much of his extremely productive career far from the elites who underwrote the cultural program of the Italian Renaissance.[1] His formative years were spent in Padua training under the famous humanist educator Gasparino Barzizza, and early in life he had the rare opportunity to spend about six years in Constantinople, where he achieved a high degree of proficiency in ancient Greek. On his return to Venice in 1427, bearing numerous Greek

manuscripts, his would become a career on the fast track. After spending a short period of time teaching in Bologna, he settled in Florence, where for the next five years he would become enmeshed in the complex fabric of Florentine social and political life. Initially sponsored as a teacher at the Florentine Studio by the oligarchs Palla Strozzi, Cosimo de' Medici, and others, his prickly personality soon provoked conflicts with other humanists supported by Cosimo, especially Niccolò Niccoli, Carlo Marsuppini, and Poggio Bracciolini. Filelfo alienated his fellow humanists by flaunting his capacities as a Hellenist and engaging in the nasty one-upmanship that was an all-too-familiar feature of early Italian humanism. From 1429 onward he began producing vitriolic satires, many of which no doubt found their way into the hands of his enemies, and eventually he was slashed in the face by a Medici partisan (apparently to disfigure and shame him rather than to kill him).[2] By October of 1433, when Cosimo de' Medici was exiled to Padua, Filelfo appeared secure, having sided with Cosimo's enemies in the established oligarchic party, Palla Strozzi, Rinaldo degli Albizzi, and Ridolfo Peruzzi. But on Cosimo's recall by the Florentine magistracy just eleven months later in September of 1434, a regime change took place, and Filelfo found himself, along with dozens of members of the Florentine *ottimati*, or oligarchs, exiled from the city.[3] After a brief teaching stint in Siena, he spent most of his later career based in Milanese territory, enjoying the patronage of the Visconti and later the Sforza dukes. Occasionally, he also attempted to establish himself in other Italian cities under more favorable conditions and under what he hoped would be more beneficent patrons.

In the last year of his life, Filelfo returned to Florence to take up a position at the court of Lorenzo il Magnifico, an ironic turn of affairs, given that the humanist had spent so much of his early career slandering Lorenzo's ancestors. But he died within a month of his arrival there; and it is perhaps because most of his career

was spent in the relatively neglected world of Milanese humanism that his modern fame as a scholar and humanist has only recently begun to equal his high fame among his contemporaries. In addition to a massive *epistolarium*, or letter collection in forty-eight books, that he carefully collected over his long career, Filelfo left behind many Latin translations of ancient Greek literature (especially Xenophon and Plutarch); miscellaneous philosophical dialogues such as the *Convivia Mediolanensia* and these *Commentationes* (and their later adaptation, the treatise *De morali disciplina*); an epic poem dedicated to Francesco Sforza, the *Sphortias*; and a host of other poetic compositions (odes, satires, epigrams) in Latin and even in Greek. His conception of himself was constantly being reshaped, but his most consistent self-image was as a poet with no small amount of Plato's *furor poeticus* in him. But in the three books of the *Commentationes* it is safe to say that Filelfo saw himself in the guise of a philosopher — or at least in the guise of a disciple of the Florentine humanist Leonardo Bruni, whose fame as a translator of Aristotle and as the most accomplished of the Italian humanists was second to none. Bruni remained friends with Filelfo even after the latter's exile, and he presides over the third book of these dialogues as a deeply respected figure.[4]

It has been suggested, quite correctly, that Filelfo's principal models in this dialogue were the Ciceronian dialogues known as the *Tusculan Disputations* and *On Duties* (*De officiis*), but in writing a work of consolation Filelfo may also have been influenced by Seneca's consolatory works.[5] Like the works of Cicero and Seneca, Filelfo's dialogue meanders broadly but retains throughout a philosophical flavor: we move from discussions of the contemporary political scene in Florence, to anecdotes containing witty observations about ancient famous men, to literary passages translated from ancient Greek, or reported speeches in *oratio recta* (such as Rinaldo degli Albizzi's exchange with Pope Eugenius IV, which is narrated by Ridolfo Peruzzi in Book 2). There are even some

rather technical philosophical discussions that occasionally become somewhat abstruse, such as the discussion of universal propositions, or category statements, at the beginning of Book 3, or the analysis of the Aristotelian *summum bonum*, or ultimate good, in Book 2, which relies heavily on the second of two commentaries on Aristotle's *Nicomachean Ethics* composed by the medieval scholastic philosopher Albertus Magnus. There are also brief comic interludes, the purposes of which are always to poke fun at his rival humanist Poggio Bracciolini, who supported Cosimo; in other works of pure invective, he and Filelfo exchanged insults in an even more unrestrained manner. The work as a whole is organized topically according to the titles of the three books — "On the Disadvantages of Exile," "On Infamy," and "On Poverty" — and we know from the marginal annotations in one manuscript that Filelfo intended the work to grow to ten books. It is unclear why the remaining books were left unwritten. The existing three books were clearly composed in the years when the hopes of Filelfo's expatriate patrons for a quick return and reestablishment of themselves in Florence were unlikely to be realized. But it may be that at some point Filelfo simply had to abandon his old Florentine patrons and turn his attention to the writing of panegyric works for his new Milanese ones. Then again, quite a few of Filelfo's other major writings fell short of their projected length.

Filelfo's dialogue is set in Florence, prior to the actual departure of the aristocrats Palla Strozzi and Rinaldo degli Albizzi, who are participants in the dialogue, but after the sentences of exile had been passed (Palla's exile was in fact ordered a few months after Rinaldo's). But Filelfo clearly wrote the dialogue after 1440, when all hope of a rapprochement between the party in exile and Cosimo's regime had failed. For in July of that year came the defeat at Anghiari by Florentine forces of a coalition made up of Milanese troops and Florentine exiles. An intermediate stage in the long

run-up to this defeat can be glimpsed in an earlier work by Filelfo, composed in 1437 and entitled the *Oration to the exiles against Cosimo de' Medici*.[6] In this unedited work, Filelfo lionized Filippo Maria Visconti, the duke of Milan, whom he believed could restore oligarchic control in Florence, and vilified Cosimo de' Medici. He accused Cosimo of murder, adultery, embezzlement of papal funds, and many other crimes. He focused in particular on slandering Cosimo's supposedly lowborn ancestry, a tactic that was frequently at the heart of invective writing at that time, inasmuch as family honor in the Renaissance, as in most cultures where shame is a motivating emotion, figured so greatly in the psychological economy of the period. In the later *Commentationes* the criticism is somewhat less libelous, though Cosimo still comes in for derisive treatment for his family's origins in the rural region of the Mugello north of Florence. In the later work, Filelfo contrasts the characters of Palla Strozzi and Cosimo, rather than of Cosimo and Filippo Visconti, and his reflections on their character traits are buttressed by philosophical discussion of relevant concepts such as virtue, pleasure, wealth, and civic responsibility. In some ways, the earlier *Oratio* is a propagandistic warm-up exercise for the later work; it is less concerned with preserving reputations than with garnering support for a political cause.[7]

Modern readers may be surprised to discover how closely the humanistic tradition adheres to teachings that we associate with psychotherapy, in particular the efficacy of talk or discussion in providing a remedy for psychological pain.[8] But here the humanists were simply following ancient Stoic tradition, and Filelfo's use of key texts from this tradition as well as from the Cynic tradition — which had laid the groundwork for Stoicism's more systematic ethical teachings — demonstrates the remarkable depth of his erudition. The central teachings of this tradition can be summarized as follows: nature has provided all that is necessary for our

happiness; culture, in the form of conventional beliefs, has distorted our relationship with nature and needs to be "unlearned"; reason, or "right reason" (*ratio recta*) is the main instrument for examining the nature of our beliefs, and it *can* succeed in controlling the passions that are inevitably stirred up by our relations with other human beings and by corrupt cultural practices; one's physical condition and one's geographical location are irrelevant to happiness, so the practicing Stoic/Cynic should consider himself or herself a "citizen of the world," or *kosmopolites*.[9] Since the overarching purpose of Filelfo's dialogue is to examine the problem of exile, it is this last teaching that is the most important, though the others certainly figure to some extent in Filelfo's arguments. Filelfo was the first humanist to use an apocryphal letter collection, the so-called *Epistolographi Graeci*, written in Greek during the Hellenistic period. These letters purported to have been written by such figures as the Cynic philosophers Diogenes and Crates, Hippocrates, Demosthenes, the Roman hero Brutus, and the Greek holy man Apollonius of Tyana. They contain interesting, witty anecdotes that epitomize much of the countercultural wisdom that we associate with the Cynic tradition, and they have a long and interesting history themselves as a philological battleground culminating in Swift's *Battle of the Books*. The next generation of humanists after Filelfo, led by the Florentine scholar Angelo Poliziano, already began to question their authenticity, but Filelfo made free use of them and never explicitly questioned their authority.

After opening his work with a flattering exordium to his Milanese patron Vitaliano Borromeo, scion of a distinguished Milanese family, in the first book of the *Commentationes* Filelfo ranges widely over numerous literary works, both classical and Christian, in order to disprove the position of Polynices in Euripides' play *The Phoenician Women*, where the latter states that exile is indeed an unhappy condition in which to live. Exile is characterized by many

incommoda (inconveniences), an adjectival substantive that figures
in the title of the first of the three books. Exile, Palla will argue,
is in fact a somewhat irrelevant circumstance, and his exchange
with his son Onofrio, who takes the more despairing position of
Polynices, dominates the discussions of this book. A fascinating
passage that Palla quotes — and Filelfo translates — from the Greek
orator Dio Chrysostom reveals interesting reflections on the role
of education in shaping civic behavior. It is the first instance in
Italian humanism of a humanist encounter with the Socratic and
Platonic critique of archaic Greek *paideia*, which centered on cho-
ral performances and gymnastic excellence. Palla somehow man-
ages to update its relevance for the contemporary Florentine scene.
Philosophical analysis follows, with Palla making distinctions between emotion and reason in terms that borrow from both the
Aristotelian and Stoic traditions. The central text of this book is
then quoted: the exchange between Jocasta and Polynices from
Euripides' *Phoenician Women*, where Jocasta's son makes observations on the features of exile that make it detrimental to human
happiness. In what follows, Palla and Onofrio exchange reminis-
cences from their reading of classical texts, many of which center
on the Cynic repudiation of power and wealth as desirable ends
for human beings. Most interesting is the quotation by Palla from
a letter by Brutus preserved in Cicero's *Familiar Letters*: Brutus
criticizes Cicero for allowing compromises to his freedom in exchange for political protection under Octavian. Petrarch, nearly a
century earlier, had famously criticized the Roman statesman for
just this same act of cowardice, and Filelfo's inclusion of this inci-
dent from Roman history indicates an important continuity in the
humanist tradition: its praise of intellectuals who preserve their
autonomy in their dealings with those in power. Filelfo's personal life was similarly characterized by ambivalent relationships
with patrons whom he alternately extolled and vilified; he even

spent some time in a Milanese jail in 1464 as punishment for disparaging remarks he had made about the recently deceased Pope Pius II.

The discussion skips to an analysis of pleasure and its role in human happiness. We do not know whether Filelfo may have been taking up this theme in part to challenge the views of the humanist Lorenzo Valla. We do know that Filelfo exchanged at least one letter with Valla and that he addressed to him an important satire critical of Valla's philosophical boldness, in particular the latter's *De voluptate* (*On Pleasure*), composed in the 1430s. The discussion also offers, naturally, a prime opportunity to satirize Poggio, who is represented as endorsing pleasure, in the form of drunkenness and gluttony, as a desirable end. The first book's closing pages focus on a conception the humanists could have found in both classical and Christian sources: the notion of the entire world as a homeland, or, what is much the same, the notion of worldly life as a state of exile from a homeland that is to be found only in a realm beyond earthly experience. Such a conception is difficult for the young Onofrio to accept, and it must in turn have been a difficult one for most of his contemporaries to embrace, rooted as they were in the urban world of Italian cities and communes with their very local networks of patronage and influence. The closing passages, in part borrowed from the Greek skeptic Sextus Empiricus, take a radical position on the deleterious influence that custom has on human nature, as Palla reminds Onofrio that the most reviled man of all was Christ himself during his earthly incarnation.[10] If his son follows the path of the sages of antiquity, he should never feel pain at the lack of a homeland or fear the world's opinion of him, even though he has lost social status and lives with a diminished reputation.

While the dialogue's first book had centered on the figures of Palla Strozzi and his son Onofrio, it is the figure of Rinaldo degli Albizzi who dominates the discussion in Book Two. The

Florentine authorities in 1434 had not only passed a sentence of exile upon Rinaldo but had also branded him with the status of an *infamato*, a disgraced or infamous man.[11] In a culture where family honor still carried a great deal of psychological power to harm, such a condition needed special therapeutic or consolatory treatment of its own. Opening with a witty Plutarchan anecdote — how the sculptor Phidias cleverly preserved his own name and fame despite his culture's disapproval of egoistic or self-regarding acts — Filelfo has his interlocutors take positions on the topic of good and bad reputations and the imperfect human judgments that shape those determinations. As the dialogue opens, Rinaldo shares his concerns over the smearing of his reputation by the citizens of Florence; in his opinion, the actions he took in the recent crisis of the regime's overthrow by Cosimo were entirely honorable, and he believes he is the victim of the duplicity of others, especially Pope Eugenius IV and the Milanese legate to the papal court, Gerardo Landriani. As one of the most powerful oligarchic leaders of the previous regime, Rinaldo had always remained loyal to the cause of the Guelf party and its traditional alignment with the papacy. He will argue in the following pages that it was largely the machinations of Eugenius that turned the papacy against the aristocrats of Florence and led it to support Cosimo and his more "popular" faction drawn from the Florentine citizenry. The rumors that Rinaldo and his colleagues had secretly tried to undermine the Medici party by seeking an alliance with Filippo Maria Visconti, it is claimed, were the motivating force compelling Eugenius to shift his allegiance. Since in recent history no power had posed more of a threat to Florence than Milan, Eugenius' support of Rinaldo became untenable, requiring him to shift his allegiance to Cosimo's faction.

The historical reality that complicates this depiction of the political situation in 1434 was that by mid-1440, just before Filelfo began composing the *Commentationes*, the aristocratic exiles had in

fact joined together with the Visconti in an attempt to seize control of Florence, but their hopes were dashed by the major Florentine victory at Anghiari. As Filelfo rewrites (and reimagines) the events that lay behind the political situation in November of 1434, when a large number of the oligarchs were awaiting their imminent expulsion from Florence as exiles, Rinaldo is presented as arguing that the rumors of the oligarchs' support of a Milanese intervention were just that — wild rumors spread about by Medici propaganda to incite popular resentment against the Florentine aristocracy. The situation years later as Filelfo wrote the *Commentationes* further complicates the presentation of Visconti's relationship to the oligarchs, given that Filelfo was writing in the early 1440s as a client and court poet of Filippo Maria Visconti.

One of the set pieces of oratory that occurs in the *Commentationes* is the rehearsal of Rinaldo's impassioned speech before Eugenius on the eve of the Medici coup; here Filelfo has it spoken by Rinaldo's friend Ridolfo Peruzzi in direct speech because Rinaldo's emotional state makes him reluctant to deliver it all over again. We are told — wrongly — that the speech succeeded in persuading Eugenius of the folly of his choice to side with Cosimo's regime, but of course we must realize that Filelfo's purpose here was in large measure to create as much anti-Medicean sentiment as he could, even after 1440.[12] The speech begins with Rinaldo acknowledging that the imminent overthrow of the oligarchic government has supplied them with no alternative other than to appeal to Eugenius for his support in preventing the Florentine "republic" from falling into the anarchic control of the Medici family and its "popular" party. It is, therefore, not just the traditional ruling elite that is threatened by the political events taking place, but the Florentine state as a whole. In attempting to dispel the rumors circulating about Milanese involvement, Rinaldo suggests that the only basis for these rumors must lie in the underhanded designs of the papal legate in Milan — Landriani — rather than in any plans laid

by Rinaldo and his associates. His arguments for his own integrity during the political events of 1434 appeal to an older, more feudal conception of the "natural" role that elites take upon themselves of guiding the state and serving as its protectors. As such, Filelfo's work can in this instance be conceived of as contributing to an important humanistic topic of debate in the Quattrocento, the debate on true nobility: was "nobility" a characteristic that was inherited, or could it be earned by meritorious acts that displayed noble values?[13] Filelfo, apparently, adhered to the older conception of nobility, but then again he did so as an individual who derived his salary and hire from aristocratic patrons whom he had no trouble telling what they wished to hear. Rinaldo closes this portion of his speech with the somewhat specious conclusion that, given the aristocratic values that require Guelf oligarchs to be the mainstays of "public honor," it is preposterous to think that they could have schemed in a dishonorable way with a ruler from Milan, the traditional enemy of Florence. Furthermore, Filelfo probably intended to classicize the Florentine political situation by portraying it as a contrast between the *optimates* and the *populus*, even though such a bifurcation of social classes did not really reflect Florentine political realities. In Florence during that period there were in fact a large number of aristocratic supporters of the Medici party, while many mercantile families whose wealth could often be much greater than that of the patrician oligarchs in a legal sense were *popolani*, or members of the old popular class.

A digression ensues that attacks Cosimo as a representative of all that the nobles and the Florentine people are not: he is a deceiver, a rapacious man who has been at the center of disastrous policies that have scandalized Europe. Specifically, Rinaldo accuses Cosimo of poisoning John XXIII and of being involved, with his father Giovanni, in masterminding a failed plot to assassinate King Ladislas of Naples. In the latter case, Rinaldo has had personal experience of the plotting of Medici family members, for

he was himself approached by the father of the plot's perpetrator as someone who might be able to protect the man's son in the aftermath of the planned crime. Rinaldo's integrity as an aristocrat bound by codes of honor necessitated his repudiation of the scheme, even though it might have been in the best interests of the Florentine state. Cosimo, his father, and his brother Lorenzo were deeply disappointed at the collapse of the plot, Filelfo claims, considering it a blow to the Florentine state's overall security; Rinaldo's steadfast commitment to the politics of virtue stands in sharp contrast to Medici methods of statecraft, reminiscent of tyranny.

After this digression, Rinaldo's speech returns to the issue of the Milanese role in the events of 1434. He rehearses the events that culminated in the Battle of Imola earlier in the year, a conflict in which Pope Eugenius' forces had defeated a Florentine and Venetian force; this account is meant to demonstrate that it is Eugenius, not the Florentine oligarchs, who cannot be trusted. Rinaldo's exposure and criticism of the fickle and self-serving politics of the pope demonstrate the inconsistency of the latter's support for Guelf states; furthermore, the pope has gladly accepted Florence as a temporary refuge for his papal court during a time when the city of Rome had become unsafe for him, but he has not been consistent in remaining a strong ally of the Tuscan city. Ironically, Rinaldo at one point turns the topic of infamy against Eugenius: he insists, disingenuously, that he does not believe the rumors that have been spread about the pope, whom the people of Florence, provoked by Medici rumormongering, are now vilifying. Rinaldo's speech ends with an appeal to Eugenius to intervene on behalf of the aristocrats. (In the fictional framing of the dialogue, they are currently under house arrest and anticipating imminent exile, so Eugenius can still presumably help their cause.) The young Onofrio enters the discussion, complaining that he is still unconvinced that possessing an infamous reputation should be of little concern to a wise man. The fundamental unfairness of the judgment passed

on the aristocrats is all the more painful when it is realized that the authority of republican *ottimati* was legitimated by its claims always to be placing "public honor" above private advantage.

Onofrio's father, Palla Strozzi, enters the discussion with a philosophical intervention meant to provide a measure of consolation for the group as they lament their currently desperate state. In the Socratic manner he initiates a series of questions designed to provide a deeper understanding of the nature of praise (or dispraise) by understanding it as an outcome of virtuous behavior. The practical issue at hand—how to cope with a distorted and defamed public image—will eventually lead him to analyze the nature of the good and of human happiness. His main argument is that human actions must be undertaken with no concern at all for the responses of others to them—one should pursue right action or virtuous action for its own sake, not out of concern for any other end or reward. The instrumental form of reasoning used by the Medici to advance their self-interested political agenda stands in sharp contrast to the "virtue ethics" here endorsed by Palla. His use of a broad range of philosophical and religious reference, comparing Stoic, Aristotelian, and Christian teachings on the subject of the virtues, allows him to arrive at a conception of human happiness grounded in virtue that completely negates the role that public perception might have in shaping human behavior: human virtue should never seek fame or a good reputation as a "mistress." Even though allegations of infamy may come from their fellow citizens, the aristocrats whom Palla is instructing must avoid concerning themselves with how they appear to others, but instead must simply carry on behaving as virtuously as possible.

The topic of the third book of the *Commentationes* is an especially relevant one that helps to complicate and deepen our understanding of the civic dimensions of Renaissance humanism. As heirs in the recent past to a powerful development in Christian theology—the Franciscan movement and its transformation of

the monastic ideal of voluntary poverty — Renaissance humanists struggled to arrive at an ethical orientation toward wealth that would reconcile Christian ideals of living one's life in conformity with Christ (*imitatio Christi*) with the social realities of living in urban communities. In such communities the accumulation of wealth was often rapid, and the patronage of social elites depended upon the large fortunes, often from banking, of families like the Medici and the Strozzi. It was these large fortunes that enabled a remarkable improvement in the quality of life for members of the elite and contributed to the enormous cultural achievements of the fifteenth and sixteenth centuries. In this book the dominant figure is Leonardo Bruni, a native of nearby Arezzo and a humanist who served a lengthy term as Florence's chancellor — functioning in a manner similar to a secretary of state for foreign affairs — and who understood as well as any Florentine citizen the importance of wealth in achieving practical security as well as in enabling an energetic pursuit of cultural progress. The immediate context of the topic of poverty is of course the changed status of the exiles themselves, who have been stripped of much of their wealth and isolated from the city in which their wealth had been created. Given both the immediate and the larger historical context of this analysis of the role that economic interests play in human societies, the third book can be seen as among the more important humanistic discussions of wealth, to be set alongside Poggio Bracciolini's *De avaritia* and Bruni's commentary on the pseudo-Aristotelian *Economics*.[14] But here the accent is on the ethical dimensions of poverty and wealth rather than, strictly speaking, their civic dimensions. It is clear at least from Filelfo's handling of the topic that his culture retained a somewhat ambivalent orientation toward wealth in all of its forms, for the discussion ultimately conveys mixed messages.

The third book opens with an anecdote about the ancient king Croesus that contrasts his great wealth with individuals who were

known for their exemplary poverty. Filelfo must then immediately perform an about-face, inasmuch as the dedicatee of his work, Vitaliano Borromeo, was a wealthy financier of Florentine extraction living among the elites of Milan during the reign of the Visconti dukes. This reversal of sentiment sets the stage for much of the discussion in Book 3, for it will be the task of Filelfo's interlocutors to arrive at an understanding of wealth that is both socially acceptable and philosophically tenable.[15] The guiding light for this symposium on wealth is Leonardo Bruni. Bruni had supported Filelfo's career when the latter arrived to teach in Florence in the late 1420s, and Bruni had been among the great champions of Greek learning in the early Quattrocento. With characteristic caution Bruni will engage Palla Strozzi — incidentally, the richest man in Florence according to the 1427 *catasto*, or tax census — in an analysis of the relative merits of wealth and poverty, and the two will together quote (in a Latin translated from Greek originals) a number of philosophical and literary texts from the classical tradition, most notably the skeptic Sextus Empiricus and Aristotle, whose *Nicomachean Ethics* Bruni had translated in the second decade of the fifteenth century.

The discussion is of course meant to console the exiles on the loss of wealth that accompanied their expulsion. With Leonardo's entrance, Filelfo makes sure to demonstrate Bruni's allegiance to the cause of the oligarchs and his disgust at the way in which the Medici used their money for political ends. Bruni casts the regime change of 1433–34 as an episode of class warfare (which it decidedly was not) and then begins to expound the Stoic classification of wealth as among those things that are indifferent (*adiaphora*) to human happiness. Following some technical discussion of terminology, Bruni arrives at what might be called a civic humanist conception of wealth: it is acceptable when linked to virtue. He proceeds to contrast the wasteful accumulations of Cosimo de' Medici (who in reality was a substantial and generous

patron of the arts) with the charitable philanthropic expenditures of Borromeo.

Francesco Soderini interrupts the discussion to suggest that poverty should be accounted an evil, but Leonardo continues to affirm the Stoic position and furthermore remarks on the close association in the classical world between philosophy and the adoption of a frugal way of life. To support this position, Filelfo has Bruni draw on the apocryphal letters of the Cynics Diogenes and Crates and the *Letters of Phalaris* as well as those of Apollonius of Tyana. Filelfo is here demonstrating the exceptionally broad basis of his Hellenic studies, and by putting much of this material in Bruni's speeches is flattering his humanist colleague while simultaneously displaying his own erudition.

The criticism of Cosimo de' Medici is sharpest in this book. Filelfo elaborates on many putative episodes from the Medici family history, details amounting to slander, which even in the fifteenth century could have drawn fines as *verba iniuriosa* had the author not already been exiled from the city of Florence. Such extreme examples of Filelfo's use of free speech remind us that this notion, while rooted in the Greek concept of *parrhēsia*, was still a developing one in Western culture — as Bruni's concluding remarks attest. Yet Filelfo's continual recourse to classical *exempla* illustrating how philosophers and intellectuals of antiquity upbraided tyrants and princes serves an exemplary function: with power comes responsibility. In a Christian society, where wealth was regarded with suspicion and poverty often praised, such a moral stance was even more compelling than it would be in a pagan world.

The final pages of the third book focus on technical philosophical treatments of voluntary and involuntary actions and on the role that rational deliberation plays in the exercise of choice — elaborate paraphrases and compilations of passages in Aristotle's *Eudemian Ethics* and *Magna Moralia*. Here the speaker is Palla

Strozzi, a patron of Filelfo in his Florentine days and an intermittent correspondent with him during his lengthy exile in Padua (he died in 1462). It is not entirely clear how this discussion relates to the topic at hand, though there is an attempt at the dialogue's close to suggest that, if the exiles consider themselves as having chosen poverty, they can perhaps avoid some feelings of shame that were meant to be part of the punishment that exiles would suffer. The dialogue closes with the anticipation of a fourth day of conversations, but Filelfo apparently never resumed working on the *Commentationes* — doubtless because he saw more rewarding opportunities with his new patrons in Milan, where he spent most of the remaining years of his long and productive life.

The *Commentationes* has, like other prose works by Filelfo, a miscellaneous character, and he can be faulted for allowing somewhat sophomoric humor and scurrilous slander to jostle alongside more profound philosophical inquiries into the nature of human happiness. But as an introduction to the varied interests of Italian Renaissance humanists, and their commitment to the five disciplines of the *studia humanitatis* (grammar, rhetoric, poetry, history, and moral philosophy), one can think of few texts of the fifteenth century that are more representative. Composed in an advanced Ciceronian Latin and modeled on that author's rhetorical and philosophical *oeuvre*, Filelfo's literary achievement is substantial, if uneven, and his work provides students of the period with a magnificent mirror of the times, at least as they were experienced by the elites of the Italian peninsula and the intellectuals they sponsored.

Written at a time when modern canons governing the presentation of "fiction" did not yet exist, Filelfo's fictional dialogue is a remarkable text, an idealized projection of cultural life at a high-water mark in Western history. It was a moment when European elites were sponsoring a massive renewal of classical literature

and philosophy in a spiritual context that remained thoroughly Christian but that was able to absorb much of the wisdom transmitted by a host of classical authors. In many ways the *Commentationes* is an excellent introduction to the world of Italian Renaissance humanism in its literary, political, and social contexts. We can perceive here the championing of "civic humanism" in what may have been its best years; the devotion to classical literature and philosophy; the competitive spirit of the age that enabled the production of so many extraordinary works of scholarship, art, and architecture; and the humanist obsession with eloquence, with well-made speeches that were deemed, both then and in the ancient world, to reflect as much on the moral character of the speaker as on his level of education and social rank. And though it is possible to complain that the work is too much of a literary potpourri, we must at the same time appreciate Filelfo's commitment to a deeply human analysis of the phenomenon of exile, of what it means to lose one's home and one's country. This focus should surely grant the work an important place in literary history.

Jeroen De Keyser would like to thank Dirk Sacré for his careful review of the Latin text and for his help with matters of punctuation. His keen eye preserved some puzzling syntax and also helped to eradicate a few particularly persistent *lapsus calami* that had stiffly resisted all collation and reviewing rounds. The manuscript research carried out in preparation for the Latin text edition was made possible in part by a research grant that was generously awarded in 2009 by the Renaissance Society of America. Scott Blanchard would like to thank John Monfasani for his aid in translating some of the more arcane philosophical passages in the second book of this work, and he would also like to thank Jeroen De Keyser for his assistance with the English translation. Shane Butler, Associate Editor of the I Tatti series for Harvard Uni-

versity Press, was also helpful in rendering the translation more
felicitous, as were Andrew Dyck and James Hankins, the General
Editor of the I Tatti Renaissance Library. Special thanks are owed
to the Faculty Research Committee of Misercordia University for
its support of the project. Any remaining errors are of course the
responsibility of the editor and translator.

NOTES

1. Carlo de' Rosmini, *Vita di Francesco Filelfo da Tolentino*, 3 vols. (Milan,
1808), is still the best overall source for Filelfo's life, though it can be valu-
ably supplemented by Rudolf Georg Adam's unpublished PhD thesis
(Oxford, 1974). The most recent survey is Diana Robin, *Filelfo in Milan:
Writings 1451–1477* (Princeton, 1991).

2. Robin, *Filelfo in Milan*, 17–21.

3. Dale Kent, *The Rise of the Medici: Faction in Florence, 1426–1434* (Oxford,
1978), is the standard account of the Medici coup.

4. On Filelfo's relationship with Bruni, see Arthur Field, "Lorenzo Bruni,
Florentine Traitor? Bruni, the Medici, and an Aretine Conspiracy of
1437," *Renaissance Quarterly* 51.4 (1998): 1109–50; for Filelfo's criticism of
Bruni after the latter's death, see Gary Ianziti, "Leonardo Bruni, the
Medici, and the Florentine Histories," *Journal of the History of Ideas* 69.1
(2008): 22n90, now incorporated into his *Writing History in Renaissance
Italy: Leonardo Bruni and the Uses of the Past* (Cambridge, MA, 2011), chap-
ter nine (see 203n89).

5. Filelfo's classical models are discussed in Giacomo Ferraù, "Le *Commentationes Florentinae de exilio*," in *Francesco Filelfo nel quinto centenario della
morte: Atti del XVIII Convegno di Studi Maceratesi*, ed. Rino Avesani et al.
(Padua, 1986), 369–88; and W. Scott Blanchard, "Patrician Sages and the
Humanist Cynic: Francesco Filelfo and the Ethics of World Citizenship,"
Renaissance Quarterly 60.4 (2007): 1107–69. Among his humanist predecessors is Petrarch, whose *De remediis utriusque fortunae* II.67 explicitly
discusses exile.

6. See Francesco Filelfo, *Satyrae I (Decadi I–V)*, ed. Silvia Fiaschi (Rome, 2005), 477–78, for a discussion of the *Oration*.

7. Silvia Fiaschi, "Deformazioni storiche e propaganda politica negli scritti antimedicei di Francesco Filelfo," in *Il principe e la storia: Atti del Convegno Scandiano 18–20 Settembre 2003*, ed. Tina Mattarese and Cristina Montagnini (Scandiano, 2005), 415–37.

8. George W. McClure, *Sorrow and Consolation in Italian Humanism* (Princeton, NJ, 1991), provides useful background.

9. Blanchard, "Patrician Sages," provides background for Filelfo's understanding of this term.

10. Gian Mario Cao, "The Prehistory of Modern Scepticism: Sextus Empiricus in Fifteenth-Century Italy," *Journal of the Warburg and Courtauld Institutes* 64 (2001): 229–80.

11. Carlo Errera, "Le *Commentationes Florentinae de exilio* di Francesco Filelfo," *Archivio storico italiano*, ser. 5, no. 5 (1890): 193–227.

12. Fiaschi, "Deformazioni storiche."

13. *Knowledge, Goodness, and Power: The Debate over Nobility among Quattrocento Italian Humanists*, ed. and tr. Albert Rabil, Jr. (Binghamton, NY, 1991), translates some key texts illustrating this important humanist theme.

14. It is worth noting that this work, finished in 1420, was dedicated to Cosimo de' Medici.

15. Gian Mario Cao, "Tra politica fiorentina e filosofia ellenistica: il dibattito sulla richezza nelle *Commentationes* di Francesco Filelfo," *Archivio storico italiano*, 155 (1997): 99–126.

FRANCISCI PHILELFI
AD VITALIANUM
BORRHOMAEUM
COMMENTATIONUM
FLORENTINARUM DE EXILIO

FRANCESCO FILELFO
FLORENTINE DISCUSSIONS
ON EXILE
DEDICATED TO VITALIANO
BORROMEO

LIBER PRIMUS

Summatim
de Incommodis Exilii

COLLOCUTORES

Pallas
Honofrius
Rainaldus
Poggius
Manettus

1 Dionysium iuniorem, Vitaliane Borrhomaee, posteaquam exciderat Syracusis aliquando interrogatum quid ei Plato philosophiaque profuisset, respondisse tradunt, 'ut huiusmodi fortunae mutabilitatem feram aeque animo.' Et graviter sane Dionysius prudenterque respondit id quod, si iampridem ante sensisset, et cum Platonis monita, tum philosophiae praecepta institutaque sequi voluisset, longe profecto tutius ac melius et sibi et suis consuluisset. Secundas enim laetasque res non munire minus et ornare philosophia

2 quam adversas atque afflictas consolari levareque consuevit. Hoc certe pro tua prudentia ipse animadvertens, ita tibi vitam perpulchre instituisti et constantissime confirmasti, ut cum apud maximum nostrum et optimum principem Philippum Mariam Anglum summa sis omnia pro tua summa virtute assecutus, idemque his omnibus cumulatissime polleas quae aut corpori aut fortunae

BOOK ONE

On the Disadvantages of Exile,
in Summary Form

SPEAKERS

Palla Strozzi
Onofrio Strozzi
Rinaldo degli Albizzi
Poggio Bracciolini
Giannozzo Manetti

There is a tradition, Vitaliano Borromeo, that when Dionysius the   1
Younger, after he had been exiled from Syracuse, was questioned
as to how Plato's philosophy had benefited him, he replied, "It
showed me how I may endure with a calm mind such fluctuations
of fortune."[1] Dionysius gave this response with wisdom and authority, but if he had recognized this fact far earlier and had resolved to follow both the advice of Plato and the teachings and
principles of philosophy, he would indeed have taken far safer and
better care both of himself and his affairs. For philosophy has a
way of strengthening and embellishing favorable and happy circumstances as well as providing consolation and relief for adverse
and troublesome ones. Since you are aware of this yourself, as be-   2
fits your thoughtful nature, you have equipped your life so very
nobly and strengthened it so consistently that during your time
with the most excellent and greatest prince of ours, Filippo Maria
Visconti,[2] you have achieved great things in line with your great
virtue; you likewise excel so very perfectly in all these qualities that
are of particular importance in respect to the body or to material
circumstances, yet in no quality are you more accustomed to shine

3

praecipua egregiaque sunt, nulla tamen re magis quam animi praestantia et virtute vel gloriari soleas vel celebrari cupias.

3   Atqui mirari nonnunquam cogor aliquorum vel inscitiam vel
inertiam qui, neglectis animi bonis, omnem suam felicitatem ac
beatitudinem in fortunae inconstantia atque fraude collocarunt.
Qui si sua omnia diligenter expenderent, si non in cute solum sed
multo magis intus sese inspicerent, si qua praecellentia ab immortali Deo praediti sunt perspicue cognoscerent,[1] aut quae sunt extra
se posita, non requirerent, si abessent, aut si forte adessent, quemadmodum tu benefice et splendidissime uterentur. Nam cum et
animo constemus et corpore, hoc nobis cum bestiis, ille cum Deo
communis est. Alii serius, alii citius, omnes tamen morimur tandem corpore, animo autem immortales sumus. Si mentis ratione,
si intelligentia uti volumus, neque inferiora haec atque temporalia
latere nos possint, nec superiora et aeterna illa esse nobis incog-
nita. Itaque studiosius inquirentibus facile nobis occurrat quid
moliendum observandumque sit, quo non pecoris sed dei vitam
4   vixisse videamur. Debet certe cogitatio nostra omnis aliud nihil
dies noctesque meditari quam quo pacto bonum illud consequa-
mur, quo ubi pervenerimus, omni demum labore vacui quietam
acturi simus atque tranquillam vitam.

Id qui non in animi bonis sed multo magis aut in corporis im-
becillitate aut in fragilitate amentiaque fortunae situm putat, et
sua ipse spe fallitur et suos labores omnis consumit frustra. Nam
tum omnia corporis quae dicuntur commoda brevi pereunt, tum
in fortuna nihil certi, nihil firmi, nihil diuturni esse potest. Quod
si animus seipsum norit, illud etiam norit, frustra ab se peti
5   aliunde quod habet ipse in sese. Quare si felicitatis est et beatitu-

or do you desire to increase your reputation more than in virtue and excellence of mind.

I am sometimes compelled to wonder at the ignorance or lazi- 3 ness of some who, having neglected the goods of the mind, have placed all their happiness and joy in the fickleness and deceitfulness of fortune. If they were to consider carefully all of their qualities, if they were to examine themselves, not only at the level of the body but much more in their innermost selves, if they clearly understood with what excellent qualities immortal God has provided them, they would either have no need for goods that are external to themselves, should they lack them, or, should they perhaps be available, they would make use of them beneficially and magnificently, just as you do. For although we are composed both of a soul and a body, the latter we share with beasts, the former with God. We all finally die in body, some sooner, some later, but in soul we are immortal. If we want to use the mind's reason, if we want to use our understanding, neither can these lower, temporal objects escape our notice, nor can those higher eternal objects remain unknown to us. And so if we investigate keenly, it should be readily apparent to us what we must undertake and heed in order for us to be seen to have lived the life not of a beast but of a god. Certainly all of our thought should day and night meditate noth- 4 ing else except how to pursue that good having achieved which we will at last be freed from all our labor and will live a life of peace and tranquility.

The man who thinks that this lies not in the goods of the mind but rather in either the feebleness of the body or the fragility and irrationality of fortune is deceived in his hope and wastes all his efforts. For just as all the so-called advantages of the body perish in a short time, so in fortune nothing can be assured, solid, long lasting. But if the mind knows itself, it knows this, too: that it seeks in vain outside itself what it contains within it. For this rea- 5 son if it desires happiness and a blessed state, it must know that

dinis cupidus, id in sua esse potestate positum non ignoret necesse est. Non enim debet excelsum atque invictum animi robur corporis illecebris et perturbationibus cedere, non ratio temeritati succumbere, non immortalitatis decus dedecori mortalium sordium probroque servire. Haec solus sapiens et videt et novit. Sapiens ipse duntaxat quod et melius et pulchrius et divinius factu sit, diiudicat ac sequitur. Solus profecto sapiens felix est, solus beatus, solus divinitatis particeps. Non enim is est qui aut fragilem caducamque fortunam virtutis stabilitati et firmitudini, aut dulcedinem corporis titillantemque laeticiam animi gravitati atque constantiae anteponendam censeat. Nam stultus, quoniam deam sibi fortunam constituerit, et quae vis animi, quae dignitas sit ignorat et omnia ad corporis voluptatem refert. Cumque maxime miser est, tum se felicitate maxima frui immortalique opinatur.

6   Quoniam igitur aliquando cum Florentiae agerem, evenit ut quorundam clarissimorum et optimorum civium et eorundem gravitate doctrinaque praestantium de exilio commentationi disputationique familiariter interessem, quae decem deinceps continuis diebus ab illis dicta eleganter, erudite, divinitus audieram, in de-
7   cem itidem libros contuli. Erant qui arbitrarentur vel uno ipso exilio ea prope omnia contineri quae miseram vitam reddant. Alii vero longe secus sentire videbantur. Itaque neque de exilio neque de miseria ipsa conveniebant. Quid autem inter se differrent, cum decem dierum commentationes percucurreris, facile perspicies. Opus quidem et longum fuit et arduum et magnificum. Quod cum plurimum ad bene beateque vivendum pertinere existimassem, tibi tali ac tanto viro pro nostra amicicia ignotum esse nolui. Ea enim in te propemodum habes omnia quae homini felicitatem

this is within its power. For the soul's noble and unconquerable strength ought not to yield to the seductions and commotions of the body, reason ought not to surrender to rashness, the glory of immortality ought not to be enslaved to the shame and disgrace of mortal squalor; the wise man alone perceives and knows these things. The wise man himself, as such, distinguishes how to act in a better, more beautiful and more godly manner and then follows it. The wise man alone is happy, he alone is blessed, he alone is a partaker in the divine. For he is not one who thinks that either fragile and fleeting fortune ought to be valued above the stability and security of virtue, nor the sweetness and enticing pleasure of the body above the dignity and steadfastness of the soul. The foolish man, because he has set up fortune as his goddess, fails to recognize what power the soul possesses, what moral worth is, and orients everything toward the pleasure of the body. And when he is most miserable, then he fancies that he is enjoying the greatest, never-ending happiness.

Once when I was living in Florence, I happened to be present at   6
a friendly discussion and debate among some of the finest and most distinguished citizens, who were likewise among the most excellent in authority and learning; the topic was exile. So I later set down in ten books what was said eloquently, learnedly, and with inspiration by these men on ten successive days.[3] There were   7
some who thought that virtually everything that makes life unhappy is comprised in the single condition of exile; others seemed to take a far different view. And so they came to no agreement either about exile or about unhappiness in general. When you have gone through the reports of the ten days, you will easily see the substance of their disagreement. The work has been long and difficult, but also illustrious. Because I reckoned it had great bearing on living well and happily, in view of our friendship I did not want this to remain unknown to a man of your distinction and importance. You possess in yourself more or less everything that bestows

afferunt. Nam et his quae in hac vita expetenda in primis sunt, non mediocriter viges, et in quibus selectionem ponunt, vaehementer affluis. Quapropter nostra haec ista cum leges, teipsum magis magisque agnosces.[2] Sed iam ut res gesta est, paucis accipe.

8   Quod omnibus humanis in rebus quae aliquam excellentiam prae se ferunt usu venire solet, cum deteriores populi Florentini melioribus inviderent ac plebei quidam et sordidi homines viros optimatis, eosdemque praestantissimos et innocentissimos civis, per omnem iniuriam atque contumeliam continuis insidiis latrociniisque vexarent, et quaeque omnia ad reipublicae perniciem, vastitatem, interitum pertinerent omni studio, omni labore, omni denique conatu molirentur et agerent, statuit ordo nobilium et ii una omnes qui per id temporis summae reipublicae praeerant, levi unius mulcta succurrere impendenti civitatis ruinae, et sic eam veluti publicam pestem extinguere. Igitur omnium illorum ignium ardentissimum fomitem atque auctorem, Cosmum Medicem, Iohannis filium, sine ulla cuiusquam prorsus aut caede aut cruciatu aut proscriptione aut detrimento ad Venetos in decennium relegant: Patavii primum, deinde Venetiis, idque Cosmo ipso supplicibus litteris ac nunciis postulante.

    Unius igitur Cosmi relegatione, eaque poene libera, perinde[3] atque alicuius teterrimi auspicii abominabilisque prodigii praesentia posteaquam est respublica liberata, tanta mox mansuetudo, tanta quies universam civitatem influxit, et ita omnes moderatione, innocentia et iusticia optimatium e prioribus illis odii et furoris procellis et tempestatibus ad pacis tranquillitatisque amorem traducti sunt, ut quod poetae de Saturno rege fabulantur quandam quasi aetatem auream vivere Florentini viderentur. Iam nullae usquam neque expilationes nec peculatus nec furta audiebantur. Nulla adulteria, nullae corruptelae, nulla veneficia patrabantur. Iam et nocturni omnes et diurni metus aberant. Nihil per libidinem et animi impotentiam agere licebat. Omnia lege, omnia more

happiness on a man. For you have an abundant supply of the things which are particularly to be sought in this life and you are mightily affluent in the things worthy of choice.[4] Therefore when you read these writings of mine, you will come to know yourself better and better. But now hear briefly how the event occurred.

As generally happens in human affairs that are endowed with some distinction, when the worse element of the Florentines hated the better ones and certain reprobate commoners were insultingly harassing the aristocrats — the very citizens who were most distinguished and blameless — with unending intrigues and robberies and were setting in motion and driving with all their energy, toil, and effort everything that contributes to the destruction, devastation, and ruin of the state, the noble class, and together with it all who at that time had charge of the commonwealth, resolved to come to the rescue of the failing state and quench the crisis as if it were a public plague by the moderate punishment of a single individual. Therefore they banned for ten years to the Veneto the hottest spark and instigator of all those fires, Cosimo de' Medici, son of Giovanni, without bloodshed, torture, proscription, or loss besides — first at Padua, then at Venice, and that upon request of Cosimo himself by written petition and messengers.[5]

Thus with the relegation of Cosimo alone, and that nearly without hardships, and after the commonwealth was liberated as if from the presence of some foul omen and unspeakable prodigy, soon such civility, such peace flowed into the entire state, and all were so transported by the moderation, blamelessness, and justice of the nobles from those previous storms and tempests of hatred and fury to the love of peace and tranquility that, as the poets tell about Saturn's reign, the Florentines seemed to be living in a golden age. No longer were any acts of pillage, embezzlement, or theft heard of anywhere. No adultery, bribery, or acts of poisoning were committed. Now all fears were gone by night and day. There was no license for acting out of lust or fury. All things were

8

9

10

maiorum, omnia aequo bonoque fiebant. Divino cultui omnes
quamrelligiosissime dediti, aliud omnino nihil nec curabant nec
meditabantur quam quod et privatae et publicae dignitati felicitati-
que conduceret.

11   At repente versutus ille et callidus veterator, circunscriptor, ve-
neficus, sacrilegus Cosmus Medices, quo mea profecto sententia
nemo est neque perniciosior nec flagitiosior, nec ad omne facinus
et nequitiam instructior, ubi simile nactus ingenium Iohannem
Vitellescum, qui Alexandrinus patriarcha idemque cardinalis et
pro Eugenio Romano pontifice vel belli dux vel atrocissima belua
modo debitas poenas tulit, Cosmus, inquam, Medices, impius
parricida, Iohannis illius Vitellesci, quem non difficile pecunia
corrupisset, non tam audacia et viribus quam fraude insidiisque
fraetus pestiferos civilium simultatum, discordiarum, seditionum
atque bellorum ignis, sopitos iam et penitus extinctos, rursus
exuscitavit, accendit, extulit, et in eas aerumnas civitatem iniecit,
12   ut iam fere serviat, imo plane serviat, ut vides. Nam ordo nobilium
et fortissimi cives, etsi nihil tale subverebantur — quid enim hominem genere humilem, moribus abiectum, infamem, sordidum,
contemptum subvereri oportebat? — cum nunquam tamen adversus eiuscemodi pecudis coniurationem imparati esse possent, ad
arma concurrunt, omnem inimicorum impetum subito proster-
nunt, comprimunt, conterunt. Quo enim pacto aut sceleri pietas
unquam cedat, aut furori constantia? Num turpitudo honestatem,
continentiam libido,[4] iniquitas aequitatem, luxuria temperantiam,
innocentiam avaricia[5] unquam superet? Facile, mediusfidius, ignaviam fortitudo, temeritatem prudentia, virtus vitium semper vin-
13   cat. Frustra enim perdita ratio cum bona confligat, amentia sanae
menti adversetur, desperatio ipsa spem bonam in discrimen pos-
cat. Cum igitur deiectae illi et debilitatae manui viri optimates

done by law, by ancestral custom, by equity. All were devoted with utmost piety to the worship of God; they concerned themselves with and took thought only for what was supportive of respect and happiness, both private and public.

But without warning that clever and crafty old fox, Cosimo de'   11
Medici — that deceiver, poisoner, and blasphemer, than whom no one, in my opinion, is more dangerous or criminal or more skilled at every kind of villainy and evil — when he met with his kindred spirit Giovanni Vitelleschi,[6] who, as patriarch of Alexandria and likewise cardinal, condottiere or rather monstrous beast in the service of Pope Eugenius, just now suffered due punishment — Cosimo de' Medici, I say, that unholy criminal, relying not so much on the daring and strength as the deceit and intrigue of the aforementioned Giovanni Vitelleschi, whom he easily bribed, once again roused, kindled, and raised the deadly fires of civil feuds, strife, sedition and war that by now were slumbering and practically snuffed out, and he cast the state into such woes that by now it is all but enslaved, nay, it is manifestly enslaved, as you see. For   12
although the nobles and the most gallant citizens feared nothing of the sort — for what need to fear a man of lowly birth, morally bankrupt, infamous, vile, despised? — since, however, they could never be unprepared against a conspiracy of this kind of beast, they rushed to arms and at once laid low, checked, and crushed every assault of their enemies. For how could loyalty ever give ground to wickedness or constancy to frenzy? Surely disgrace could never prevail over honor, lust over continence, wickedness over justice, luxury over temperance, greed over blamelessness? As God is my witness, courage could always vanquish cowardice with ease, prudence rashness, virtue vice. An addled faculty of reason-   13
ing would struggle in vain against a good one, madness be pitted in vain against a sound mind, desperation would vainly challenge hope. When therefore the nobles had pitted the flower and strength of the most gallant men against that outcast and enervated

fortissimorum hominum florem ac robur opposuissent et illico
impurissimi latrones essent in fugam versi planeque iam victi cap-
tique tenerentur, Iohannis unius Vitellesci (qui facinus immane
animo anhaelans se ab Eugenio missum dictitaret ad sedandas atque componendas procellas omnis fluctusque civiles) dolis ac periuriis inclyti victores, ipsi patriae patres, nulla pugna, nullis armis,
nullis opibus victi sunt.

14   Quas quidem insidias proditionesque detestabiles quoniam longiore illa ad optimatis exules oratione sumus persecuti, recte ad-
monemur ne impraesentiarum longiores simus. Ubi ergo in urbem
Cosmus per tanti sceleris furorem legibus iuribusque contemptis
prostratisque rediisset, nulli rei magis studuit quam bonis et sanc-
tis viris eiiciendis, id est diripiendae evertendaeque reipublicae.

15   Itaque universa nobilitate perculsa, posteaquam primarii et inno-
centissimi cives, qui fraude doloque circunventi apud Eugenium
asservabantur, exilio impie damnati iam essent, ob eamque rem
plaerique omnes tantae calamitatis acerbitatem indignitatemque
fortunae et indignius et acerbius vel quererentur vel ingemiscerent
vel deflerent atque afflictarentur, Pallas Stroza, vir omnibus rebus
ornatus, qui semper in optima pacataque civitate princeps fuerat
essetque et Graece et Latine non doctus minus quam eloquens,
quo praesenti aegritudini mederetur, de exilio sermonem cum Honofrio filio, verecundo et probato adolescente, opportune aggredi-

16   tur. Huic tum ipse Honofrius tum alii non nulli respondent ac
varias quisque suas sententias proferunt. Permulta disseruntur
utrinque et gravia et utilia et memoratu digna. Quae quoniam pro
mea cum illo ordine consuetudine ac benivolentia praesens coramque audivi, existimavi operae precium fore ne tantam et tam salu-
tiferam disputationem oblivionis interitus caperet. Quamobrem
iam Pallantem ipsum, qui tuas quoque maximas immortalisque

band and instantly the foul brigands were put to flight and, by now clearly defeated, were being held in captivity, by the trickery and lies of Giovanni Vitelleschi alone (who, lusting to commit a monstrous crime, kept claiming that he had been sent by Pope Eugenius to allay and calm all the storms and waves of civil strife), the illustrious victors, the true fathers of their homeland, were defeated without a battle, without arms, without resources.

Since I have narrated these intrigues and loathsome treacheries 14 in that lengthy speech to the exiled nobles,[7] I need to remind myself to refrain from prolixity at present. So when Cosimo had returned to the city through outrageous crime, holding the laws and justice in contempt and trampling them under foot, he aimed at nothing more than that the good, patriotic men be driven into exile — that is, that the republic be ransacked and overthrown. And thus the whole of the nobility was struck down, the leading 15 citizens of the greatest integrity, who, tricked by fraud and deceit, were being kept under close guard at Eugenius' palace.[8] They had already been unjustly condemned to exile and for this reason most were indignantly and bitterly lamenting or bewailing or crushed by the bitterness of the enormous disaster and the injustice of fortune. At this point Palla Strozzi, a man thoroughly accomplished, who had always been a leading citizen in the fine and peaceful republic and who was just as learned as he was eloquent in both Greek and Latin, in order to provide relief for their present suffering, began a timely conversation on exile with his son Onofrio, a young man both modest and well regarded. Both Onofrio and 16 some others replied to him and offered each his own differing opinion. Many things were discussed on both sides which were weighty, beneficial, and worth remembering. Since I was present at the discussion, owing to my familiarity with and goodwill toward men of this class, I reckoned it would be worthwhile if oblivion were not to befall so important and beneficial a discussion. Hence, if you pay close attention to Palla himself (who used to make

virtutes frequentissime usurpare dicendo consuevit, dicere incipientem si diligenter attenderis, quae primo die de incommodis exilii disputata summatim fuerint, liquido cognosces.

17 *Pallas.* Quid ita, fili, tristis es? Quid suspiras? Quid gemis? Quur adeo te affligis?

Honofrius. Non iure trister, mi pater, meritoque affligar, cum e felici me video nulla mea causa infelicissimum factum? Possumne, vel potius debeo, non suspirare atque ingemiscere, vel teipsum intuens tantis fortunis ac tam florenti spoliatum statu et domo et urbe pelli, et — quo nihil acerbius esse puto — perinde[6] ac[7] hostem et inimicum patriae mulctari exilio? An est quicquam exilio aut aerumnosius aut miserius?

18 *Pallas.* Profecto, fili, quod usurpari a sapientibus quibusdam solitum accepi, iuventutem, quoniam rudis quodam modo humanarum rerum imperitaque[8] sit prudentiae, laudem non mereri, verum esse liquido perspicio. Nam utrum intelligeres vel exilium vel miseriam, plane iudicares tua te opinione plurimum falli.

Honofrius. Scio equidem, mi pater, eum et esse et appellari 'exulem' qui 'extra solum' (hoc est locum patrium) sit, 'miserum' vero qui et pluribus et maximis prematur malis. Quod si extrudimur patria, si omni dignitatis atque honoris gradu deiicimur, si cunctis denique fortunae commodis ornamentisque orbati ludibrio sumus flagitiosissimis abiectissimisque hominibus — si homines ii tandem appellandi sunt qui non modo nihil habent humanitatis, sed etiam feri sunt et immanes et tetri — nonne sumus non modo exules, sed omni miseriarum aerumna acerbitateque oppressi?

19 *Pallas.* At ego me nec miserum nec exulem volo. Nam nec patria pellor nec durius quicquam accidit quod miseriam mihi afferre

frequent reference to your great and immortal virtues) as he begins
to speak, you will clearly understand what was said summarily on
the first day about the disadvantages of exile.

Palla. Why, my son, are you so sad? Why do you sigh? Why are   17
    you groaning? Why are you causing yourself such distress?

Onofrio. Am I not rightly sad, father, and am I not distressed with
    good reason when I see myself changed from happy to wretched
    through no fault of my own? Can I or should I, rather, not sigh
    and groan when I see you robbed of such fortune and such a
    distinguished position and driven from the city and — than
    which I think nothing more bitter — punished with exile as an
    enemy of our homeland. Is there anything more wretched or
    miserable than exile?

Palla. I see clearly, my son, that the saying is true that, I've heard,   18
    used to be uttered by wise men, namely that young people,
    since they are more or less untrained in human affairs and un-
    skilled in wisdom, do not deserve commendation. For if you
    understood either exile or misery, you would judge that you are
    much mistaken in your view.

Onofrio. I know, father, that he is and is called "exile" (*exul*) who is
    "outside the land" (*extra solum*) (that is, his ancestral place); he
    is and is called "wretched" who is hemmed in by many great
    evils. But if we are expelled from our homeland, if we are thrust
    out of every rank of respect and dignity, if finally, bereft of all
    the goods and embellishments of fortune, we are made sport of
    by the most reprobate and worthless men — if they ought to be
    called men who have no particle of humanity but are savage and
    monstrous and foul — are we not merely exiles but crushed by
    bitter misery?

Palla. But I claim to be neither wretched nor an exile. For I am   19
    neither being expelled from my homeland, nor has anything
    untoward occurred which can bring misery upon me. This is

possit. Sic enim puto. Nam 'scire' nequaquam audeo dicere, propter sapientem illum gravissimumque Socratem. Itaque[9] diligenter expende quid ipse te scire asseveres.

20 *Honofrius.* Auges mihi, mi pater, aegritudinem, cum eam pergis excutere. Nam exules negare, qui non modo urbe patriaque arceamur, verum etiam omni Tuscia, si id exilium non est, quid sit exilium nescio. Huic autem cum alia permulta, tum intolerabilia haec mala deinceps adiuncta esse, infamiam, paupertatem, servitutem, contemptum, intempestivam senectutem, aegrotationem, nonnunquam etiam carcerem ac mortem, quis dubitet? Quae si vitam miseram non efficiunt, quibus miseria constet malis, non facile assequor. Quare abs te peto, mi pater, et quibus possum obsecro precibus ut, quandoquidem nullo iniquae fortunae impetu nec frangeris nec moveris, si quid habes — quid enim non habes? — quo hanc infesti fati necessitatem moderate

21 feram, et latius et apertius proferas, modo tamen id possis. Vereor enim quod de Aenea prudenter scripsit Maro, 'Spem vultu simulat, premit altum corde dolorem,' ne identidem tibi accidat hoc tempore. Vix enim credendum est eadem te esse animi qua oris tranquillitate. Nec fieri ulla ratione posse crediderim quin hanc tantam calamitatem atque contumeliam persentiscas.

Pallas. Animadverto, fili, longiore tecum oratione utendum esse, et ea quidem dierum complurium. Non enim exilium duntaxat male interpretaris, sed quanti infamiam ac paupertatem fieri oporteat, non sane intelligis. Servire vero, contemni, consenescere, aegrotare plurimum metuis. Carcerem autem ac mortem videris non solum in malis ponere, sed etiam in summis malis. Et his tu quidem rebus constare miseriam putas quae nulla

22 utique sit, si in hisce quidem sit posita. Verum huiusmodi tibi orationem obscuram esse non miror. Nam si reliqua etiam tibi

what I *think*, for owing to the wisdom and authority of Socrates I do not by any means venture to say that I *know*. Therefore weigh carefully what you yourself assert that you know.[9]

Onofrio. You increase my misery, father, when you try to drive it 20 away. For to deny that we are exiles, we who are not only relegated from city and homeland but even from all Tuscany — if this is not exile, I fail to understand what exile is. Moreover, who would doubt that not only are many other things connected with exile but also these intolerable evils: infamy, poverty, slavery, contempt, a premature old age, sickness, sometimes even prison and death? If these do not make life miserable, it is difficult for me to grasp what evils comprise misery. Therefore I beg you, father, and beseech you with what prayers I can muster that, since you are neither broken nor moved by any blow of unjust fortune, if you have — and what do you not have? — the means by which I can bear with moderation this necessity of fate, that you set it out comprehensively and explicitly, provided that you can. For I fear lest the very same thing happen to you 21 at this time that Vergil wisely wrote of Aeneas: "He feigned hope with his countenance but suppressed sorrow deep in his heart."[10] It is scarcely credible that you have the same calmness of heart as of face. Nor would I by any means believe it possible for you not to feel keenly this enormous disaster and insult.

Palla. I see, my son, that we require a longer discussion, in fact, one of several days. Not only do you misinterpret exile but you fail to understand the value to be set upon infamy and poverty. You have great fear of being a slave, being despised, growing old, being sick. Moreover, you seem to class prison and death not only among evils but even among the worst evils. And you think that wretchedness consists in these things which, if it really resided in them, would be no wretchedness at all. But I am 22 not surprised that discourse of this type is obscure to you. For even if you possessed the other prerequisites for perceiving the

adessent ad veritatem perspiciendam, multum tamen ac varium rerum usum, qui prudentiam efficit, humanae magistram vitae, negat annorum paucitas. Quo fit ut, perturbationibus deditus, quod in re sit ne internoscere quidem possis. Laetor autem et gaudeo plurimum, quandoquidem quod ex teipso nequis, ex altero cupis intelligere. Nam ut pulchre simul et graviter praecipitur iis versibus quos Philelfus noster ex Hesiodo ad nos traduxit:

23

> Optimus hic equidem, qui per sese omnia novit,[10]
> consiliis praevisa suis meliora secutus;[11]
> rursus et ille probus qui paret recta monenti.
> Sed qui nec per se valuit monitusque refugit
> recta sequi, cuiusque vir est is muneris expers.

Quapropter quoniam et ociosum me Vitellescus reddidit et perturbationibus nequaquam obruor, morem geram voluntati tuae, et libenter id quidem. Nam et res quam petis studio memoratuque digna est, et te in dies magis ad constantem animi probitatem institui et confirmari cupio.

24   Sed priusquam ad rem venio, placet in medium referre quaedam Socratis verba, quibus magnus ille vir et eruditus in primis multitudinem imperitam, quotiens in eam incideret, severe simul et graviter castigabat: 'Heus,' inquit, 'homines, quonam ruitis, et quae ignorantia vestra est? Nihil quod deceat, quod oporteat agitis. Vos parandis pecuniis omnem operam, omne studium indulgetis, quibus et ipsi abundetis et filios item abundantioris[12] deinceps reddatis. Ipsos autem filios priusque[13] vos

truth, your scant years deny you the plentiful and varied experience in human affairs that produces wisdom, the teacher of human life. The result of this is that you cannot even discern what are the facts of the matter, since you have abandoned yourself to your emotions. But I am happy and rejoice, since you are eager to learn from another what you cannot know on your own. For this message is beautifully and profoundly taught 23 in those verses of Hesiod that our friend Filelfo has translated for us:

> The best man is he who understands all things for himself,
> Who follows the better course, foreseen by his own
>   deliberation.
> And again, he is virtuous who obeys a good counselor.
> But the man who has not the wherewithal on his own and
>   refuses to follow
> True counsel when so advised, that man is bereft of any
>   gift.[11]

Therefore since Vitelleschi has put me at leisure and I am by no means overwhelmed with emotion, I will oblige your wish, and willingly. For the subject that you inquire about is worthy of earnest discussion, and I want you to be trained and strengthened day by day to the greatest constancy of mind.

But before I come to the topic, it seems appropriate to quote 24 some words of Socrates with which that great and extremely learned man severely and solemnly criticized the ignorant crowd every time he encountered it:[12] "Alas, men, where are you rushing, and what is this ignorance of yours? You are doing nothing that is appropriate or needful. You devote all your effort and energy to acquiring money so that you may not only have it in abundance yourselves but make your children in turn more wealthy. But you are neglecting the children themselves, as your parents in their turn neglected all of you, since you have found

parentes neglegitis identidem omnes, quippe qui nullam neque
sufficientem nec utilem hominibus disciplinam aut exercitationem reperiatis, qua instituti pecuniis recte ac iuste, non prave et
iniuste et cum vestro ipsorum detrimento uti possint. Cui rei
magis studendum quam pecuniis esse ducitis et liberis et uxori-
bus et fratribus et amicis? Ac illi item vobis?

25   'Verum si citharam, si palaestram, si litteras a parentibus
discitis, filiosque docetis, futurum existimatis ut et temperan-
tius et melius urbem habitetis? Atqui siquis coegerit et citharis-
tas et paedotribas et grammaticae professores qui haec singula
optime teneant, et iis colonis civitatem constituerit aut etiam
gentem, quemadmodum vos olim Ioniam, cuiusmodi ea vobis
urbs videatur et quo pacto habitari? Nonne multo etiam peius[14]
ac turpius quam ea quae in Aegypto est urbs tabernariorum,
ubi tabernarii omnes habitant et viri iuxta et mulieres? Nonne
longe ridiculosius habitaturi hi sunt quos dico vestros filiorum-
que magistros, paedotribae, citharistae et grammaticae professores, assumptis etiam poetici carminis recensitoribus atque his-
trionibus?

26   'Et enim quaecunque homines discunt, huiusce rei gratia
discunt, ut quandocunque opus fuerit, quisque ea quam didicerit utatur arte, ut gubernator cum navim inscenderit, eam clavo
dirigat; ob hanc enim rem didicit gubernandi artem. Medicus
vero cum adversa valitudine laborantem acceperit, ut et utilibus
venenis et iis quae ad ordinatum victum pertinent curet. Nam
27   huius rei gratia peritiam illam adeptus est. Nunquid igitur vos
etiam,' inquit, 'cum quid de republica consultandum fuerit, ubi
in concionem conveneritis, assurgatis alii cithara utentes, alii
palaestra, alii Homero Hesiodove accepto legatis Homericum

no education or training that is sufficient or useful for men, on the basis of which they might be able to spend money rightly and justly, rather than wrongly and unjustly, to your own detriment. What matter do you think that your children, wives, brothers, and friends should give more attention to than to money? And to what matter do they, likewise, think that you should?

"But if you learn from your parents how to play the lyre and wrestle, to read and write, and teach these things to your sons, do you think you will lead a more moderate and better life in the city? And yet, if one were to assemble all the cithara players and gymnastics masters and schoolmasters and grammarians who have the best knowledge of each of their subjects, and if one were to found a city, or even a nation, with them as the colonists, as you once colonized Ionia, what kind of city would this seem like to you and how inhabited? Would it not be worse and more shameful than that city of shopkeepers in Egypt,[13] where all live as shopkeepers, both men and women alike? Will it not be a far more ridiculous city when lived in by those whom I call your teachers and the teachers of your children—the gymnastics masters, cithara players, schoolmasters, along with the rhapsodes and actors into the bargain? 25

"For whatever people learn they learn for this reason, that whenever the need arises, someone can practice the art he has learned: when, for instance, a pilot has boarded ship, he guides it with the rudder; for this is the reason he learned piloting. When a physician has taken charge of a patient in poor health, he does so in order to cure him with medicines and a dietary regimen; for this is the reason he acquired that art." He continued: "Now for your own case, when there is need of any deliberation concerning the state and you have convened in the Assembly, surely some of you do not get up and play the cithara, others wrestle, and yet others take a copy of Homer or Hesiod 26 27

aliquid aut Hesiodicum? Haec enim melius quam alii scitis,
putatisque ab his vos optimos viros fore, et qui publicas priva-
tasque res quamrectissime gesturi sitis. Ac nunc quidem harum
spe rerum urbem habitatis filiosque instruitis, tanquam sint
futuri qui et suis rebus et publicis uti possint, quicunque vel
"Pallada, Persepolin, Minervam" cithara reddiderint aut pede ad
lyram incesserint. At quo pacto eorum quae vobis patriaeque
conducant cognitionem sitis habituri, et ut pro legibus ac iure
civitas vobis gerenda sit, neque didicistis hoc unquam, nec an-
28   tea unquam nec etiam hoc tempore vobis est curae. Atque trag-
oedos assidue spectatis in liberalibus, et infortunati hominum
in tragoediis casus in sui[15] commiserationem vos trahunt. Veruntamen nunquam memoriae vobis fuit non eos in hisce versari malis qui et illiterati sint et male canant et palaestram nes-
ciant. Nec etiam eo quisque tragoediam docuit, quod pauper
quispiam sit. Nam contra intueri licet omnes tragoedias loqui
Atreos, Agamemnonas, Oedipodas, qui plurimas et auri et argenti et terrae et pecorum pecunias possederunt. Et qui maxime
adversa fortuna in iis fuerit, pecudem ei auream fuisse ferunt.
29   Eninvero Thamyras, qui optime citharam sciret, et cum ipsis
Musis de harmonia contenderet, tum excaecatus est, tum etiam
citharisticam dedidicit. Et ipsum Palameden nihil iuvit quod
litteras invenisset, ne iniuste ab Achaeis lapidibus atque ab iis
obrutus quos ipse erudiisset necaretur. Sed quoad litterarum
huiusque disciplinae expertes fuerant, eum vivere permiserunt.
Ubi vero cum aliis tum Atridis in primis scilicet litteras tradidit, et cum litteris quo pacto flammis signa efferenda essent,
numerandique exercitus, quoniam ne numerare quidem ut par
esset turbam sciebant, quemadmodum pastores pecudes solent,
tunc sapientiores melioresque effecti ipsum interemere.

and read some passage of theirs, do you? For you know these things better than others, and you think you will, as a result, become the finest men and will manage public and private affairs in the best way. And now in the expectation of these results you dwell in the city and educate your sons as if whoever can perform a rendition of 'Pallas, Persepolis, Minerva' with the cithara or tap with the foot in time to the lyre will be able to handle both private and public affairs. But you have never previously learned, nor even at this time do you take thought, how you will know what is in the interest of you and your country and how you should govern the state in accord with the laws and justice. Moreover, during festivals you avidly view the trage- 28 dians, and people's catastrophes in the tragedies draw you to feel pity for them. Nonetheless you never recalled that it was not those who are illiterate and sing badly and are ignorant of gymnastics who were involved in these troubles. Nor has anyone produced a tragedy because someone was a pauper. On the contrary, one can observe that all tragedies speak of men like Atreus, Agamemnon, and Oedipus, who held most of their wealth in gold, silver, land, and herds; and they say that he among them who had the worst fortune was the one who had a golden ram.[14] In fact, Thamyras,[15] who was a virtuoso of cit- 29 hara and competed with the very Muses in harmony, was both blinded and deprived of his ability in the art of the citharode. It did not avail Palamedes to have invented the alphabet to avert his being stoned to death unjustly by the very Achaians he had educated; but as long as they had been without training in literacy they allowed him to live. But when he passed on literacy to others and the Atridae in particular and along with literacy how signs were to be produced by fire and armies numbered — since they did not even know how to count the mob correctly, as shepherds do sheep — then, when they had been made wiser and better, they killed him.

30 'Sin autem oratores,' inquit, 'eos esse censetis qui satis ad consultandum valeant, et ipsorum arte bonos effici viros posse, miror equidem qui minus rerum ipsarum iudicium illis permiseritis, sed vobis ipsis potius, neque iustissimos illos optimosque duxeritis, nec etiam rerum gerendarum munus illis concesseritis. Identidem enim facturi sitis ac si gubernatores et triremium praefectos declaraveritis aut remiges aut qui remigi-

31 bus facienda iubent. Quod si quis tandem vel ex his qui rempublicam gerunt vel ex oratorum numero ad eum diceret ut hac utentes disciplina Athenienses quo tempore Persae cum tot hominum millibus bis deinceps adversus urbem et adversus aliam Graeciam duxerunt exercitum, et primum quidem viribus ac ducibus a[16] rege missis, postea vero ipso etiam Xerxe cum omni Asiatica multitudine adveniente, hos tamen vicere omnis et ubique eos tum consilio tum etiam pugna superarunt, et quonam pacto superare potuissent talem apparatum et tantas copias ni virtute quoque praestitissent, aut qui virtute praestare potuissent, si non optima disciplina sed et prava et inutili fuis-

32 sent, ad eum qui talia diceret, respondebat ne illos quidem venisse in Graeciam ulla disciplina institutos, nescientes etiam quid consilii de rebus agendis capiundum esset, sed qui sagittandi equitandique ac vaenandi peritiae studuissent. Atque nudari corpore et spuere[17] in propatulo turpissimum eis videbatur. Verum haec illis nihil erant profutura. Itaque nullus erat illorum imperator, nullus rex, sed infinita hominum millia aderant, qui et amentes omnes miserique essent. Quod siquis in iis foret qui et tiaram haberet rectam sederetque in aureo solio, ab quo tanquam a numine violentissime agerentur, alii in mare,

"But if you reckon," said he, "that the orators are the men   30
equal to the task of deliberation, and that by their art men can
be made good, I am surprised that you have not granted them,
but rather yourselves, the power of judging matters of state and
have not considered them to be the most just and best citizens
nor yielded to them the task of managing affairs. For you would
be doing the same thing if you were naming oarsmen or those
who give orders to the oarsmen as the captains and commanders of your triremes. Suppose, then, that some public official or   31
orator were to say to Socrates: 'Practicing this education at the
time when the Persians twice brought an army of many, many
thousands of men against Athens and the rest of Greece—the
first time an army with forces and generals sent by the king, the
second time when Xerxes himself marched with the multitudes
of Asia—the Athenians nevertheless defeated them all and defeated them everywhere, both in strategy and fighting. How
could they have achieved victory over such an assemblage and
so many forces if they had not also excelled them in courage?
Or how could they have excelled in courage if their education
had not been the best but both defective and useless?' To the   32
man who would say things like this, [Socrates] used to reply
that the enemy that had come against Greece had been brought
up without any education, not even knowing what sort of policy should be adopted in state affairs, but had trained in the
skills of archery, riding horses, and hunting. And to them it
seemed the vilest thing to strip naked and spit in public.[16] But
those qualities did them no good. And so they had neither a
general nor a king, just countless thousands of men who were
all foolish and wretched. But if there were someone present
among them who had an upright tiara and sat on a golden
throne, by whom they would be powerfully driven as if by divine power, they would be forced to die, some by plunging into

33 alii adversus montes, et caesi verberibus et perterriti et trusi trementesque mori cogebantur. Quemadmodum igitur si homines duo palaestricae artis ignari palaestram luserint, et alter aliquando prosternat alterum, ac ne id quidem ulla peritia sed fortuna quadam, saepe autem ipse bis etiam deinceps prosternatur, sic Atheniensibus quoque congressi Persae quandoque sunt ab Atheniensibus superati, quandoque superaverunt Athenienses, veluti postero tempore cum urbis etiam muros bellum adversus Lacedaemonios gerentes solo aequarunt. Nam possis mihi dicere an unquam Athenienses minus vel musicis vel litteris eruditi fuerint? Deinde rursum cum Cononis ductu navali ad Cnidum pugna victoria potiti sunt, num melius vel luctabantur vel canebant?'

34 Haec sunt illius Socratis verba, quem non modo rex Macedonum Archelaus, vir certe et suopte ingenio et multarum maximarumque rerum peritia et[18] eruditissimorum hominum consuetudine permagnus atque perillustris, quo talia disserentem audiret, ingentibus ad se praemiis pulcherrimisque muneribus invitavit, sed etiam Apollinis iudicio sapientem appellatum tradit antiquitas. His, inquam, verbis Socrates eos acriter castigabat homines qui rebus vanis inutilibusve dediti animi sapientiaeque praestantiam negligerent ac pro nihilo haberent. Non enim in cantu et fidibus, non in harena, non in ambitione, non in contentionibus puerilibus positum est vitae humanae decus.

35 Sed cum duae sint animi partes, quarum altera continet rationem, altera est rationis expers, utriusque vis perdiscenda est omnis. Nam cui vel metus vel cupiditas inhaerescit, cui aut aegritudinis aut voluptatis faces admotae sunt, non potest is recte neque iudicare nec sentire quicquam. Ut igitur communem[19] illam vegetandi quam vocant ac nutriendi vim omittamus — non enim humanae virtutis est particeps — volunt aliam quandam

the sea, others pinned against mountains, cut by lashes, terrified, thrust back, trembling. Just as if two men, ignorant of the   33
art, were to play at wrestling and the one were eventually to lay
the other flat, not by any skill but by some chance — even if the
same man were thrown flat on his back twice — so also the Persians fought with the Athenians and were sometimes defeated
by them and sometimes defeated them, just as, later, waging
war against the Spartans, they even razed the city walls. Can
you tell me whether the Athenians were never uneducated in
music and illiterate? Surely later on, when through Conon's
admiralship they gained victory in battle at Cnidus, they were
not any better at wrestling and singing, were they?"

These are the words of Socrates, whom Archelaus, king of   34
Macedonia, a very great and distinguished man both for his
own genius and experience in numerous and important affairs
and through consorting with the most learned men, invited to
his court with rewards and splendid gifts in order to hear him
discoursing on such matters; and antiquity relates that he was
called wise by the judgment of Apollo. With these words, then,
Socrates fiercely excoriated those who had given themselves
over to empty or pointless activities and neglected the priority
of the mind's wisdom and held it of no importance. For the
splendor of human life does not reside in singing and lyre play-
ing, in the arena, in ambition, in childish quarrels. But since the   35
soul has two parts, one of which contains reason, the other of
which lacks reason, the entire power of each of them needs to
be thoroughly learned. For the person to whom either fear or
desire attaches or who has been beset by the fires of illness or
pleasure cannot judge or perceive anything correctly. Therefore,
setting aside that common power that they call vegetative or
nurturing, as it has no share in human virtue, philosophers
claim that there is a certain distinct nature of the irrational

27

36   esse animi irrationalis naturam, quae etsi ipsa quoque ratione caret, rationem tamen potest admittere. Nam quamquam appetitus, quoniam repugnat nonnunquam adversaturque rationi, irrationalis dicitur, persaepe tamen solet veluti fraeno generosus equus obtemperare parereque rationi, et ita eius quoque fieri quodammodo particeps. Quid enim et incontinentem vituperare et continentem laudare consuevimus? Nempe quod in altero appetitus perinde[20] atque perturbatione effraenatus ac praeceps non solum rationem non sequitur, sed aspernatur potius, odit, contemnit, ab eaque vaehementer abhorret atque avertitur, in altero autem non resistit rationi appetitus, verum et libenter admittit et amat et admiratur, et eidem sese tradit ac omni ex

37   parte obsequitur. Quo fit ut altera pars animi et ipsa in se rationem habeat, et parti alteri largiatur, cum sua natura propemodum aeque appetitio atque vegetandi vis ratione careat, quanvis nutritivae sensitiva vis non mediocriter antecellat. An haec ignoras?

38   *Honofrius.* Ignorabam equidem antea, mi pater. Sed nunc ita perspicue de istis es cumulatissimeque locutus, ut nulla me omnino dubitatio teneat. Verum quia ratione appetitionem quasi fingi ac regi, perturbatione autem irritari et inmoderatius ferri videris dicere, quid utraque tandem sit, cupio scire.

39   *Pallas.* Et recte quidem cupis, o fili. Nam quaecunque ulla de re instituta praeceptio fuerit, tum recte potest eleganter explicari, si a definitione proficiscatur. Quare tametsi noster hic sermo de exilio sit futurus, non alienum fuerit quid ratio, quid perturbatio sit paucis ostendere, praesertim cum moralis virtutis perturbatio sit materia, ratio vero forma. Ut igitur a perturbatione primum sermo noster proficiscatur — ita enim voco quod Graeci πάθος nominant, eandem non nulli tum 'passionem,' tum

soul, which, while it lacks reason itself, can nonetheless be open to reason.[17] For although appetite is said to be irrational since it sometimes resists and opposes reason, it is often nonetheless accustomed to acquiesce in and obey reason, as a thoroughbred horse does a bridle, and thus in a certain sense comes to partake in it. Why do we habitually upbraid the incontinent man and commend the man who shows self-control? Clearly because in the one, appetite, as if set loose and driven headlong by emotion, not only fails to follow reason but spurns, loathes, and despises it, shrinks and turns away from it with vehemence. In the other, however, appetite does not resist reason but even takes it in, loves it, looks up to it, surrenders itself to it, and offers wholehearted obedience. From this it follows that one part of the soul contains reason in itself and bestows it on the other part since by their own nature the appetite and the vegetative power are almost equally lacking in reason, even though the sensible power enormously excels the vegetative one. Are these matters unknown to you?

Onofrio. They were previously, father, but you spoke so clearly and perfectly about these topics that I am free of all doubt. But since you seem to maintain that appetite is, as it were, molded and guided by reason but provoked and carried along uncontrollably by emotion, I wish to know what each of these two is.

Palla. Rightly so, my son. Whatever instruction has been begun about any topic, it can be explained elegantly if it proceeds from a definition. Therefore, although this conversation of ours will concern exile, it is not out of place to indicate briefly what reason is and what emotion is, especially since emotion is the matter, while reason is the form of moral virtue. So inasmuch as our conversation starts out with emotion — for this is what I call what the Greeks refer to as *pathos*, some people being accustomed to translate this word sometimes as "passion,"

'morbum,' tum 'permotionem,' tum pro variis et locis et rebus,
variis item nominibus interpretari consueverunt²¹ — hanc multi-
40 pliciter dici non absurde licet. Nam aut id quidem 'passio' dicitur quod in corruptionem agit, aut quod agit in perfectionem.²²
Sic enim lignum *pati* dicitur ab igni, perinde²³ atque in corruptionem agatur. Pati etiam sensus dicuntur a sensibilibus, eo
quod et ab illis perficiantur aganturque e virtute in actum. Dicitur item 'passio,' ut Aristoteli placet, qualitas qua potest quippiam in suum transire contrarium, ut albedo in nigredinem,
dulcedo in amaritudinem, gravedo in levitatem, reliquaque
huiusmodi. Alio autem modo, ut haec aguntur iamque mutantur, quae quidem prima materia caliditas frigiditasque recipit.
41 Praeterea quae magis nocet mutatio ipsa atque permotio maxi-
meque et tristis et damnosa, identidem 'passio' appellatur. Su-
binde quod ex iis accidit quae maximam aut aegritudinem aut
voluptatem afferunt, 'passio' nominatur. Et quanvis quaeque
partis nutritivae vis activa sit, sensitivae autem passiva, mentalis
vero alia activa, alia passiva, tamen, ut uno verbo multa complectar, quaevis animi actio potest 'passio' vocari. Quibus quidem de rebus singillatim transigendi non est praesentis neque
42 temporis neque loci. Quid vero perturbatio ipsa sit, alii aliter
definiunt. Nam alii sunt qui dicant passionem esse motum ex
alterius in alterum operatione qui principium in agente habeat,
finem vero in patiente. Alii dicunt passionem esse mutationem
huiusce cuiuspiam cuius erat, sive propter bonum, sive secus.
Item passio est quod mutari potest in hoc quod prius non erat.
Verum omissis aliis aliorum definitionibus, nos una hoc tempore — et ea quidem Aristotelica — contenti simus. Est igitur

sometimes as "disease," sometimes as "the stirring of feelings,"
varying the translation in accordance with subject matter and
context—this multiplicity of names is not absurd. For "passion"   40
can refer either to what leads to ruin or to what leads to perfection. A piece of wood is said to "be affected" (*pati*) by fire precisely when it is being corrupted, but the senses also are said to
"be affected" (*pati*) by sensible objects just because they are perfected by them and reduced from potency to act. A quality by
which anything can change into its opposite is called a "passion," as Aristotle holds: for example, from white to black,
sweetness to bitterness, heaviness to lightness, etc.[18] But passion is spoken of in another way when the things that heat and
cold receive via prime matter are being reduced and are already
changing. Furthermore, the [kind of] change that is more   41
harmful and the extreme of motion which is particularly harsh
and damaging are likewise called "passion." What immediately
results from the things which bring the greatest suffering or
pleasure is called "passion." And even though every power of the
nutritive part is active and of the sensible part passive, while
some mental powers are active and some passive, nonetheless,
to use a blanket category, any action of the soul you like can be
called a "passion." However, now is neither the time nor the
place to deal with these matters individually. As to what emo-   42
tion itself is, people define it in different ways. For there are
some who say that passion is a movement from the natural pro-
cessing of one thing into another that has its origin in an active
thing and its end in a passive thing. Others say that passion is a
change in any kind of thing, whether for better or worse. Likewise passion is the capacity for something to be altered into
what it was not beforehand. But having set aside all the other
definitions of other men, let us be content, at least for the
moment, with one, namely Aristotle's. Passion is an emotion,
therefore, that moves men and sets them in opposition to their

43 perturbatio qua homines permoti iudicio repugnant. Nam quod Andronicus Peripateticus perturbationem definierit esse animi propter existimationem mali aut boni permotionem quae ratione careat et praeter naturam appetitioni adhaereat, vel quod sit animi motus rationi non obediens, vel, ut Zeno Citieus ille, aut aversa a recta ratione contra naturam animi permotio vel appetitus ipse vaehementior, caeteraeque huiuscemodi de perturbatione definitiones novi aliud nihil afferunt quod superiore una ac brevi Aristotelis descriptione minus contineatur. Num tandem quid perturbatio sit intelligis?

44 *Honofrius.* Satis a te mihi hac in re, mi pater, superque factum est. Verum quandoquidem ita perturbationem definieris, scire admodum cupiam et eius genera et generum partes, modo id quidem probes aut tempestivum ducas.

Pallas. Probo equidem, fili, sed quod Pittacus monebat: 'Tempus cognosce.'[24] Non enim omnia nunc doceri possunt quae tibi expedit scire. Non multo post, cum occasio dabitur, obsequar fortasse desyderio isti tuo. Deinceps quod alterum erat abs te quaesitum, de ratione ipsa, nunc percurramus. Hanc item multipliciter dici manifestum est. Sed nos, reliqua omittentes quae hoc de nomine ab his notantur qui grammatici dicuntur, ea brevi perstringamus quae a philosophis disseruntur.

45 Sunt qui rationem et animum idem esse velint, quare etiam[25] immortalem. Alii rationem dicunt animi aspectum, quo per seipsum quid veri sit, non per corpus intueatur. Et ipsam veri contemplationem rationem volunt. Ad haec ratio, quam alii a corporis sensibus inchoatam, alii ab intelligentia mentis inventam probant, tum animi caput, tum oculus dici solet, eandemque ita habere[26] ad mentem ut aspectum ad oculum ostendunt.

judgment. The Peripatetic philosopher Andronicus'[19] under-   43
standing of emotion as a disturbance of the soul owing to a
judgment of evil and good, a judgment that is lacking in reason
and that clings to appetite, contrary to its nature; or the view
that it is a motion of the soul that does not obey reason; or the
renowned Zeno of Citium's[20] view that it is a movement of the
soul that is at odds with right reason and contrary to nature; or
[the definition of it as] a violent appetite; and other definitions
like this of "emotion" — none of these definitions bring anything
new beyond what is comprised in the few words of Aristotle's
definition, given above. So do you now understand what emotion is?

Onofrio. You have more than satisfied me on this topic, father. But   44
since you define emotion in this way, I would very much like to
know its genera and species, provided you approve of this and
consider it an opportune time.

Palla. Indeed, I do approve, son — that is, I approve the warning
Pittacus issued: "Know the time."[21] For not everything can be
taught now that is helpful for you to know. I shall perhaps
oblige that wish of yours before long, as occasion offers. But let
us now go over that other topic you asked about, the one concerning reason itself. It is clear that this is likewise spoken of in
many senses. But setting aside what has been observed about
the term by the so-called grammarians, let me touch briefly
upon the philosophers' arguments.

There are some who claim that reason and the rational soul   45
are the same and therefore that reason is also immortal; others
say that reason is an aspect of the soul by which it contemplates
through itself, not through the body, what truth is. And they
claim that reason is the very contemplation of truth. In addition, reason is generally called the "head" or the "eye" of the soul
because some say that it originates with the bodily senses,
others that it was discovered by the mind's intelligence. In the

33

Quare mentem et rationem eodem saepe nomine appellant. Verum hac de re nixius est urgendum. Qui subtilius de ratione, quam natura humana in mente[27] inesse volunt, et constantius disputant, hanc dupliciter dici arbitrantur: et superiorem et inferiorem. Ac illa quidem sapientiae est, qua aeterna et incommutabilia contemplamur, haec autem scientiae, qua in rerum temporalium atque mutabilium actione versamur. Differt enim a sapientia scientia, ut a contemplatione actio, id quod etiam eruditus ille sanctissimusque Paulus non obscure ostendit, inquiens, 'Alii quidem per spiritum datur sermo sapientiae, alii sermo scientiae secundum eundem spiritum.' Idem etiam docet innocentissimus Iob, cum ait, 'Ecce pietas est sapientia. Abstinere autem a malis scientia est.'

Qua certe distinctione satis liquido declaratur sapientiam contemplationis, scientiam esse actionis. Nam pietas hoc loco ea est virtus qua Deum colimus. Hanc autem Graeci tum εὐσέβειαν, tum significantius θεοσέβειαν nominant. Cum igitur iis in rebus quae aeternae immutabilesque sunt, nihil Deo sit maius, nihil excellentius, nihil praestantius, ad divinum cultum contemplatio nostra omnis referatur oportet. Hac enim illustri una felicique virtute et via pervenimus ad Deum. Hac omni labore negocioque vacui mundique, omni corporis sorde et omni denique labe penitus loti ac nitidi, et videmus Deum et in Deo quamsuavissime conquiescimus. At scientia quam non eorum quae necessitate sunt, ut Aristoteles probare nititur, sed rerum temporalium esse ostendimus. Nam et quaecunque a nobis vitia perpetrantur, secundum tempus perpetrantur; quorum evitatio ad aeterna nos illa dirigit bona. Et quidquid prudenter, iuste, fortiter, temperanter agimus, eius est disciplinae

latter way they demonstrate that reason relates to the mind as
vision relates to the eye. For this reason they often call mind
and reason by the same name. But we must pursue this topic
more strenuously.[22] Those who discuss reason more subtly and
consistently claim that it is naturally present in the human
mind and that it is spoken of in two ways: as higher and lower.
The higher belongs to wisdom, by which we contemplate eter-   46
nal and unchanging objects; the lower belongs to knowledge, by
which we act upon temporal and changing things, for knowledge is distinguished from wisdom as action from contemplation. That most learned and holy man Paul demonstrates this
clearly, saying: "To one is given through the Spirit the utterance
of wisdom, and to another the utterance of knowledge according to the same Spirit."[23] That most blameless man Job also
teaches the same thing when he says: "Behold, piety is wisdom,
and to depart from evil is understanding."[24]

By this distinction it is clearly shown that wisdom concerns   47
contemplation and knowledge concerns action. For in this passage piety is that virtue with which we worship God. The
Greeks speak of this as *eusebeia* (piety) or, with greater weight
of meaning, *theosebeia* (godliness). Since therefore among those
things that are eternal and unchanging nothing is greater than
God, nothing more excellent, nothing better, all our contemplation must be oriented to the worship of God. For by this one
splendid and happy virtue and path we arrive at God; by means
of this, freed from all toil and trouble and pure and spotless,
thoroughly cleansed of all the filth of the body and finally of all
sin, we see God, and in God we enjoy the sweetest possible
peace. We have shown that knowledge is not of those things   48
that exist by necessity, as Aristotle endeavors to prove, but of
temporal things. For whatever sins are committed by us are committed in time; the avoidance of these points us to those eternal goods. Whatever we do wisely, justly, bravely, temperately

qua tum evitamus turpia, tum honesta expetimus. Scientia, inquam, ipsa quoddam veluti iter paratur nobis eundi, non perveniendi, ad immortalem et sempiternum Deum. Scientia enim quae in huius exercendae temporalis vitae praeceptis est, non autem in illius aeternae caelestisque doctrina, in eo maxime laboramus operamurque, ut per animi ab omni terreno coeno ac sordibus mundationem atque abstersionem Deum aliquando videamus coramque fruamur. Nec illud tamen praeterire nos debet, solere aliquando 'scientiam' pro 'sapientia' appellari. Cum enim idem Paulus ait: 'Nunc scio ex parte, tunc autem cognoscam sicut et cognitus sum,' huiusmodi scientiam atque cognitionem non in agendo sed in contemplando versari manifestum est; sicuti etiam illustris aliquos artifices (ut Praxitelen, Copam, Phidiam, Apellen, Apollodorum, Parrhasium, Euphranorem, Polycletum) et egregios poetas (ut Homerum et Hesiodum) sapientes vocabat antiquitas, quos omnes nequaquam est dubium in his versatos quae et temporis sunt et corporis.

Ut igitur ad rem ipsam de qua loqui coeperamus nostra revertatur oratio, ratio inferior ea est quae ad hasce pertinet res sciendas quae corporis et temporis mutabilitati ac loeto subiectae sunt, superior vero quae illa respicit quae interitum nesciunt, mutabilitatem omnem et inconstantiam aspernantur, suntque divina. Ratio autem ipsa, ut a genere definitio oriatur, est quaedam mentis motio, quae eius quod discitur distinguendi et connectendi vim habet. Rationis vero inquisitio ratiocinatio dicitur; aeque enim ratione inquirimus ut intelligimus intellectu. Nam et ratio mentis aspectus et intellectus visio mentis est; at mens ipsa quasi oculus quidam animi. Dictam autem 'mentem' puto non solum quia *meminerit*, sed eo potius quia *emineat* in animis nostris, vel etiam quia *maneat* sitque et sempiterna et immortalis — nam μένειν Graece 'manere' significat — vel, ut

belongs to that teaching by which we both avoid disgraceful things and seek honorable ones. Knowledge itself, I say, is prepared for us as a kind of route for going to, not for arriving at, immortal and eternal God. By knowledge which consists in the precepts for leading this temporal life, not in the teaching of that eternal and heavenly life, we particularly toil and busy ourselves so that, with the mind cleansed and purified of all the earthly filth and squalor, we may at long last see God and enjoy His presence face to face. Nor should we fail to note that sometimes "knowledge" is used as a synonym for "wisdom." For when Paul likewise says, "now I know in part, but then I shall know as I am known,"[25] it is clear that knowledge and understanding of this kind involves not acting but contemplating, just as antiquity called wise some distinguished artists (such as Praxiteles, Copas,[26] Phidias, Apelles, Apollodorus, Parrhasius, Euphranor, Polycletus) and outstanding poets (such as Homer and Hesiod), all of whom were clearly engaged in temporal and corporeal matters. 49 50

To return to the matter about which we began to speak, the lower reason is the one that pertains to knowing things that are subject to the mutability and filth of time and the body, the higher reason the one that has reference to things that cannot perish, that spurn all mutability and inconstancy, and that are divine. Let our definition begin with the genus. Reason itself is a certain movement of the mind which has the power of taking apart and putting together what is learned. The investigation of reason is called theorizing (*ratiocinatio*); for we investigate by reason just as we understand by the intellect. For reason is the mind's act of seeing and intellect its vision; and the mind itself is as it were the eye of the soul. I think it is called "mind" (*mens*) not only because it remembers (*meminerit*) but because it is prominent (*emineat*) in our souls or even because it "remains" (*maneat*) and is both eternal and immortal—for *menein* in Greek 51

quibusdam placet, nomen a luna mens traxit, quam Graeci
52 μήνην vocant. Ut enim luna crescendo et decrescendo ac variae
vicissitudinis commutatione quadam in id se tandem quod
modo fuit mirabili quapiam opportunaque novitate restituit, ita
etiam mens ab qua intelligentia quam eius esse visionem diximus procedit, nunc veluti volitans ab inferioribus ad superiora
tollitur, nunc descendit ad infima, modo sese referens ipsa sibi a
falsis vera distinguit, modo ad ea regenda atque moderanda
quae vel corpori vel tempori tributa sunt circunflectitur, tum
aeternis rationibus contemplandis consulendisve tota intendi-
53 tur. Et quoniam plaerunque adverti non nullos huiusce tempestatis philosophos et alios quosdam eruditos viros qui non Grae-
cae modo sed Latinae etiam linguae proprietatem differentiasque
contemnunt, pro intelligentia eodemque intellectu mentem de-
pravate appellare solitos, et pro mente intellectum, mentem appello quem Graeci νοῦν, intelligentiam vero quam iidem διά-
νοιαν nominant. Mens enim inseparate secundum Platonicos
et indivise in iis intelligendis versatur quae intelliguntur. Intellectus autem transitio quaedam est ex propositionibus in conclusiones, et ea quidem ratiocinatione utens[28] ad rem eam quae
54 intelligitur compraehendendam. Sed nequis sua fallatur opinione, hic accipiendum velim τὸ διανοεῖσθαι (id est 'intelligentia uti'), ut intelligamus multa sciri simul posse, at circa
multa simul intelligentiam versari non posse. Ut enim multa
simul verba dicere non possumus, ita circa multa simul cum
intellectu versari non possumus. Nam intellectus quaedam est
animi oratio,[29] qua secum ipse loquitur. Quare quisquis intelligentia utitur, circa aliquid unum utitur. Num igitur, fili

signifies "remain" (*manere*) — or, as some hold, mind derives its
name from the moon, which the Greeks call *mene*. For just as   52
the moon, by waxing and waning and by a kind of alteration of
different states, restores itself, with a marvelous and timely renewal, to what it once was, so the mind also advances by this
intelligence that we have called its vision: now, as if flying, it is
lifted from lower to higher realms, then it descends to the bot-
tom; now bringing itself back, it distinguishes true from false,
now it is turned round to guide and control the things that have
been assigned to time and the body, then it focuses entirely on
contemplating and taking thought of eternal principles. Since I   53
have often noticed that some philosophers and other learned
men of our time who despise the proper usage and distinctions,
not only of the Greek, but even of the Latin language, are accustomed, perversely, to speak of "mind" in lieu of "intelligence"
and "intellect," and to use the term "intellect" instead of "mind,"
I call "mind" what the Greeks call *nous* and "intelligence" what
they call *dianoia*.[27] For according to the Platonists, the mind is
engaged undividedly and wholly in understanding those things
that are understood. The intellect, on the other hand, is a kind
of transition from propositions to conclusions and uses the
drawing of inferences (*ratiocinatio*) to grasp the thing that is
understood. But lest anyone be misled, I would like *to dianoeis-*   54
thai (that is, "to employ the intelligence") here to be understood,
[namely] that we understand that many things can be known
simultaneously, but intelligence cannot simultaneously be engaged upon many things. For just as we cannot pronounce
many words simultaneously, so we cannot be engaged simultaneously with the intellect upon many things. For the intellect is
a kind of speech of the mind by which it speaks to itself. Therefore whoever uses intelligence, uses it upon some one thing.

Honofri, quicquam habes quod in his quae breviter perstrinximus, enodatius aut latius exponi cupias?

55 *Honofrius.* Haberem equidem permulta, mi pater, quae nisi permolesta haec exilii aerumna me vaehementius premeret, libenter ex te perdiscerem. Sed quoniam animi partes luculenter complexus es, et non solum quae ad perturbationem rationemque pertinebant, es omnia mea sententia elocutus et diligenter et plane, verum etiam quod ex aliis pluribus qui existimantur[30] doctissime eruditi et poene sapientes cognoscere nunquam potui, qui mentem, qui intellectum accipi oporteat (quod minime petieram), es non minus opportuna quam mihi admodum grata oratione complexus, iam siquid habes ad hanc exilii levandam acerbitatem, ut in medium proferas etiam atque

56 etiam te[31] et rogo et oro. Nam siquid de his voluero quae non perspicue minus quam subtiliter persecutus es vel audire prolyxius vel intelligere explicatius, licebit postea, cum praesentem mihi animi maerorem paululum oratione sedaveris, per tempus inquirere. Quare nunc, si placet, de exilio.

Pallas. Faciam equidem quod petis. Sed interim quae singillatim disseruimus, ne excidant provideto. Erunt enim medicamenta quaedam ad praesentem animi tui morbum.

Honofrius. Memoriter, mi pater, et quae locutus es et quae deinceps loqueris, meminero omnia.

Pallas. Audistine unquam quae apud Euripidem Polynices loquitur?

Honofrius. Quaenam? Non enim memini.

57 *Pallas.* Facit, inquam, Euripides in *Phoenissis* Polynicem cum Iocasta matre talia quaedam disserere.

> *Pol.* Mater, quod ad viros mihi infensos ierim,
> et mente ducor sana et insana. At solum
> necessitas omnis agit, patrium ut colant.
> Quod qui secus dicit, thriumphat vocibus

Now then, Onofrio my son, is there any point in what I have
briefly touched upon that you would like explained with greater
clarity or at greater length?

Onofrio. There are a great many things, father, that I would gladly   55
learn from you were not this misery of exile weighing heavily
upon me. But since you have brilliantly expounded the parts of
the soul, and not only the ones that bear upon emotion and
reason, in my opinion you have expressed everything carefully
and clearly, but also you have encompassed in a speech no less
opportune than pleasing to me what I could never grasp from
others who are thought to be highly educated and virtually
sages, namely how the mind and intellect are to be understood,
something I had not requested. But now, if you have any means
of alleviating this bitterness of exile, I must beg and pray you
with great insistence that you share it. If I shall want to listen at   56
greater length or to understand more fully any of these things
that you have pursued with clarity and subtlety, we can do so
later on, once you have allayed my present sorrow a bit with
your discourse. So now, please speak about exile.

Palla. I will certainly do what you ask. But in the meantime, see
that you don't forget the individual points we have been discussing, because they will constitute remedies for your current
soul sickness.

Onofrio. I will remember well, father, everything you have said and
what you soon will say.

Palla. Have you ever heard Polyneices' speech in Euripides?

Onofrio. What speech? I don't recall.

Palla. In the *Phoenissae* Euripides has Polynices say the following   57
to his mother Jocasta:[28]

> *Polynices.* Mother, when I meet my enemies I am partly sane,
> partly mad. But necessity always forces men to love their
> ancestral soil. If anyone says otherwise, he is vaunting

inanibus. Nam mente patriam canit.
Cura metuque sic premor, nequis dolus
me fratris opprimat, manus uti meas
armatus ense venerim per oppidum,
faciem rotans circum. Sed unum me iuvat
et foedus et fides tua. Hac ducor libens
in patria moenia, lachrymas post diutinas
fumum domesticum deumque aras videns,
gymnasiaque in quis ductus et Dirces aquam.
Quibus omnibus depulsus iniuste, colo
urbem peregrinam. Genae lachrymis madent;
ad pristinum dolorem alius item dolor
accedit, ut te, mater, et rasam caput
atramque peplos video, vae misero mihi!
Ut, mater, est grave sanguinis cognati odium,
et quam nequit dissolvi! At age, senex pater
dic quid domi facit, tenebris aevum agens,
quidque soror utraque. Num meum exilium dolent?

58   *Iocasta.* Laevus deorum quispiam Oedipi genus
olim interimere coepit, unde perperam
peperi, paterque perperam nupsit tuus
ac perperam ventri meo te conseruit.
Sed his quid usus? Quaeque caelites iubent,
mortalibus ferenda sunt modice omnia.
Sed qui rogem? Mentem tibine mordeam
quae cupio, vereor, vel tibi tristis rogem.

Pol. Verum roga, ne tu tibi ipsa defueris.
Nam quae ipsa vis, haec sunt mihi carissima.

Ioc. Tandem rogo te scire quod primum velim:
quid exilium ais, nate? Num magnum malum?

Pol. Quammaximum, maiusque re quam oris sono.

Ioc. Quonam modo? Quae est exulibus acerbitas?

with empty words, for inwardly he sings of his country. I am so weighed down by anxiety and fear that some trick of my brother may crush me that I pass through the town, my hands armed with a knife, turning my gaze round and round. But the truce and your pledge are my sole aid. In reliance on this I am led willingly into my city's walls, seeing my hearth and home and the altars of our gods after such long-lasting sorrow and the gymnasium in which I was trained and the fountain of Dirce, from all of which I was unjustly driven out and inhabit a foreign city. My cheeks are wet with tears; another sorrow is added to the original one as I see you, Mother, your head shaven, dressed in a black robe—woe is me! How burdensome and incurable is hatred for one's own blood, Mother! But tell me how my aged father is faring at home, spending his life in darkness, and how both my sisters are faring. Do they lament my exile?

Jocasta. Some god hostile to Oedipus began long ago to destroy his family, from the time when I gave birth unlawfully, and your father wedded unlawfully and unlawfully sowed you in my womb. But what good are these recriminations? Mortals must bear with moderation all that the gods bid. But why should I ask? I fear causing you anguish with my request, or growing sad by asking you. 58

Polynices. Ask so as not to disappoint yourself. For what you wish is very dear to me.

Jocasta. I ask you what I wish to know first: what do you mean by exile, son? Is it a great evil?

Polynices. The greatest possible, greater in reality than words can express.

Jocasta. How so? What bitterness do exiles feel?

Pol. Quo durius nihil est, oportet exulem
demittat ipse se, nec audeat loqui.
Ioc. Servile puto nequire quod sentis loqui.
Pol. Ineptiasque principum ferat, est opus.
Ioc. Et hoc grave est, aliorum ut ullus particeps
amentiae fiat. *Pol.* Lucrique gratia
servire cogitur. *Ioc.* Sed, ut dici solet,
spes exules pascunt. *Pol.* At hae pulchris quidem
luminibus aspiciunt, nimis at amant moras.
Ioc. Neque longa vanas indicat dies eas?
Pol. Habent voluptatem malorum quampiam.
Ioc. Verum unde quaerebas cibum ante nuptias?
Pol. Modo diurnum habui, modo carui miser.
Ioc. At patris amici et hospites nil proderant?
Pol. Utere secundis. Nullum amicum miser habet.
Ioc. Nec magnitudo sustulit generis boni?
Pol. Malum est egere. Me genus aluit nihil.
Ioc. Patria, ut videtur, est homini amicissimum?
Pol. Amicum ut est patria, loqui nequeam quidem.

59 *Honofrius.* Profecto, mi pater, adhuc meam causam agis, Euripidis etiam testimonio, apud quem Polynices, patria sponte cedens ac etiam rem et gloriam extra patriam nactus adeptusque, quam tamen molestum sit patria carere, satis id certe liquido

Polynices. The hardest thing of all is that the exile must humble himself and not dare to speak his mind.

Jocasta. I think it is a slave's lot to be unable to say what you think.

Polynices. The exile must put up with princes' follies.

Jocasta. This, too, is oppressive: to share in others' madness.

Polynices. One is forced, for gain, to be a slave.

Jocasta. But it is said that exiles feed on hope.

Polynices. Hope appears with a lovely countenance but is too fond of delay.

Jocasta. Does length of time not reveal that she is vain?

Polynices. Hope takes a sort of pleasure in misfortunes.

Jocasta. But before you married, where did you seek your food?

Polynices. Wretch that I was, I supplied myself day by day, sometimes going without.

Jocasta. Did your father's friends and clients supply you nothing?

Polynices. Enjoy fortune's favor while you can; the unhappy man has no friends.

Jocasta. Your distinguished lineage did not help you?

Polynices. To be needy is an evil; my fine pedigree brought me no food.

Jocasta. Is a man's greatest treasure, as it seems, his homeland?

Polynices. How treasured it is I cannot even say.

Onofrio. So far you are arguing my case, father, with the testimony 59
of Euripides, in whose work Polynices is voluntarily departing from his country and, even after obtaining and acquiring wealth and fame outside of his homeland, showing clearly how grievous a thing it is to be deprived of one's country when he calls

demonstrat, cum dicit exilium non solum magnum malum, sed
adeo maximum, ut re maius quam verbo esse convincat.

Pallas. Quam ego causam ago tuam, postea viderimus. Verum dic
mihi, quibus Polynices argumentis convincere tibi videtur exilium malum esse quam maximum?

60 *Honofrius.* Primum, ut iam sua ipsius utar sententia, quoniam necesse admodum sit ita se gerat demissum exul ut — quod servile
est — ne verbum quidem facere audeat. Idque aut infamia aut
inopia aut etiam utraque re accidere arbitror. Qui enim mulcta-
tur exilio, ob aliquod facinus exilio mulctatus vulgo existimatur.
Quare ab omnibus monstratur digyto: 'Hic est,' inquiunt, 'ab
hoc tibi cave. Non temere hunc sui cives exosi sunt. Machina-
batur immane scelus in patriam. Hoc iam fecerat. Illud propediem factum ire meditabatur. Quos non decipiebat? Quos non
61 fallebat? Quos non inducebat?' Omnes coronae, consessus omnes exulem carpunt. Alii ebriosum, alii voracem, alii iniustum,
alii raptorem, adulterum, flagitiosum, nequam accusant. Nulla
innocentia, nulla pietas, nulla fides, nulla sanctimonia, nulla
temperantia, nulla frugalitas, nulla denique virtus vitam exulis
tuetur. Prudentiam exulis maliciam nominant. Simplicitatem
invidioso calliditatis vocabulo depravant. Vultum, quem veluti
quendam mentis sermonem dicunt, variis calumniis signant.
Fiduciam in confidentiam trahunt. Sapientis aequabilitatem at-
62 que constantiam ignaviam et stuporem interpretantur. Quid
pluribus? Quidquid in exule boni praeclarive extiterit, per omne
cavillum ludibriumque invertunt. Quo fit ut nihil sibi taciturnitate tutius et ad tranquillitatem et ad quietem exules ducant.
Egestate vero atque inopia quam esse demisso animo exulem
oportet, idem Polynices paulo post declarat, cum ait, 'Pauper est
nihil vir nobilis.' Itaque[32] non inepte apud Virgilium Aeneas,
cum miseriae suae cumulum esset ostensurus, non sine magna
quadam ac tristi animi permotione subdidit:

exile not just a great misfortune, but the greatest by far, so that he demonstrates his point more by facts than by words.

Palla. We shall afterward see to what extent I am arguing your case. But tell me the arguments Polynices uses that seem to convince you that exile is the worst possible misfortune.

Onofrio. First of all, to adopt his own view, the exile must carry 60 himself so humbly that he does not dare utter a word—the behavior of a slave. And this I think happens either through infamy or poverty or both. For a man who is punished by exile is commonly thought to have been punished because of some crime. For this reason everyone points a finger at him; they say: "That's the man; beware of him. His fellow countrymen had good reason to detest him. He plotted a monstrous crime against his country; he already carried it out; he has been thinking about carrying out the next one very soon. Whom has he not cheated? Whom has he not deceived? Whom has he not misled?" All the bystanders, the entire assembly upbraid the 61 exile: some accuse him of being a drunk, others a glutton, others a cheater, others a rapist, an adulterer, a worthless disgrace. No innocence, no piety, no trustworthiness, no holiness, no restraint, no self-control, in short, no virtue protects the exile. The exile's prudence they term maliciousness; they pervert his "straightforwardness" to "shrewdness." They brand his face, which they say is the mind's speech, with various insults. They call his confidence arrogance. They pervert a sage's calmness and constancy to laziness and stupidity. Why go on? They in- 62 vert in mockery all the exile's good qualities. The result is that exiles hold nothing safer than silence for their peace of mind and rest. How humble the exile must be in his poverty and want Polynices shows a bit later when he says, "A pauper is by no means a noble man."[29] And so, when Aeneas is about to show the mass of his afflictions—not without great sorrow and emotion—Vergil aptly adds:

47

> Ipse ignotus, egens, Libyae deserta peragro,
> Europa atque Asia pulsus.

63   Se, inquam, tanquam ignotum aiebat esse, quoniam egeret exul. Nam quanti secundus rumor faciundus sit, et quam formidandus adversus, satis modo ostenderat, cum ita de se loqueretur:

> Sum pius Aeneas, raptos qui ex hoste Penates
> classe veho mecum, fama super aethera notus.

64   Quod si utrunque malum, et infamia et paupertas, accesserit, nihil profecto exule miserius, nihil infelicius, nihil infortunatius. Deinde non loqui solum quod recte senserit prohibetur, sed etiam ineptitudinem principum stulticiamque ferre, et cum iisdem insanientibus simul insanire, et eorum libidini quasi mercenarius servus et sponte miser per omne probrum ac de-
65   decus servire cogitur. Quibus profecto rebus nihil esse puto nec aerumnosius nec luctuosius. Nonne igitur rectissimis Polynices rationibus convincit exilio nihil esse durius[33] nec gravius quicquam? Nam quod exuli amicus nullus est reliquus nec quisquam fert opem, nemo est qui neget. Quis enim res prosperas et securas non libenter malit quam desperatas et perditas sequi atque complecti? Praeterea quis eum aut amet aut ullo vitae auxilio prosequatur, a quo nullum commodum expectet, incommoda autem et pericula pertimescere multa possit?

66   *Pallas.* Quod non te statim dedis neque facile sinis moveri loco, haud omnino vitupero. Quo enim acriorem te praestiteris ad id

Driven from Europe and Asia, I wander the Libyan desert
without name or goods.

He spoke of himself as "without name," I think, because as an   63
exile he was in need. How much value should be attached to a
favorable reputation and how much a negative one should be
dreaded, he sufficiently showed when he spoke of himself as
follows:

I am faithful Aeneas, whose fame flies beyond the heavens,
Who carries in his ship the Penates seized from the
    enemy.[30]

But if both infamy and poverty fall to his lot, there is nothing   64
unhappier, nothing more miserable, nothing more unfortunate
than an exile. Besides, not only is he forbidden to speak what
he truly thinks, but he is also forced to endure the folly and
stupidity of princes, to play the madman along with them when
they are raving, and like a hired slave is compelled to minister
willingly to their whims through a gamut of disgrace and dishonor. I believe there is nothing more vexatious or grievous   65
than these conditions. So doesn't Polynices show clearly with
cogent arguments that there is nothing harsher or more oppressive than exile? No one would deny that there is no friend left
for an exile nor anyone to bring him assistance. Who indeed
would not gladly follow and embrace prosperity and security
rather than desperation and bankruptcy? Moreover, who would
love or provide sustenance to a man from whom he expects no
benefit but on whose account he can fear many troubles and
dangers?

Palla. I don't reproach you at all for not immediately conceding   66
the argument or refusing to alter your position. The keener you
show yourself in defending your view, the more you will be

tuendum quod sentis, eo magis veritatem, ubi cognoris, admittes teque nequaquam demisso animo probabis.

Honofrius. Et quonam modo?

Pallas. Quia exilium tibi loquendi disceptandique fiduciam minime subtraxerit.

67 *Honofrius.* Verum uberius de his velim.

Pallas. Sed quid dixeris si probabo exilium non modo non esse summum maximumve malum, at ne magnum quidem? Vel potius non modo non esse magnum, sed nullum omnino malum esse?

Honofrius. Audiam equidem te, mi pater, hac de re disserentem non libenter minus quam diligenter. Sed ne—quod Polynices monebat—aliud sentias, aliud disseras, ipse videris. Ego tamen ad audiendum me paravi.

68 *Pallas.* Non is sum qui verbis gaudeam. Menti oratio respondebit. Non enim aliter te institui cupio quam meipsum instituerim. Ad haec neque mentitur vir bonus, nec prudens mendacium dicit. Vano autem futilique homine levius nihil existimo. Primum igitur hoc mihi responde: de cuius exilio loqueris? De sapientisne atque boni viri, an de stulti et improbi hominis exilio?

Honofrius. De sapientis quidem. Stultus enim quocunque in loco fuerit, sive exul seu in patria, miser est, ut opinor.

69 *Pallas.* Si ergo stultus ubique est miser, qui minus opinaris ubique item sapientem felicem esse?

Honofrius. Quoniam, ut diximus, conscius suae sibi fortunae loqui quod recte senserit non audet, aliorum stulticiae obsequi et ad suam utilitatem servire etiam interdum cogitur.

Pallas. Nunquid Annibal videtur tibi ulla ex parte demisso animo fuisse aut quod prudentissime sentiebat dicere veritus, cum maximis rebus gestis apud Antiochum regem exularet? Omitto

open to the truth when you recognize it, and you will show that
you have by no means conceded in an attitude of dejection.

Onofrio. How so?

Palla. Because exile has not taken away your confidence in speaking and debating.

Onofrio. I should like to hear you expound this at greater length.   67

Palla. What would you say if I show that exile is not only not the
supreme and greatest evil but not even a great one? Or rather,
not only that it is not a great evil but that it is not an evil
at all?

Onofrio. I will listen to you willingly and attentively, father, as you
discuss this topic. But beware of saying one thing and thinking
another — a point that Polynices cautioned against. Nonetheless, I am resolved to listen.

Palla. I am not one to take delight in words; my speech will cor-   68
respond to my thoughts. For I want you to be instructed no
differently than I have instructed myself. Moreover, a good man
does not lie, and a wise man tells no falsehood. I think nothing
more frivolous than a hollow and empty man. First tell me this:
whose exile are you talking about? That of a wise and good
man, or of a fool and reprobate?

Onofrio. That of a wise man. For wherever a fool finds himself,
whether as an exile or in his own country, he is, I think, unhappy.

Palla. If then the fool is unhappy everywhere, why do you not   69
likewise think that the wise man is happy everywhere?

Onofrio. Because, as we said, conscious of his misfortune, he does
not dare to say what he truly thinks, and he is compelled to
humor others' foolishness and even sometimes to be a slave for
expediency's sake.

Palla. Surely you do not think Hannibal was in any degree hum-
bled or feared to speak his wise thoughts when, after his great
exploits, he lived in exile at the court of King Antiochus? I set

quae de Phormione philosopho cavillatus fuerit. Sed audi eius

70 duo dicta in regem. Cum Antiochus Romanis bellum illaturus quas ingentes pedestris equestrisque copias ex omnibus gentibus compararat Annibali ostentaturus eduxisset in campum, currusque falcatos et elephantos cum turribus numero magno circunductaret, et cataphractis admodum abundaret, nec militum arma duntaxat, sed equorum etiam fraenos, monilia, phaleras multo et argento et auro atque gemmis longe fulgentes miraretur, iactabundus ad Annibalem versus, 'Et putasne,' inquit, 'conferri posse ac satis esse credis Romanis haec omnia?' At Annibal, militum preciosissime armatorum ignaviam secordiamque eludens, nihil cunctatus urbanissime simul gravissimeque respondit: 'Satis plane, o rex, satis esse credo Romanis haec

71 omnia, etiam si avarissimi sunt.' Quaesierat rex insulsus per comparationem aequiperationemque suarum et Romanorum virium de exercitus magnitudine ac robore. Poenus autem de praeda non insulse respondit, et id prudenter quidem ac vero. Nam et Syros coram intuebatur et Romanos, diuque et multum per varias fortunae vices expertus fuerat. Idem cum aliquando ineundi praelii tempus videretur, regem hortabatur hostes invaderet. Sed ubi augur dixisset id aestis hostiae prohiberi, ob idque Antiochus adoriri hostem vereretur, eundem obiurgavit Annibal, inquiens, 'Tu quod caro dixerit, facis, et non quod

72 homo praeditus mente?' Abunde insensatum illum atque fatuum demonstravit, qui plus fiduciae in pecoris cadavere quam in se tanto tamque exercitato et imperatore et duce reposuisset. Idem etiam obiurgasse in Prusiam Bithiniae regem traditur.

aside his cutting remarks about the philosopher Phormio,[31] but
listen to his two sallies against the King. When Antiochus was   70
on the point of attacking the Romans, in order to show Hannibal the massive forces of cavalry and infantry he had assem-
bled from all peoples, he led them out into the plain: he led
around scythe chariots and turreted elephants in great numbers, and he had a great abundance of men in full armor; nor
did he marvel only at the soldiers' arms but also at the horses'
bridles, necklaces, bosses flashing far and wide with a great deal
of silver, gold, and jewels. Turning to Hannibal he boasted, "So
do you think that all this is comparable to what the Romans
have? Will it be enough for them?" But mocking the cowardice
and laziness of soldiers so expensively armed, Hannibal replied
most wittily and profoundly without hesitation, "Your highness,
I think it's clear enough that all this will be enough for the Romans, even if they *are* extraordinarily greedy." The foolish king   71
had aimed at a comparison and weighting of his and the Romans' forces in relation to the size and strength of the army, but
the Carthaginian replied, not without wit, about spoils, and did
so indeed prudently and correctly. For he had personally observed both the Syrians and the Romans and had long experience of the shifting changes of fortune. Again when it finally
seemed time to initiate battle, he urged the king to attack the
enemy. But when the augur said that this was forbidden by the
entrails of the sacrificial animal, and for that reason Antiochus
feared attacking the enemy, Hannibal scolded the king, asking,
"Are you acting on the recommendation of a piece of meat, not
what a man supplied with reason tells you?" He gave ample   72
proof that the king was foolish and silly, a man who placed
more trust in an animal's cadaver than in himself, a great and
seasoned commander. He is said to have scolded King Prusias
of Bithynia in similar terms.

Honofrius. At Annibalem istum qui domo pulsus atque opis indigens ad Antiochum sese Prusiamque recepisset, simusne sapientem habituri? Nam haud scio quam eius sales vel Prusiae
vel Antiocho grati essent, iucundi certe non poterant.

Pallas. De Annibalis sapientia non facile tibi responderim. Sed
audisti unquam quid Socrates ei responderit qui an regem Persarum felicem arbitraretur inepte quaesierat?

Honofrius. Quid tandem?

73 *Pallas.* 'Fortassis,' inquit, 'est felix.' Sed id tamen nescire se, quoniam illius consuetudine usus nunquam esset, neque cuiusmodi
intellectu foret, exploratum haberet. Nam recte Socrates non in
argento et auro, non in margaritis ac gemmis, non in urbium
agrorumve dominatu, in nullis denique eiusmodi rebus summum bonum constituebat quae in nostra potestate non sunt.
Sed ita quenque felicem arbitrabatur, ut se quisque cognosce-
ret[34] atque sequeretur, nec a se unquam discederet. Talem au-
74 tem sapientem esse, quis ambigat? Ea est, mediusfidius, sapientis absoluta fortunataque felicitas, ut nihil eum impedire queat,
nihil prohibere, quippe qui nulla re egeat, is ad decus et ad gloriam natus, adeo est magno et forti animo, ut humana omnia
despiciat ac pro nihilo putet. Ea in eo inest animi stabilitas, ea
firmitas, ea constantia, ut laborem doloremque non modo non
pertimescat, sed intrepide etiam atque libenter subeat. Et quoniam nullum humanum bonum ab interiore mentis bono segre-
gatum putat, quidquid aut dicit aut facit, continuo quantum in
se est, et cumulate et omni ex parte tum dicit perfecte, tum
etiam facit. Quare qui statuit mali quicquam sapienti accidere

Onofrio. But are we to consider Hannibal, who was driven from home and betook himself, resourceless, to Antiochus and Prusias, a wise man? Though I suspect that his witticisms were gratefully received by Antiochus and Prusias, they surely cannot have been amused.[32]

Palla. I could not easily reply to you on the subject of Hannibal's wisdom. But have you ever heard what Socrates said to the man who boorishly asked him whether he thought the king of the Persians was a happy man?[33]

Onofrio. What, then?

Palla. He said, "Perhaps he is happy," but that he did not know   73
this because he had never experienced the man's company and had not investigated what sort of understanding the king had. For Socrates correctly established that the highest good lies not in silver and gold, not in pearls and gems, not in ownership of cities and territories, and, in sum, in none of the kinds of things that lie outside of our power. Rather he thought that someone was happy to the extent that he knew himself and followed his natural inclinations and never departed from his true self. Who would doubt that such a man is wise? So help me   74
God, this is the perfect and blessed happiness of the wise man: that nothing can obstruct him, nothing get in his way; he is indeed a man who has no need of anything. As one born for honor and fame, his soul is so great and strong that he despises all human affairs and accounts them as nothing. He has such steadiness of mind, such strength, such stability, that not only does he not fear hardship and sorrow but fearlessly and gladly endures them. And since he considers no human good to be separate from the inner goodness of his mind, whatever he says or does, he both says and does it instantly to the best of his ability and completely and perfectly in every respect. The man who has decided that something evil can befall the wise man is

75 posse, is certe sapiens non est. Itaque de Annibalis sapientia nihil habeo certi. Nam illo familiariter uti nunquam potui. Sed illud affirmare ausim, multa in eo fuisse—quantum habeo auditu—quae sunt sapientis et boni viri, et hoc in primis, quod Antiocho atque Prusiae verum locutus est nec assentari voluit. Praeterea si cum Polynice contuleris, Annibalem virum sapientemque invenias, istum autem deliram mulierculam. Omitto res gestas ingentes illas atque formidabiles, quibus Romanum imperium unus omnium post hominum memoriam miserrime attrivit ac prope delevit. Quando Poenus dixisset unquam se cura et metu premi? Nam lachrymas fundere non magis voluisset

76 quam mortem. Quinimo memoriae proditum est in rebus adversis suis et in totius exercitus maerore non modo non collachrymasse, sed risisse potius, et ea fuisse frontis serenitate, ut omnes in meliorem fiduciam converterit. Non igitur hic tacebat aut ad aliorum voluptatem loquebatur, neque cum insipientibus desipiebat etiam ipse, neque servitutem ullam[35] metuebat. Sciebat mortem libertatis esse refugium et tanquam asylum quoddam, idem[36] quod re quoque ad ultimum probavit. Eninvero praestantis et magni hominis animus nunquam ita cedet fortunae, ut quicquam vel faciat vel loquatur quod humile et abiectum sit, sed habet vim impetumque fortunae quasi gymnasium aliquod ac palaestram virtutis suae.

77 Num Privernas ille quicquam de sua suorumque salute humilius cogitavit, cum interrogatus in curia quam Privernates poenam mererentur, respondit, 'Quam ii merentur qui se libertate dignos iudicarent.' Et rursus cum, eo dicto exasperatis patrum animis et ira vaehementius incensis ac iam de Privernatium poena et supplicio acerbius cogitantibus, interrogatus a

surely not himself a wise man. And so I am in doubt about   75
Hannibal's wisdom, since I never was personally acquainted
with him. But I would venture to assert that—as far as I have
heard—he had many qualities of a wise and good man, and in
particular the fact that he spoke the truth to Antiochus and
Prusias and was unwilling merely to voice his agreement. Moreover, if you compare him with Polynices, you would find the
former a man and a sage, the latter an effeminate lunatic. I set
aside those major and awe-inspiring exploits of his by which,
unique in human history, he ground down Rome's empire and
all but destroyed it. When did the Carthaginian ever say that
he was overwhelmed by worry and fear? He no more wanted to
shed tears than to meet death. Indeed, it has been recorded that   76
during his misfortunes and while his entire army was grieving,
not only did he not shed tears, but rather laughed, and his
countenance was so serene that he gave everyone greater self-
confidence. He therefore did not keep silent or converse at the
prompting of others. Neither did he play the fool along with
fools, nor did he have any fear of enslavement. He knew that
death was a refuge and, as it were, a sanctuary of freedom,
something he actually experienced at the end of his life. For the
soul of a great and eminent man will never submit to fortune in
such a way that he does or says anything that is base and lowly;
rather, he considers the power and force of fortune as a sort of
training ground for his own virtue.

Surely that famous man from Privernum did not think more   77
humbly about his own safety and that of his men when, asked
in the senate what punishment his fellow citizens deserved, he
replied, "The punishment that those who judge themselves
worthy of liberty deserve." And again, when with that answer
he had exasperated the senators' hearts and made them burn
with still fiercer anger, and they were contemplating a sharp
penalty and punishment for the citizens of Privernum, he was

consule qualem cum eis pacem Romani forent habituri, donata impunitate, subdidit eadem animi vultusque constantia: 'Si bonam dederitis, perpetuam quidem; at si malam, nequaquam diuturnam.' Diogenes vero ille Sinopeus cognomento Cyon, quanto erat quamque invicto animo, cum in Philippi depraehensus exercitu, quo is tempore cum Graecis esset praelio decertaturus, et ad eum actus ut speculator coram accusaretur, 'Ita,' inquit, 'Philippe rex, speculator veni inexplebilis tuae cupiditatis atque amentiae, qui ita venias ut et de imperio simul et de corpore aleam iacias.' Audi etiam Theodorum Cyrenaicum philosophum non ignobilem, cui cum rex Lysimachus exprobrando dixisset, 'Patria te quoniam talis esses eiecit?', 'Certe,' inquit, 'eiecit me, quoniam ferre non posset, quemadmodum Liberum patrem Semele.' Cumque idem huic ostendisset in vinclis augurem, effossis oculis et amputatis naribus excisisque auribus ac lingua, subdidissetque, 'Sic illos afficio qui mali in me quippiam perpetrarunt,' et ad haec mortem minitaretur, 'Magnifica profecto,' inquit, 'tibi res contigit, quod vim cantaridis assecutus es.' Quo dicto Lysimachus accensus, cum eum cruci suffigi iussisset, 'Terribile,' ait, 'hoc sit purpuratis tuis. Nam mea quidem nihil interest, humine putrescam an sublimis.' Innocens quidem et bonus vir suaeque vitae conscius ac plane sapiens non modo non recusat dolorem aut mortem, modo animadvertat nihil a se factum iri quod ab honestate sit Deoque alienum, sed ultro etiam deposcit. Norit enim ita sese in clarissima luce versari, ut nihil nec dicat nec faciat quod in obscuro esse ullo modo possit. Nam tum omnium oculos in se esse coniectos qui et quid agat et quomodo vivat diligenter

78

79

80

asked by the consul what sort of peace the Romans would enjoy with them if pardons were issued, and he added with the
same steadiness of mind and facial expression: "If you were to
grant a good peace, it will, of course, last forever, but if a bad
one, it will last not even a single day."[34] In fact, what a great and   78
invincible mind that famous Diogenes of Sinope, nicknamed
"The Dog," demonstrated when he was detected in the army of
Philip of Macedon as the latter was about to join battle with
the Greeks. Diogenes was brought to Philip's presence to be
charged as a spy. "Very well, King Philip," he said, "I have come
to spy on your insatiable greed and madness, you who come in
such a way that you are casting dice for both your kingdom and
your life." Listen also to Theodorus, a renowned philosopher   79
from Cyrene: when King Lysimachus said to him insultingly,
"Did your country expel you for being the man you are?" Theodorus said, "Of course. It cast me out because it could not bear
me, just as Semele could not bear Bacchus." And likewise, when
the king showed him an augur in chains, with eyes gouged out
and nose, ears, and tongue cut off, and added, "This is the way
I treat those who commit crimes against me," thus threatening
him with death, Theodorus replied, "Certainly an outstanding
turn of events has befallen you, to acquire the power that poison possesses." King Lysimachus was incensed at this remark.
When he ordered him to be crucified, Theodorus said, "This
will frighten your courtiers, but to me it makes no difference
whether I rot on the ground or in the air."[35] An innocent and   80
good man, one who reflects upon his own life and is clearly
wise, not only does not refuse pain or death, provided that he is
mindful that he has taken no action at odds with honor or
God, but even willingly asks for them. For the wise man knows
that he dwells in a light so very bright that there is nothing he
says or does that can by any means be kept in the dark. For he
knows that not only are the eyes of all turned toward him,

inquirant, tum etiam Deum ipsum mortem quasi calcem aliquam totius superioris vitae decursus pulcherrimis cum prae-
81   miis aeternisque expectare. Non ergo loqui vereatur unquam vir
sapiens, qui ne mortem quidem pertimescat. Praeterea nec illud
omnino servile est quod quis loqui quod senserit nequeat, sed
loqui potius vel scurrile vel ineptum nonnunquam. Num censes
Pythagoram ad servitutem auditores discipulosque suos an ad
libertatem instituere voluisse?

Honofrius. Ad libertatem quidem.

Pallas. At quid illius ἐχεμυθία vellet, nondum accepisti?

Honofrius. Ea 'silentium' significari audio.

82   *Pallas.* Recte interpretaris. Nam quoscunque Pythagoras sua doctrina dignos statuisset, simul atque in discipulos admiserat, ne-
quid prorsus loquerentur, sed quidquid audissent taciturnitate
atque mysterio tuerentur summopere iubebat. Itaque taciturni-
tas erat eorum prima disciplina, quam et triennium et qua-
driennium et amplius multi, sed minus quam biennium nemo
quisquam servavit. Non enim eum recte locuturum existimabat,
qui quod tacendum foret nondum didicisset. Memoriae etiam
proditum est regem secundum Romanorum, Numam, qui ut
aetate Pythagorae, ita et prudentia et iusticia caeteris regibus
anteiverit, Romanos docuisse Tacitam sibi deam in primis vene-
randam. Hanc autem Musarum unam in quas plurima vaticinia
83   referebat aiebat esse. Vel raro tacendo vel nunquam peccari solet, loquendo vero erratur saepe. Itaque illud Xenocratis dictum
iure laudatur, quem dicere solitum aliquando tradunt sui se
quandoque sermonis poenituisse, taciturnitatis autem nunquam. Et silentium igitur opportune aget vir sapiens, et loque-
tur etiam audacter atque constanter cum id sibi vel ad rem vel

sedulously asking who he is and what he is doing and how he is
living, but also that God Himself awaits his death as if it were
a goal with the most beautiful and eternal rewards for the
course of his whole previous life. The wise man, since he does 81
not fear even death, is therefore never afraid to speak. Moreover, it is not altogether slavish for someone to be unable to say
what he thinks, but it is slavish for him to say something scurrilous or impertinent. Do you think that Pythagoras wanted to
train his listeners and students for slavery or freedom?

Onofrio. For freedom, of course.

Palla. But have you understood what he means by that word of
his, *echemythia?*

Onofrio. I understand that it means "silence."

Palla. You understand its meaning correctly. As soon as he ad- 82
mitted them to his school, Pythagoras ordered any whom he
deemed worthy of his teachings not to say anything but to
guard whatever they had heard in silence and mystery. Thus
this restraint in speech was their first training, one that many
adhered to for a three- or four-year period or more, but no one
for less than two years. For he thought that a man would not
speak rightly who had not yet learned to keep silent. It has been
also recorded that Numa, the Romans' second king, who lived
before the time of Pythagoras, and surpassed the other kings in
wisdom and justice, taught the Romans that they ought to devote special worship to the goddess Tacita.[36] He said that she
was one of the Muses, to whom he attributed many prophecies.
But seldom or never is it the case that one errs by keeping si- 83
lent, whereas one often goes astray by speaking. And so that
saying of Xenocrates is rightly praised, who, tradition relates,
was wont to say that he was often sorry for his speech but never
for his silence.[37] The wise man will therefore practice silence at
the right moment and will speak — even boldly and firmly —
when he believes it will be beneficial either to the matter at

ad dignitatem conducturum iudicabit. Nec enim infamiam formidet qui ne famam quidem cupierit unquam. Nam suae sibi conscius vitae, conscientiae mentisque suae testimonio sit contentus. Ad haec non quid imperita multitudo de nobis loquatur, sed quid boni sentiant, pensitandum est. Qui rumores curat, qui populorum aura ducitur, semper animo sollicito sit oportet. Sed perturbatio in sapientem non cadit. Itaque infamiam aeque ac famam nihilipenderit, quippe qui norit eam esse vulgi consuetudinem ut nihil sani nec sentiat nec loquatur. Facile improborum susurrationes maledictaque contempserit quisquis vel Iohanni Baptistae innocenti et sancto viro daemonium vel ipsi Christo—id est immortali et sempiterno ac rerum omnium conditori et regi—voracitatem, vinositatem et cum publicanis atque peccatoribus amiciciam obiectam meminerit. Nec enim stultorum calumnias metuat qui multo sibi potius duxerit quod ad Sinopeos scripsit Diogenes, vituperari a pravis impurisque hominibus quam laudari. Non possum equidem Phocionem Atheniensem non probare, cum alias saepenumero, tum maxime, cum per id temporis quo redditum est Atheniensibus oraculum unum esse in urbe virum qui a caeteris omnibus dissentiret, et quinam is esset Athenienses clamoribus quaerendum iuberent, Phocion se hunc esse respondit; nam sibi soli eorum probari nihil quae multitudo ageret ac diceret. Non igitur iniuria G. Iulius Caesar, tantus ille talisque vir, eorum stulticiam ridebat a quibus et reginam se et adulterum appellari audiebat. Sciebat homo sapientissimus eam esse pravitatis et sceleris naturam, ut virtuti semper illustrique praestantiae invideret, lacesseret, morderet, insimularet; et propterea[37] insipientium atque flagitiosorum obtrectationem in lucro ponendam esse; nam malos recte vel iudicare vel loqui neque velle nec scire. Qua certe opinione ductus idem Phocion, cum aliquando

84

85

86

hand or to his status. The one who has never even desired fame
will not fear infamy. For, conscious of his own way of life, he
would be content with the testimony of his conscience. Besides,   84
one should weigh not what the ignorant multitude say concerning us, but what sound men think. He who concerns himself
with rumors, who is guided by the winds of fashion, must always be troubled. But emotion is alien to the wise man. And so
he holds infamy and renown to be equally worthless, since he
knows that it is the habit of the masses to think or speak nothing sound. Whoever remembers the demon that was imputed
to John the Baptist, an innocent and holy man, or the gluttony,
wine bibbing, and consorting with publicans and sinners that
was cast in the teeth of Christ himself—that is, the immortal
and eternal Founder and King of the universe—will easily despise the whisperings and slanders of villains. Nor would he   85
fear the slanders of fools who has considered it better for himself, as Diogenes wrote to the people of Sinope, to be excoriated
rather than commended by wicked and base men.[38] There are
many reasons why I cannot fail to approve of Phocion of Athens, but one in particular. Once when an oracle was brought
back to the Athenians saying that there was one man in the city
who differed from all the others, and the Athenians with a
shout ordered an investigation as to who this might be, Phocion
replied that it was he;[39] for he alone approved of none of the
things which the masses did or said. Thus the great and noble
Julius Caesar was right to deride the stupidity of those from
whom he heard that he was being called a queen and an adulterer.[40] For this man of consummate wisdom knew that such is   86
the nature of wickedness and crime that it envies, provokes,
carps at, and accuses virtue and distinction; moreover, the dis-
paragement of fools and reprobates should be accounted as
profit; for the wicked neither wish nor know how to judge or
speak correctly. The same Phocion was surely guided by this

oratione ad populum habita laudibus efferretur et aeque omnis eadem voce eodemque consensu, in sententiam suam ire intueretur, ad amicos conversus ait: 'Num mali quippiam prorsus mihi dicenti excidit?'

87   At nec ignorabit[38] scriptum esse: 'Perdes omnes qui loquuntur mendacium.' Scietque illum qui mentiatur ex Deo non esse. Et quod sapiens ille propheta inquit, intelliget, 'os eorum obstructum esse qui loquuntur iniqua.' Et enim facile et expedite vir sapiens omnem aciem calumniae, quam acutissimam Thearidas ostendebat, vitae innocentia et sanctimonia hebetabit ac

88 retundet. Memineritque se nequaquam imperitae multitudini vivere, sed sibi ipsi, sed virtuti, sed Deo, ad quem ipsum suam omnem intelligentiam, omnem actionem — ad quae quidem duo nos Aristoteles natos ait — referre debeat. Itaque non mortalibus sese sed immortali Deo, cui nihil occultum esse possit, probatum iri omni opera, omni industria, omni diligentia molietur. Gaudebit enim exultabitque plurimum, cum secum ipse versabit mercedem suam copiosam in caelis esse, et quo plura maledicta insectationesque pertulerit, cum quidquid mali adversus se dicatur, aequo animo tolerarit, eo se beatiorem vel

89 evangelica promissione existimabit. Praeterea qui a stultis, qui ab improbis laudatur, stulticiae et improbitatis suspicione haud omnino vacat. Quis enim ignorat ingenii ac morum similitudine benivolentiam, dissimilitudine odium nasci solere? Nam quod ais paupertate animum demitti, quasi permagna sit quaedam in divitiis commendatio, non sentis cum Diogene, qui nihil fere maiore studio quam paupertatis nomen complexus est, et cum

90 dives esse posset, certe noluit. Non enim vestium, non aedium, non epularum magnificentia, nullo denique exteriore corporis ornatu ducebatur. Et recte id sane, quippe qui omne divitiarum

view when on one occasion, having delivered a speech to the people, he was praised to the skies and saw them all alike, with one voice and accord, voting for his motion; thereupon he turned to his friends and said: "Did some bad advice slip out while I was speaking?"[41]

But the wise man will not fail to recognize that it has been   87 written: "You shall destroy all who speak a lie."[42] And he will know that he who lies is not from God. And he will understand what the wise prophet said, that "the mouth of those who speak evil has been blocked."[43] For the wise man will easily and quickly blunt and beat back with the innocence and holiness of his life the entire cutting edge of calumny, which Thearidas showed to be so very sharp.[44] And he will recall that he never   88 lives for the ignorant multitude, but for himself, for virtue, and for God, to whom he must answer for all his thoughts and actions — the two things that Aristotle says we are born for.[45] And so he will endeavor, by all his effort, hard work, and commitment to win the approval, not of mortal men, but immortal God, from whom nothing can be hidden. He will indeed feel much joy and inspiration when he reflects that this ample reward is in heaven, and the more insults and verbal attacks he endures — when anything evil is spoken against him but he bears it calmly — the more blessed will he consider himself according to the gospel's promise. Besides, he who is praised by   89 fools or scoundrels is liable to be suspected of folly and wickedness. For who does not know that goodwill usually arises from a similarity of mind and character, and hatred from their dissimilarity? In saying that the mind is cast down by poverty, as if there were some great praise to be had for possessing wealth, you are not of the same mind as Diogenes, who embraced nothing with greater passion than the reputation for poverty. Although he could have been wealthy, he refused. For he   90 wasn't motivated by splendid clothing, houses, or feasts, nor

decus, omnem splendorem, omnem elegantiam in animi praestantia bonitateque posuerat. Reliqua vero omnia supervacanea
quaedam et inimica virtuti iudicabat. Eum divitem, eum magnum virum, eum imperatorem, eum regem arbitrabatur, qui
nulli dedecori obnoxius naturam sagacem ac prudentem vivendi
91   ducem sequeretur. Nam quam et parvis paucisque rebus natura
contenta est, id non obscure ea nobis ostendit epistola quam
Apollexidi scripsit:

> Diogenes Cyon Apollexidi salutem. Eorum multitudinem,
> quibus pera gravabatur, abieci, paraxida[39] quoniam didi-
> cissem esse in pane concavitatem et poculum pro quo
> manibus uti possem. Nec dedecet qui aliis praesit, ut se
> adhuc puerum esse dicat. Non enim par erat eam inven-
> tionem quae bono usui sit, ob aetatem praetermittere po-
> tius quam admittere.

92   Audi eius alteram eadem de re epistola:

> Diogenes Cyon Crateti salutem. Memento paupertatis
> principatum a me tibi datum in omnem vitam. Itaque tibi
> opera danda est ne hunc istum aut ipse deponas aut ab
> alio auferri patiare. Consentaneum enim est Thebanos,
> miseriae obnoxios, eiecturos te rursum. At tu velim existi-
> mes pallium esse leonis pellem, baculum vero clavam, pe-
> ram autem terram ac mare unde alimentum accipis. Sic
> enim in te surrexerit Herculea quaedam animi elatio,
> omni etiam fortuna melior. Quod si tibi aut lupini aut
> caricae supersint, mitte etiam nobis.

93   Videsne, fili, quanti Diogenes paupertatem faciebat? Sciebat
certe vir sapiens eum qui sese divitiis dedidisset, libero esse
animo nunquam posse; at hominem quidem ad libertatem,

any external adornment of the body. Rightly so; for he assigned all the beauty, splendor, and elegance of wealth to the goodness and excellence of the soul. He thought everything else truly superfluous and at odds with virtue. He considered that man to be rich, a great man, an emperor, a king, who followed as his guide for living the wisdom and prudence of nature and was not vulnerable to anything disgraceful. For in a letter he wrote 91 to Apollexis he showed how content nature is with the smallest and most insignificant of things:

> Diogenes the Dog to Apollexis: Greetings. I have jettisoned a great number of things that weigh down my sack, since I have learned that a hollow made in bread can serve as a plate, and I can use my hands as a cup. Nor is one who has charge of others disgraced by saying that he is still a boy. For it is not right to ignore because of its age a discovery that is still useful, rather than to welcome it.[46]

Listen to another letter of his on the same subject: 92

> Diogenes the Dog to Crates: Greetings. Remember that I bestowed on you a regimen of poverty for all your life, and so it should be your job neither to cast it aside nor allow someone else to take it from you. For it is likely that the Theban people, subject to their own unhappiness, will throw you out again. But I would like you to think of your philosopher's robe as a lion's skin, your walking staff as a club, your sack as the land and sea from which you derive your nourishment. For in this way a sort of Herculean loftiness of spirit has risen in you better than any good fortune. And if there are some lupines or dried figs left, send these also to me.[47]

Do you see, son, how Diogenes valued poverty? This wise man 93 surely knew that one who has committed himself to wealth can never possess a free spirit, and that man is born for freedom,

non ad servitutem natum. Quare quaecunque mortales minus liberos esse sinunt, ea recte abiicienda arbitrabatur. Haec autem eiusmodi omnia esse censebat quae fortunae temeritati subiecta sunt; satis enim nos esse commendatos naturae, quae necessaria nobis omnia nullo etiam nostro labore subministrarit. Itaque dum paraxida,[40] dum poculum abiiceret, aliud nihil, ut opinor, significabat quam omne a nobis curiosius vivendi studium omnesque delicias amovendas. Haud enim delicatos et mollis, sed animi robore et gravitate fraetos dignos esse qui viri appellentur. Non igitur Cretensis, non Cyprii, non Meroici vini indigebat qui sitim aqua restinguere didicisset, ac ne Choaspia illa quidem qua Persarum reges sola propter dulcedinem usi perhibentur, sed tam Panopis quam et Calliroes et Cephisi aqua. Nec obsonia dapesve regias desyderare cogebatur, qui ad sedandam famem caricis et lupinis quamiucundissime vesceretur. Non ergo insulse dicere visus est, prandere Aristotelem cum Philippo videretur, at Diogenem cum Diogeni. Intelligebat profecto vir gravissimus non eum qui divitias, qui voluptates, qui fortunae illecebras sequeretur, sed qui et parvo et pauco, qui seipso contentus esset, et liberum esse et magnificum. Quare cum saepius accerseretur ab Alexandro in Macedoniam, non modo ad eum perhumane invitatus profectus non est, sed litteris quoque illum ineptitudinis arguere non infacete est ausus:

> Diogenes Cyon Alexandro regi Macedonum salutem. Adnuncias regem Macedonum vaehementer cupere aspectum meum. Fecisti autem bene quod regi Macedonas addidisti, quippe qui non esses nescius nos regi non esse

not for servitude. For that reason he thought that whatever things compromise the freedom of mortals should rightly be rejected. He considered the things that are subject to the accidents of fortune to be all of that sort. For it is sufficient to have placed our trust in nature, which supplies all our necessities, even without our effort. So in throwing away his plate and cup Diogenes indicated, I think, nothing else than that we ought to put aside any excessive care in pursuing one's livelihood and refined pleasures, for it is not the overrefined and soft, but those who rely on the mind's strength and authority, who are worthy to be called men. The man who learned to quench his thirst   94
with water had no need for Cretan, Cypriot, or Meroean wine, and not even for the finest water of the Choaspes—which alone, because of its sweetness, the kings of Persia were said to drink—but Diogenes drank the water of Panops as well as of Callirhoe and the Cephisus. He who would happily dine on figs and lupines to satisfy his hunger felt no desire for royal delicacies or feasts. Therefore it did not seem foolish for Diogenes to say that Aristotle dined at Philip's pleasure but Diogenes at Diogenes' pleasure.[48] For that most serious of men certainly knew that the man who was content with a few small things, and with himself, enjoyed both liberty and bounty—not the one who pursued riches, pleasures, and the seductions of fortune. For that reason, when summoned as he frequently was by Alex-   95
ander to Macedonia, and despite the high courtesy of the invitation, not only did he not go, but he even dared in a letter to accuse Alexander himself, very wittily, of ineptness:

> Diogenes the Dog to Alexander, King of the Macedonians: Greetings. You bring me a message that the king of the Macedonians is extremely eager to lay eyes on me. But you did well to add "of the Macedonians" to "the king," for you are not unaware that I am not one of the king's subjects. No

subiectos. Videre autem mea corporis liniamenta ac figuram nullus ut peregrinam et admirandam velit. Quod si uti Alexander voluerit nostris vitae morumque institutis, ei dicito quantum ex Athenis in Macedoniam, tantundem etiam esse e Macedonia Athenas.

96   Deinde sollicitatus ab Alexandro crebrius ad se iret, multisque et blandiciis fatigatus et precibus, ita rursus scribere non dubitavit:

Diogenes Cyon Alexandro regi Macedonum salutem. Si vis et aequus et bonus fieri, abiecto e capite diademate ad nos veni. At nullo modo possis tu quidem: detineris enim ab Hephaestionis femoribus.

Etsi Cynice, aperte tamen ac vero virtutem et divitias simul esse non facile posse Diogenes — ut vides — ostendit. Sunt enim eae voluptatis ac libidinis instrumenta.

97   *Honofrius.* Num fortasse, pater, eum censes vituperandum qui divitias quoque cum virtute coniunxerit?

Pallas. Virtus ipsa satis per sese ad felicitatem munita est. Satis armata adversus omnem fortunae impetum atque naufragium. Nullius opis indiget, nullius subsidii. Praeterea, ut inquit Pindarus:

Cum virtute simul divitiae insitae rarae
sunt homini.

Honofrius. Verum, pater, siquem reperias qui virtute et sapientia sit, eundem quoque divitiis praeditum, putasne huic vitio dandum quod locuples sit?

98   *Pallas.* Respondeat tibi, quandoquidem tam summopere divitiis delectaris, non Pallas sed Sappho illa doctissima:

one should wish to see the frame of my body and its shape as a thing that is foreign and to be marveled at. But if Alexander should wish to put into practice our training in life and character, tell him that the distance from Macedonia to Athens is the same as from Athens to Macedonia.[49]

Later, when repeatedly asked by Alexander to visit him, he was so tired of the numerous flatteries and requests that he did not hesitate to write back: 96

Diogenes the Dog to Alexander, King of Macedonia: Greetings. If you wish to become a good and upright man, cast the crown from your head and come to me. But you certainly cannot, for you are held fast by the thighs of Hephaestion.[50]

Although in a Cynic mode, yet in an open and truthful one, Diogenes, as you see, demonstrated that virtue and riches could not easily coexist, for the latter are the tools of pleasure and lust.

Onofrio. Surely you do not think, father, that the man who combines wealth with virtue should be criticized? 97

Palla. Virtue by itself is sufficiently fortified to secure happiness. It is sufficiently armed against fortune's every blow and disaster. It lacks no resource, requires no assistance. Moreover, as Pindar says,

Riches are rarely planted in a man along with virtue.[51]

Onofrio. But father, were you to find someone endowed with both virtue and wisdom who also possessed riches, do you think that the fact that he is wealthy should be considered a fault?

Palla. Since you are so mightily drawn to wealth, let not Palla, but the most learned Sappho furnish you a response: 98

Absque virtutis sciae decore
sunt opes pravae; cumulant beatam
additae vitam.

Fateor equidem eas divitias quae et solae et sine virtute sunt,
non modo non esse utiles humano generi, sed admodum perni-
99 ciosas atque funestas. Nec maiorum exempla ad hanc rem com-
memoremus est opus. Videmus in hac urbe nostra, cum alias
alios saepe multos, tum maxime hoc tempore Cosmum Medicem, qui vi pecuniarum quas omni sibi flagitio, omni scelere et
comparavit et comparat, quantas calamitates, quantos ignis,
quantas pestes in rempublicam intulit. Qui si pecuniis nudus
foret, nec nocuisset, nec nocere non modo nequivisset, sed ne
fortasse voluisset quidem. Nam cum intellexisset frustra fore
conatus suos, rationem quam libidinem sequi, quo rectius rebus
suis sibique consuleret, plane maluisset. Quod si minus maluisset, saltem quas ingenti pecuniarum corruptela paucorum con-
iuratione effugit, in carcerem vinclaque publico decreto coniectus debitas poenas meritaque supplicia dedisset.
100 Sin autem huic divitiae contigerint qui iam in patritam hae-
reditariae virtutis et avitam possessionem pervenerit, ac totius
controversiae victor libere et tranquille consederit, virtutem quidem ipsam maiorem non reddent, at facient fortassis opis
huiusmodi indigentibus aliquanto iucundiorem. Nam si divitiae
propter sese in precio habendae⁴¹ forent, nunquam illud Domini praeceptum, qui se salvos vellent adeo vaehementer tuerentur ut vaenderent omnia quae haberent et ea pauperibus

> Without the splendor of virtue, riches are a bad companion;
> when they are joined together, they crown a blessed life.[52]

I assert that those riches that exist alone by themselves and not
alongside virtue not only are not beneficial to the human race
but are even dangerous and fatal. There is no need for us to   99
recall for this purpose the examples of our ancestors. In this
very city of ours we have seen many [examples of riches without virtue] at various times, but in our time we have the greatest example of all in Cosimo de' Medici, who, through the
power of the money he has procured and continues to procure
for himself by all manner of outrage and crime, has inflicted
upon the republic innumerable disasters, conflagrations, and
plagues. Were he stripped of his money, he would have done no
harm, and not only would he not have been able to do any
harm, but perhaps he would not even have desired to do so. For
when he understood that his efforts would be in vain, he would
clearly have preferred to follow reason rather than impulse so as
to take better care of himself and his interests. Had he not so
preferred, then he would have been thrown in prison by public decree and loaded with chains, and he would have paid his
due penalty and had just punishment. He escaped this through
a massive bribe of money and a conspiracy with a few confed-
erates.

But if riches befall a man who has already come into paternal   100
and ancestral ownership of hereditary virtue, and if, as a winner
of the whole dispute, he settles down quietly of his own free
will, then his riches will not raise his virtue itself any higher,
but perhaps will make him somewhat more congenial to those
lacking such wealth. For if riches are to be reckoned valuable for
their own sake, then never will that teaching of our Savior be
observed so earnestly by those who wish themselves saved, that
they should sell all the things they have and give to the poor

darent, Deumque sequerentur. Et enim nemo virtutem sequitur, qui Deum non sequitur. Nulla enim virtus est quae Deo vacat. In quo Deus non est, is omni turpidini atque probro et nequitiae est addictus. In homine vero etsi non improbo et facinoroso, nondum tamen perfecto ac plane bono, nihil est mea sententia paupertate nec tutius nec securius. Itaque principio danda est opera boni ut simus, id quod in paupertate melius quam in opulentia consequemur. Post adeptam autem confirmatamque probitatem si nummi quoque accesserint, honestate parti, quibus subveniatur indigentibus, admittendos potius quam excludendos puto. Sed cum ea et nunc est et antehac semper fuerit hominum insania, ut summum bonum in divitiis vulgo statuerint, rectissime paupertatem Diogenes quasi compendiariam quandam et expeditam ad virtutem viam amplectitur. Non inepte ea omnia contemnebat quae virtutis essent expertia. Probo viro et sapienti nihil deesse posse arbitrabatur. Itaque ne cochleae quidem exemplo uti ad incolendas aedes, ut Apollexidi scripsit, turpe sibi ducebat. Et Alexandro ipsi siqua ei re opus foret interroganti, in sole sedens respondit nulla sibi re alia opus esse nisi ut sua se umbra paululum liberaret. Quo quidem dicto Alexander eius animi magnitudinem admiratus in stuporemque adductus ad amicos conversus ait: 'Ni Alexander essem, Diogenes utique essem.' Neque igitur divitiis sapientis viri animus attolletur, neque demittetur paupertate. Nam is satis est dives, qui modice potest et inopiam ferre et opulentiam contemnere. Quod si infamia simul paupertateque urgeatur, non magis movebitur quam elephantus Indus sive ab uno seu a pluribus culicibus temptetur. Quam me Diogenes vaehementer delectat, cum alias semper, tum maxime ea epistola qua veluti iocatur cum patre:

101

102

103

104

and follow God.⁵³ And no one acquires virtue who fails to follow God, for there is no virtue that lacks God. The man in   101
whom God is not present is entirely addicted to infamy, disgrace, and wickedness. However, in a man who, even if he is
not wicked and villainous, is nonetheless not yet perfect and
completely good, there is, in my opinion, nothing safer or more
secure than the state of poverty. And so to start with, we must
take pains to be good, something that we can achieve in poverty
more easily than in wealth. After integrity has been achieved
and strengthened, if money should be added, honestly acquired,
in order to give assistance to the poor, I think that it should be
permitted, rather than forbidden. But since such is now and   102
always has been the delusion of men that they class riches as
the highest good, Diogenes quite rightly embraced poverty as a
kind of short and easy path to virtue. He appropriately condemned everything that is devoid of virtue; an honest and wise
man, he thought, could not lack anything. And so, as he wrote
to Apollexis, he did not even consider it a lowly thing for him
to follow the example of a snail regarding housing,⁵⁴ and to   103
Alexander himself, who asked him if there was anything he
needed, he replied as he was sitting in the sun that there was
nothing else he needed except to be freed somewhat from Alexander's shadow.⁵⁵ At this remark Alexander marveled at his
greatness of soul and turned, stupefied, to his friends and said:
"If I were not Alexander, I would certainly be Diogenes."⁵⁶
Riches therefore will do nothing to elevate the soul of a wise
man, nor will poverty lower it. He is a sufficiently wealthy man
who can moderately endure poverty and who holds wealth in
contempt. But if he is burdened by infamy and poverty at the
same time, he will be no more agitated than Indian elephants
are annoyed by fleas, whether singly or in a swarm. Diogenes   104
always delights me in general but especially in that letter in
which he jokes a bit with his father:

Diogenes Cyon Hycetae patri salutem. Ne te, pater, sollicitet quod Cyon dicor, ac duplici pallio amicior et humeris peram fero atque habeo manu baculum. Indignum est
enim horum causa sollicitari te, quinpotius laetandum est
et egere paucis tuum filium et a gloria, cui omnes tum
Graeci tum barbari serviunt, liberum esse. Nam hoc nomen splendidum est quodammodo. Non enim rebus naturaliter respondet, sed signum est. Vocor enim Cyon
(hoc est canis) caeli, non terrae, quod illius in me imaginem repraesento; quippe qui non e gloria sed e natura
vivo sub divo ac Iove liber, ad quem ipsum summum bonum rettulerim. Stolam autem Homerus etiam scribit
Ulyssem, qui Graecorum esset sapientissimus, indutum
fuisse per id temporis quo domum ex Ilio revertisset, et id
quidem Minerva praecipiente. Quae quidem stola adeo et
pulchra est et praeclara, ut ne humanae quidem inventioni
sed divinae potius concedenda sit.

> Cuique stolam primum et tunicham porrexit, amictus
> sordidulos, tristis, fumi caligine tetros.
> Ac circum celeris dedit hinc ingentia cervi
> tergora, tum sceptrum et peram superaddidit atram.

Bono igitur animo sis, o pater, tum nominis quo nos appellant, tum etiam stolae gratia. Nam et canis est apud
deum et stola inventum dei.

Referebat, inquam, ad deum Diogenes summum bonum. Quare
et quid stultorum greges de se dicerent contemnebat, et sibi
(hoc est animo) quam insatiabili corporis cupiditati vivere ma-
lebat. At si iam Cynici ac Diogenis te saties forsan ceperit, audi
et Pythagoreum et sapientem et magnum virum Apollonium
Tyaneum; quem si diligentissime consyderabis, nihil tibi ad

105

106

Diogenes the Dog to Hicetas, his father: Greetings. Let it not upset you, Father, that I am called a dog and put on a double coarse cloak, carry a sack over my shoulders, and hold a staff in my hand. It is not worth your distressing yourself over such matters, but you should rather be glad that your son is satisfied with little and is free from glory, to which all, both Greeks and barbarians, are enslaved. This word is somehow resplendent. It has no correlate in nature but is a sign. For I am called Cyon (that is, dog) of heaven, not of earth, since I reflect heaven's image, since I live not from glory but from nature, free under the open sky and Jupiter, to whom I assign the supreme good. Homer writes 105 that Ulysses, who was the wisest of the Greeks, put on a robe during the time when he returned home from Ilium, and that on the advice of Minerva. This robe is so beautiful and outstanding that it should be acknowledged to be the discovery, not of men, but of a god.

> First she offered him a robe and tunic, filthy garments black-ened by soot. Next she put round him a large hide from a swift deer and gave him a staff and added a black bag.[57]

Be of good cheer, Father, in gratitude for the name by which they call me, and even for my clothing, since the dog lives with god and his garments are god's invention.[58]

Diogenes, let me add, attributed the highest good to God, and 106 for this reason scorned what the crowds of fools said about him, and he preferred to live for himself, that is, for his soul, rather than for the insatiable desires of the body. But if by now you have had your fill of Diogenes the Cynic, listen to a Pythagorean, a wise and great man, Apollonius of Tyana. If you

107   hanc rem quod desyderes reliquum fuerit. Is enim in epistola ad Diotimum ita scribit:

> Si de me bifariam et nunc loquuntur et loquentur in posterum, quaenam est admiratio? Necesse est enim, ut de omni excellentia (quacunque tandem ea de re esse videatur), in utranque partem disceptari. Sic de Pythagora, de Orpheo, de Platone, de Socrate non dicta solum contraria sed etiam scripta sunt. At boni quidem viri veram orationem admittunt, quasi aliqua sibi similitudo cum ea sit, improbi vero falsam. Sed huius generis homines ridendi sunt. Deteriores dico. Tantum hoc duntaxat de meipso nunc est commonefaciendum, quod de me dei non secus quam de viro divino locuti sunt. Et id quidem non privatim modo quibusdam saepe dixere, verum etiam publice. Sed quoniam qui aut plus aut minus de sese loquitur molestus est, te bene valere opto.

108   Aeque sane Apollonius Tyaneus quid de se invidorum inimicorumque et inertium hominum oscoena garrulitas effutiret, pro ridiculo habebat, et virorum integritate et relligione sanctimoniaque praestantium tanquam divino testimonio laetabatur. Quam vero pecuniam virtuti obesse arbitraretur, non est difficile ex ea brevi coniectare epistola quam ad Histiaeum dedit:

> Apollonius Histiaeo salutem. Virtus et pecunia apud nos vaehementissime invicem adversantur. Nam et ex alterius dimminutione alterum crescit, et ex incremento dimminuitur. Qui ergo fieri potest ut utrunque penes eundem sit? Ni fortasse — ut fatuorum proverbio dicitur — apud quos divitiae virtus habentur. Nolim igitur istis gratificando assentiare nos tibi esse adeo ignotos, nec patere nos

carefully reflect upon this man, you will be fully satisfied on this topic. For in his letter to Diotimus he writes as follows: 107

> If they talk about me now and in the future in two distinct ways, is that a surprise? For just as in anything that is excellent, whatever seems to be at issue, it is inevitable that opinions divide pro and con. Concerning Pythagoras, Orpheus, Plato, and Socrates, contrary opinions were not merely spoken but committed to writing. Good men are amenable to true speech almost as if it bore some resemblance to themselves, whereas bad men open the door to false talk. People of this sort deserve ridicule — the bad ones that is. Now as to myself, I must merely give this advice, that the gods have spoken about me no differently than about a divine man, and this not only to certain persons in private but even publicly. But since the man who speaks about himself either too much or too little is tiresome, I hope that you will keep well.[59]

The offensive things that envious, hostile, and lazy men babbled   108
about him Apollonius of Tyana rightly held to be ridiculous, and he rejoiced in the integrity, scrupulousness and holiness of excellent men as if they were a god's testimony. How detrimental to virtue he considered money is easy to surmise from this brief letter to Hestiaeus:

> Apollonius to Hestiaeus: Greetings. In our culture money and virtue are very much at odds. For the one grows from the lessening of the other, and the other decreases with the increase of the other. How could it then be that both were lodged in the same man? Unless, perhaps — as is stated in a proverb about the foolish — among fools, riches are accounted a virtue. Therefore I would not wish in obliging these sorts of people to flatter them that we are so very unfamiliar to

divites potius quam philosophos suspicentur. Et enim turpissimum est videri nos peregre proficisci atque abesse
quorundam eorum pecuniarum gratia qui malint nomen
suum immortalitatis memoriae consecrare quam virtutem
amplecti.

109   Abunde mihi videor superiore oratione complexus quid maximi
praestantissimique philosophi et de paupertate et de aliorum in
se cavillis, conviciis, maledictis senserint. Quorum quidem iudicium etsi non dubito maxime apud gravissimos viros probatum
iri, opera tamen nobis danda est ut nostrorum quoque exemplo
aliquo confirmemur. Omitto autem hoc tempore G. illum Iulium Caesarem, quem utique unum in omni praestantiae et
probitatis genere fuisse puto, qui non modo cum omni Graecia,
cum omni barbaria, cum omni antiquitate, sed cum universo
plane humano genere et cum ipsa prope natura contendere de

110 laude potuerit. At quid (dii boni!) in hunc talem tantum tamque divinum virum vel dictum oscoene vel scriptum improbe
non legimus? Indignor equidem perturborque vaehementer cum
dicta quorundam in Caesarem audio vel foeda vel impia. Nam
qui innumerabiles virtutes huius tam claras, tam dilucidas minus videt, mentis caecitatis est accusandus. Quod si videt, nec
laudat tamen, est is sane vel invidiae vel ingratitudinis arguen-
dus. Sin autem laudantibus reluctatur, non stultus solum, sed et
demens et insanus iudicandus est.

111   Verum P. Scipionem Africanum illum superiorem paulisper
nunc consyderemus. Si quibus vir ille virtutibus claruerit oratione complecti velim, dies me deficiat. Nam qua fuerit ab ineunte
aetate pudicicia, qua deinceps continentia, qua demum in omnem vitam innocentia et animi magnitudine atque splendore,

you, nor to allow them to suspect that we are rich men rather than philosophers. For it is the vilest thing for us to appear to travel abroad and to be away from home for the sake of money belonging to those who would rather dedicate their name to immortal memory than embrace virtue.[60]

I have, I believe, just discussed at length what the greatest and most outstanding philosophers have thought about poverty and about the criticisms, reproaches, and insults of others against them. But although I have no doubt that their judgment will meet with approval among the most serious men, yet it is my task to strengthen my argument with an example from our culture. For the moment I set aside Julius Caesar, whom I consider to have been unique in every kind of excellence and virtue; he could compete for praise not only with all Greece, with all barbarian nations, and all of the ancient world, but clearly also with the entire human race and almost with nature herself. But, good gods, what don't we read that has either been spoken scurrilously or written infamously against such a distinguished and divine man? Indeed, I am offended and deeply disturbed when I hear things said by certain persons against Caesar that are either foul or disrespectful. Someone who fails to see the numerous virtues of this man, virtues so renowned and resplendent, ought to be accused of mental blindness. But he who sees them but does not praise them is certainly to be charged with either jealousy or ingratitude. If he is opposed to those who praise Caesar, he ought to be judged not only a fool but an insane lunatic.

But let us now reflect for a little while on the elder Publius Scipio Africanus. Daylight would fail me if I wished to discuss the virtues for which this man was renowned. For both Greek and Latin books proclaim the modesty he possessed from an early age, the self-control, the blamelessness, the greatness and

109

110

111

et Latini et Graeci codices praedicant. At huiusmodi virum invidiae morsus effugere nequivisse constat. Nam cum esset adolescens, impudiciciae notatus est nomine; id quod et alii Romanarum rerum scriptores et Gn. Naevius poeta hisce versibus non obscure significavit:

> Etiam qui res magnas manu saepe gessit gloriose,
> cuius facta viva nunc vigent, qui apud gentes solus praestat,
> eum pater cum pallio uno ab amico abduxit!

112 Valerius autem Antias eundem Scipionem tradere non erubuit virginem pulcherrimam et illustri inter Celtiberos loco natam et illustri iuveni Indibili desponsam, cum vi oppressa in Hispania Carthagine una cum aliis plaerisque obsidibus quos ea in urbe Poeni asservabant suam in potestatem redegisset haberetque captivam, non modo eam patri restituere ac reddere noluisse, sed etiam in deliciis et amoribus habuisse. Idemque ad postremum repetundarum et tanquam peculatus accusatus quod praeda ex Antiocho rege capta aerarium fraudasset, coactus tandem est per voluntarium exilium invidorum et inimicorum

113 insimulationi et furori cedere. Nam de eiusdem rei familiaris tenuitate nemo est qui dissentiat. Nec tamen vel paupertas ipsa vel petulantissimorum hominum convicia illius animi magnitudinem neque dimminuere nec labefactare usquam potuerunt. Eninvero abstinentissimae suae integerrimaeque vitae ac recte factorum conscius, non solum non demittebatur animo aut minus de sese loqui magnifice sentireque audebat vir clarissimus ob aliorum in se maledicta atque contumelias, sed non etiam eos quos suae virtuti advertebat infestos dignos existimabat[42]

splendor of his soul throughout his entire life. But it is a fact that a man of this sort could not escape the malicious attacks of jealous persons. For as an adolescent he had a reputation for being immodest, a fact that some authors of Roman history have clearly indicated, as well as Gnaeus Naevius in these verses:

> One who often gloriously accomplished great things in battle, he who stands out alone among the nations, whose deeds are celebrated even now — his father dragged him away from his boyfriend with only his shirt on![61]

Yet Valerius Antias was not ashamed to relate that this same 112 Scipio, after he had beaten back Carthage by force in Spain, brought under his power and held captive a beautiful young woman along with many other hostages whom the Carthaginians had protected in that city. She had been born to a distinguished family among the Celtiberi and was betrothed to Indibilis, a wellborn young man. Not only did he refuse to restore and return her to her father, but he kept her for pleasure and lovemaking. Similarly, at the end of his life he was accused of extortion and corruption in office on the grounds that he had defrauded the treasury of spoils taken from King Antiochus. In the end, accepting voluntary exile, he was forced to yield to the angry accusation of jealous and hostile men. There is no one 113 who would disagree that this man's property was modest. Nor could poverty itself or the insults of the most impudent men ever lessen or weaken that man's greatness of soul. Being conscious of his supremely self-denying and upright life and of his right actions, not only did this most famous man not become despondent and not refrain from speaking or thinking about himself in the grand manner because of the slander and abuse of other people toward him, but he did not even consider those

quibus invide et petulanter insimulantibus quicquam prorsus
pro causa respondisse videretur. Eos enim esse iudicabat quorum vituperatio non plus obesset quam laudatio prodesset.

114   Quare et ab ipso Marco Naevio peculatus, quod modo dicebam, insimulatus et aliis quibusdam indignis se criminibus ho-
neratus, tum Scipio ea praefatus quae suae et vitae et gloriae
dignitas postulabat:

> Memoria (inquit) Quirites, repeto, illum hunc esse diem
> quo Annibalem Poenum, vobis et vestro imperio inimicis-
> simum, magno praelio in terra Africa superavi, vobisque
> insperantibus et pacem et victoriam peperi. Ne igitur ad-
> versum deos immortalis ingrati simus moneo, simulque
> censeo ut isto relicto nebulone eamus nunc protinus Iovi
> optimo gratulatum. Quod siquis etiam velit, ut adversum
> me suffragium ferat iubeo. Nam ego coronatus in Capito-
> lium sacrificium facturus ascendo.

Quibus dictis cum in Capitolium coepisset ascendere, eum universus populus relicto accusatore etiam dicente secutus est.

115   Videsne, fili, quantam vim virtus habet? Multitudo etiam
ipsa, quae in deteriorem partem inclinare saepius solet, veretur
eos aliquando quos sui maxime dissimiles norit. Et quibus per
nefas omne inviderit, admirari pientissime,[43] et quos iniuste
oderit, amare etiam iustissime cogitur. At magnus vir et invictus neutram in partem multitudinis iudicio se accommodat.
Nihil honestum, nihil bonum existimat, nisi quod sua sponte,
sua vi, sua natura et honestum et bonum sit. Satis se laudatum
116   censet si laude dignum se praestiterit. Nec enim cum Calli-
macho sentit, inquiente:

people who he noticed were jealous of his virtue worth replying
to, given the jealous and impudent character of their accusations; for he considered that these were men whose vituperation
would not harm any more than their praise would help. There-   114
fore Scipio, accused, as I said, by Marcus Naevius of corruption
and burdened with certain other unworthy charges, opened his
speech as the honorableness of his life and the worth of his renown required:

> I recall, citizens, that this is the day on which I conquered
> Hannibal the Carthaginian, a man most hostile to you and
> your empire, in a great battle in Africa and brought you
> peace and victory when you had lost hope. I warn you that
> we ought not to be ungrateful toward the immortal gods,
> and at the same time I propose that we now abandon this
> trickster and go to give thanks to Almighty Jupiter. But if
> anyone should still wish to vote against me, I bid him do so.
> For I, wearing a crown, am going to ascend the Capitoline to
> offer sacrifice.

When he had spoken these words and had begun to ascend the
Capitoline, the entire people followed him, leaving behind the
accuser still talking.[62]

Don't you see, son, how much power virtue has? For the   115
crowd itself, which often is inclined to choose the worse option,
sometimes fears those who it knows are quite different from itself. It is forced to admire with great affection those whom it
wrongly envies and is forced to love most justly those whom it
unfairly hates. But a great and unshakable man is not swayed in
either direction by the opinion of the crowd. He considers
nothing virtuous or good unless it is so on its own, through its
own power and nature. He thinks that he has been sufficiently
praised if he shows himself worthy of praise. He does not share   116
the view of Callimachus, who says:

Nec virtutis inops aurum nec tollit in altum
virtus aeris inops.

Eiusmodi esse virtutem ducit, quae nullis etiam loculis, nullis
honerata nummorum sacculis, nullis prorsus adminiculis alienis
fraeta et facile et expedite sese in altum tollat et omnibus con-
spicuam splendidissimamque ostendat. Nam quod ait poeta,

Non facile emergunt quorum virtutibus obstat
res angusta domi,

non de sapiente ac perfecta virtute viro dictum putet, sed de
sapientiae et virtutis simulatore, qui non se aliter gloriosum
opinatur, nisi ab insaniente populo et probetur et honoretur.
Quam me delectat Paulus Aemylius,[44] qui cum secundum con-
sulatum petens repulsam habuisset ac non multo post nec petens nec cupiens consul declaratus esset, quoniam bellum quod
Romanis adversus Persen ac Macedonas gerebatur, imperatorum inscitia atque inertia prolyxitatem capere videretur, 'Ego,
Quirites,' ait, 'vobis gratias nullas habeo, quippe qui non tam eo
imperatorem me delegistis, quod mihi imperio foret opus, quam
quod vobis imperatore.' Atqui huius filius Africanus minor libertatem patriam gravitatemque imitatus, ubi capta Numantia
secundum thriumphasset, et G. Gracchum, cuius sororem in
matrimonium haberet, Gn. Carboni, tribuno plebis seditioso
pestiferoque civi, quid ei de illius nece videretur interroganti,
sibi iure caesum videri respondisset, atque ei dicto tribunicio
furore instigata concio succlamasset, in ipsumque Scipionem
qui esset pro tribunali populus turbatus tumultuaret, tunc ipse,
inquam, Africanus, 'Nunquam nos,' ait, 'legionum vociferatio

117

118

Wealth stripped of virtue does not exalt on high,
Nor does virtue without wealth.[63]

He considers virtue to be such that it is not burdened by any
coffers or sacks of money, does not rely on the support of others, and easily and quickly raises itself up on high and shows
itself visible to all and resplendent. For what the poet says,

Those whose merits are blocked by straightened domestic
    circumstances
Have difficulty rising to the top,[64]

would not be said about a wise and completely virtuous man,
but about a counterfeiter of wisdom and virtue who does not
believe himself renowned unless he receives the approbation
and respect of the insane crowd. How delighted I am by Aemil-   117
ius Paulus, who suffered rejection when seeking his second
consulate. Not long afterward he was declared consul when he
neither sought nor desired the office because it appeared that
the war the Romans were waging against King Perseus and the
Macedonians was dragging on because of the inexperience and
laziness of the commanders. "I feel no gratitude toward you,
citizens," he said, "since in fact you have not chosen me as a
commander so much because I needed a command, as because
you needed a commander."[65] After his son, Scipio Africanus the   118
Younger, imitating the freedom and gravity of his father, captured Numantia, he celebrated his second triumph. To Gnaeus
Carbo, tribune of the plebs, a seditious and vexatious citizen,
who asked Scipio what he thought about the murder of Gaius
Gracchus (to whose sister Scipio was married), he replied that
he appeared to have been justifiably murdered. When the assembly, stirred up by the tribune's rage at that pronouncement,
raised a shout, the unruly mob rose up against Scipio himself,
who was in front of the tribunal. Then Africanus said, "I have

perterruit, nedum hominum confluctuatio atque confusio, quibus non matrem Italiam sed novercam potius esse scio.' Et orto
deinde murmure, 'Nunquam,' ait, 'efficietis ut solutos verear
quos ligatos adduxi.' Cumque ab amicis Gracchi de interfi-
ciendo[45] tyranno clamor sublatus esset, 'Recte,' subdidit, 'qui
patriam oppugnant, me prius volunt de medio tollere. Non
enim Romam casuram putant Scipione superstite, neque victu-
rum Scipionem si Roma ceciderit.' Contemnit, inquam, vir sapiens et magnanimus omnem populi favorem. Nihil est omnium sua sibi probitate carius, nihil gloriosius. Malit non modo
non laudari, verum et exilium et mortem quoque (si opus sit)
pati quam officium decorumque deserere. Idem superior Africanus, cum Paetilius et Quintus tribuni plebis instantissime agerent in senatu ut rationem et pecuniae et praedae Antiochinae
redderet, exurrexit[46] aliquantisper pro sua gravitate indignatus
aitque: 'Hoc in libro, patres conscripti' — nam continuo librum
e sinu togae protulerat — 'et Antiochina omnis pecunia et praeda
omnis scripta est; quem eo tuleram mecum, quo et palam reci-
taretur deferreturque ad aerarium. Sed id certe iam facturus
non sum. Nec enim me ipse afficiam contumelia.' Quae tum
voce fiduciae suae plena, tum vultu constantissimo locutus, statim eum librum suis ipse manibus coram discidit atque discerp-
sit. Non enim aegre pro sua innocentia Scipio ferre non potuit
quod pecuniaria ab se ratio posceretur, qui non praedam et
manubias solum, sed salutem ac libertatem reipublicae attulis-
set. Maluitque in exilium sponte proficisci quam non modo
supplicem se demissumque praestare, sed respondere etiam pro
sua causa quippiam apud invidum et ingratum populum. Eadem ratio fuit Socratis, qui coniectus in carcerem quoniam

never been afraid of the shout of armed hosts, let alone that of a disorderly rabble of men of whom Italy is not the mother but the stepmother." And when a murmur of disapproval then 119 arose, he said, "You will never make me fear unbound men whom I once brought in bound." When a shout arose from Gracchus' followers that the tyrant ought to be killed, he said, "It is right that those who attack their homeland want first to get rid of me; they think Rome will not fall while Scipio stands, and that if Rome has fallen, Scipio will not survive." The wise and great-souled man, then, holds the people's favor in contempt. For there is nothing at all more precious to him, nothing more glorious, than his own integrity. He prefers not only not to be praised but to suffer exile and even death, if necessary, to deserting his duty and his honor. Likewise when the tribunes 120 of the plebs, Paetilius and Quintus, were insisting most urgently in the senate that Scipio Africanus the Elder render an account of the money and spoils from Antiochus, taking umbrage in view of his standing, he got to his feet and said, "In this book, senators"—for he had immediately drawn out a book from the folds of his toga—"all the money and spoils of King Antiochus have been recorded. I had brought it with me to have it read out and deposited in the treasury. But I am not about to do this now, for I would not submit myself to insult." When he had spoken these words, filled with self-confidence 121 and with a steadfast expression, in their presence, with his own hands, he at once tore apart and scattered the book. For in view of his innocence Scipio could not but feel pain that a monetary account was being demanded of him, a man who had delivered to the republic not only plunder and spoils, but also safety and freedom. Rather than simply show himself submissive and humiliated, or give some reply in his own defense before the jealous and ungrateful people, he preferred to go voluntarily into exile. Socrates followed the same principle: he was thrown into

deum habere in se diceret (hoc est mentem ipsam, qua nihil est ab immortali Deo divinius homini datum), nec iudicibus supplex fuit, nec facere pro causa verbum voluit.

122 *Honofrius.* At propterea et ille exilio et hic morte mulctatus est?

Pallas. Verum neutrum mea sententia malum est, id quod postea plane me puto ostensurum. Sed supplicem se praestare ac mentiri aut quicquam inepte loqui indignum viris gravissimis oscoenumque videbatur. De Aenea vero quae addidisti, facilis est solutio. Nec de viro sapienti Virgilius est locutus, nec Aeneas sapiens adhuc erat. Sed quoniam humanam vitam secundum aetates omnis ac varios cuiusque aetatis mores perpulchre poeta prudentissimus effingeret, Aeneae, quem pro ea posuit animi parte quae sua natura rationis est expers, non inepte perturba-

123 tiones addidit. Quare cum nondum Sibyllae rationisque ductu is uteretur, non quae ratio consuleret, sed quae perturbatio cogeret loquebatur. Nam vir sapiens nihil de se unquam istiusmodi loqueretur. Sed ut magnifice de sese verissimeque sentit, ita si conducturum sibi intellexerit, omnia pro sua fiducia loquatur. Nam tacebit quoque si opus fuerit idque dignitatis suae interesse duxerit. Sed quae loquatur, non abiecte aut falso ulla rerum externarum inopia infamiave deterritus, sed magnifice de

124 se omnia verissimeque loquatur. M. Brutus, vir fortis et gravis, non potuit M. Tullio Ciceroni, homini amicissimo et optime de se merito, non acriter succensere, quod se Octaviano, qui Augustus postea cognominatus est, humilius commendarat.

prison for saying he had a god within him (that is, his mind: nothing more divine than that has been given to man by immortal God[66]). He did not supplicate the judges, nor did he wish to utter a word in his own defense.[67]

Onofrio. Was that the reason the former was punished with exile, the latter with death? 122

Palla. Yes, but in my opinion neither is an evil. This is something that I think I will show clearly later on. To play the suppliant and to lie, or to speak about anything inappropriately, has seemed unworthy and disgusting to the most serious men. There is an easy solution to what you said about Aeneas. Vergil did not speak about a wise man, nor was Aeneas as yet a wise person. But since the shrewdest of poets brilliantly fashioned human life according to all its ages and the varying characters of each age, to Aeneas, whom he made stand for that part of the soul that by its nature lacks reason, he aptly added emotions. Therefore since he was not yet taking advantage of the Sibyl's 123 guidance and of reason, he was speaking not what reason recommended, but what his emotions compelled him to. For a wise man would never say anything of this sort about himself. But if he knows it is going to be in his interest, he should speak everything openly with self-confidence, as he has a grand and accurate view of himself. He will also remain quiet if necessary and if he considers it in the interest of his standing. What he says he ought not to say in a disparaging or false manner, frightened by lack of wealth or a concern for infamy, but he should speak about himself in a splendid and true way. Marcus 124 Brutus, who was a courageous and respected man, could not rightly be other than angry at Marcus Tullius Cicero, a very good friend of his and one who had done him good service, for recommending him in too groveling a manner to Octavian, who later received the cognomen Augustus:

Particulam (inquit) litterarum tuarum, quas misisti Octavio, legi missam ab Attico mihi. Studium tuum curaque de salute mea nulla me nova[47] voluptate affecit. Non solum enim usitatum, sed etiam quottidianum est aliquid audire de te quod pro nostra dignitate fideliter atque honorifice dixeris. At dolore me quammaximum capere animo possum eadem illa pars epistolae scripta ad Octavium de nobis affecit. Sic enim illi gratias agis de republica, tam suppliciter ac demisse? Quid scribam? Pudet conditionis ac fortunae, sed tamen scribendum est. Commendas nostram salutem illi—quae morte qua non perniciosior?

125 Deinde non multo post: 'Rogas enim,' ait, 'velit nos salvos esse. Videmur ergo tibi salutem accepturi cum vitam acceperimus? Quam, si prius dimittimus dignitatem et libertatem, qui possumus accipere?' Nunquid hic erat vel demisso animo, vel minus de se magnifice loqui verebatur? An quid de se alii dicerent, aut ullam fortunae invidiam insectationemque cogitabat, qui nihil sibi melius quam memoriam rectefactorum duceret ac libertate 126 contentus negligeret humana? Nec eum latebat quanta esset Octaviani potentia, quantae vires, quantus principatus. Verum secum ipse decreverat aut vincere aut mori potius quam alicuius dominantis inscitiam et ineptiam perpeti et aliorum se insaniae participem fieri. 'Quare non Octavius est,' inquit, 'rogandus ut velit nos salvos esse. Magis tu te exuscita, ut eam civitatem in qua maxima gessisti liberam et honestam fore putes, si modo sint populo duces ad resistendum improborum consiliis.'

I have read a small portion of the letter you sent to Octavian, forwarded to me by Atticus. Your concern and care for my safety gives me pleasure, which is nothing new. Hearing something that you have spoken faithfully and honorably on behalf of my worthiness is not merely a usual but even a daily occurrence. But that same portion of your letter to Octavian about me caused me distress as great as my heart can contain. Are you thanking him on behalf of the commonwealth in such a suppliant and humble tone? What can I write? I am ashamed so to write to one of such position and high estate, yet I must do it: you recommend to him our lives and safety! Could any death be more disastrous than this?

Then not much further on he says: "For you ask for him to 125 agree to our safety: do we therefore seem to you about to accept immunity, since we have accepted life? How can we accept this if we have previously surrendered position and liberty?" Was he ever the least bit downhearted, did he ever shrink from speaking grandly about himself? Did he think about what others were saying about him or give any thought to any envious attack of fortune — a man who considered nothing better for himself than a record of his good deeds and, happy with his liberty, remained indifferent to human concerns? For it did 126 not escape him how great the power, the resources, and the status of Octavian were. But he decided either to conquer or die rather than to suffer the ignorance and folly of any master and become a participant in others' madness. "Hence Octavian ought not to be petitioned to agree to our safety. Instead, spend your energy to assure yourself that the state in which you have performed the greatest deeds will be free and of good standing, which it will be if only there are leaders to help the people resist the plots of traitors."[68]

127 *Rainaldus.* Ego te profecto, Pallas, cum Honofrio tuo, vel nostro potius, de exilio graviter docteque disserentem non invitus — id quod ex attentione mea potes animadvertere — et audivi et audio. Fuerunt autem mihi quae locutus es omnia non mediocriter grata, sed nihil profecto gratius quam quod de M. Bruto, viro maximo et fortissimo, in medium protulisti. Mors enim mea sententia ei saluti quae libertatis sit et dignitatis expers, est admodum praeferenda. Quid enim acerbius ea vita quae et[48] obscura est et servilis et tetra? An ego Florentiae velim vivere, ubi omnia geri perspiciam pro furore ac libidine Cosmi unius Me-

128 dicis? Malim equidem non modo exilium pati, sed et dolorem et mortem, quam et memoriam rectefactorum oblivisci et, quam a maioribus firmam florentemque rempublicam acceperam, hanc imbecillam languentemque deserere. Itaque ipse quoque si teipsum audies, et exuscitabis te quamprimum, et qua in patria, cum natus, altus educatusque es, tum plurima pulcherrimaque facinora tua maxima cum laude gessisti semper, ut hanc liberam et honestam velis, omni studio atque viribus moliere.

129 *Pallas.* Ego te, Rainalde Albizi, et civem optimum semper duxi et ingenti animo virum et in nostra republica plane principem. Utinam tibi esset iampridem obtemperatum, patriae nostrisque rebus integris! Nam si tuum grave sanumque consilium sequi voluissemus, non de nostro nunc, sed de inimicorum vel exilio vel capite quaereretur. Sed quae tempora secuta sint, vides. Quos nobiscum et sentire et esse par fuerat, ii nos maxime oppugnant. Verum nos de his postea, si videtur, inter nos commentabimur, et quod utilius factu censueris sequemur.

Rinaldo. Without any reluctance I have listened and am now lis- 127
tening to you, Palla, seriously and learnedly discussing with
your — or rather our — Onofrio about exile, a fact that you can
gather from my attentiveness. All the things that you said were
very agreeable to me but none more agreeable than what you
related about that greatest and most courageous man, Marcus
Brutus. For in my opinion death is to be preferred to a safety in
which freedom and good standing are absent. What is more
bitter than a life that is obscure, slavish, and foul? Would I
want to live in Florence when I see everything being carried out
in accordance with the rage and lust of one man, Cosimo de'
Medici? I would certainly prefer to suffer not just exile but even 128
pain and death rather than forget the memory of just actions
and to leave the commonwealth feeble and weak, when I inherited it from my ancestors strong and flourishing. And so if you
listen to your own discourse, you will rouse yourself as soon as
possible, and for that homeland where you were born, raised,
and educated, and where you have always performed all your
countless and splendid exploits to the greatest praise, you will
then work with all your energy and power to keep it free and
virtuous.

Palla. I have always considered you as the finest citizen, Rinaldo 129
degli Albizzi, and a man with a great soul, and clearly a leader
in our republic. Would that your advice had been followed long
ago when our interests and those of our homeland were still
intact! Had we been willing to follow your weighty and sensible
advice, there would now be no question of our own exile and
death but of our enemies'. But you see what crises followed.
Those who ought to have been of our sentiment and party
most attack us. We will talk among ourselves afterward about
these matters, if it is agreeable, and we will follow what you
consider the more expedient course.

130 *Rainaldus.* Placet id quidem fietque commodius. Nunc perge quod coepisti. Nec aegre tuleris si te aliquando disserentem interpolabo.[49] Nam in hac ista exilii disputatione communis optimatium omnium et innocentissimorum civium causa agitur.

Pallas. Immo ut me loquentem pro tuo arbitratu interpoles,[50] non solum non aegre fero, sed et laetor et rogo. Cum enim et honestam et nostram causam agimus, veritatem debemus, non contentionem sequi. Nullus, inquam, fortunae impetus sapientis animum retardabit quin fidenter[51] et pro dignitate sua omnia loquatur quae senserit. At inconstanter obsequi cuiquam aut assentari sibi mortis instar iudicabit.

131 *Honofrius.* At Aristippum, mi pater, sapientem habitum audio; nec is tamen non assentabatur cum id sibi profuturum sentiebat. Nam ut alia conticescam, cum is apud Dionysium seniorem Syracusarum tyrannum aliquando versaretur et ab eo quiddam[52] pro amico nixius peteret nec tamen assequeretur, illius genua suppliciter tetigit. Quo facto cum sibi quod poposcerat contigisset, intelligeretque eiusmodi assentationem a praesentibus vitio dari, 'Non ego,' inquit, 'huiuscemodi assentationis auctor sum, sed Dionysius, qui in genibus aures habet.'

132 *Pallas.* At non attendis teipsum abs te refelli?

Honofrius. Cur?

Pallas. Quia si sapiens cuiquam assentetur, idque tibi recte fieri videtur, nihil est quod exulem vituperes si suae conscius fortunae ineptias principum tulerit. Verum iste quem laudas Aristippus non magis in tangendis Dionysii genibus mihi sapere visus est quam cum et saltandi se principem exhiberet et Diony-

133 sium ipsum superare potando niteretur. At vir sapiens idemque

Rinaldo. This is agreeable and will be appropriate. Now continue 130
to the goal you have set out for. Please do not be annoyed if I
occasionally interrupt you as you are speaking. For in this discourse of yours about exile the common cause of all the aristocrats and faultless citizens is at stake.

Palla. On the contrary, not only am I not annoyed, but I beg you
and am delighted for you to interrupt my discourse as you see
fit. For as we are pleading a case that is both honorable and our
own, we must pursue truth, not quarrels. No blow of fate will
hinder the heart of the wise man from speaking all his thoughts
confidently and in line with his rank. But he will reckon that
for him the unprincipled humoring or flattering of anyone is
tantamount to death.

Onofrio. But I have heard, father, that Aristippus was considered a 131
wise man, yet he indulged in flattery when he thought it would
further his interests. Not to mention other instances, once
when he was spending time at the court of Dionysius the Elder,
the tyrant of Syracuse, and he earnestly petitioned something
from him for a friend but failed to attain it, he touched the
king's knees in suppliant gesture. After doing so, when it fell to
him to ask what he wanted, he knew that obsequiousness of
this kind was reckoned a vice by those present. He said, "I am
not the originator of flattery of this kind, but Dionysius, who
has ears in his knees."[69]

Palla. But don't you see how you are contradicting yourself? 132

Onofrio. Why is that?

Palla. Because if a wise man flatters someone, and you take this to
be acceptable, there is no reason why you should criticize a man
in exile if he, aware of his fate, were to put up with the follies of
princes. But that very man whom you praise, Aristippus, did
not appear to me to be any more wise in touching the knees of
Dionysius than if he had presented himself as a dancing master
and attempted to outstrip Dionysius himself in drinking. But 133

constantissimus nihil profecto unquam facturus sit, nihil dicturus, cuius non possit et probatam et rectam reddere rationem.
Neque supra se quempiam vereatur qui humana omnia infra se
ducit. Nec enim cuiuspiam etiam lucri gratia servire is velit qui
se solum liberum novit. Nam ut est excelso animo et invicto,
nullo quaestu, nulla re cogi queat ut qui natura sit liber natus et
perpetuo animi iudicio atque institutione ad libertatem confir-
matus, servitutem perpeti ullam possit. Intelliget sane et naturae rationisque constantiae et firmitati potius quam vel fortunae
vel temeritatis inconstantiae ac fragilitati se tradere oportere.
Itaque nihil esse ducendum lucro quod dedecus, quod indignitatem ullam afferre possit. Atqui bonae spei plenus malit vel
Camillum vel Ciceronem quam Polynicem meditari. Nam et
Camillum qui secundis in rebus suis urbe expulerant, Ardeae
exulantem extrema pressi calamitate implorantes Romani dicta-
torem dixerunt, ab eodemque praesenti periculo internicioque
liberati in urbe ipsa retenti sunt; et Ciceronem Clodiana coniu-
ratione eiectum Roma atque Italia non multo post Italia suis
humeris reportans sibi Romaeque restituit. G. vero Marius
cum magnas res illustresque gessisset ac sexto iam consulatu
fungeretur, et a L. Sylla victus et a senatu patriae hostis iudica-
tus est. Cumque in Minturnensium paludibus lateret ac inde ab
oppidanis extractus esset, Gallum ad se occidendum missum a
Sylla, nulla insectante fortuna fractus, sed sperans semper meliora, sola vultus maiestate deterruit. Exulavit is tandem; et diu
ac multum in Africa exulavit. Sed ad postremum in Italiam

the wise man and the man of firm principle will never do anything, will never say anything, for which he cannot deliver both
an acceptable and correct justification. A man who considers all
human affairs beneath him should not be afraid of anyone
above his station. A man who knows that he is alone free would
not desire to serve anyone for the sake of any monetary gain.
For since he is possessed of a lofty and unshakable mind, he
cannot be compelled by any reward nor by anything else, being
naturally born free and forever strengthened for freedom by his
judgment and training to tolerate any kind of slavery. He will
know that he must entrust himself to nature, to the consistency
of reason, and to strength rather than to fortune, wavering im-
pulsivity, and weakness. Nothing is to be considered a gain that   134
can bring any shame or disgrace. The wise man prefers being
full of optimism and to take to heart Camillus and Cicero
rather than Polynices. For the same Romans who had driven
Camillus out of the city in good times, when they were threatened with utter disaster, begged his aid when he was living in
exile at Ardea and named him dictator. The same man freed
them from imminent danger and carnage and kept them in the
city itself.[70] When Cicero was banished from Rome and Italy
because of the Clodian conspiracy, not long afterward Italy carried him back on her shoulders and restored him both to Rome
and to herself.[71] Although Gaius Marius had performed great   135
and distinguished exploits and was serving his sixth term as
consul, he was defeated by Lucius Sulla and judged by the senate an enemy of his country. When he hid in the swamps of
Minturnae and was exposed by the townspeople, when a Gaul
was sent by Sulla to kill him, he was not broken by the Fortune
that harried him but, sustained by the hope of a better future,
he overawed his would-be assassin with the majesty of his
countenance alone.[72] He finally lived in exile; he spent a long
exile in Africa. But at the end of his life he was recalled to Italy

Urbemque revocatus et magnas res gessit et septimum consul diem obiit.

136   Sperabit, inquam, semper meliora vir sapiens. Nec interim tamen ita parabit sese ut sua spe delusus videatur. Ut enim doctus peritusque gubernator, cum etiam a puppi optatum ventum flaturum sperat, non secus et rudentibus malum munit et anchoras parat totamque navim ornat quam si continuo nova sit eum aliqua procella tempestasque invasura, ita vir huiusmodi patria fugatus, cum maxime celerem et secundum sperabit in patriam reditum, tum potissimum ipse armabit sese fortitudinis robore, prudentiae praesidio atque omnium denique virtutum

137   subsidiis adversus vim omnem impetumque fortunae. Nec metuet diurnum sibi cibum vel diuturnum etiam defuturum, cum secum ipse repetierit quid Hiero post Gelonem tyrannus Xenophani Colophonio responderit. Nam cum Xenophanes saepius dicere consuesset vix se alere duos servos, 'At Homerus is,' ait, 'cui tu detrahis, pluris quam decemmillia vel mortuus alit.' Facile se unum alat qui animi et sapientiae alimento alios alere

138   multos possit. Quod si corporis imbecillitas nos sollicitet, poterimus etiam eam corporis famem loci mutatione non admodum difficile vitare. Qua in re sanctissimos illos imitabimur patriarchas, qui non dubitaverunt Palestina relicta in Aegyptum descendere. Quod si quam parvo natura contenta est consyderemus, et quanta nobis nullo etiam nostro labore terra sua sponte suppeditat, non ad victus necessitatem modo, sed etiam ad voluptatem, sane intelligamus deesse alimentum nemini posse.

and Rome; he performed great exploits and died serving as
consul for the seventh time.[73]

The wise man, I insist, will always nurture hope for better   136
days. Yet in the meantime he will not allow himself to appear
deluded by his hope. For just as a trained and seasoned admi-
ral, even while he hopes that a favorable wind will be blow-
ing behind his stern, nonetheless secures the mast with ropes,
makes his anchors ready, and equips the entire ship just as if
another squall or storm is about to fall upon him at once, in the
same way a man of this sort who has been driven from his
homeland will put hope in a swift and happy return to his
country, but he will still arm himself against every blow and
assault of fortune with courageous strength and the protection
of wisdom and the assistance of the virtues. He will not be   137
anxious about lacking his daily or even his long-term sustenance, since he will remind himself of what Hiero, the tyrant in
power after Gelo, replied to Xenophanes of Colophon. For
Xenophanes used to say that he could barely feed two slaves:
"But Homer," said Hiero, "whom you disparage, is feeding
more than ten thousand, even as a dead man."[74] The wise man,
who can feed many others with the nourishment of his mind's
wisdom, would easily feed himself alone. But if weakness of   138
body is to distress us, we may with no difficulty at all avoid
bodily hunger with a change of dwelling place. In this way we
shall follow the example of the most holy patriarchs, who did
not hesitate to leave the land of Palestine behind and descend
into Egypt. But if we consider with how little nature is satisfied, how much the earth freely furnishes us, even without our
effort — not just the bare need for food but enough for our enjoyment — we should doubtless realize that nourishment cannot
be lacking for any human being.

139 *Honofrius.* Verum alius quidam sapor atque iucunditas in carnibus est et piscibus delicatissimisque obsoniis quam in olusculis et pomis et nucibus.

Pallas. Istiusmodi voluptates facit opinio, non natura. Persae, ut scribit Xenophon, ad panem nasturcio utebantur obsonio, et eo iucundissime vescebantur. Ac ne mirandum id quidem. Caena-bant enim non ad libidinem et luxum, sed ut levata fame imbe-

140 cillitati naturae satisfacerent. Qualis Lacedaemoniorum victus esset, declaravit Dionysius tyrannus, qui quoniam accepisset ius nigrum quod dicitur adeo apud eos probari ut seniores ipsi ne carne quidem egerent, emit huius rei gratia adolescentem Laco-nicum, cui ut ius illud sibi pararet impensaeque nulli parceret imperavit. Deinde cum ius gustatum despuisset, coquum dixisse tradunt: 'O rex, hoc ius tibi vescendum est, ubi te et Laconice exercueris et in Eurota laveris.' Non carnibus ei, non piscibus, nullis deliciis opus est qui animi rationem quam corporis ha-bere malit.

141 *Honofrius.* Quamobrem istud ais, mi pater? Num eo fortasse car-nium et piscium esum damnas, quod in iis aut patris aut matris aut alicuius amici secundum Empedoclen animus violetur?

Pallas. Dixit id quidem Empedocles, dixit et Pythagoras, aliique non nulli Pythagorei. Verum illos aliud sensisse arbitror.

Honofrius. Et quidnam?

Pallas. Carnium, inquam, aescae ac itidem vinum et reliquarum huiusmodi delicatiora videntur humanum corpus validius red-dere atque robustius, sed imbecillum atque infirmum animum sua repletione et crassitate efficiunt.

142 *Poggius.* Audi, Pallas Stroza, paulisper, nisi molestum est, Pog-gium tuum Bambalionem. Habeo enim quod dicam. Si omnis

Onofrio. There is one kind of flavor and enjoyment in meats and 139
fish and in the most delicate sauces, and another in vegetables,
fruits, and nuts.

Palla. Convention fabricates pleasure of this kind, not nature. The
Persians, as Xenophon writes, used cress as a spread on their
bread, and it should be no wonder that they ate this most en-
joyably.[75] For they were dining not for pleasure or indulgence,
but compensating for nature's weakness by having their hunger
alleviated. Dionysius the Tyrant showed the nature of the Spar- 140
tan diet. Because he had learned that the so-called black sauce
was so popular among them that their elders required no meat,
he bought a young Spartan whom he ordered to spare no expense in preparing him that sauce. Then when he had spat out
the sauce he had sampled, the cook said: "Your majesty, you
should eat this sauce after you have exercised like a Spartan and
have washed in the Eurotas."[76] The man who prefers to take
account of his mind, rather than his body, has no need for
meats, fish, or delicacies.

Onofrio. Father, why are you saying this? Do you perhaps con- 141
demn the eating of meat and fish because, according to Empedocles, in them the soul of either a mother or father or some
friend may be violated?[77]

Palla. Empedocles did indeed say this, as did Pythagoras as well as
some other Pythagoreans. But I believe they had something else
in mind.

Onofrio. What is that?

Palla. Let me note that the eating of meats and likewise wine and
other delicacies of this sort appear to make the human body
stronger and more robust, but by their fullness and fattiness
they make the soul weak and compromised.

Poggio. If you do not mind, Palla Strozzi, listen briefly to your 142
friend Poggio Bambalio,[78] for I have something to say. If all the
pleasure of the soul, than which nothing better nor more divine

animi voluptas, qua nihil est humano generi ab immortali Deo neque divinius datum nec melius, a corporis voluptate proficiscitur (id quod Cyrenaicis etiam placet), corpus autem ex huiusmodi aesculentis atque potulentis voluptatem maximam capit, quid est quod tantopere cum carnium et piscium usum tum suavissimum vini haustum non probes? An ignoras lac senis vinum esse? Nam etsi omni aetati vinum est iucundum, tamen senectuti nectar quoddam opinor. Quid illa videntur tibi:

143

Laudibus arguitur vini vinosus Homerus.

Et:

Ennius ipse pater nunquam nisi potus ad arma
prosiliit dicenda.

Atque illud quoque:

Exul ab octava Marius bibit et fruitur diis
iratis.

Nonne hisce omnibus luce clarius monstratur et Homerum, divinum poetam, et Ennium, poetam et ipsum quoque non ignobilem, et G. Marium, virum fortem et imperatorem illustrem, cum aut illi dicere aut hic facere robustius et gloriosius quicquam vellent,[53] ad vinum sese tanquam ad firmissimum aliquod certissimumque praesidium recipere solitos? Itaque ut inflatae repletaeque tibiae sonare consuevere modulatius, ita qui epulis se absumptis meroque referserint et contemplando et agendo et dicendo sunt ad omnia nimirum aptiores, idque non solum corporis robore, sed etiam vi atque virtute animi. Ego enim facio de meipso coniecturam, cui cum intestina prae inanitate murmurant atque aridum guttur est, meipsum odi, morosus sum, nullus sum. Crede, inquam, mihi: animus recte habet cum corpus recte habet.

144

has been given to the human race by immortal God, originates
in the pleasure of the body (a view that the Cyrenaics also
held), yet the body takes the greatest pleasure in eating and
drinking of this kind, then why do you so strongly disapprove
of the enjoyment of meats and fish and the pleasurable quaffing
of wine? Don't you know that wine is the old man's milk? For
even though wine is enjoyable for every age group, I consider
it a kind of nectar of old age. What do you make of the fol- 143
lowing?

By his praise of wine Homer convicts himself of tippling

and

Father Ennius himself never broke out singing of arms
Unless he was drunk.[79]

and again

The exile Marius drank from the early afternoon on and
    took pleasure
In the gods' anger.[80]

Don't these examples show more clearly than daylight that the
divine poet Homer and Ennius, himself a distinguished poet,
and Gaius Marius, a courageous man and distinguished general, when the former wanted to say and the latter to do anything of vigor and renown, were wont to have recourse to wine
as the strongest and most reliable defense? Just as pipes that 144
have been blown in and filled generally make a more melodious
sound, so those who have filled themselves with feasting and
wine are more skillful at thinking, acting, and speaking, not
only in bodily strength but also in force and power of mind. I
infer this from my own case: when my guts grumble for food
and my throat is dry, I am depressed, fussy, good for nothing.
Believe me: the mind is well when the body is well.

145 *Rainaldus.* Cuperem equidem tibi, Poggi, respondere, si liceret id
mihi per Pallantem.

Pallas. At licet istud quidem tibi, Rainalde, modo ipse velis. Erit-
que longe mihi gratius audire quam loqui. Quid enim dicturus
non es et prudenter et erudite?

Rainaldus. Quid ais, Poggi Bambalio? Num ista e philosophia didicisti?

Poggius. Obsecro, Rainalde, si mecum verba facturus es, ut barbam
tuam hirsutam istam quam nescio qua tibi gravitate indueris,
primum abradas. Nam cum aspicere te volui, mihi terrori es!

146 *Rainaldus.* Haud miror, Poggi, si tibi barba non placet. Nam ne
gravioribus quidem annis delectaris. Verum si infra quintum et
quadragesimum annum aetatem agerem, si tibi obsequerer in
radenda barba, minus forem fortasse repraehendendus. Sed
cum non senior modo sed iam sum plane senex, utpote qui iam
prope septuaginta sum natus annos, qui pulcherrima veste hac
nudari faciem iubes? Ni fortassis propterea istud nobis faciundum censes, quoniam nullus sit in pugnando, ut Alexander
Parmenioni aliquando respondit, quam barbae captus alius melior. Nos autem non manibus neque pugnis, sed mentis inter
nos ratione verboque contendimus. At si barbam omnino exosus es, abradam equidem barbam atque capillum omnem, modo
tu lyppitudinem istam ex oculis abradas tuis.

147 *Poggius.* Age, age, ut libet. Quid tandem ais ad nostra?

Rainaldus. Num ista, inquam, e philosophorum scholis accepisti?

Poggius. Quaenam? Nam ego philosophis durioribusque hominibus minime delector. Omninoque ipsum philosophari mihi
nunquam placuit.

Rainaldus. Et ostendis id quidem non vita minus quam oratione.
Num quae modo dicebas de voluptate, de epulis, de mero, eiusmodi esse statuis ut in sapientis domicilium recipi possint?

Rinaldo. With Palla's permission, I should like to reply to you,   145
Poggio.

Palla. Indeed you have permission, Rinaldo, if that is what you
wish. I much prefer to hear rather than speak. For you could
only speak wisely and with learning.

Rinaldo. What are you claiming, Poggio Bambalio? Surely philosophy has not taught you *that*?

Poggio. I beg you, Rinaldo, if you are going to speak with me, first
shave off that shaggy beard of yours which you have adopted
along with a certain air of authority. For when I look at you, I
am terrified!

Rinaldo. I am hardly surprised, Poggio, that you dislike my beard.   146
You don't even like people of riper age. But if I were below the
age of forty-five, if I were to follow your advice in shaving my
beard, perhaps I would be more acceptable. But seeing that I
am not only older but already clearly an old man, since I am by
now almost seventy, why force me to strip my face of this lovely
garment? Unless perhaps you think I should do so since, as
Alexander once replied to Parmenio, there is no better hold in a
fight than by the beard.[81] However, we are not competing with
each other with hands or fists but with the mind's logic and
eloquence. But if my beard is so loathsome to you, I shall shave
it off and all my hair provided that you clear the bleariness from
your eyes.

Poggio. Go on, go on as you wish. What do you say to my thesis?   147

Rinaldo. You surely have not derived this notion from the teachings of the philosophers, have you?

Poggio. What notion? I dislike philosophers and dour people. Phi-
losophizing in general has never held any charm for me.

Rinaldo. And you show it no less in your life than in your words.
Surely you don't fancy that what you were just now saying
about pleasure, feasts, and wine are such that they can be welcomed into a wise man's house, do you?

148 *Poggius.* Imo, debeant sane, non possint; debent autem, quare
etiam possunt. Non enim sapiens ille est qui sibi ipse non sapit.
Non autem sapit qui voluptatem ignorat, qui non corporis ha-
bitudini et firmitati consulit, qui animum curis pressum ac veluti a se distractum quibus artibus, quibus remediis colligat non
tenet.

149 *Manettus.* Certe, Poggi, non omnino erravit Hesiodus, cum ait:

> Fama quidem populis celebrata frequentibus ore
> nunquam tota perit, nanque immortalis et ipsa est.

Nam quae de quopiam fama mentitur, etsi principio incrementa
apud stultos aliquando suscipiat, deficit tandem paulatim ad
veritatis radios ac veluti nebula omnino evanescit. Sed quae veris initiis profecta est, etiam si primos favores habeat imbecilliores, erumpit tandem, 'viresque acquirit eundo.' Putabam equidem falsa quae de tua ista voluptaria vita homines, Poggi,
loquebantur. Sed posteaquam te coram audivi, iam omni sum
errore liberatus. Nulla es enim usus circuitione. Doleo autem
vicem tuam, qui iam homo sexagenarius—non enim possum
me continere—ita vivas ut inter hominem et inertem aliquam
pecudem nihil interesse putes.

150 *Poggius.* Rainalde, dimittamus Iannocium Manettum cum sophis-
matis suis, et quod dicere coeperamus, siquid reliquum est
quod perdiscere cupias, prosequamur.

Rainaldus. Perdiscere cupio permulta. Sed vide, obsecro, ne tua me
doctrina ex stulto insanum reddas.

Poggius. Imo, e prudente sapientem sane te efficiam, si institutis
meis obtemperabis.

Rainaldus. Obtemperabo equidem, modo recte instituas. Sed dic
mihi: 'voluptatem' istam quid esse vis?

151 *Poggius.* Et ipse quod loquor intelligo, et abs te intelligi cupio.
Ego eam loquor voluptatem quam a Graecis ἡδονήν appellari
audio. Nec istam sentio quam umbra quaedam virtutis inani

Poggio. No, not that they can but that they ought to. Moreover, 148
they ought to, therefore they also can. For no man is wise who
is not wise for himself.[82] Moreover, he is not wise who knows
nothing of pleasure, who takes no thought for the condition
and strength of his body, who does not know by what arts and
remedies he can repair a mind weighed down by cares and, so
to speak, alienated from itself.

Manetti. Surely, Poggio, Hesiod was right when he said: 149

> Reputation spread by the lips of popular throngs
> Never wholly dies, for it is itself immortal.[83]

For whatever lies reputation tells about anyone, although they
gain ground among fools, finally dissipate before the rays of
truth and disappear altogether like a cloud. But a reputation
that is built upon a foundation of truth, even if its initial re-
ception is weak, finally bursts out and "gathers strength as it
goes."[84] But now that I have heard you in person, I am dis-
abused of any misconception. You did not resort to any circum-
locution. Your change pains me: you, a man already sixty — I
cannot hold back — live as though you think there is no difference between a human being and some lazy beast!

Poggio. Rinaldo, let us leave Giannozzo Manetti to his sophistries, 150
and let us pursue what we had begun to discuss, if anything
remains that you wish to learn.

Rinaldo. I wish to learn a great many things. But beware, please,
lest your teaching turn me from a dunce into a madman.

Poggio. No, I shall turn you from a prudent man into a wise man
if you follow my teachings.

Rinaldo. I shall indeed, provided that you teach rightly. But tell
me: what do you mean by that term of yours, "pleasure"?

Poggio. I understand what I am saying and want you to under- 151
stand. I call that pleasure which I hear is called *hedone* by the
Greeks. I do not have in mind that pleasure which a certain

honestatis nomine conficere dicitur, sed hanc potius quam sensus accipiens quadam titillatione movetur et suavi iucunditate perfunditur. Id autem — si verum fateri volumus et non ad aliorum sed ad nostram opinionem loqui — et vescendo et potitando maxime assequimur. Rectissime enim Chremes apud Terentium: 'sine Cerere et Libero friget Venus.' Nulla, inquam, nobis voluptas est ieiuno stomacho, nullum prorsus nec corporis nec animi bonum.

152 *Manettus.* Tametsi me paululum audaciorem cognosco, velim tamen, Rainalde, aequum te mihi aliquantisper exhibeas, et hanc mihi ad Poggium respondendi atque refellendi provinciam concedas. Nam nihil profecto unquam absurdius dici audivi.

Rainaldus. Geramus, Poggi, Manetto morem, si videtur. Est enim et acutus scilicet, et in dicendo subtilis. Itaque nihil oberit huius viri oratio.

Poggius. Ut libet, Rainalde. Nihil enim repugno. Sed sophistam garrulum audiemus.

153 *Manettus.* Quod obest, Poggi, bonum esse non potest. Nunquid aliter sentis?

Poggius. Nequaquam, sed isto modo. Nam voluptas et corpori prodest et animo.

Manettus. Istud paulo post viderimus. Quae maxima voluptas sit, ea ex epulis ac mero maxime proficiscitur, secundum tuam orationem. Aisne ita?

Poggius. Recte accipis.

Manettus. Et quo magis epulis sese quispiam sufferserit et vino ingurgitaverit, eo maiorem voluptatem putas?

Poggius. Certe.

154 *Manettus.* At istiusmodi repletio et turpis est et detrimentosa.

shadow of virtue is said to produce with the empty name of moral goodness; but this, rather, is pleasure that causes the senses, when they receive it to be moved by a certain titillation and suffused with sweet enjoyment. Moreover, if we are willing to speak the truth and speak in tune not with others' opinions but our own, we achieve this best by eating and drinking. For Chremes in Terence was quite right: "Venus freezes without Ceres and Bacchus."[85] We have, I maintain, no pleasure with an empty stomach, nothing good for the body or soul.

Manetti. Though I know I am being a bit overbold, I would none- 152 theless like, Rinaldo, for you to show me kindness and yield to me the task of replying to and refuting Poggio. For I have never heard a more absurd proposition.

Rinaldo. Let us indulge Manetti, Poggio, if you please. For he is indeed an acute and subtle speaker, so his words will do no harm.

Poggio. As you please, Rinaldo. I make no objection. But we will be listening to a longwinded sophist!

Manetti. What is harmful, Poggio, cannot be good. Or do you 153 think otherwise?

Poggio. By no means, but in this sense: pleasure benefits both the body and the mind.

Manetti. We shall see about that later. The greatest pleasure de- rives especially from food and wine according to your speech. Is that your position?

Poggio. Correct.

Manetti. And you think that the more food a person has choked down and the more wine he has imbibed, the greater the plea- sure?

Poggio. Certainly.

Manetti. But being stuffed this way is both disgraceful and harm- 154 ful.

Poggius. Cur, quaeso, turpem appellas, cum turpe natura nihil est, sed inepta quadam consuetudine et tristiore vestro iudicio?

Manettus. Dicerem te plane Pyrrhonium, nisi viderem alia quaedam te in vita sectari a quibus Pyrrho abhorruit. Nihil igitur putas turpe natura?

Poggius. Neque turpe natura quicquam nec malum existimo. Sed ne ab eo quod frustra probare nitebaris, aberrato. Aiebas huiusmodi repletionem detrimentosam. Hoc proba, si potes. De turpitudine alias. Facile enim tua sophismata confutabo, cum voluero.

155 *Manettus.* Profecto, Poggi, totus es tui similis. Sed ne Pallantis disputationem retardemus, nunc paucis agamus. Detrimentosam esse et perniciosam in primis cibi potusque repletionem hominis declarat et corpus et animus. Primum enim qui parvo cibo contenti sunt, facile possunt, cum opus est, vel cibo vacui labores ferre ac diutius eo carere, nec indigentes obsonii omnem aescam admittere. Quae quidem res et ad bonam valitudinem et ad status proceritatem conducit plurimum.

Poggius. Et quonam modo?

156 *Manettus.* Alimenti, inquam, paucitas et valentiora efficit corpora et vegetiora. Et quod ad corporis incrementum mirabiliter accedit, spiritus ipse vi atque honere alimenti in profunditatem corpus et latitudinem premit, at ea mole liberior atque levior idem illud in altum tollit facitque pulcherrimum. Quis enim ignoret gracilis et macilentos habitus parere agilitati artuum, tumentes vero et pinguis honere suo reluctari? Corpus, inquam,

Poggio. Why, I ask, do you call it disgraceful when nothing is disgraceful by nature but by an absurd convention and your austere opinion?

Manetti. I would declare you a Pyrrhonian if I did not see you follow in your lifestyle certain other elements far removed from Pyrrho.[86] Do you, then, think that nothing is by nature disgraceful?

Poggio. I hold that nothing is by nature disgraceful or bad. But do not wander off from what you were vainly endeavoring to prove. You claimed that being stuffed in this way was harmful. Prove that if you can. We will discuss disgrace another time. For I will easily refute your sophistries whenever I wish.

Manetti. Poggio, you are truly through and through the same   155
man. But so as not to impede Palla's discourse, let us now be brief. Both body and mind show that for a man to fill himself up with food and drink is harmful and deadly. In the first place, those who are content with scant rations can easily, when need arises, endure hard labor without food and go without it for longer periods, nor do they crave delicacies but accept any fare. This circumstance greatly enhances good health and tall stature.

Poggio. How so?

Manetti. A small quantity of food, I maintain, makes the body   156
stronger and more active. And in addition to promoting the body's growth, surprisingly, by the force and weight of the food the spirit itself presses the body toward greater depth and breadth, but when it is free of that mass and light, it raises the same body high and makes it beautiful. For everyone knows that slender and lean constitutions obey the agility of the limbs, whereas obese and fat ones struggle against it because of their own weight. The body, then, is raised in height whenever the

in longum fertur quandoquidem spiritus neque retardetur nec laboret. Laborat autem atque retardatur quotiens alimenti copia atque[54] vi in profunditatem et latitudinem fertur. Emergit autem spiritus petitque superiora in corporis levitate solute faleque crescentis. Itaque vel in convivio Lacedaemonii vetere Lycurgi instituto utebantur parsimonia, ut assuescerent repleri nunquam. Ita enim in fame toleranda longe se utiliores et in belli et in pacis artibus futuros arbitrabantur. Quod si omnis repletio fugienda est, tum obsonii potissimum et delicati quidem preciosique obsonii, quale est et carnis et piscis. Illudque Laconis meminerimus dictum haud insulsum, qui cum in cauponula quem emerat pisciculum parandum cauponi tradidisset, isque et caseum et acetum et oleum peteret, 'At si quidem ista mihi fuissent,' inquit, 'piscem non emissem!' Sed hoc tempore ad id insaniae ventum est ut iam non carne, non pisce obsonio, sed cibo utantur vulgo, vixque illa iam obsonio sint quae Cyprus, quae Syria, quae Arabia, quae remotissimae orbis regiones vel ad condenda cadavera vel ad condienda obsonia produxerint. Haec, Poggi, crede mihi, et corpus deformant et animum. Nec hominem sinunt ulla sibi ex parte constare. Nonne ipsa repletione et crapula — quod ex te ipso facile diiudices[55] — et in podagram et in laterum dolorem et in stranguriam et in alios innumerabiles morbos incidunt? Nonne quottidie multi alii vitam, alii mentem amittunt? Nam quid ego de vino dixerim? Quo ipso vinci et obrui nihil esse turpius arbitror, nihil foedius, nihil magno et claro viro indignius. Apte idem Chremes apud Terentium, in *Eunucho*, ut opinor:

spirit is neither slowed down nor struggling. Moreover, it is slowed down and struggling whenever it is extended in depth and breadth by the quantity and amount of food, whereas the spirit rises and seeks the heights in a light body that grows freely and without constraint. Therefore even at banquets, by   157
old precept of Lycurgus, the Spartans used to practice parsimony so that they acquired the habit of never filling themselves up. They thought that in this way they would be more useful in enduring hunger and in the arts of war and peace. But if any overeating is to be avoided, then it is especially filling oneself with refined and costly delicacies, such as meat and fish.[87] Let us recall the famous and witty *mot* of the Spartan, who, in a cookshop, when he had turned over to the proprietor a small fish he had bought and the other asked him for cheese, vinegar, and oil, replied, "If I had those things, I wouldn't have bought the fish!"[88] But in our time we have come to such a pitch of   158
madness that people commonly use meat or fish not merely as a delicacy but as food, and those items scarcely now count as delicacies that Cyprus, Syria, Arabia, and the remotest regions of the world have produced for preserving meats or seasoning delicacies. Believe me, Poggio, these things deform both body and mind. They do not allow a man to remain himself in any degree. Do people not by overindulgence in food and drink — a point you can easily determine from your own case — incur gout, asthma, bladder trouble, and numerous other diseases? Do some not lose their lives, others their minds on a daily basis? What should I say about wine? I think nothing more disgraceful, nothing more foul, nothing less worthy of a great and distinguished man than to be conquered and overmastered by drink. Chremes in Terence again speaks aptly, in the *Eunuch*, I   159
believe:

Atat data hercle verba mihi sunt: vicit vinum quod ego bibi.
At dum accubabam, quam videbar mihi esse pulchre
sobrius!
Postquam surrexi, neque pes neque mens satis suum
officium facit.

Ait ille deceptum sese quod a vino sit victus, quare neque corpore sibi neque mente constare. Nam quod et inclytum centau-
rum illum Eurytionem et Cyclopa,[56] qui corporis et magnitudine et viribus hominem excedebat, vinum ipsum perdiderit
Homerus, quem tam imprudenter vinositatis insimulas, testis
est.

160 *Poggius.* At hominibus ego vinum bibendum, non bestiis censeo.
Eurytionem enim equum homini admixtum fuisse omnes ludi
magistri, omnes pueri norunt. Cyclopa[57] vero natum esse Nep-
tuno patre, quid aliud significat quam omnis illum humanitatis
expertem habitum? Num enim ignoras qui prudentia praestitissent humanissimique essent, eos 'Iovis filios' a veteribus dici solitos? Inhumanissimos autem atque ferocissimos eosdemque
stultissimos omnis omnium poetarum chorus 'Neptuni filios'
concinit. Nam quanti vini vim atque virtutem Homerus fecerit,
si quemadmodum tu e Philelfo tuo Graecas litteras didicissem,
facile tibi probarem illis ipsis versibus quos laudibus in caelum
161 Nicolaus Nicolus crebro effert. Ait enim et creberrimo usurpare
sermone meus Nicolaus consuevit nihil sibi tantopere, cum e
Manuele Chrysolora Homerum audiret aliquando placuisse
quantopere versus illos quibus Hecuba Hectorem filium e diffi-
ciliore quodam praelio in urbem sacrificii gratia redeuntem allo-
quitur. In illis sane quanti sit vinum faciundum, Homerus
perspicue complectitur. Doleo autem maiorem in modum quod
illos mihi proferre non liceat. Intelligeres profecto me nihil de
vini laudibus locutum absurde.

> Ah! Words have been put in my mouth! The wine that I
>   drank has got the better of me.
> But while I was at table how splendidly sober I thought
>   myself!
> After I got up, neither foot nor mind did its job.[89]

He claims that he has been duped because he was overcome by wine; on that account he was himself in neither body nor mind. Homer, whom you so unwisely accuse of being a wine lover, bears witness that wine was the ruin of the illustrious centaur Eurytion and of the Cyclops, who excelled human beings in bulk and strength of body.[90]

Poggio. But I think that people, not beasts, should drink wine. All 160 schoolmasters and boys know that Eurytion was a horse joined to a human body. Doesn't the fact that the Cyclops was born the son of Neptune show that he was thought to be devoid of any human quality? Aren't you aware that those who were outstanding in wisdom and humanity used to be called by the ancients "the sons of Jupiter"? The entire chorus of all poets has sung of all the most inhuman, fierce, and at the same time stupid ones as "sons of Neptune." I would easily prove to you how much value Homer attached to the strength and power of wine, if, like you, I had learned Greek from Filelfo, namely by those very verses which Niccolò Niccoli frequently praises to the skies.[91] For my friend Niccolò asserts, and used to invoke the 161 point frequently in conversation, that once, when he heard Homer from the lips of Manuel Chrysoloras, nothing delighted him so much as those famous verses with which Hecuba addresses her son Hector as he returns from a hard-fought battle to the city to offer sacrifice. In them Homer clearly explains how much value should be attached to wine. I keenly regret that I cannot quote them. You would then understand that I have made no absurd claims about the merits of wine.[92]

162 *Manettus.* Verum, Poggi, quos ipse nequis, Homericos istos versus quoad potero interpretabor, nequa re disputatio nostra intercludatur:

> Quid Martem indomitum linquens huc, nate, redisti?
> Nempe piis manibus summa qui praesidet arce
> sacra Iovi facturus ades, furor asper Achivum
> usque adeo exuperans urbem premit. Ast age vinum,
> nate, mane, tibi dulce feram, quo prima tonanti
> caelicolisque aliis facias libamina, prosis
> potans inde tibi. Vires nanque acrius augent
> vina fatigato, qualis tu, nate, labore
> lassus es, auxilio dum cives eripis hosti.

Quos proferre versus cupiebas, hine, Poggi, an alii fortasse?

163 *Poggius.* Imo, illi isti prorsus. Nam tametsi Nicolaus neque Latine neque tam apte referre posset — nam Graecam litteraturam libarat, non ebiberat, Latinam autem, ut scis, negligit — tamen istiusmodi de bibendo sententiam referebat. Et Hecubam illam ut peritam prudentemque faeminam Homeri testimonio laudabat.

Manettus. Nunquid unquam commemoravit quid Hector responderit?

Poggius. Minime. Sed dic, obsecro, quam libenter vir ille splendidissimus matris consilium persecutus est.

164 *Manettus.* Quid credis? 'Ille impiger hausit spumantem pateram et pleno se proluit ore.' Respondit autem ita vir fortissimus:

Manetti. Well, Poggio, I shall, insofar as I can, translate those very   162
verses of Homer that you do not know, so that our discussion
may not be stalled for any reason:

> Why, my son, have you left invincible Mars and returned
>   here?
> Surely you are here to offer with devout hands sacrifice to
>   Jupiter,
> Who presides over the sacred citadel. The Achaeans' bitter
>   rage
> Mounting to this point is weighing on the city. But come,
>   son,
> Wait, I shall bring you sweet wine that you may first pour
> Libations to the Thunderer and the other gods, and that
>   you may benefit
> By drinking from it. For wine keenly adds strength
> To a weary man, as you, my son, are worn out
> From toil, bringing aid and rescuing citizens from the
>   enemy.

Are these the verses you wanted to quote, Poggio, or were there
others, perhaps?

Poggio. No, these are the very ones. For although Niccolò couldn't   163
translate them correctly into good Latin (for, as you know, he
had sampled but not deeply imbibed Greek literature and neglected Latin literature), yet he reported such an opinion about
drinking. And on the testimony of Homer he used to extol
Hecuba as an experienced and wise woman.

Manetti. But did he ever mention what Hector said in response?

Poggio. No. But please tell me how readily that splendid man followed his mother's advice.

Manetti. What do you think? "He vigorously drained the foaming   164
bowl and drenched himself from the golden vessel"?[93] In fact
that most courageous of men made the following reply:

Mellifluum, genetrix, vinum mihi ferre caveto,
ne natum enerves corpusque animumque relinquat
vis roburque suum.

Poggius. Isti, mediusfidius, eiusmodi sunt versus quos in Homeri
poesi scriptos nusquam reperiri putem. Quod si uspiam forte
reperiantur, ex eorum sunt numero quos prudentissimus Aristarchus Homeri esse neget.

165 *Manettus.* Si rei vim atque naturam, Poggi, pensitares, longe secus
sentires. Sed tuae tu isti de vinositate sententiae adeo te ad-
dixisti ut nihil omnium minus velis quam veritatem admittere.
Hinc enim et Ennium et Homerum vinolentiae facis obnoxios,
quasi Horatius Flaccus non modo vitia in claris viris non sec-
tanda ostenderit, sed Cratinum quoque illum Priscum non
inscite momorderit, qui avidus vini veteres illustrisque poetas
sui similes voluerit. Videmus enim, Poggi, hac etiam nostra
tempestate qui se cuipiam turpitudini dediderunt, non tam laborare ut ea se liberos aliquando faciant, quam ut magnos aliquos praestantissimosque viros per omnem calumniam sui si-
166 miles arguant. Nam quam vinositatem Flaccus vitio det, cum
alias saepe tum ad Torquatum scribens his versibus manifestis-
sime docet:

Quid non ebrietas designat? Operta recludit,
spes iubet esse ratas, ad praelia trudit inermem,
sollicitis animis honus eximit, addocet artis.
Faecundi calices quem non fecere disertum?
Constricta quem non in paupertate solutum?

Mother, do not bring me wine, which goes down like honey,
Lest you weaken your son and he lose his body, his mind,
And his strength, and vigor abandon him.[94]

Poggio. My God, these are verses of the sort that I thought I'd
never find written in Homer's poem. But if by chance they are
to be found somewhere, they are among those that the very
wise critic Aristarchus denies as Homeric.

Manetti. If you were to weigh, Poggio the essence and nature of
the matter, you would think far differently. But you are so fixed
in that opinion of yours concerning wine loving that you want
nothing less than to admit the truth. You therefore represent
both Homer and Ennius as dipsomaniacs, just as Horace not
only showed that vices in famous men should not be emulated,
but even wisely attacked old Cratinus, who, himself an avid
drinker of wine, cleverly claimed that the old and the famous
poets were like him.[95] Even in our own time, Poggio, we see
people who have been dedicated to shameful behavior of any
kind not so much trying to free themselves from this behavior
as pretending, with all kinds of slander, that some great and
very illustrious men behaved like them. How much Horace
criticized the love of wine he teaches very clearly in many other
places, and especially in these verses to Torquatus:

What *doesn't* drunkenness perpetrate? It reveals secrets,
It turns hopes into confirmed facts, it thrusts an unarmed
    man into battle,
It lifts the burden from troubled minds, it teaches new arts.
Whom have ample chalices not made eloquent?
What man in the toils of poverty have they not cleared of
    debt?[96]

167   Et Demosthenes quidem, quoniam nunquam sit usus vino, eloquentia minus valuit? Nam quod G. Marium Iuvenalis ebriositatis accusat, verissime quidem accusat. Bibebat, inquam, Marius fusius, non ut quicquam ageret, sed ut nihil ageret. Nam ut Plutarchus Cheronensis locuples testis est, quoniam Marius a L. Sylla victus exulque Italia sollicitus praesentibus animi aerumnis se quieti dare ac dormire nullo modo posset, veritus ne vigilia nimia in duriorem aliquam aegrotationem incideret, morbo statuit morbum amovere. Bibebat igitur ut solveretur in somnum Marius, non ut robustius quicquam et gloriosius faceret.

168   *Poggius.* Dixeram tibi, Rainalde, Manettum esse captiosum et propterea dimittendum. Hic rem naturamque depravat. Est homo contentiosus, ineptae victoriae quam opportunae veritatis studiosior. Itaque suis loquacioribus captionibus fraetus nihil curat quid dicat, modo dicat. Verum ego te separatim, cum voles, plane quae locutus sum omnia e Minervae officina deprompta edocebo. Nunc Pallas prosequatur quod coeperat, si videtur.

        Rainaldus. Videtur sane. Nam tu docebis quae voles ad Kalendas Graecas.

169   *Pallas.* Carnium, inquam, aescae ac vini potus reliquaque huiusmodi pinguiora delicatioraque obsonia corpus quidem et validius reddunt et firmius. At mentis rationem atque intelligentiam perinde ac debilitant atque enervant. In pavone et squilla, in vino Cretensi et Cyprio nemo se nisi vir absoluta sapientia continuerit. In nasturtio et aqua ne stultus quidem sit multus. Quod si cogitare incommoda ipsa poene infinita calamitatesque velimus quae ex crapula et ebriositate proveniunt, si clades, si miserias meminisse, intelligemus exulem in paucitate victus atque vilitate felicem atque fortunatum. Nam ut morbus calculo-

170   rum, debilitas artuum, stomachi, dentium, oculorum et capitis

Was Demosthenes any less eloquent because he never used 167
wine? Juvenal quite rightly charged Gaius Marius with drunkenness.[97] Marius, let me note, drank copiously, not in order to
accomplish anything, but to accomplish nothing. For Plutarch
of Chaeronea is an eloquent witness that Marius, after he was
defeated by Sulla and banished from Italy, because he was mentally troubled, was completely unable to rest and sleep; fearing
that he would fall into still worse illness because of insomnia,
he decided to drive out one disease with another. Therefore
Marius drank to allow himself to sleep, not to perform any energetic or magnificent exploit.[98]

Poggio. I told you, Rinaldo, that Manetti is captious and should 168
therefore be dismissed; he perverts the topic and its nature. He
is a quarrelsome man more eager for an awkward victory than
for serviceable truth. And so relying on his own bombastic
sophistries, he cares not at all what he says, provided that he
says something. When you like, I shall give you a clear explana-
tion in private of all that I said, brought from Minerva's work-
shop. Now, if it is agreeable, let Palla continue what he began.

Rinaldo. Indeed it is, for you will teach whatever you like at the
Greek Calends.[99]

Palla. I maintain that consumption of meat and wine and other 169
such fatty and rich foods makes the body healthier and stronger
but in turn weakens and enfeebles the mind's reasoning power
and intelligence. No one except a perfectly wise man would
limit himself in regard to peacock, shellfish, and Cretan and
Cyprian wine; in salad greens and water not even a fool would
indulge to excess. But if we wish to consider the evils and almost numberless dangers that derive from drunkenness and
excess, the disasters and miseries, we will understand that the
exile is happy and fortunate in the meagerness and cheapness
of his food. For to say nothing of kidney stones, weakness of 170
the joints, stomach aches, toothaches, aching eyes, headaches,

dolor, vomitus, oris faetor, tremor corporis, membrorum stupor atque alia innumerabilia mala taceantur: quando primi nostri parentes illi paradisum amiserunt? Nempe cum statuto cibo contempto e prohibito ligno comedere ausi sunt. Cain tunc se fecit reum sceleris, dum gulae indulgens primitias primus degustare non erubuit. Filii Iob quando aedium ruina oppressi sunt? Nonne in cibo et potu? Nam Esau quis ignorat tunc primogeniti primatu privatum esse, cum lenticulae avidus ventrem

171 suffarcinavit? Ionathas mellis favo mortis sententiam meruit. Aegyptiacae mensae desyderium iratum Israelitico populo Deum reddidit. Ophni et Phinees, Eli filios, quid aliud morti tradidit quam sacrificii carnes fuscinulis raptae? Opimae boves voracitati servatae Saulem regno eiecerunt. Quid Sodomitas ad immanis coitus, libidinem ac rabiem compulit? Nonne perpetua epularum illecebra?[58] Nonne priscus ille populus cum primum in stratis, in conviviis, in gulae ventrisque fomentis consenuerunt, pudorem cum pudicicia amiserunt? At Belis sacerdotes nonne sunt debitas passi poenas a Daniele in ebrietate confusi?

172 Quando autem Noe Cam filius oscoene dormientem vidit irrisitque? Nonne cum sensum vino amiserat? Qua Lot fuisse tunc credimus mente, cum causam didicit quamobrem cubaret inter filias? Sed quid pluribus utamur exemplis? Nonne in evangelio legimus divitem illum qui quottidie splendidissime epulabatur, sepultum esse in inferno? Oh mortalium caecitatem atque insaniam, qui animi immortalitatis obliti per omnem turpitudinem ac dedecus corporeis sordibus obsequuntur et sese ipsi prudentes scientesque interimunt!

173 *Manettus.* Profecto, Pallas, vera sunt quae dicis omnia, meque tua mirifice delectat oratio. Soleo enim nonnunquam mirari quorundam inscitiam, qui cum aliquod aut exemplum aut dictum e

vomiting, bad breath, shakiness, rigidity of the limbs, and countless other ills — when did those first parents of ours lose Paradise? Surely when they had shunned licit food and dared to eat from the forbidden tree. Then Cain became a criminal when, indulging his appetite, he brazenly helped himself to the first fruits.[100] When were Job's sons crushed by their collapsing house? Was it not amid feasting and drinking? Everyone knows that Esau lost the birthright of the firstborn when he greedily stuffed his belly with lentils. Jonathan earned a death sentence   171 because of a honeycomb. Their longing for the feasts of Egypt made God angry with the people of Israel. Were Hophni and Phineas, sons of Eli, consigned to death for any other reason than that they snatched the sacrificial meat with forks? Fine cattle kept for consumption cost Saul the throne. What compelled the Sodomites to their monstrous intercourse, their frenzied lust? Was it not the unending seduction of feasts? Did not that ancient people, having grown old on couches, in banquets, in lenitives for throat and stomach, lose their sense of shame along with their chastity?[101] Did not the priests of Bel, confounded in their drunkenness, suffer deserved penalty at Daniel's hand?[102] When did his son Shem see and mock Noah   172 sleeping in his nakedness? Was it not when the latter had lost his wits to wine? In what state of mind do we suppose Lot was when he learned the reason why he slept with his daughters? But what need of more examples? Do we not read in the gospel that the rich man who dined in sumptuous fashion each day was buried in hell?[103] Alas for the blind insanity of mortals who, forgetting the soul's immortality, through all kinds of disgrace and dishonor oblige the disreputable body, and with eyes open and knowingly destroy themselves!

Manetti. Certainly, Palla, all that you say is true, and your words   173 provide me with marvelous pleasure. I am sometimes accustomed to marvel at the stupidity of certain persons who, upon

fidei Christianae relligione vel tempestive apteque depromptum
audierint, tanquam offensi et mutant vultum et avertunt faciem.
Iidem siquid e poetarum fabulis atque gentium diis exceperint,
laeti exhilaratique exultant. Si Sardanapallum audiunt cibi potusque luxui et nequissimis voluptatibus deditum occidisse, non
solum veritati ducunt,[59] sed quasi divinum oraculum admiran-
174   tur. Massagetas et Thomyridos[60] filium Spargapisen epulis vinoque confectos facile a Cyro superatos tradit Herodotus. Ilium
somno vinoque sepultum captum a Graecis volunt. Leonidas
praepotentem illum atque incredibilem Xerxis exercitum solutum in vinum noctem diemque cecidit. Alexander quibus ami-
cissime familiarissimeque uteretur, occidit ebrius. Durum ac
robustum Annibalis militem, quem neque itineris longitudo nec
Alpium frigora nec arma Romanorum potuere, convivii Cam-
pani luxuries ita demollivit effaeminavitque ut et saepe in fugam
175   versus et extrema tandem strage percussus perierit. Haec ho-
rumque similia tanquam e caelo delapsa excipiunt plausu, admirantur, concinunt. Quae tametsi ipse non vitupero, tamen eiusmodi esse statuo, ut eorum omne — ut ita dixerim — lumen ad
nostrae relligionis veritatis radios immensumque splendorem
obscuretur, offendatur, obruatur, intereat. Delectas me, inquam,
Pallas, cum tua omni oratione, tum ista exemplorum comme-
moratione quae e Christiano sacrario depromis. Quis enim
fastidiosus adeo morosusque fuerit, cuius aures non demulceat
pulcherrimum illud consilium ac facinus, quo prudentissima illa
176   fortissimaque Iudith Holophernen vino pressum interemit? Et
Iahel, eadem prudentia et animi magnitudine mulier, quando
clavum supra Sisarae tempus positum percussumque malleo ad

hearing some example or saying drawn in timely and apt fashion from the Christian faith, change their countenance and
avert their eyes as if offended; the same men, upon hearing
something from the poets' tales or the gods of the heathen,
display joy and exhilaration. If they hear that Sardanapalus
died, given over to luxurious food and drink and wicked pleasures,[104] not only do they consider it true, but they marvel at it
as if it were a divine oracle. Herodotus records that the Mas-   174
sagetae and Spargapises, son of Thomyris, weakened by feasting and wine, were easily defeated by Cyrus.[105] They claim that
Troy, buried by sleep and wine, was captured by the Greeks.
Leonidas cut down that massively powerful and unbelievable
army of Xerxes day and night when it was relaxed over wine.[106]
When drunk, Alexander slew his best and closest friends.[107]
Though neither long marches nor the Alpine cold nor Roman
arms could break Hannibal's tough and mighty soldiers, the
luxury of Campanian banqueting softened and emasculated
them to such an extent that they often turned tail and ran, and
at length they were shattered and perished in a final massacre.[108] These and suchlike things they welcome with applause,   175
wonder at, and celebrate as if they had fallen from heaven.
Though I do not criticize these examples, I nonetheless find
that all of their light, so to speak, is eclipsed, opposed, up-
ended, and undone in the presence of our religion's rays of
truth and enormous brightness. I repeat, Palla, your entire discourse gives me pleasure and especially the citation of examples
that you have brought out from the Christian shrine. For who
would be so overrefined and ill-tempered that his ears would
not be soothed by that splendid plot and crime by which the
wise and brave Judith slew Holofernes when he was drunk from
wine? And when did Jahel, a woman of the same wisdom and   176
greatness of soul, place a nail above Sisara's temple and strike it
with a hammer into his brain until she pinned it to the ground?

terram usque defixit in cerebrum? Nonne cum vaehementius
appotus vaehementius dormisset? Nam Ioseph quando execra-
biles fratres vaendiderunt? Nonne cum ventre suffarcinato per
ebrietatem convivii in eum sunt invidiae ignibus inflamati? Im-
pudica et nefarria meretricula quando impollutum ac sanctum
Iohannis Baptistae caput recepit in disco? Nonne in crapula
atque insania intemperantis convivii?

177 *Pallas.* Adiuvas me, Manette, et recte quidem. Nam qui abhorret a
dictis atque exemplis Christianae fidei, is certe Christianus non
est. Verum quid longiores sumus in re perspicua? Quando
Christus ipse — omitto enim sobrietatem ac ieiunia apostolo-
rum et reliquorum sanctissimorum hominum — quando, inquam, Christus Deus in civitate commedit nisi Pascha? Et id
quidem nullam aliam ob causam, puto, nisi ut mysteria adim-
pleret. Quid autem praecipiebat discipulis, cum ait: 'Operamini
178 non pereuntem sed permanentem cibum?' Quando illum lar-
giore aut prolyxiore convivio usum accepimus? At in quadragesimum usque diem ieiunium et inediam pertulisse scimus. Non
igitur, fili Honofri, qui animi bono divinitatique maluerit quam
corporis infirmitati et fragilitati prospicere, qui sui ipsius rationem quam fortunae inconstantiam sequi, ita sese unquam
abiiciat ut in alimenti paucitate vilitateve aut minor sit aut hu-
milior. Et quo permanentem cibum operetur, quasi pereuntis
oblitus, vel[61] Zenonis illud secum ipse repetet, qui cum audisset
navis quam reliquam habebat et eorum quibus erat navis honerata in mari naufragium atque amissionem, 'Bene,' inquit, 'facis,
o fortuna, quae nos ad pallium vitamque philosophi compulisti.'
179 Fortunae hic gratulatus est, quod se philosophum e mercatore[62]
reddiderat, hoc est e servo liberum, nullius non modo cibi sed

Was it not when he was extraordinarily drunk and had fallen into an extraordinarily deep sleep? When did Joseph's loathsome brothers sell him? Was it not after stuffing their bellies during the drunken revelry of a party that they were fired with flames of envy against him? When did the brazen and wicked little whore receive the pure and holy head of John the Baptist on a platter? Was it not amid the stupor and madness of an immoderate party?[109]

Palla. You are helping me, Manetti, and rightly so. For he who   177
shrinks from the sayings and examples of the Christian faith is assuredly no Christian. But why go on when the point is clear? When did Christ himself—I set aside the sobriety and fasting of the apostles and the other saints—when, I ask, did divine Christ eat in the city except during Passover? And he did so for no other reason, I think, except to fulfill the prophecies. Moreover, what did he instruct his disciples to do when he said: "Do not work for perishable but lasting food"?[110] When did we hear   178
of him participating in a sumptuous or lengthy banquet? But we know that he endured fasting and abstinence from food for forty days. So, Onofrio my son, he who prefers to look out for the goodness and divinity of the mind rather than the weakness and fragility of the body, to follow his reason rather than the vagaries of fortune, never abases himself to the degree that he be a lesser or more humble man in view of the small quantity or cheapness of his food. And in order to work for lasting food he forgets, as it were, the perishable kind, or he will remind himself of Zeno's comment when he heard of the loss at sea and shipwreck of the last remaining ship he owned and of the goods with which it was loaded: "Well done, Fortune, you who have forced us to the rough cloak and the philosopher's life!"[111] He   179
congratulated Fortune since it had transformed him from a merchant into a philosopher, that is, from a slave into a free man, one in no need of food or anything else. Content with

ne rei cuiuspiam prorsus indigentem. Nam animi virtute sapientiaque contentus humana et caduca omnia contemnebat.

Et huiusmodi quidem vir, aut etiam hoc melior, nunquam se paternis hospitibus et amicis orbatum desertumve queratur. Satis sibi amicorum superesse arbitrabitur si virtus, si prudentia superfuerit. Honestatis utetur semper sapientiaeque hospitio. Quibus ipsis rationibus ducti duo illi Pythagorei Phytias et 180 Damon ne in morte quidem se mutuo deseruerunt. Omitto Thesea[63] et Perithoum. De Achille et Patroclo verbum facio nullum. Oresten et Pyladen conticesco. Praetereo Epaminondam atque Pelopidam. Haec enim quinque sunt amicorum paria Graecorum litteris celebrata. Nulli bono et sapienti et sancto viro vel paternus vel suus aut amicus aut hospes unquam defuerit. Quinetiam hoc ipso exilio quod admodum tibi acerbum ducis, cum alia plurima, tum id boni contineri video, quod facile praestet ut assentatorem ab amico iudicemus. Non enim qui statu fortunaque florentem vel officio prosequitur vel studio, sed qui calamitosum et afflictum auxilio tuetur, iuvat opibus, assistit, consolatur, fovet, amici nomen meretur et laudem. 181 Nam qui eo te amat, quoniam aliquid commodi ad se perventurum expectet, non is meo iudicio est amicus dicendus, sed assentator et perniciosus et impius. Amicus enim non tua minus quam sua ipsius omnia et cogitet et curet. Et quamquam prosperas tibi ac securas res quam desperatas perditasque maluerit, eundem se tibi tamen et hospitem et amicum et familiarem et benivolum praestabit semper in omni fortunae vicissitudine. Nam quod ad generis claritudinem pertinet, Euripideus Polynices cum ait maiorum splendorem sibi profuisse nihil, et virum nobilem nihil esse in paupertate, quam se mendacii arguat,

wisdom and the virtue of the soul, he despised all things human and perishable.

This sort of man, or one even better than he, would never complain that he has been orphaned and abandoned by his paternal connections and friends. He will think that he still has enough friends if virtue and wisdom remain his. He will always have the benefit of the hospitality of moral goodness and wisdom. Guided by such principles the two famous Pythagoreans, Pythias and Damon, did not even abandon each other in death. I set aside Theseus and Peirithous; I make no mention of Achilles and Patroclus; I hold my peace about Orestes and Pylades; I pass over Epaminondas and Pelopidas. For these are the five pairs of friends celebrated in Greek literature. A good, wise, and holy man would never lack a friend or connection, whether inherited or his own. What is more, I see that this very exile, which you consider so bitter for you, contains many good features, including what is easily best: that we may distinguish a flatterer from a friend. For it is not he who pursues with services or attentions the man who is at the height of public standing and fortune but he who guards with his aid the victim of disaster, helps him with resources, stands by him, consoles, and cherishes him who deserves the commendable name of friend. For he who loves you because he anticipates that some benefit will fall to him is not in my view to be called a friend but an insidious and wicked flatterer. For a friend thinks of and takes care for all your affairs no less than his own. And although he would prefer for your affairs to be in a favorable and secure position, rather than desperate and abandoned, in every fluctuation of fortune he will show himself the same connection and friend, an intimate and man of goodwill. As to the fame of one's line, when the Euripidean Polynices asserts that he reaped no benefit from the distinction of his ancestors and no man living in poverty is noble, his connection by marriage with

180

181

Adrasti regis affinitas declarat. Nullo unquam somnii praesagio ille motus ascivisset sibi Polynicem generum, si aut me aut Poggio patre natum didicisset.

182 *Poggius.* Pallas, afficis me convicio quia humilioribus parentibus natus existimor. Quod si me penitus noris, aliter sentias.

Pallas. Ita est, Poggi, ut dicis. Nec ego te prius noram. Verum ignosce. Clarum nomen maiorum opinor non mediocriter conducere posteris si ad parentum lucem suum ipsi quoque lumen accenderint. Quis enim ambigat Latinum regem longe libentius Aeneam, Anchisae filium, generum sibi delegisse, cum animadvertisset id quod Dardanum conciliavit Teucro, ad eius animi praestantiam maiorum etiam splendorem accedere? Num Dardanum putas aut Arcadiam aut Samothraciam aut etiam Corithum unquam desyderasse, rem cum gloria adeptum in Phrygia? An fortassis Aeneam censes Italiae imperantem Ilii se civem
183 quam Italiae regem maluisse? Quid enim Florentia pelli adeo miserum ducimus? Danda est opera ne nosmetipsi nobis defuisse existimemur. Ego longe et quietius et tranquillius ubivis gentium me futurum spero quam Florentiae. Non virtus fortunam, sed virtutem fortuna sequitur. Enitere igitur ut maiorum tuorum claritudini respondeas. Quod si feceris, Florentiae desyderium moderate feres.

Honofrius. Verum, mi pater, patriae benivolentia magna est. Durum est peregrinum dici, durissimum exulem atque proscriptum.

184 *Pallas.* Si mihi de patria conveniret tecum, quid aut durum esset aut non durum, fortasse conveniret. Sed tu patriam, reor, Florentiam dicis?

Honofrius. Et quamnam aliam? Nam Florentiae nati sumus.

King Adrastus convicts him of lying. For Adrastus would never, influenced by a prophetic dream, have joined Polynices to him as his son-in-law if he had learned that he was the son of me or of Poggio.

Poggio. Palla, you are taunting me because I am thought to be of   182
humble parentage. But if you knew me well, you would think otherwise.

Palla. It is as you say, Poggio. I did not previously know you. Pardon me. I believe that a distinguished ancestral name benefits the descendants if they themselves add luster to their parents' light. Who doubts that King Latinus far more readily chose Aeneas, son of Anchises, as his son-in-law, once he had noticed what had commended Dardanus to Teucer, namely that to the excellence of his mind the glory of his ancestors was added as well?[112] Surely you do not fancy that Dardanus ever felt any longing for Arcadia or Samothrace or even Corinth once he had attained a glorious position in Phrygia? Or do you perhaps suppose that Aeneas, when ruling over Italy, would have preferred to be a citizen of Ilium rather than king of Italy? Why do we   183
still consider it so wretched to be driven from Florence? We must exert ourselves lest we be thought to have failed our own cause. I expect that I shall live a more peaceful and undisturbed life anywhere in the world other than in Florence. Courage does not follow fortune but fortune courage.[113] Strive, then, to replicate your ancestors' distinction. If you do so, you will bear your longing for Florence with moderation.

Onofrio. But, father, the benevolence of one's homeland is an important thing. It is hard to be branded a foreigner, hardest of all a proscribed exile.

Pallas. If we agreed about the term "homeland," perhaps we would   184
agree about what is hard or otherwise. But you are, I believe, calling Florence our homeland?

Onofrio. What other? We were born in Florence.

Pallas. At Lysias orator non est Athenis natus sed educatus. Nec Sami Pythagoras philosophus. Et tamen hic Samius, ille Atheniensis appellatus est. Educatio igitur atque institutio vitae plus interdum valet quam ortus. Quod si tantam vim is locus habet ubi primum emersisti in lucem, quid magis tibi urbem totam patriam ducis quam cubiculum illud quod e matris utero te primum excepit?

185 *Honofrius.* Atqui, mi pater, cubiculum illud, ita ut aedes, Florentiae est.

Pallas. Et Florentia quidem in Tuscia; haec autem in Italia. Cur igitur, ne procedam longius, Florentiam tibi magis patriam vocas quam aut Tusciam aut Italiam?

> Argivus sum, ait Hercules, aut Thebanus.
> Non enim me ex una appello urbe.
> Omnis mihi Graecorum turris patria est.

186 Pulcherrime de se Hercules loquebatur, sed longe pulchrius Socrates atque constantius, qui cuias esset interrogatus, non Atheniensem aut Lacedaemonium sed mundanum se esse respondit. At ego dum mecum diligentius mundum ipsum consydero, in eam sententiam ducor ut ne Socratem quidem sapienter omnino ac vero respondisse iudicem. Nam quo pacto mundum ego patriam mihi appellarim, quem videam non communem urbem atque civitatem et Dei et hominis, ut Stoicis placet, verum potius molestum quendam teterrimumque carcerem ab immortali Deo humano generi constitutum? Quando enim eandem vel aeris temperiem vel terrae bonitatem aspicimus? Modo frigore, glacie, vento, coeno, aqua, nive compleri videmus omnia, calores modo aestusque sentimus. Perparum

187 anni tempus moderatum est. Quo fit ut nunc nimio frigore, nunc fervore nimio et culta omnia et sata pereant. Hinc

Palla. But the orator Lysias was not born but educated at Athens. And the philosopher Pythagoras at Samos. And yet the latter has been called a Samian, the former an Athenian. So education and training for life sometimes has greater influence than birth. But if the place where you first emerged into the light has such great power, why do you rather consider the entire city your homeland rather than the crib that first received you from your mother's womb?

Onofrio. And yet, father, that crib belongs to Florence, just as the house does. 185

Palla. And Florence is in Tuscany, and it in Italy. Why, then, to proceed no further, do you call Florence your homeland rather than Tuscany or Italy?

> I am an Argive, Heracles said, or a Theban
> For I do not name myself after a single city.
> Every tower of Greece is my homeland.[114]

Heracles spoke eloquently of himself, but far more eloquent 186 and consistent is Socrates, who, when asked from what country he hailed, replied that he was neither an Athenian nor a Spartan, but a citizen of the world.[115] When I contemplate this "world" more carefully, I am led to conclude that not even Socrates replied with complete wisdom and truthfulness. For how should I call the world my homeland when I see that it has been set up by immortal God not as a city and state common to God and man, as the Stoics hold,[116] but as a kind of grievous and foul prison for the human race? When do we find an even temperature of the air or quality of the soil? We see that the whole world is sometimes filled with freezing cold, ice, wind, mud, water, snow; at other times we experience heat waves and sweltering summers. Temperate weather amounts to a tiny part of the year. The result is that at one time the cultivated 187 and sown crops perish from excessive cold, at another from

procellae, turbines, fulgura, fulmina, typhones pestem ac perniciem minitantur. Hinc ex inferis regionibus tantus tam terribilis motus fit ut nemo sibi satis constare possit. Maris vero et fluviorum impetus atque vastitates quot quamque horrendae sunt, quottidie vel experimur vel audimus. Haec autem omnia supplicia nostra sunt. His enim et antequam accidant commovemur, et cum acciderint, metu exanimati amentesque conficimur. Nos autem adeo mentis sumus et sensus inopes ut, non hoc naturae carcere contenti, angustiores alios nobis carceres moliamur, aedes et urbes lignis atque lapidibus anxii ac solliciti fabricantes, veluti siquis in magna aliqua custodia breviores alias construxerit.

188   Quare ad ea quae nobis divina censura supplicia sunt constituta, addimus stulticia nostra graviores alios cruciatus. Praeterea quaeque hic gignuntur, quique fructus humo egreditur, ad huiusmodi nostram asservationem egreditur tanquam triste aliquod vileque alimentum, quod datur iis qui sunt in vincula coniecti. Et quemadmodum iis qui a nobis plectuntur qualiscunque praebuerimus cibos videntur ob famem consuetudinemque iucundi, ita etiam nos ob necessitatem atque indigentiam huiusmodi alimentis, quae et prava et perniciosa sunt, admodum delectamur. Nam quanta est horum pravitas atque pernicies, ex infirmitate calamitateque corporea compraehendi potest. Et quod etiam est miserius, ut improba sunt detrimentosaque alimenta, neque his tamen ex aequo omnes affluimus, neque sine labore maximo. Ad haec ut et animo constamus et corpore, alii sunt animi, alii corporis morbi. Animus enim dolori atque voluptati, formidini cupiditatique obnoxius, quasi intimis quibusdam et efferatis beluis et dies sollicitatur et noctes. Nam etsi rationis medicamentis eas pestes aliquantisper

189

excessive heat. On one side hurricanes, lightning, thunder, ty-
phoons threaten plague and devastation, on the other a quake is
produced in the nether regions so great and so terrifying that
no one can stand on his own. Each day we experience or hear
of the many horrific devastations caused by the incursion of
seas or rivers. All these are our punishments: we are shaken by
them before they occur, and when they do, we are driven out of
our minds with fear. We are so lacking in intelligence and good
sense that, not satisfied with this prison of nature, we construct
other, more confining prisons for ourselves; anxious and troubled, we build houses and cities with wood and stone — just as
if someone were to build, inside of some large prison, other,
smaller prisons.

Therefore to the punishments that have been put in place for   188
us by divine censure, we add, by our own stupidity, other, more
severe tortures. Moreover, everything that is grown here and
whatever fruit comes out of the soil is produced for our preser-
vation, as some bitter and cheap food to be given to prisoners in
chains. And just as whatever foods we offer to those we are
punishing appear enjoyable to them because of hunger and habituation, so we too out of necessity and need for such nourishment take delight in foods that are both bad and harmful. For
the amount of harm and danger present in these foods can
be gathered from our body's weakness and deterioration. And   189
what is even more unfortunate is that, as vile and harmful as
this nourishment is, not all of us are provided with it in the
same degree or without the greatest effort. In addition, since we
are composed of mind and body, some illnesses are of the mind,
others of the body. For the mind, being subject to pain and
pleasure, fear and desire, is afflicted day and night as if by some
savage inner demons. For even if the mind were to alleviate its
diseases somewhat with the pharmacopeia of reason, yet it can
never be rid of its torments altogether; for as long as it is

137

sedat, non tamen earum ignibus vacat unquam omnino. Quos enim motus e corpore animus accipit, eorum, quandiu est in corpore, esse omnino expers nullo modo potest. At corporis morbos siquidem non dico enarrare, sed nominare voluero, 'ante diem clauso componet Vesper Olympo.'

190   Partem totius naturam sequi necesse est. Corpus, quod animi carcer est, pars est totius mundi, quem hominis carcerem esse paulo ante dicebamus. Hinc sanguinis est spiritusque plenum, constatque et[64] carnibus et nervis et ossibus. Et hisce quidem singulis aliis mollibus, aliis duris, aliis calidis, aliis frigidis, aliis humidis, aliis siccis, quae quidem quam invicem repugnant suntque inter se contraria, quis non videt? His autem et conquassari mortalium corpora et tandem corrui dubitandum certe non est. Atque tum malignitas ciborum, tum caeli inclaementia partim auget morborum novorum numerum, partim qui minus antea videbantur inesse — cum inessent tamen in corporum na-

191 tura — rursum movet, ac veluti dormitantes excitat. Nam caetera quidem supplicia, siquis ea his comparet quae natura insunt, extrinsecus fiunt. Nemo enim nescit vel ignis vel ferri vel verberum vel aliorum huiuscemodi cruciatuum natura vaehementius etiam atque celerius quam aegrotationibus ipsis sensu corpus privari atque interire. Hisce igitur et animi et corporis suppliciis obnoxii, relegati sumus in hoc mundano carcere. Plectimur enim non nostris duntaxat malis quae quottidie perpetramus, sed etiam nostrorum parentum, eorum culpa qui primi extiterunt in Deum ingrati, et constitutum quidem tempus relegati ab Deo sumus. Non enim exilium nostrum est, non proscriptio, sed relegatio. Nam nostra nobis amicissima patria caelum est, non Florentia, non Tuscia, non Italia, non Europa, non totus denique terrarum orbis, non mundus hic universus infer-

192 ior. Apte igitur ac perdocte Plato, 'Homo,' inquit, 'non terrae

housed in the body, it can never be free of the passions it receives from the body. But if I wished — I do not say to give a full account of — merely to name the body's diseases, "beforehand the evening star will close the heavens and put the day to rest."[117]

The part must follow the nature of the whole. The body,   190
which is the soul's prison, is part of the whole world, which we just now said is man's prison. Hence it is full of blood and spirit and is composed of flesh, sinew and bones. And who does not see how in every single one of these there are conditions that are mutually incompatible and at odds with one another, with some that are soft, others hard, some warm, others cold, some wet, others dry? There should be no doubt that mortals' bodies are shaken and finally destroyed by these opposing elements. The harmfulness of food as well as the harshness of the weather partly increases the number of new illnesses and partly resuscitates and awakens as if from sleep illnesses that did not appear to be present before, even though they were still present in the nature of the body. The remaining afflictions originate   191
from external sources, if one compares them to those that are present in us by nature. For no one is unaware that because of the nature of fire, steel, the lash, or other kinds of torture, the body is deprived of sense and dies even more violently and quickly than by illnesses. Subject, then, to these torments both of body and soul, we have been relegated to this earthly prison. The fact is that we are being punished not only for our own crimes, which we perpetrate each day, but also those of our parents, for the guilt of those who first showed themselves ungrateful to God, and we have been relegated from God for a fixed time. For our fate is not exile, not proscription, but relegation. For our friendliest homeland is not Florence, not Tuscany, not Italy, not Europe, not the whole earth, not this entire sublunary world, but heaven. Plato said with great aptness and   192

neque immobilis planta est, sed caeli,' cuius quidem caput quasi radix corpus erigit sursum ad caelum versum. Ita enim natura creati sumus ut non aliorum animalium instar proni terram despiciamus, sed caelum, unde nobis est ortus noster, divina lege suspiciamus. Nam quod Ovidius novit, nos, qui veri Dei praecepta sequimur, ignorare turpissimum est. Is enim de Deo loquens ait in suo maiore carmine:

> Pronaque cum spectent animalia caetera terram,
> os homini sublime dedit, caelumque videre
> iussit, et erectos ad sydera tollere vultus.

193   Iussit sane Deus immortalis deum mortalem (id est hominem, quem ad suam ipsius quantum ad excellentiam immortalitatemque mentis attinet imaginem fecit), ore sublimi atque elevato caelestem suspicere patriam et ad sydera immensumque splendorem veritatis aeternae omnem animi voluntatem contemplationemque intendere. 'Vultus' enim a 'volendo' nomen sumpsit. Est autem signum quod pro motu animi apparet in facie. Qui ergo in huius mundani carceris relegatione ita sese comparavit offirmavitque ut vel nullam ceperit loci contagionem aut labem, vel siquam forte ceperit, ea se continuo per multam scientiae exercitationem lavando terendoque purgarit ac praeterea sapientiae lucem ante oculos semper habuerit, revocat hunc tandem non post longum temporis curriculum Deus ex hoc inferiore atque polluto coeno lotum ac nitidum in illam sanctam, in illam supernam et desyderatam atque amicam patriam, et se tanquam[65] redeunti concivi illabens coniungit, totum se penitus

194   visendum, se quamfamiliarissime fruendum tradit. Qui vero sui Deique oblitus rationem temeritati submisit atque prostravit,

learning, "Man is not a plant of the earth," an unmoving thing, "but a plant of heaven," whose head, like a root, raises the body up toward heaven.[118] For we have been so created by nature that we do not look at the earth face down like other animals but by divine statute we look up at heaven, from which we derive our origin. For it is an utter disgrace for those of us who follow the teachings of the true God to fail to know what Ovid knew. For in speaking of God in his more important poem he says:

While the other animals look face down at the earth,
He gave the human being an upraised face and bade him
To contemplate heaven and to lift his gaze up to the
   stars.[119]

Immortal God bade the mortal god (that is, the human being, whom He made according to His own image, as far as concerns the excellence and immortality of his mind) with face lifted and raised up to look up at his heavenly homeland and to focus his mind's will and contemplation on the stars and the boundless radiance of eternal truth. For "countenance" (*vultus*) has derived its name from "will" (*volere*);[120] it is a sign of emotion that appears on the face. Therefore he who has so prepared and strengthened himself during his relegation to this prison of the world that he has been infected by no contagion or stain of the place or, if perhaps he has, he has immediately, through a concerted exercise of knowledge, cleansed himself of it by washing and wiping and has always kept the light of wisdom before his eyes — this man, after no long period of training, is summoned back by God from this lower, polluted filth to go, washed and radiant, to that upper, longed for and welcoming homeland. Like one who warmly greets a returning fellow citizen, God unites himself entirely with this man and yields himself entirely to him to be seen and intimately enjoyed. The man, however, who, having forgotten himself and God, has subjected reason to

193

194

tanquam is qui ob continuas tenebras visum amisit, veritatis omnem exosus lucem existimat suam omnem felicitatem in huius mundi miseria sitam esse, et quo turpibus corporis dirisque satellitibus magis servit, eo se liberiorem iudicat. Is, quoniam et ratio ab se sua et intellectus exulat, nec inferiora inquirere nec superiora discernere valet, tunc se censet exulem cum ex parvo mittitur et angusto in latiorem ac patentiorem carcerem. Non enim is est cui dicere liceat: 'Ego mea omnia mecum porto.' At istiusmodi homines, vel furentes potius insanaeque beluae, quippe qui in hominis figura immanitatem beluarum et diritatem gerunt, continuo sempiterno mulctantur exilio proscribunturque a divino censore. Itaque humi remanent extremis pressi intolerabilibusque aerumnis. Ego igitur, fili Honofri, exulem me neque puto neque volo. Sum in hac mundana insula relegatus, idque ad certum tempus. Et ab eo sum relegatus imperatore qui tanta claementia est, ut non fisco, non aerario bona mea vendicet, sed mihi potius, modo iniussu suo hanc insulam non egrediar, integra esse velit. Quare ut et bona mea omnia et alia iura omnia retineo, ita etiam te reliquosque liberos in potestate retineo. Cum nihil mihi iuris ademptum est, nec tibi quoque, si paterno exemplo uteris, si paternis monitis pares, si te iuri haereditario non subtrahis, adimi potest, qui ergo te exulem, te proscriptum quereris, cum ipse nec exilio nec proscriptione mulctatus sum? Num alia causa tua est quam nostra?

195

196 *Honofrius.* Nequaquam. Sed eadem ista, mi pater. Verum tu aliter de exilio loqueris quam vulgo solent. Nec ullus mihi reliquus est contradicendi locus. Sed quid mihi in mentem venit, audi, rogo. Tu hominis patriam caelum dicis. Et mundum hunc modo

impulse and subverted it, like one who has lost his sight from
time spent in continual darkness, hating all the light of truth,
thinks that his entire happiness is placed in the misery of this
world, and the more he is enslaved to the shameful and sinister
servants of the body, the freer he thinks himself. Since he has
abandoned both his reason and intellect, he can neither inquire
into nor distinguish lower and higher; he considers himself an
exile when he is released from a small and narrow prison to one
that is wider and more spacious. He is not the man who can
say: "I am carrying all my goods with me."[121] Such men, or
rather raving and insane beasts, since they conceal the sinister
monstrousness of beasts in a human form,[122] are punished and
proscribed by the divine Censor with unremitting and eternal
exile. Therefore they remain on the ground, burdened by ex-   195
treme and unendurable miseries. So, my son Onofrio, I neither
consider myself an exile nor wish to be one. I have been relegated to this island of the world, and that for a fixed time. And
I have been relegated by an Emperor of such clemency that he
does not claim my goods for the fisc or the treasury but wishes
them to be intact for me, provided that I not depart this island
unless He gives the order. Therefore as I retain all my goods
and other rights, so I retain in my power you and my other
children. Since no right has been taken from me, no right can
be taken from you either, if you follow your father's example, if
you obey his precepts and if you do not remove yourself from
your hereditary rights. Why, then, do you complain that you
are an exile, a man proscribed, when I myself have been punished neither with exile nor proscription? Surely your case is no
different from mine, is it?

Onofrio. By no means, for it is the same, Father. But you speak of   196
exile in a different sense from the common man, and no room
is left for me to voice an objection. But please listen to what has
struck me. You call heaven a man's homeland, and you call this

carcerem, modo insulam vocas. Hic nos ab Deo relegatos ad constitutum tempus existimas. Et qui divinae legi paruerit, huic brevi reditum patere in caelum atque aevum cum Deo futurum. Repugnantibus vero atque rebellibus et relegationem perpetuum fieri exilium et proscriptionis iure sempiternae mortis poenas paratas esse. In hanc puto sententiam tua omnis tendebat oratio.

Pallas. Bene interpretaris.

197 *Honofrius.* Non saepe contingit ut in quibuspiam amplis aedibus aut caenaculum tibi aut atrium aut cubiculum aut etiam bibliothecam aliquam aedifices quae omni reliquo apparatu aedium et commodior sit et pulchrior et gratior? Si ergo in hac urbe, quam ad longitudinem latitudinemque universi mundi angustum aliquem carcerem ducis, et natus sum et altus et educatus, delectorque huius consuetudine unice (hic enim et paterna mihi substantia et amici et fortuna omnis collocata est), cur ab hac tam commoda, tam pulchra, tam grata, tam amoena tamque suavi sede et — ut ita dixerim — hospitali patria eiici non feram

198 aegerrime, et eiici quidem iniuste, eiici cum ignominia? Siquis te, cum aut Graece aut Latine quicquam studiosius lectitas, ex tua tibi iucundissima bibliotheca expulerit, qua aequitate animi contumeliam sis laturus? Adverti equidem aliquando cum in bibliothecam lecturus aliquid concessisses, a quopiam vel officii gratia postulatum, facie te non admodum hilari bibliothecam egressum. Et ego tam indigna, tam acerba, tam luctuosa contumelia affectus non mihi dolendum censeam?

199 *Pallas.* Tu tibi, quantum intelligere videor, Florentiam omnino vis patriam. Hac utcunque extrudi molestum iudicas, iniuste extrudi molestius, ignominiose extrudi molestissimum.

world sometimes a prison, sometimes an island. You think that we have been relegated here by God for a fixed time. He who has obeyed divine law will in a brief time be permitted to return to heaven and to spend eternity with God; but for those who resist and rebel, the relegation becomes a perpetual exile and by the law of proscription the penalties of eternal death are in store. I believe that your entire discourse comes down to this idea.

Palla. You have understood me well.

Onofrio. Isn't it often the case that in a spacious house you build   197 for yourself one room, whether a dining room, a living room, a bedroom, or even a library, that is more comfortable, beautiful, and more pleasant than any other feature of the house? If therefore in this city, which you consider a narrow prison in relation to the length and breadth of the entire world, I have been born, raised, and educated, and if I take unique delight in this familiar setting—for here my familial wealth, friends, and fortune are all located—why should I not feel distress at being driven out of such a comfortable, beautiful, pleasant, lovely, and agreeable place, and—so to speak—a welcoming homeland, and to be driven out unfairly and in disgrace? If when you were   198 keenly reading some work in Greek or Latin, someone drove you out of your library, so pleasurable to you, with what calmness would you bear the insult? I have on occasion noticed that, upon withdrawing to your library to read something, when you have been summoned by some person or duty, you have emerged with a face that was not exactly cheerful. And should I, so unworthily, bitterly, and grievously affronted, not feel pain?

Palla. As far as I understand, you lay absolute claim to Florence as   199 your homeland. You consider being driven out from it offensive, to be driven out unfairly more offensive, to be driven out in disgrace the height of offense.

Honofrius. Ista mea prorsus sententia est. Nam quamquam et veram et propriam et sempiternam patriam caelum puto, hanc tamen impraesentiarum quam omnes et indocti et docti uno nomine ubi nati et educati sumus patriam appellant, itidem ipse patriam mihi et haberi et dici volo.

Pallas. Geratur ergo mos tibi, quandoquidem nondum fortiora excipis, agamus tecum mollioribus remediis. Num malum putas patria carere?

200 *Honofrius.* Quid malum ais? Puto equidem summum malum. Cum enim animus patitur, non pati corpus non potest. Patitur igitur totus homo. Quid autem amplius restat quin me plane miserum fatear?

Pallas. Putasne sapientem miserum esse posse?

Honofrius. Minime omnium. Nam sapiens semper felix, semper beatus est.

Pallas. Non igitur patria carere miserum est?

Honofrius. Cur, quaeso?

201 *Pallas.* Quoniam patria carere sapiens nonnunquam potest. Bias fuit unus ex eorum numero quos universae antiquitatis iudicio sapientes et dictos et habitos audimus. Is non solum patria caruit, sed eam verti in praedam vidit. Diogenes patria pulsus nunquam Sinopen desyderavit. Solon ultro se patria abdicavit. Crates Thebanus exul factus a suis civibus potius ipse Thebis quam ei Thebae desyderio fuere. Lycurgus Lacedaemonius, qui rex in patria esse posset, semel et iterum patriam reliquit. Et cum primum suorum atque amicorum et litteris sollicitatus et nunciis vix tandem rediisset, mox, ubi salutiferis et institutis et legibus principatum patrium muniisset, in perpetuum exilium profectus est, cavitque moriens ut ne corporis quidem relliquiae

202 referrentur Spartam. Anaxagoras Clazomenius, Lampsaci cum moreretur, interrogatus velletne mortuus reportari Clazomenas,

Onofrio. That is indeed my view. For although I consider heaven
my true and proper and eternal homeland, nonetheless I want
this present one, which all persons, ignorant and learned alike,
call by the single name homeland, namely where we have been
born and educated, to be considered and called my homeland.

Palla. Let me humor you: since you cannot yet take stronger remedies, let me treat you with milder ones. Do you think it an evil
to be deprived of one's homeland?

Onofrio. What do you mean an evil? I consider it the worst evil.   200
For when the mind suffers, the body cannot fail to do so. So
the whole person suffers. What more remains but for me to
confess that I am wholly miserable?

Palla. Do you think that a wise man can be miserable?

Onofrio. By no means: the wise man is always happy, always
blessed.

Palla. So to be deprived of one's homeland is not wretched?

Onofrio. Why?

Palla. Because a wise man can sometimes be deprived of his home-   201
land. Bias was one of the number of those whom we have heard
were said and considered to be wise men in the opinion of all of
antiquity. He not only was deprived of his homeland but saw it
turned over to pillaging. Diogenes, though driven from his
homeland, never felt any longing for Sinope. Solon went into
voluntary exile. When Crates of Thebes was sent into exile,
Thebes felt a longing for him rather than vice versa. Though
Lycurgus of Sparta could have been king in his homeland, he
left his country twice. The first time, he returned with reluctance, begged by letters and messages of relations and friends;
then when he had fortified his homeland's leadership with salutary teachings and laws, he departed for perpetual exile and,
when dying, took precautions that his bodily remains not be
brought back to Sparta. When Anaxagoras of Clazomenae lay   202
dying at Lampsacus and was asked whether he wanted his body

respondit undique ad inferos tantundem esse itineris. Aristoteles et Thrax fuit et Stagerites; qui tum Athenis, tum in Macedonia versatus, non Stageris neque in Thracia, sed Chalcide mori voluit. Cuius auditores Theophrastus Ephesius idemque Lesbius, Aristoxenus Tarentinus, non ille Epheso aut Lesbo, nec hic Tarento, sed alter Athenis, alter Mantinea usi sunt. Diogenes Babylonius fuit et eius discipulus Antipater Tarseus. Neuter tamen se minus aut felicem aut magnum existimavit quod solo patrio caruisset. Si requiras quo in loco Pythagoras aut educatus fuerit aut mortuus, reperias neque ubi natus esset

203 neque ubi educatus eum degere voluisse. Archedemus fuit Atheniensis. Reliquit is cum transisset ad Parthos successionem Stoicae disciplinae apud Babylonios. Athenas Zeno Citio praetulit. Plato tantus ille ac tam illustris philosophus, Athenis natus institutusque, Academiam sibi locum admodum tenuem atque angustum patriam selegit. Hunc Polemo secutus est, hunc Xenocrates. Nam Xenocrates quando unquam Athenas ventitabat, nisi semel annis singulis, quo liberalium celebritatem sua praesentia decoraret? Atqui paucissimos summos viros reperias qui vel in patria claruerint vel gloriam assecuti diutius in patria esse potuerint. Aut enim ineptias civium ac principum,

204 aut invidiam fugere coacti sunt. Omitto Cleanthen Lysium, omitto Chrysippum Soleum, omitto Carneaden Cyrenaicum, omitto Clitomachum Carthaginensem. Quid enim meminero aut Aristonem Chium aut Lampsacenum[66] Stratonem aut Critolaum Phaselitam aut Demetrium Phalereum aut Lysaniam

brought back to Clazomenae, he replied that the route to Hades was just as long from any point.[123] Aristotle was both a Thracian and a Stagirite; though he lived now at Athens, now in Macedonia, he did not want to die in Stagira or in Thrace but in Chalcis. His pupils were Theophrastus of Ephesus[124] and of Lesbos and Aristoxenus of Tarentum; the former did not live at Ephesus or Lesbos nor the latter at Tarentum, but one lived at Athens, the other at Mantinea. Diogenes was a Babylonian and his pupil Antipater came from Tarsus; neither of them felt unhappy or diminished because they were deprived of their homeland. If you ask where Pythagoras was educated or died, you would find that he wanted to live neither where he was born nor where he was educated. Archedemus was an 203 Athenian; when he crossed over to the Parthians, he left a tradition of the Stoic school with the Babylonians.[125] Zeno preferred Athens to Citium. Though a great and distinguished philosopher, born and educated at Athens, Plato chose for himself a thin and narrow place, the Academy, as his homeland. Polemo followed him in this as did Xenocrates. For when did Xenocrates ever visit Athens except once a year to honor the great assembly of free men with his presence?[126] In fact, you would find very few outstanding men who were either distinguished in their homeland or, once having attained glory, could live any longer in their homeland. They were compelled to flee either the idiocy of citizens or leaders or envy. I leave to one 204 side Cleanthes the Lysian,[127] Chrysippus of Soloe, Carneades of Cyrene, and Clitomachus of Carthage. Why mention Aristo of Chios or Strato of Lampsacus or Critolaus of Phaselis or Demetrius of Phalerum or Lysanias of Sphettus or Cebes of

Sphettium aut Thebanum Cebetem aut Brysonem Heracleo-
tam, atque alios fere innumerabiles qui aliam sibi quam ubi nati
sunt patriam non inviti vel paraverunt vel admiserunt?

205　*Manettus.* Quoniam Honofrium video nescio quid secum meditari
quod respondeat, tantisper ego, dum ipse sese accingit, capiam
eius partes, non tam ut cum ipso sentiam quam nequa mora
utilissima haec et pulcherrima disputatio deserta videatur. Tu
quidem, Pallas, sapientes multos et claros viros in medium eleganter ac memoriter protulisti qui aut voluerunt aut coacti sunt
patria carere, eosdemque videris ostendere nulla in re minores
neque fuisse nec habendos esse quod patria abessent. Sed Homero quid respondebimus, apud quem Ulysses, quem Graecorum prudentissimum esse vult, ita loquitur, credo, apud Alci-
noum?

> Quippe videre aliud patrio nil dulcius usquam
> ipse solo possum.

206　Ac tanti quidem patriae dulcedinem Ulysses faciebat ut modo
Ithacae fumum videre posset, continuo mori vellet. Nam in iis
quae de Ulysse cum Iove Minerva loquitur, huiusmodi versus
ab Homero referuntur:

> At patriae fumum surgentem noscere terrae
> si queat, extemplo cupidus moriatur Ulysses.

207　*Pallas.* Facilis est, Manette, et expedita responsio. Nam et Homerus, qui ista opportune scripserit, mendicus esse quam habitare
in patria maluit, quo factum est ut eius etiam patria ignoretur.
Et Ulysses, qui de se talia locutus pro tempore fingatur, si tanti
fecisset patriam, in patriam quamprimum revertisset potius
quam

Thebes or Bryso of Heraclea and countless others who prepared for themselves or accepted a different homeland from the
one where they were born?[128]

Manetti. Since I see that Onofrio is pondering his reply, while he   205
is preparing himself I shall take his part, not so much since I
am of his mind as lest by some delay this most beneficial and
noble discussion appear to have been abandoned. Palla, you
have elegantly and from a well-stocked memory adduced many
wise and distinguished men who either wished or were forced
to be deprived of their homeland, and you appear to show that
they were and should be considered in no respect diminished
because they were absent from their country. But what reply
shall we make to Homer, in whose work Ulysses, whom he
claims is the wisest of the Greeks, speaks as follows, I believe,
at Alcinous' palace?

> I can nowhere see anything else sweeter than my ancestral
> land.

Ulysses attached such value to his sweet homeland that he was   206
willing to die at once provided that he could see the smoke rising from Ithaca. For in the conversation that Minerva had
with Jupiter about Ulysses the following verses are related by
Homer:

> But if he could see the smoke rising from his native land,
> Ulysses would be eager to die at once.

Palla. The reply to that is easy and quick, Manetti. For Homer,   207
who wrote those words appropriately, preferred to be a beggar
than to live in his homeland; the result is that his homeland is
unknown. If Ulysses, who is represented speaking this way
about himself for expediency's sake, had attached such value to
his homeland, he would have returned to it as soon as possible
rather than

> moenia Troiae
> post eversa sacrae multumque diuque pererrans
> et mentes[67] hominum multorum nosset et urbes.

Eodem etiam modo Zeno, Cleanthes, Chrysippus, qui patriam
et honorandam et plurimi faciundam esse dicerent, domi tamen
non manserunt. Itaque oratores potius quam philosophi videntur aliud dicere, aliud sentire. Quid enim solum natale adeo
sollicitare nos debet? 'Ubi cuipiam bene est,' ut ait Aristopha-
neus ille Mercurius, 'ibi patria omnis est.' Qua ratione ductus P.
Virgilius Maro, natus Mantuae, Brundusii mortuus, Neapoli
sepultus est. L. Annaeus Seneca, vir Stoicae disciplinae, et Lu-
canus poeta, eius fratris filius, Romae mori quam vivere Cordubae maluerunt. Itemque M. Annaeus Seneca, cuius adhuc extant luculentissimae tragoediae, Romam Cordubae praeposuit.
Eodem etiam modo Statius aliam ipse sibi patriam delegit
quam ei natura contigisset. Alcuman, inter lyricos non vulgaris
poeta, Spartiatam se longe maluit quam Sardianum. Euripides,
qui et ipse patriam laudibus ad caelum extulisset, in Macedoniam profectus apud Archelaum vita defunctus est. Fuit et
Aeschylus Atheniensis, at eundem Sicilia sepellivit. Et Stesi-
chorum et Simonidem alio in loco natos, in alio sepultos invenias. Non Herodotus historiarum pater, Alicarnasi natus, Thu-
ris habitavit? Nam M. Tullius Cicero, natus Arpini, eam est
nominis claritudinem Romae assecutus ut pater patriae dicere-
tur, idque non a fartoribus aut cauponibus quorum studiis
Cosmus ducitur, sed a M. Catone, viro magno et severo. Et
ne invidere nostrae tempestatis hominibus putemur: Iaco-
bus Bucellus, et civis Florentinus et nobili familia natus, qui

208

209

210

After the overthrow of
The walls of sacred Troy, wandering much and long,
He came to know both the minds and cities of many
men.[129]

In the same way Zeno, Cleanthes, and Chrysippus, who said
that one's homeland should be honored and considered of great
importance, nonetheless did not stay home. Therefore as ora- 208
tors rather than philosophers these men appear to be saying one
thing but thinking something else. Why should our native soil
so trouble us? As Aristophanes' Mercury says, "One's entire
homeland is wherever one is well."[130] Guided by this principle,
P. Vergilius Maro was born at Mantua, died at Brundisium,
and was buried at Naples. L. Annaeus Seneca, a Stoic, and the
poet Lucan, his brother's son, preferred to die at Rome than to
live at Corduba. Likewise M. Annaeus Seneca, whose brilliant
tragedies are extant, preferred Rome to Corduba.[131] Similarly,
Statius chose himself a different homeland than the one that
fell to him by nature. Alcman, a distinguished lyric poet, far 209
preferred a Spartan homeland to a Sardian one. Though he
praised his homeland to the skies, Euripides set out to Macedonia and died at the court of Archelaus. Aeschylus, too, was an
Athenian, but Sicily was his burial place. You would find that
both Stesichorus and Simonides were born in one place but
buried in another. Did not Herodotus, the father of history,
though born at Halicarnassus, inhabit Thurii? M. Tullius Cicero, born at Arpinum, attained such distinction at Rome that
he was called the father of his country, and that not by the
poulterers and tavern keepers, by whose partisan zeal Cosimo is
guided, but by M. Cato, a great man and stern critic.[132] Lest we 210
seem to envy the men of our own time: Jacob Bucellus,[133] a
Florentine citizen of noble family, who could have lived most

153

honestissime in patria esse posset, nostri huius Francisci Philelfi
maternus avus, Tholentinum sibi patriam delegit, fuitque apud
Rhodulfum illum seniorem — quo et ipsi fortunatissimo imperatore et Picentes iustissimo principe usi sunt — omnium primus. Quid dicemus de Philippo Scholari? Num hic miser habendus est quod mercator[68] in patria in clarissimum belli ducem
apud regem Sigismundum evaserit? Vitalini Borrhomaei nomen
si cuiquam sit obscurum, se sibi ipsum obscurum fateatur licet.

211 Vivit enim in clarissima virtutis ac nominis luce. Num ei molestius quicquam accidisse arbitremur quod Insubres Venetis,
quod Mediolanum Patavio anteposuerit? Nam quantum et auctoritate valet et gratia apud potentissimum ac maximum Insubrium ac[69] Ligurum principem, quis non novit? Ubicunque sapiens vivendum sibi statuerit, aut princeps eo in loco aut inter
principes continuo est futurus. Nam stulti prudentibus cedant
necesse est. Non lati enim, secundum Sophocleum
Agamemnona,[70]

> patente nec tergo feri,
> ubique praestant, mente sed sana viri.
> Et latere magno fraetus ictu verberis
> parvi tamen bos rectus incedit viam.

212 Sertorium urbe expulsum et magnum vidit Hispania et clarum
imperatorem. Coriolanus, quem optime de republica meritum
invidiae rabies in patria esse vetuit, Volscis[71] nominis Romani
infestissimis hostibus immortali sua cum laude admirationeque
omnium imperavit. Lucumo, exulis Corinthii Damarati filius,
qui postea L. Tarquinius Priscus dictus est, Romae regnavit.

honorably in his homeland, the maternal uncle of our friend
Francisco Filelfo, chose Tolentino as his homeland and was the
most honored of men at the court of Rodolfo the Elder, whom
the Piceni have had as their fortunate general and just prince.
What are we to say of Filippo Scolaro? Surely he should not be
considered unhappy because, though a merchant in his homeland, he emerged as the most distinguished general in the service of King Sigismundo? If the name of Vitaliano Borromeo is
obscure to anyone, that person should admit to himself that he
is himself obscure; for Borromeo lives in the brightest light of
virtue and fame. Do we think anything offensive that happened   211
to him because he preferred the Lombards to the Venetians,
Milan to Padua? Who is unaware how preeminent in authority
and affection he is at the court of the most powerful and greatest prince of the Lombards and Ligurians? Wherever a wise
man has decided to live, he will always live there either as the
first citizen or among the first. For fools must give way to wise
men. According to Agamemnon in Sophocles, not only those
who are

> broad and fierce in body
> Everywhere excel, but men with a sane mind.
> And with a light lashing of the whip, however large the
>   flank,
> A bull moves straight upon the path.[134]

Spain saw Sertorius, though exiled from Rome, as a great and   212
famous commander. A man whom the madness of envy prohibited from living in his homeland, though he had served the republic in the best way, Coriolanus ruled the Volsci, who were
the fiercest enemies of Rome, to his own immortal praise and
everyone's admiration. Lucumo, the son of the Corinthian exile
Damaratus, ruled at Rome; he was afterward called Lucius Tarquinius the Elder. And if being absent from one's birthplace is

Atque si carere solo natali adeo durum esset, durum fuisset
Noe Armeniam visere, durum Abrahae Aram Chaldaeosque
relinquere. Non Isahac, non eius filius Iacob Abrahae nepos
exulavit? Exulavit Moses. Hebraei denique omnes, cum per
desertum in quadraginta usque annos exulavissent, eam patriam
nacti sunt ubi nati non fuerant. Num apostoli Christum imitati
eandem obitus quam ortus patriam habuere?

213 *Manettus.* Probas mihi, Pallas, quae dicis. Nec habeo quicquam
quod repraehendam. Sed Honofrium iam meditatum video
quae loquatur. Itaque suam sermonis vicem ipse recipiat.

Honofrius. Equidem, mi pater, non parum referre puto siquis spontene patria careat an vi. Quod sponte libenterque fit, non modo
non aut miserum est aut durum, sed et gratum certe et periu-
cundum. Sed quod vi coactus quis facit, non triste esse non
potest. Et philosophos mihi et poetas et patriarchas et aposto-
los memoras qui in patria esse noluerunt. At mihi de illorum
exilio habetur oratio, qui dum maxime in patria esse cupiunt, in
ea esse non possunt. Quare vi carent patria vel inviti.

214 *Pallas.* At sapienti vis nulla afferri potest.

Honofrius. Quur igitur in patria minus manes?

Pallas. Ut patriae caritati consulam.

Honofrius. Et qui consulas, cum hanc sacrilegis, latronibus, sica-
riis, parricidis lacerandam interimendamque deseris?

215 *Pallas.* Tempori nonnunquam parendum est. Et sapientis est, cum
plurima sibi mala proposita viderit, id eligere quod minus habet

so very difficult a thing, it would have been difficult for Noah to see Armenia, hard for Abraham to leave behind Aram and the Chaldeans. Didn't Isaac, didn't his son Jacob, the grandson of Abraham, go into exile? Moses lived in exile and in the end all the Jews had been living in banishment, wandering in exile through the desert for as long as forty years, when they found a homeland where they had not been born. Did the apostles who imitated Christ have the same homeland for their deaths as for their births?

Manetti. You are proving what you have spoken, Palla, and I believe there is nothing I would challenge. But I see now that Onofrio has considered what to say, so let him take his turn to speak. 213

Onofrio. My father, I think it makes no little difference whether someone lacks a homeland of his own free will or by coercion. For what is done willingly and by one's own choice is not an unhappy or a distressful condition but a desirable one and very pleasing. But what one does compelled by force cannot fail to be unhappy. You draw my attention to the philosophers, poets, patriarchs, and apostles who did not want to live in their homelands, but for me the topic is the exile of those who, though they very much desire to live in their native land, cannot do so. They are therefore living without a homeland under compulsion or unwillingly.

Palla. But no coercion can be exercised upon a wise man. 214

Onofrio. So why aren't you remaining in your homeland?

Palla. To take thought for my affection for my homeland.

Onofrio. How are you taking thought when you leave her to be cut to pieces and destroyed by blasphemers, thieves, cutthroats, parricides?

Palla. One sometimes must obey circumstances. It is the nature of 215 a wise man, when he sees many evils placed before him, to choose the course that holds least danger or trouble for himself.

157

in sese vel periculi vel molestiae. Et nostrae nunc et sociorum vires ad Immolam fractae sunt. Et exercitus et imperator et duces omnes sunt in hostium potestate, et id nostra quidem stulticia. Nam cum iniquum et nefarrium bellum cum Philippo Maria quam et necessariam et honestam et utilem pacem malumus, non iniuria nostrae dementiae poenas damus. Itaque si a nobis ille vel summo nostro cum detrimento ac dedecore iniuria lacessitus, nos inter nos senserit armis dissidere, etsi humanissimus claementissimusque est, opportunitatem fortassis amplectatur ac nostram rempublicam in servitutem agat.

216 *Rainaldus.* At ego, Pallas, hac una re omnino abs te dissentio. Malim enim Philippo Mariae tanto et tam benigno principi patriam servire, si fortasse — quod omen Deus avertat — serviendum sit omnino, quam ineptissimo nebuloni Cosmo Medici.

Pallas. Verum, Rainalde, non modo Philippus nobis metuendus est, sed Eugenius multo magis. Quae una ratio me potissimum movit, ut quod ipsum unum nostram victoriam impedivit atque intercepit, et te et reliquos optimatis ac bonos civis ab armis consiliis improborum deceptus revocarim. Videre enim videbar et Eugenium et alios quosdam aliud nihil meditari atque machinari quam ut nostram rempublicam perderent. Ea vero mea sententia semper fuit, longe nobis conducibilius esse, et ad privatam et ad publicam dignitatem, ut mala etiam obscuraque libertas anteponeretur cuivis utili servituti.

217 *Rainaldus.* Quod si libertas potestas est vivendi ut velis, quid hanc libertatem appellas, qua nulla servitus est turpior, nulla foedior, nulla nequior?

Pallas. Veruntamen utcunque res habet, Florentinus dicitur principatus.

Our troops and those of our allies have recently been crushed at Imola. The army and its general and all the leaders are in the enemy's power, and all this because of our stupidity. For when we prefer a dangerous and criminal war with Filippo Visconti, rather than a necessary, honorable, and beneficial peace, we rightly pay the penalty for our madness. So if he were unjustly provoked by us, even to our own extreme harm and shame, and were to know that among ourselves we are in armed conflict, then even though he is a most humane and forgiving man, he might perhaps seize the opportunity and drive our republic into slavery.

Rinaldo. But, Palla, I completely disagree with you in this one re-   216
spect: I would rather prefer the country to be subject to Filippo Maria, so great and benign a prince, than to a bumbling trick-ster like Cosimo de' Medici, if we must—may God avert the omen!—be slaves at all.

Palla. But, Rinaldo, we must not only fear Filippo but much more Eugenius. The one consideration that particularly troubles me and the one thing that hindered and cut short our victory is that, tricked by the plots of scoundrels, I called you and the rest of the nobles and sound citizens back from armed resistance. For it seemed to me that Eugenius and certain others were de-vising and plotting nothing less than to destroy our republic. My view always has been that it is far more advantageous for us, both for our private standing and our public image, that a bad and barely distinguishable liberty be preferred to an expedi-ent slavery of any sort.

Rinaldo. But if liberty is the power of living as you wish, what do   217
you call this liberty, which is more disgraceful, more foul, more worthless than any slavery?

Palla. But however the matter stands, it is called the Florentine Principate.

Rainaldus. Sed sanius profecto dicatur vel Mucellensis vel carbonarius. Non enim te praeterit senior ille Cosmus qui primus est, pro Medico non illepide Medices appellatus, et quinam fuerit et quam artem tenuerit et quod praemium ob indignitatem oscoeni facinoris acceperit.

218 *Pallas.* Haec nunc, Rainalde, missa faciamus. Facile enim, cum voles, rempublicam nostram pro dignitate constitues. Sed nunc, mihi crede, si temporis naturam sequi volueris, tutius nomini Florentino nobisque consulueris si exules nos malis quam victores.

Rainaldus. Ut libet, Pallas, tametsi futurum vereor ut, iam senectute occupatus, quod ipse non imprudenter expectas, visurus nunquam sim. Sed de his, ut paulo ante dicebas, ipsi postea inter nos commentabimur.

219 *Pallas.* Recte mones, fietque id et commodius et melius. Nunc autem — quod modo dicebam — et temporis ratio est habenda et e malis id eligendum quod minimum sit.

Honofrius. Nos tamen, pater, et vi pellimur et innocenter et cum ignominia.

Pallas. Utrum facere an pati vim malis?

Honofrius. Neutrum profecto, mi pater. Nam alterum est iniusti, alterum calamitosi. Sed iniuriam propulsare et iusticiae esse puto et fortitudinis et illustris perfectaeque virtutis.

220 *Pallas.* Nulla sine prudentia virtus est. Cum navis in magna aliqua periculosaque tempestate agitatur undique contrariis ventorum flatibus, nonne tibi propinquior naufragio videatur siquidem ii qui sunt in navi contendant inter se mutuo quam si pars altera alteri tantisper cedat, dum extrarii turbines fluctusque resederint?

Rinaldo. It might more sensibly be called the Mugellan or the Charcoal Burner's Principate. It won't have escaped you who that elder Cosimo was, wittily called a mayor (*medix*) instead of a "physician" (*medicus*), and of what craft he was master and what reward he received for his dishonorable and disgusting crimes.[135]

Palla. Rinaldo, let us set these matters aside for now. For you will 218 easily, when you wish, set our republic in order consistent with its dignity. But now, believe me, if you are willing to adapt to the circumstances, you will take counsel in a safer way for the nation of Florence and for us if you prefer to regard us as exiles rather than victors.

Rinaldo. As you please, Palla, although I fear it will be the case that, already well advanced in age, I shall never see what you yourself wisely anticipate. But we will discuss these matters, as you said a little earlier, among ourselves.

Palla. You rightly caution us, and that will prove to be a more 219 convenient and better course. But now — as I was just saying — we must take circumstances into account and choose the least of evils.

Onofrio. All the same, Father, we have been driven out by force, though innocent, and in disgrace.

Palla. Do you prefer to inflict or suffer force?

Onofrio. Surely neither, Father. For the one is characteristic of an unjust man, the other of a ruined man. But to fend off injury I consider the part of justice and courage, and of a distinguished and perfect virtue.[136]

Palla. Without wisdom there is no virtue. When a ship is being 220 tossed about in some great, dangerous storm by crossing gusts of wind, wouldn't a shipwreck seem to you more imminent if the crewmen struggle with each other rather than if one group were to yield to the other until the storms and waves have subsided?

Honofrius. Videtur sane. Sed iniuste patria privari ita et durum et molestum censeo, ut aliud nihil neque durius neque molestius accidere posse putem.

Pallas. Nunquid unquam audisti quid uxori Xanthippae Socrates in carcere aliquando responderit?

Honofrius. Qua de re?

221 *Pallas.* Socrates, inquam, ipse cum in tyrannide illorum triginta ageret omnia quae Atheniensi populo profutura crederet, nec ullam sibi cum improbis et flagitiosis familiaritatem vellet, quique ad Leontem Salaminium ab eisdem triginta cum mitteretur, minime paruisset ac tyrannis coram malediceret, eos improbis bubulcis similes esse inquiens qui boves quas et robustas et multas acceperint paucas imbecilliorisque[72] facerent, nihilque omnino neque publicis neque privatis officiis usquam omitteret quod Atheniensibus conduceret, idem tamen postea, secundis in rebus, ab eodem populo pro quo ipse nullum vitae periculum subterfugerat, calumnia invidorum accusatore Melito, qui ab eo diceret adolescentes pravis imbui et disciplinis et moribus, et non Atheniensium deos sed suum aliud numen inusitatum coli, et alias quasdam inanis huiusmodi insimulationes obiiceret, idem, inquam, Socrates, innocentissimus et optimus plane vir, 222 ab eodem ipso ingrato Athenarum populo enecatur. Cum igitur forti animo et invicto nulla trepidatione, nulla neque oris neque vultus mutatione e manu carnificis potionem veneni accepisset et, admoto iam labris mortifero illo poculo, Xanthippe uxor inter flaetum et lamentationem vociferaretur eum innocentem periturum, 'Quid ergo,' inquit, 'vociferaris, o mulier? Nunquid mihi mori nocenti satius esse duxeris?' Longe satius esse

Onofrio. It does seem so. But I think that being unfairly banished from your country is so difficult and offensive that I wonder whether there is anything else that can be experienced that is more difficult or more troubling.

Palla. Have you ever heard the reply Socrates made to his wife Xantippe, when he was in prison?

Onofrio. On what topic?

Palla. During the rule of the Thirty Tyrants, Socrates did every- 221 thing he thought would benefit the people of Athens and re- fused to have any dealings with those criminal and shameful men. When he was dispatched by the Thirty to Leon of Sala- mis, he disobeyed and taunted the Tyrants to their faces, saying they were like bad cowherds who received cows who were strong and numerous and made them fewer and weaker;[137] he never missed any opportunity, in a public or private capacity, to do what would benefit the Athenians. All the same, afterward, during good times, Socrates was killed by the same people on whose behalf he had shirked no danger. He was charged on the basis of the slanders of envious persons, with Melitus as the prosecutor, who said that young boys had been corrupted with vile teachings and habits and that he worshipped not the gods of the Athenian people but his own peculiar divinity, and Meli- tus hurled at him other empty fabrications of this sort. Socra- tes, then, the most innocent and finest of men, was put to death by the same thankless people of Athens. When, with 222 courage, without fear, with no change in countenance or ap- pearance, he had taken the deadly potion from the executioner's hand and moved the fatal cup to his lips, amid her wailing and sobbing his wife Xantippe blurted out that he was going to his death an innocent man. "What are you bawling, woman?" he said. "Would you reckon it preferable for me to die as a guilty

arbitror, fili Honofri, nos iniuste et innocenter Florentia pelli quam siquid nostra culpa mereremur.

223 *Honofrius.* At hanc tantam tamque intolerabilem ignominiam qua aequitate animi quisquam ferat, quod hostes patriae, quod proditores, quod impii iudicemur?

Pallas. Et istudne est quod tu maxime omnium molestum putas?

Honofrius. Hoc certe, mi pater. Nam si honorationem virtutis et rectefactorum praemium volunt, quid est de ignominia iudicandum?

224 *Pallas.* Qui virtutem honorant, seipsos honoratos reddunt, quoniam ex officio facientes se gratos dici quam ingratos malint. Qui vero ignominia virtutem dedecoreque afficere conantur, non virtuti faciunt (quae per seipsam honoratissima est), sed sibiipsis iniuriam. Nam in virtute violanda se vitii arguunt, se ignominia dedecoreque afficiunt. Praeterea cum et animo constemus et corpore, cumque et bona quaedam sint natura terminata ac item mala, quidquid in his peccatur, et nocet id quidem

225 et turpe putandum est. Quod autem recte fit, non ex omni parte prodesse in omnem eventum non potest. Caetera vero illa dedecora et ignominiae et quaecunque alia huiusmodi sunt, lege quadam, non tam ratione quam arbitrio constituta atque opinione, turpia malaque dicuntur, quae si corpori etiam quandoque possunt, animo certe nihil officiunt. Nunquam enim sapientis et iusti viri animum vel exilio vel ignominia improbum factum reperias. Quod certe alia nulla re fit, nisi quod nihil huiuscemodi natura malum est.

226 At ne redire quidem in patriam nec manere quoque in patria in bonis duci oportet. Sed qualia quisque haec opinatur, talia videntur esse. Quo fit ut eadem saepe res apud alios laudi, apud

man?"[138] I think, my son Onofrio, that it is far preferable for us to be driven from Florence unjustly and guiltlessly rather than deserve expulsion by our own guilt.

Onofrio. But how can anyone calmly endure so great and intolerable a disgrace, judged as we are enemies of our country, traitors, and blasphemers? 223

Palla. Is this what you consider the greatest affliction of all?

Onofrio. Indeed it is, father. For if people want approbation to be the reward of virtue and deeds performed justly, what view must one take about disgrace?

Palla. Those who respect virtue make themselves honorable since those who act out of a sense of duty prefer to be called deserving rather than undeserving. Those who try to attach dishonor and disgrace to virtue do no harm to virtue, which, on its own, is the most respected of things, but to themselves. For in violating virtue they convict themselves of vice and bring on themselves disgrace and dishonor. Furthermore, since we are composed of both mind and body, and since some actions are defined as good by nature, just as some are bad, whatever is sinful in the latter is harmful and must be considered shameful. Yet what is done rightly cannot fail to be beneficial in every respect and toward every outcome. On the other hand, those behaviors that are truly shameful and dishonorable, and any other actions of this kind, are said to be shameful and evil by a principle that is established not by reason but by whim and opinion. Even if these actions can at some point bring harm to the body, they certainly cannot harm the mind. You will never find the mind of a wise and just man that has become base through either exile or disgrace. Surely this happens for no other reason than that no outcome of this kind is by nature evil. 224 225

There is no need to consider returning to our homeland, or even remaining there, as a good thing. These things appear to be whatever someone believes them to be.[139] For this reason it 226

alios vituperationi danda existimetur, apud alios in praecio habeatur, contemnatur apud alios. Aethiopes pulcherrimam mulierem putant quae maxime et sima et nigra sit. Persae vero
quae sit tum naso maxime adunco, tum etiam albissima. Alii
vero neutram probant, sed eam omnibus forma praestare dicunt
227 quae media quaedam sit et figura et colore. Zeno autem ille
Citieus, quem in Stoica disciplina unice admirantur, in disputa-
tionibus *De instituendis pueris* nihil differre ait vel uti puerorum
amoribus vel non uti, eodemque modo interesse nihil aut pueris
aut puellis congredi; haec enim non diversa sed eadem esse, et
itidem decere[73] eadem esseque decora. Ad haec quae Oedipus
in fabulis cum Iocasta matre perpetrasse dicitur, nullam afferre
turpitudinem probare argumentatur. At haec nos non turpia et
foeda modo, sed scelerata et impia non iniuria censemus.

Poggius. At non omnes, Pallas, sententiam tuam istam admittant.

228 *Pallas.* Non hic, Poggi, vel de Cosmo et Medicibus, quibus omne
vetitum licet, vel de Bambalione quopiam, cui nihil sanctum
est, habetur sermo, sed de viro et severo et pudico. Longeque
melius et gravius et illustrius Christianos philosophatos puto
quam vel Zenonem vel reliquam omnem illam antiquitatem,
quae veri Dei legem praeceptaque ignorabat. Quid enim Chrysippo stultius, qui in libro *De iusticia* ita scripserit: 'Quod si
membrorum pars aliqua abscidatur quae ad alimentum usui sit,
neque ea defodienda est, neque aliter iacienda, sed esu absu-
menda potius, quo pars altera in nobis fiat.' Hoc illi turpe non
229 videbatur, at nobis immanitatis plenum. Aitque idem Chrysippus in libro *De officio* de parentibus sepelliendis, loquens ita
ad verbum: 'Cum autem parentes diem obierint, sepulturis
utendum est iis quae maxime simplices sint, quasi corpus sicuti

happens that a trait considered praiseworthy by some people is treated with scorn by others; one that is considered valuable by some is held in contempt by other. The Ethiopians think that the most beautiful woman is the one that is in the highest degree snub-nosed and black, but the Persians the one who has a hooked nose and is white; still others hold neither one in high regard but say that the woman who excels all others in beauty is the one who is a kind of mean in form and complexion. Zeno 227 of Citium, whom the Stoics uniquely admire, in his books *On Educating Boys* says that it makes no difference whether love for boys is practiced or not; likewise it does not matter whether sex takes place with boys or girls. For these are not different things, but the same, and these same practices are likewise equally suitable and honorable. As for what Oedipus is said in myth to have committed with his mother Jocasta, he asserts that there is nothing shameful about it. But we rightly consider these actions not just shameful and defiling, but wicked and impious.

Poggio. But not everyone, Palla, agrees with this opinion of yours.

Palla. This discussion, Poggio, is not about Cosimo and the Med- 228 ici, who allow themselves all that is forbidden, or some Bamba-lio, to whom nothing is sacred, but a man who has high standards and is chaste. I consider that the Christians have philosophized with far greater authority and distinction than Zeno and all the rest of antiquity, a culture that was in ignorance of the law and teachings of the true God. What could be more stupid than Chrysippus, who wrote in his book *On Justice:* "If one of our members that are useful for nutrition is cut off, it should neither be buried nor discarded but rather consumed so that we may grow another part." Though this seemed no disgrace to him, to us it seems utterly monstrous. Chrysippus 229 likewise in his book *On Duty* on the subject of burying one's parents says, verbatim, the following: "When our parents pass away, we ought to use the simplest forms of burial, since the

unguis aut capilli nihil nostra intersit, nec curiosiore nobis diligentia huiusmodi in rebus opus sit. Quare etiam si carnes fuerint ad alendum utiles, iis utentur quemadmodum propriis
partibus. Sin autem inutiles, aut iis defossis monumentum im-
ponent, aut concrematis cinerem dimittent, aut aeminus proiec-
tis non magis eas curabunt quam vel praesegmina vel capillos.'
Nec turpia Chrysippo Stoico haec prodigia nec mala videbantur. Apud nos vero non modo hominum, sed ipsius naturae et
institutis et legibus habentur inhumana, dira, tetra, horrenda.

230   Sed quo nostra tendit oratio? Ut intelligamus non nihil esse
natura et turpe et malum, quod apud aliquos neque turpitudini
est neque malo cuipiam obnoxium, non nulla etiam turpia et
mala duci quae natura non sunt; et idem esse apud alios turpe
ac malum, quod apud alios et honestum et bonum iudicetur.
Dandam igitur operam puto, ut aut quae honesta et bona natura sunt, aut quae secus, nequaquam nos fugiant. Nam siquid
in his deliquerimus, etiam si nulla nos afficiamur ignominia,
231   dedecorosi sumus. At illa quae hominum duntaxat opinione
talia esse iudicantur, contemnenda nobis omnino non sunt. Id
enim et fastidiosi esset et intemperantis ingenii. Sed quorum
opinio iudicium faciat, consyderandum est etiam atque etiam.
Non enim quid insipientes et improbi, sed quid probi et sapientes de nobis sentiant, movere nos debet.

   Honofrius. Verum, pater, hanc ignominiam publici nobis magistratus inferunt.

232 *Pallas.* 'Magistratus,' ut inquit Bias, 'virum ostendit.' Ii profecto
nunc Florentiae magistratus gerunt, qui aut quid aut quantum
magistratus valeat neque re neque nomine cognorint. Quid
enim recti sanive quicquam intelligant ii quorum deus venter

body, like a hair or a nail, makes no difference to us, nor have we need of any great amount of care in such matters. Therefore if the flesh be useful for food, they will use it as they would their own members. If not, they will either bury them and set up a marker, or cremate them and scatter the ashes, or cast them at a distance and take no more thought for them than for the clippings of nails or beards." Nor did these practices seem uncouth or wicked to Chrysippus the Stoic. But in our culture these practices are considered inhuman, terrible, offensive, and repulsive not only by the teachings and laws of men but of Nature herself.

But what is the point of my discourse? That we understand 230 that there is something disgraceful and evil by nature, which in the eyes of some is neither disgraceful nor evil; that some things are held to be disgraceful and evil that are not such by nature; and the same thing is disgraceful and evil in the eyes of some that others regard as honorable and good. Therefore we must take pains that it not escape us which things are honorable and good by nature and which are otherwise. For if we err in these matters, even if no disgrace attaches to us, we are dishonorable. But we should not altogether despise the things that are merely 231 judged to be such by men's opinion. For to do so shows an overfastidious and immoderate character. But we must earnestly consider by whose opinion the judgment is made. For we ought to be influenced by what good and wise men think of us, not fools and scoundrels.

Onofrio. But, father, the public magistrates are inflicting this disgrace upon us.

Palla. "The magistracy," as Bias remarked, "shows the man."[140] At 232 Florence currently men exercise magistracies who do not understand, either in practice or in theory, the meaning and extent of a magistrate's power. For what correct or sound principle would men understand whose god is their belly and their

est immanisque libido? Qui aliud nihil cogitant, nihil curant quam omnia per intemperantiam, per avariciam, per flagitium, per contumeliam, per dedecus agere. Istiusmodine igitur pecudum ignominiam verearis, a quibus ornari dedecorosum admodum sit? Non pluris, mediusfidius, istorum helluonum iudicium bono viro faciendum puto quam si Galilaeus Bufonius, qui medicinae omnino ignarus se medicorum peritissimum profitetur, quempiam extenuari et aegrotare iudicet qui bona prorsus habitudine valitudineque sit. Quamobrem huiusmodi ignominia sua natura mala non est, neque in exilio mali quicquam inesse potest. Quot homines invenias qui tanquam ex omni loco depellerentur, omnem ferme aetatem peregre consumpserunt? Quod cum summis etiam cum laboribus et periculis facerent, tamen cum non nihil in videndis variis et locis et urbibus, in cognoscendis hominum aliis atque aliis moribus ad prudentiam sibi accedere animadverterent, libenter id omne exilium atque incommoda perferebant. Quam certe rem in Ulyssis erroribus Homerus eleganter docet. Et Apollonius ille Tyaneus, si Philostrato credendum est, totum prope terrarum orbem peragravit. Atque sacerdotes Aegyptiorum, ut ex iis patet quae leguntur in sacris libris, ad se traiecisse tradunt priscis temporibus et Orpheum et Musaeum et Melampoda[74] et Daedalum et Homerum ipsum poetam et Lycurgum Spartiatam et Solonem Atheniensem et Platonem philosophum et Pythagoram Samium et Eudoxum mathematicum et Democritum Abderitam et Oenopiden Chium. Quorum omnium signa non nulla afferunt aliorum imagines quasdam, aliorum vero appellationes, quibus aut loca aut aedificia et monumenta illorum nomina repraesentant. Utunturque certissimis argumentis, quibus ostendunt eos omnis in quibus maxime rebus apud Graecos claruerunt, disciplinam apud Aegyptios assecutos. Quos tamen eosdem ipsos non Aegyptum duntaxat, sed ultimas terras propter discendi cupiditatem peragrasse accepimus. Itaque nobis

boundless lust? They think and care about nothing else than to act intemperately, greedily, disgracefully, insultingly, and dishonorably. Should you, then, fear disgrace inflicted by beasts of such a nature that it would be a dishonor to be honored by them? I think the good man should make no more of the judgment of such wastrels than if Galileo Bufonio, who, though an ignoramus in medicine, claims to be the most skilled physician, judges that a man of excellent constitution and health is feeble and sickly. Therefore such disgrace is not by its own nature an 233 evil, nor can there be any evil in exile. How many men would you find who have spent practically their entire life abroad, as if they had been driven from every place? Though they did this with the utmost toil and danger, nonetheless since they have noticed that in seeing various places and cities, in getting to know other people and their customs, they have gained in wisdom, they gladly endured the entire exile and its disadvantages. Homer elegantly taught this point in the case of Ulysses' 234 wanderings. If Philostratus is to be believed, Apollonius of Tyana traveled over practically the entire world.[141] As is clear from their sacred books, the priests of Egypt record that in ancient times many crossed over to them: Orpheus, Musaeus, Melampus, Daedalus, the poet Homer himself, Lycurgus of Sparta, Solon of Athens, Plato the philosopher, Pythagoras of Samos, the mathematician Eudoxus, Democritus of Abdera, and Oenopides of Chius.[142] They adduce tokens of all of them, 235 statues of some, of others designations by which either places or buildings or monuments provide the equivalent of their names. They put forward reliable arguments by which they show that all those persons in the skills in which they were particularly distinguished among the Greeks obtained training among the Egyptians. We have received the tradition that these very same men wandered not only over Egypt but the remotest lands because of their eagerness to learn. Therefore we too

quoque laborandum est ut ex hoc praesenti nostro quod tu exilium vocas (ego 'peregrinationem' malim), id nos emolumenti consecuti existimemur ut et prudentiores redditi melioresque videamur. Quod si fecerimus, non tam Florentia nobis quam nos Florentiae desyderio futuri sumus. Nec admodum referre putandum est, spontene solum hoc natale relinquamus an inviti, modo scilicet hoc studeamus, ut prudentia aucti probitateque putemur. Exercitum propterea ita nominatum volunt, quod exerceri plurimum oporteat; ut enim ocio et quiete languidior atque hebetior solet, ita exercitatione laboreque frequenti et robustior efficitur et acrior. Non minus igitur utilitatis milites consequantur si invite quam si sponte exerceantur. Neque is qui mercator[75] invite navigat, minores adipisci pecunias solet quam qui sponte id faciunt. Nec minore illum gaudio affici oportet cui invito vel oratoria vel philosophia vel alia huiusmodi praestantia aut boni aliquid contigerit, quam id ipsum cupienti et[76] studenti cuipiam.

236

237   Verum quod adolescens ille Terentianus Clitipho secum loquitur, ne iure dici de nobis queat, diligenter curandum est:

> Nulla est enim tam facilis res quin difficilis siet
> quam invitus facias.

Debet enim vir sapiens nihil invite agere. Id sane iure laudatur quod recte fiat, at recte fieri nihil ducitur, nisi idem sit ultroneum.[77] Quidquid acciderit nobis, aut etiam accidat, ita est accipiendum quasi ex sententia contingat. Non enim quae pro libera voluntate,[78] sed quae invite homines faciunt, graviter ferunt. Nec quaecunque cupiunt ut ea contingant, par est, sed omnia quae necessitate proveniunt cupienda sunt. Nam neque vivendi modum pro nostra electione habere possumus, nec adeo dissoluta quaedam nobis data est libertas ut nostri omnino

238

should exert ourselves that out of this present fate of ours that you call an exile (I would prefer "travel abroad") we be thought to have gained the benefit that, when restored, we seem to be wiser and better. If we have done so, Florence will not so much be the object of our longing as we of Florence's. Nor should we think that it matters greatly whether we are leaving our native soil willingly or unwillingly, provided that we eagerly pursue this goal: to be thought to have been improved in wisdom and uprightness. Some say that an army (*exercitus*) has been so named because it requires a great deal of training (*exerceri*),[143] for as it tends in times of peace and quiet to be rather slow and dull, so by exercise and repeated toil it is made stronger and sharper. Soldiers, then, gain no less benefit if they train unwillingly than if they do so willingly. Nor does the man who sails as a merchant unwillingly gain less money than those who do so willingly. No less enjoyment should be afforded to someone unwillingly by rhetoric, philosophy, or other such excellent pursuits than to one who desires and eagerly pursues them.

236

We must take special care that what Terence's young man Clitopho says in his monologue cannot rightly be said of us:

237

There is nothing so easy but that it is difficult
If you do it against your will.[144]

The wise man ought to do nothing unwillingly. What is done correctly is rightly praised, but nothing is considered done correctly unless it is voluntary. One must accept whatever has happened to us or what is happening, as if it befalls us according to our wishes. For people are troubled not at what they do in accord with their free will, but what they do against their will. It is not fair for them to gain whatever they wish, but all things that come about by necessity are to be wished. For neither can we have a way of life in accord with our own choice, nor have we been given such unfettered liberty that we are completely

238

simus. Sed ut fortunae visum sit, et ut cuique nostrum sors ea quae cuiusque fatum absolvat pro divina voluntate data fuerit, ipsi quoque faciamus necesse est. Necessitati autem repugnare et insolentis est et insani.

Honofrius. At haec in nos hominum ingratitudo dolenda non est, ut pro ingentibus et immortalibus beneficiis quibus patriam semper prosecuti sumus, patria pellamur?

239 *Pallas.* Nil tibi durius accidit quam Cadmo, Agenoris filio, quem Thebarum conditorem Thebanus populus iam senio confectum Thebis Boetiaque exegit. Nil gravius quam Theseo, qui cum Athenienses passim vagantes ac longe lateque dispersos et ritu ferarum vitam agentes urbe civitateque ornasset et privatim et publice summis beneficiis affecisset, ab eisdem ipsis Atheniensibus in exilium actus est. Eadem Athenienses ingratitudine in Solonem sunt usi, eadem in Aristiden, eadem in Themistoclem, eadem in Demetrium Phalereum. Socratem unicum virtutis
240 speculum veneno interemerunt. Nam Miltiaden, qui eos ad Marathonem a barbarorum vinclis et carcere liberarat, in vinclis et carcere mori coegerunt; cuius etiam cadaver noluerunt prius humatum iri quam Cimon mortui patris miserabiles cathenas subiisset. Phocionem vero non solum per extremos corporis cruciatus enecarunt, sed eius ossa exterminarunt ex omni Attica. Sed ne videamur Athenienses infestius insectari, quanto se meliores in Lycurgum Ladaemonii praestiterunt? Nonne in eum, optime de se meritum, lapidibus insurrexerunt? Non eius
241 oculum eruerunt? Nam Herculis filios non ii sunt duce Eurystheo per omnem contumeliam aerumnasque insectati, quos ille contumelia saepius aerumnisque liberarat et splendidissimos per omnem terrarum orbem potentissimosque reddiderat? Quid

our own man. But as Fortune has seen fit and as a fate that brings an end to our destiny has been allotted to each of us in accord with divine will, we ourselves must also act. To resist necessity is to be an arrogant madman.

Onofrio. But should people's ingratitude toward us not be lamented, that in return for the enormous and immortal benefits we have always conferred on our homeland we are driven out?

Palla. Nothing harsher has happened to you than to Cadmus, 239 Agenor's son, whom, though he was the founder of Thebes, the Theban people drove out of Thebes and Boeotia when he was already afflicted by old age. Nothing more grievous has happened to you than to Theseus, who, though he supplied the Athenians, who were wandering here and there, scattered far and wide and living like animals, with a city and a state, and with the finest benefits both publicly and privately, yet was driven into exile by those same Athenians. The Athenians practiced the same ingratitude toward Solon, Aristides, Themistocles, Demetrius of Phalerum. Socrates, a singular mirror of human excellence, they executed by means of poison. Miltiades, 240 who at Marathon had freed them from the chains and prison of the barbarians, they forced to die in chains and prison; they refused burial to his corpse until Cimon had put on his father's wretched chains. They not only put Phocion to death through a series of brutal tortures but banned his bones from burial in all of Attica. But lest we seem to be criticizing the Athenians with excessive hostility, how much better did the Spartans show themselves toward Lycurgus? Did they not, for all his services toward them, rise up against him with stones? Did they not gouge out one of his eyes? Did they not, under the leadership 241 of Eurystheus, pursue the sons of Heracles through a course of insult and miseries, the very ones whom Heracles had often freed from insult and miseries and made the most splendid and powerful people in the world? Why should I mention

autem Romulum meminero, quem ad Paludem Caprae dum exercitum lustraret, Romani ipsi quibus et urbem ille et nomen et rem et gloriam pepererat, e medio crudeliter sustulerunt? Fuerunt itidem in Camillum, fuerunt in Coriolanum ingrati. Si maioris exilium, si minoris Africani necem cogitemus, nihil Romanis intelligamus ingratitudini magis obnoxium. At Scipio Nascica, qui prostratam rempublicam solus erexit, Pergami diem obire coactus est. Omitto Ahallam, omitto Ciceronem, omitto Iulium Caesarem, in quos invidorum faces per omnem ingratitudinis vim atque incendium exarserunt. Non satis id nobis exemplo sit egregiam singularemque praestantiam semper invidiae esse odio, quod Christus Deus, qui se ut humano generi salutem immortalitatemque afferret, et hominem voluit et mortalem, ab iis est invidia cruci affixus quorum aeternae beatitudini potissimum consulebat?

Quid ergo nos homunciones adeo turbare debet si beneficiis in alios tum publice, tum privatim semper usi exemplo Dei patimur ingratitudinem hominum improborum? An forte malimus beneficium foenerari? Non multo et melius est et gloriosius beneficum et esse et dici extorrem quam vel maleficum vel ingratum manere domi? Fugienda nobis est non Florentia quidem, sed isti potius qui omne flagitium et scelus in Florentiam machinantur. Itaque exules isti plane ac vero putandi sunt, a quibus omne animi bonum exulat. Nos autem quandiu rationis utemur ductu, etiam si Florentia caruerimus, nunquam exulabimus; quin omni demum relegationis munere functi in veram patriam brevi revocabimur. Nam quod non multo ante monuimus, nostra patria non est in hisce terrenis fluctibus, sed in illa caelesti plaga, cuius regio domicilio qui se dignum fecerit,

Romulus, whom the Romans themselves cruelly dispatched at the Goat's Swamp while he was ritually purifying his army, the Romans to whom he gave a city, and a name and a state, and glory?[145] They were likewise ungrateful to Camillus and Coriolanus. If we consider the exile of the Elder Africanus and the death of the Younger, we would understand that no nation was more guilty of ingratitude than the Romans. Scipio Nasica, who alone raised up the republic as it lay in ruins, was forced to die at Pergamum. I leave aside Ahala, Cicero, Julius Caesar, against whom the torches of envious persons flared with all the incendiary violence of ingratitude. Would it not suffice us as an example of the fact that outstanding and unparalleled excellence is always loathed by envy that divine Christ, who, to bring salvation and immortality to the human race, was willing to make Himself a human being and mortal, was nailed to a cross in envy by those whose eternal blessedness he cared for above all?   242

Why, then, should we poor mortals be so upset if, after always having conferred benefits both publicly and privately to others, we follow God's example in suffering the ingratitude of wicked men? Or would we perhaps prefer to lend our beneficence out at interest? Is it not much better and more glorious to be and be called a benefactor in exile than to be called a malefactor or to remain at home as *persona non grata*? We must flee not Florence, but rather those who plot every outrage and crime against Florence. Therefore those persons should clearly and truly be thought exiles, from whom every good quality of the mind is in exile. As long, however, as we use reason's guidance, even if we have been deprived of Florence, we will never be in exile. What is more, when we have finally fulfilled every task of our relegation, we will soon be called back to our true homeland. For as we cautioned not long ago, our homeland lies not in these earthly tempests, but in that heavenly region; he who has made himself worthy of this royal dwelling mocks all those   243

244

Polynicea illa quaeque incommoda deridet. Non paupertatem
metuit, non infamiam perhorrescit. Nihil servile, nihil demissum sapit. Non ad aliorum libidinem quicquam vel dicit vel facit, sed seipsum audit, sibi obtemperat, omnia pro sua constantia et animi iudicio moderatur. Non amicis, non hospitibus
245   caret. Nulla re eget. Solus sapiens magnus est, solus potens,
solus fortunatus, solus suus. Novit sibi vim nullam afferri posse.
Aliorum iniuriam non sibi sed inferentibus perniciosam putat.
Nec ulla se ignominia notari posse intelligit quem animi probitas honoratum reddit. Siquid nobis dolendum est, non nostra
sed istorum causa dolendum est qui se ingratitudinis reos ultro
facientes, nullius prorsus sceleris expertes (ut sunt impudentissima nequitia) argui volunt. Haec, fili Honofri, si tecum diligenter cogitabis, non modo non cruciaberis animi, sed gaudebis
potius nos talis esse quos improbi oderint.

246   *Honofrius.* Quae mihi, mi pater, saluberrime praecepisti et audivi
libenter et mihi omnino probari vaehementer cupio. Sed si tempestivum ducis, paululum etiam quiddam mihi superest quod
rogem.

Pallas. Quidquid tibi reliquum est, quod velis, postridie quaeras
licet. Nunc enim advesperascit. Et nos alia quaedam pro communi causa acturi sumus. Idemque Rainaldo videri intelligo.

Rainaldus. Rectissime, Pallas, monuisti. Idemque Rhodulphus hic
Pyrucius innuerat.

"disadvantages" of Polynices.[146] He does not fear poverty or
recoil before infamy. There is nothing slavish, nothing lowly
about him. He does not say or do anything at the pleasure of
others but heeds himself, obeys himself, moderates everything
in accord with his steadfast judgment. He lacks neither friends
nor guests; he lacks nothing. The wise man alone is great, pow-   245
erful, fortunate, his own man. He knows that no violence can
be applied to him. He thinks that harm done by another is
damaging not to himself but to the one who inflicted it. He
knows that he on whom his integrity has bestowed honor can
be marked by no disgrace. If we must take offense at anything,
we must do so for the sake of those who, spontaneously making
themselves guilty of ingratitude, claim, with the most brazen
wickedness, to be proven innocent of any crime. If, my son
Onofrio, you carefully contemplate these points, not only will
you not be distressed, but you will rather rejoice that we are the
kind of men that scoundrels hate.

Onofrio. I have gladly listened, father, to the salutary message you   246
have taught and want very much to be completely convinced by
it. But if you consider the time right, a small question remains
that I should like to pose.

Palla. You can ask tomorrow about any remaining point you wish.
For now evening is coming on, and we are going to discuss certain matters in relation to our common cause. I know that this
is also Rinaldo's view.

Rinaldo. You have advised quite rightly, Palla. Ridolfo Peruzzi here
has also signaled his approval.

LIBER SECUNDUS

De Infamia

COLLOCUTORES

Rainaldus
Pallas
Rhodulphus
Honofrius
Nicolaus
Poggius
Manettus
Soderinus

1 Phidiam qui famae cupiditatis magnitudinem ostendunt proferre quasi locupletissimum testem quempiam volentes, aiunt ita suam effigiem in eburneae illius Minervae clipeo illigasse ut nulla omnino arte sine totius operis dissolutione convelli posset. Huic enim cum non liceret in eiusmodi sigillo nomen suum inscribere, hoc pacto nominis celebritatem apud posteros proinde[1] atque egregiam et singularem aliquam tam praeclari muneris mercedem vaenari libuit. Neque fortassis absurde quis censeat mortales tam summopere duci famae dulcedine, quippe quae non secus virtutis prae-
2 mium vulgo iudicetur quam vitii poena solet infamia. Et profecto quod aliorum sermo de nobis gratum ac secundum testimonium facit, non iniuria nos delectat. Non enim videmur omnino vel hac ista qualicunque aura frustra plurimos maximosque labores diu multumque subiisse. Itaque consuerunt non nulli non parum perturbari siquidem quos praestantiae probitatisque meruerunt, quasi

180

BOOK TWO

On Infamy

SPEAKERS

Rinaldo degli Albizzi
Palla Strozzi
Ridolfo Peruzzi
Onofrio Strozzi
Niccolò della Luna
Poggio Bracciolini
Giannozzo Manetti
Francesco Soderini

Those who make clear the great extent of the desire for fame,   1
meaning to appeal to some trustworthy witness, say that Phidias
bound his own self-portrait on the shield of the famous ivory
statue of Minerva in such a way that it could not be detached by
any means at all without destroying the whole sculpture.[1] For although he was not allowed to inscribe his name on a statue like
this, he wished by this means to seek renown among later genera-
tions and a distinctive and unique reward for such an outstanding
work. Nor should anyone consider it an absurd thing for mortals
to be tremendously seduced by the sweet taste of fame; indeed,
fame is considered to be the reward for virtuous behavior by the
common man just as infamy is considered to be the punishment
for vice. And certainly we are justly pleased by what others say   2
about us when it makes for pleasant and favorable evidence of our
character. For then we do not appear to have taken upon ourselves
for so long so many and such great tasks in vain, just for the sake
of some publicity such as this. And so some men tend to be upset

abiecti ipsi et nullo hominum numero improbitatis ac nequitiae titulos ferant.² Quod eo videatur molestius, quo quis ab omni turpitudine alienior sit. Nam neque putari non iniustum potest ut qui propter illustris atque optimas actiones praemium debet, poe-
3 nam recipiat. Atqui ea res cum in iudicium venit, aliter atque aliter definitur. Non enim eadem mente et vulgus et sapientes iudicant. Alii temeritatis, alii rationis lance veritatem expendunt. Quare ut quid pro nobis aut adversus nos dicatur cogitandum est, ita opera danda maxime ut nihil nisi decore et splendide dici possit. Malle-que debemus esse, si utrunque fieri nequeat, quam videri boni. Nam plaerique opinionis errore (qui aliud nihil est quam falsi pro vero approbatio), non nulli animi perturbatione (quae iudicium
4 omne pervertit) in iudicando falluntur. Atque permultos quottidie intueri licet qui, fucata quadam subdolae virtutis imagine, cum omnium facinorosissimi flagitiosissimique sunt, et innocentes et sancti viri existimantur, dicuntur, praedicantur. Alii rursus, quos et aequos et bonos tum haberi, tum omnium sermone celebrari par sit, per omnem infamiae labem atque ignominiam in omnium prope ore versantur. Cui male iudicantium morbo cum alii multi praestantes et magni viri videntur obiecti, tum hi maxime, quos vel civilis furor vel invidorum insania contumeliosissime patrio solo
5 eiecerit ac exterminarit. Quo fit ut qui imbecilliore³ sunt animo, tanquam rerum humanarum imperiti ac rudes, non mediocrem sibi miseriae portionem accidisse arbitrentur, cum adversis rumoribus laborant. Cum igitur postridie eius diei quo de incommodis exilii summatim Florentini illi optimates quos impia inimicorum

if, though they have deserved the labels of excellence and integrity, they must tolerate reputations for wickedness and vice, as if they were contemptible men and nobodies. This is more difficult to bear the further someone is from any taint of shame, for it cannot be considered fair for someone to be punished who deserves a reward because of his distinguished and outstanding actions. When 3 the matter comes under scrutiny, it is explained one way by some, another way by others. For wise men and the common crowd do not make judgments with the same attitude. The latter weigh matters rashly, the former on the balance of reason. Therefore, just as what is said for or against us needs to be considered carefully, special efforts must be made so that nothing can be said unless it is said properly and honorably. We ought to have a preference, if both options are not possible, for being good rather than seeming good.[2] For many people are mistaken in forming judgments because of an error in their opinion (which is nothing other than approving of what is wrong instead of what is right), some because of emotion (which distorts every judgment). And it is possible to 4 observe on a daily basis many who, even though they are the most criminal and wicked of all, through a kind of cosmetic image of counterfeit virtue, are considered, spoken of, and proclaimed as holy and innocent men. On the other hand, there are others who deserve to be regarded as honest and good and to be praised by all who are labeled with every kind of stigma and disgrace of infamy in nearly everyone's gossip. Many other eminent and great men seem to have been exposed to this disease of bad judgment, but especially those whom either civil strife or the madness of envious men have, with gross insult, cast out and banished from their homeland. Whence it happens that those who have a rather weak 5 soul, inexperienced and untrained, as it were, in human affairs, think that they have incurred no small portion of bad fortune when they struggle against hostile gossip. So when on the day after the Florentine nobles, whom an ungodly conspiracy of their

coniuratio patria bonisque mulctarat commentati inter se sunt,
eodem ad Rainaldum Albizium vel salutandi vel consolandi gratia
venissem, audivi, cum ibi adessem, quonam modo et de bona et
mala fama iudicandum esset et quanti eam per sapientissimos et
gravissimos viros fieri oporteret, quidque sequendum et quid fu-
6 giendum foret. Nam cum essent qui infamiam in maximis malis
numerarent, multa ab iis prudentissimis viris subtiliter in eam rem
et copiosissime disputata sunt. Ac eum quidem omnem sermonem
summa cura memoriaque collectum in secundum hunc *De exilio*
librum contuli. Quem — quod de primo antea feceram — propterea
ad te dedi, Vitaliane Borrhomaee, quo id etiam unum quo aeque
ac lautissimis amplissimisque divitiis ornatus es, in teipso animad-
vertas: nihil pluris quicquam ducendum esse quam verum atque
solidum et idem omnium maximum virtutis praemium, quod aliud
nihil est, ut opinor, quam secundum virtutem ac Deum et operari
7 et agere. Id enim non in alieno arbitrio aut testimonio, sed in nostra potestate positum est neque nobis eripi a quopiam potest.
Quam quidem rem non prisci modo et eximia nobilitate philosophi videntur intellexisse, sed multo etiam firmius ac melius per
expressum indubitatumque testimonium et intellexit et confirmavit
virgo illa sanctissima pientissimaque[4] Iustina, Vitaliani regis filia,
quem auctorem fuisse constat paterni tui et generis et nominis. Illa
enim non apud humanam insaniam, sed apud Christum optimum
maximum per relligiosissima et constantissima sanctae pietatis
opera illud sibi praemium expetivit, paravit, consecuta est, quod
non solum a nemine aut auferri aut labefactari potest, verum et
8 sempiternum est et stabilissimum et maximum. Nunquam certe
qui accuratissime seipsum expenderit et mores suos quamdiligentissime exquisierit, aut multitudinis magis quam suo iudicio

enemies had punished with the loss of their homeland and possessions, were discussing the inconveniences of exile in general, I had
come to the home of Rinaldo Albizzi both to greet and console
them, I heard, while I was there, how good and bad reputations
should be considered, how much importance should be attached
to reputations by the wisest and most authoritative men, and what
ought to be pursued and what avoided. For even though some   6
people counted infamy among the worst of evils, many aspects of
this topic were discussed minutely and at length among these wise
men. And I have gathered and set down that entire discussion
with care and keen memory in this second book *On Exile*. Moreover, I have dedicated it to you Vitaliano Borromeo, as I did the
first one previously, so that you may notice in yourself the one
thing you have been graced with in the same degree as your most
splendid and ample wealth, that is, that there is nothing to be
reckoned of greater value than the true and solid, and even greatest of all rewards for integrity, which is, in my opinion, nothing
other than living and acting in accordance with virtue and God.
For this resides in our power, not in a stranger's opinion or testi-   7
mony, and it cannot be taken away from us by anyone. Not only
do the ancients and philosophers of the most uncommon excellence seem to have understood this fact, but Justina, that most
holy and reverential daughter of King Vitaliano, understood and
confirmed it much more confidently and better through her distinct and faithful example, a woman who is known to be the
founder of your paternal lineage and name. She sought, prepared,
and obtained that reward for herself not amid the insanity of human beings, but with Christ, the Best and Greatest,[3] through her
most holy and faithful works of sacred piety, a reward that not
only cannot be undermined or carried away by anyone but which
also is eternal, unshakable, and greatest. For the man who has   8
weighed himself carefully and investigated his own character with
utmost diligence would never rely more on the crowd's judgment

nitatur, aut apud homines quam apud Deum praemium malit. Sed
hanc rem omnem et facilius cognosces et melius si, quasi ea coram
geratur, audieris quonam pacto iidem summi viri de infamia, quae
ad exilium vel in primis videtur comes accedere, inter sese disse-
ruerint. Rainaldus enim Albizius, ingenti animo vir idemque prudentissimus, posteaquam intueretur et eosdem fere omnis quos
hesterno die et alios quosdam non infimae sortis homines apud
se convenisse, ita cum Pallante Stroza opportune sermonem aggre-
ditur.

9 *Rainaldus.* Quae nobis, Pallas, famae nota inusta est inimicorum
insidiis, ex animo exuri meo nunquam poterit; quod idem tibi
videri puto.

Pallas. Quidnam, Rainalde, novi accidit? Quae te tanta movere
possit infamia?

Rainaldus. Quod hesterno vesperi constitueramus, mane cum primum illuxisset, Rhodulphus hic et ego ad Eugenium accessi-
mus, quem non tam querentes — quod iustissime facere licebat — quam versi in preces omni ingenio solertiaque studuimus

10 causae nostrae patronum reddere. Nec tam quibus esset a nobis
affectus beneficiis commemoravimus, quam leniter monuimus
ne utilitatem cum honestate pugnare unquam arbitraretur, mal-
letque horum causam decorumque amplecti quos in difficillimis
rebus suis esset expertus, quam illis adesse quorum tum studia
olim habuisset adversa, tum praesens causa et turpis esset et
impia.

Pallas. Ille autem quid?

11 *Rainaldus.* Respondit is primum perhumane cum summa testifica-
tione et plurimorum et maximorum nostrorum erga se merito-
rum, cum nihil se magis cupere, nihil magis optare diceret
quam nobis nostraeque reipublicae gratias quamcumulatis-
sime aliquando relatum ire. Deinde altius suspirans ait: 'Doleo
equidem, filii, etiam atque etiam, quod is de vobis rumor

than his own or prefer a reward at the hands of men, rather than God. But you will more easily and better understand this entire topic if you hear, as if it were carried out in your presence, how the same great men discussed infamy, which seems to be especially associated with exile. Rinaldo degli Albizzi, a man of great soul and great wisdom, after he saw that nearly all the same men from the previous day, and some others of the highest rank, had gathered at his house, began a timely conversation with Palla Strozzi.

Rinaldo. The unfair stigma that has been affixed to us by our enemies can never be blotted out of my mind; I believe you are of the same opinion. 9

Palla. Rinaldo, what new disaster has befallen us? What infamy could so deeply unsettle you?

Rinaldo. As we decided yesterday evening, Ridolfo and I approached Eugenius at dawn this morning, whom we were keen to win over as a supporter of our cause. We did this without complaining — though that would have been perfectly justifiable — but besought him on bended knee with all the wit and cleverness at our disposal. Nor did we so much call to mind the 10 favors he had received from us as gently caution him against supposing that interest is ever at odds with the good[4] and that he should rather embrace the cause and honor of men whom he had tested in their most trying circumstances than lend support to those whose opposition he had once faced and whose present cause was both shameful and dishonorable.[5]

Palla. What did he say?

Rinaldo. He at first replied with great kindness citing our numerous and substantial services toward himself since he claimed that he hoped and wished for nothing more than that he could someday render the fullest possible thanks to us and to our republic. Then, sighing deeply, he went on: "I am pained, my sons, again and again that the rumor about you has been 11

dispersus in populum longe lateque sit, ut nobis minus licere videatur tueri causam vestram. Nam vulgo praedicant sensisse vos cum Philippo Maria. Quid inquam sensisse? Imo vestram vos illi rempublicam tradere constituisse cum Gerardo Landriano Laudensi pontifice, eius impraesentiarum ad nos oratore. Id si quidem ita est, quam possim honeste favere causae vestrae, ipsi iudicate.'

Pallas. At vos, Rainalde, quid tandem ad ista?

Rainaldus. Exponat id tibi Rhodulpus velim. Nam ego sum non mediocriter permotus.

Pallas. Quid, inquam, ad ista, Rhodulphe, responsum a vobis est?

Rhodulphus. Profecto, Pallas, cum semper antehac Rainaldum tum vel maxime hoc die sum admiratus. Cum enim in dicendo antea reliquos omnis nostrae civitatis sapientes et perdisertos viros semper consuevit, tum ita nunc apud Eugenium communem causam egit, ut non solum superasse seipsum, sed divinum quoddam eloquentiae numen secum habere videretur. Quanta enim, proh Deum atque hominum fidem, eius in dicendo copia, quanta vis, quanta gravitas, quanta maiestas![5] Quid non acutissime invenit, non subtilissime locutus est! Quocunque oratione invaderet, et disturbabat cuncta et dissipabat. Nec vires tantum in verbis inerant insuperabiles, sed nitoris quoque ac palaestrae plurimum. Quare cum principio vaehementer Eugenium quo voluit movisset, ita reliquo decursu orationis, cum fidem faceret, mirabili quadam rerum continuatione ac serie — nam quae dicebat alia ex aliis nexa omnia et omnia inter se apta quodam quasi artificio ita erant et colligata, ut nemo inveniri posset adeo indocilis ac tardus, adeo durus atque inexorabilis, qui insignes

12

13

14

disseminated so far and wide among the people that it would seem impossible for me to defend your cause. For the common gossip has it that you sided with Filippo Maria [Visconti]. Why do I say 'sided with'? Rather, that you had decided to be- 12 tray your republic to that prince in collaboration with Gerardo Landriani,[6] bishop of Lodi, his current ambassador to us. If that is so, you yourself may judge how I could honorably take your side."

Palla. But, Rinaldo, what did you say in response to these rumors?

Rinaldo. I would like Ridolfo to expound that to you, since I am overcome by emotion.

Palla. What response, I repeat, was made by you, Ridolfo, to these allegations?

Ridolfo. Palla, though in the past I have always held Rinaldo in the 13 highest esteem, I did so particularly on that day. For he was previously accustomed to excel the rest of the wise and eloquent men of our state, so now he pleaded our common case before Eugenius in such a way that he not only seemed to surpass himself but to have with him a kind of marvelous, supernatural gift of eloquence. By the faith of God and men, how rich was his supply of arguments, what power, what authority, what grandeur! What argument did he not shrewdly discover and express with fine nuance! Whatever direction he took in his speech, he threw all opposing arguments into confusion and scattered them. His words not only possessed invincible power but a good deal of polish and training. Therefore after he had 14 at the beginning of the speech taken hold of Eugenius and moved him in the desired direction, in the further course of the speech, when he won his trust with an amazing string and se- ries of points — for his arguments were all bound one to the other and coordinated with each other as if by some craftsman- ship so that no one could be found so doltish and slow, so

illas illustrisque sententias vel minus assequeretur vel non facile
indubitatoque probaret — ita, inquam, deinde, cum fidem faceret, eum constituit, ut ubi ad perorationem ventum est, quam-
minimo labore impelleretur, palamque et clara voce fateretur
nobis rem esse cum sordidis impiisque latronibus, qui nihil
15   pensi habeant, nihil sancti; verum debere nos malle Christum
imitari quam Iudam (nam pati quam facere iniuriam longe
praestare) sibi vero hoc tempore aliud quicquam quam et com-
misereri et solita mentis pietate nos complecti, prorsus licere
nihil, sed brevi futurum sperare se ut nos vel inopinantis e mor-
tuis vivos reddat et e tenebris reducat in lucem, quippe qui
suopte ingenio improborum omnium perpetuus atque acerri-
mus hostis sit, eorum vero qui probitatem ac laudem foveant et
amicus diligens et propugnator invictus.

16   *Pallas.*[6] Quantum intelligere possum, vincere nos, Rhodulphe,
oportuit. Tamen, utcunque futurum est, bona nos Eugenius
spe, bono animo esse iubet. Ac ita certe faciundum censeo.
Nam multa dies affert,[7] multa ratio.

     Rainaldus. Oh, nox illa, Pallas, fausta malis, funesta bonis, quae et
e manibus nostris paratam certamque victoriam extorsit, et
seditiosis consceleratisque latronibus lacerandam patriam atque
interimendam tradidit!

17   *Pallas.* Fateor, Rainalde, me totius huius nostrae calamitatis et
auctorem et ducem et principem fuisse. Qui dum publicae
quieti bene consultum cupio, inertissimorum nequissimorum-
que hominum dolis ac periuriis circunventus, omni quiete atque
ocio disturbato, non alui solum spem impiorum parricidarum,
sed impetum quoque et furorem corroboravi. Itaque fateor
me stultum et imperitum, qui nefarrios eorum coeptus non

unfeeling and unpersuadable that he would not follow those distinguished and brilliant thoughts or not, easily and without question, grant approval—then, when he won his trust, I say, he so disposed him that, when he came to the close of the speech, with only the slightest effort he prompted Eugenius to acknowledge openly and explicitly that our opponents are vile and wicked cutthroats who have no authority, no scruples. We 15 ought rather to imitate Christ than Judas, since it is far better to suffer than to commit wrong; at this time he can do nothing, other than to offer his condolences and embrace us with his usual loyalty, but he hopes that he can in a short time, though we little expect it, restore us as living men from the dead and bring us back from darkness to light, since he is by his nature an unremitting and ferocious enemy of all scoundrels, but a committed friend and invincible champion of those who cherish virtue and excellence.

Palla. As far as I know, Ridolfo, we ought to prevail. All the same, 16 whatever will be, Eugenius bids us be of good hope and good cheer. I think we should do so, for time and thought bring many things to light.

Rinaldo. Ah, Palla, that night, propitious for the wicked, ill-omened for the good, was one that wrested a well-founded and assured victory from our hands and delivered our homeland to treasonous and wicked cutthroats for them to attack and destroy!

Palla. I admit, Rinaldo, that I was the author, leader, and prime 17 mover of this disaster of ours. While I was aiming to insure the tranquility of the state, I was ensnared by the tricks and lies of lazy and worthless men; once all tranquility and peace were upset, I not only fed the hopes of the wicked parricides, but I even added strength to their violent madness. So I acknowledge that I was stupid and foolish in failing to perceive their wicked agenda; they, however were worthless scoundrels who

adverterim, eos vero nequam et improbos, qui nihil nisi de flagitio et scelere cogitarint. Quae quidem iniuria quo durior est, pestilentior, atrocior, ferior, eo minus — siquidem maximi animi haberi et esse volumus — commoveri nos decet. Ita enim et fruemur iniuria et omnem contumeliam vertemus in nostram laudem.

18 *Rainaldus.* At ego magni profecto interesse arbitror ad decus et ad laudem nostram si non adeo nosmetipsos vel segnis vel stupidos praestiterimus ut nostrum atque bonorum civium patrocinium deseruisse reliquisseque iudicemur, nec eam existimemur neglexisse defensionem quam nostrae ac patriae libertatis ratio praescribat. Quare siqua est reliqua in nobis diligentia, siqua virtus, siqua consensio, omni via et arte temptandum est, elaborandum, efficiendum ut quae scelerum omnium et inveterati furoris adultaeque audaciae maturitas in nostram tandem aetatem eruperit, etiam si in maximis periculis insidiisque versamur,

19 ea omnis contabescat, solvatur, intereat. Nec enim ferendum est ut qui lucem huic reipublicae per omne facinus ac probrum eripuerunt et noctem quasi quampiam offuderunt, illustres ipsi atque praeclari fiant, nos autem obscurati nominis tenebras subeamus. Et quamquam secus sum modo visus apud Eugenium dicere, adversi rumores negligendi non sunt, neque famae nota contemnenda.

Honofrius. Equidem, Rainalde, si mihi a patre ignosci existimarem, interpolator[8] paululum accederem.

Rainaldus. Quid ais, Pallas?

Pallas. Loquatur quae velit, quandoquidem ociosi sumus.

Rainaldus. Cedo igitur, Honofri. Nam tuae me argutiae delectant.

20 *Honofrius.* Faciam, Rainalde, et eo quidem libentius quod Nicolaus hic Luna, quo familiarissime et coniunctissime utor, ut est eloquentiae et bonarum artium studiosus, iamdudum mecum

had nothing in mind except their outrageous crime. The harsher, more deadly, more outrageous, more savage that wrong is the less fitting it is for us — if we want to be considered and to be of great soul — to be shaken. For in this way we shall reap benefit of the wrong and convert all insult to our glory.

Rinaldo. I think it makes a great deal of difference to our honor 18 and glory that we not show ourselves so sluggish or dimwitted that we be thought to have abandoned our advocacy on behalf of ourselves and the sensible citizens or to have taken lightly the defensive action dictated by a policy of liberty for ourselves and our country. Therefore if we still have any care, courage, or consensus left, we must endeavor, work, and engineer by every means and skill that the ripe harvest of all crimes, of deep-seated madness, and full-grown criminality that has finally burst out into our times waste away, be dissolved, perish, even though we are beset by extreme dangers and plots. It is 19 indeed intolerable that those who by every crime and disgraceful act have robbed this republic of its light and have poured, as it were, a kind of night over it, become distinguished and famous, whereas we enter the darkness of an eclipsed reputation. And although I appeared to say otherwise just now at Eugenius' house, one should not make light of hostile rumors, nor should a black mark on one's reputation be despised.

Onofrio. Rinaldo, if I thought my father would pardon me, I would join in with a brief intervention.

Rinaldo. What say you, Palla?

Palla. Since we are at leisure, let him speak his mind.

Rinaldo. I yield you the floor, Onofrio, since I find your cleverness charming.

Onofrio. I shall speak, Rinaldo, and all the more gladly since my 20 very close friend Niccolò della Luna here, being a keen student of oratory and the liberal arts, has for some time now been

agit ut abs te petam—quod sine tua molestia fiat—ut quam
mane ad Eugenium orationem habuisti in medium proferas.
Quam ipse quoque audire mirifice percupio, non solum quod
vel Rhodulphi testimonio, viri omnibus rebus ornati, gravitate
et sapientia tua dignam fuisse audio, verum etiam quia discendi
sum avidus quid de rumore adversus innocentiam nostram dis-
21   perso in populum, quid de infamia sis locutus. Nam cum alia
quaedam hesterno vesperi, tum hac de re, quo doctior fierem,
dicturus eram ad patrem. Nam quae antea de infamia locutus
fuerat, satis quidem pro tempore locutus est, sed mihi non satis
omnino, id quod etiam tibi ex iis quae modo dicebas videri arbitror. Quamobrem si pro tua humanitate tuam nobis orationem recensueris, non modo meo huic Nicolao, sed mihi etiam
morem gesseris.

22   *Rainaldus.* An idem sentis tu, Nicolae?

    Nicolaus. Maxime. Nam ex iis quas de tua eloquentia laudes quot-
tidie audio ex patre, incredibilis me cupiditas tenet audiendi tui.
Quare cum inter inambulandum modo in forum obviam ha-
buissem Iannotium istum Manettum, qui cum hoc isto Francisco Soderino hesternam et Pallantis et tuam de incommodis
exilii disputationem efferret ad caelum, meque ut ad audiendum
accederem invitaret—se enim et Soderinum ad vos maturare—
non fuit longa cohortatione opus. Itaque ut tam diuturnum
desyderium meum ex aliqua parte expleri sinas, te plurimum
obsecro. Erit enim hoc mihi tam gratum quam quod omnium
maxime.

23   *Rainaldus.* Obsequerer sane tibi, Nicolae, ac item Honofrio nostro, si quod petistis praestari a me posset. Sed quia sum paulisper animo perturbato ex hac rerum indignitate, patiamini licet
aequo animo silentium meum. Praeterea nec meditatus ad dicendum accesseram (nam qui scire poteram Eugenium de infamia responsurum, qui vel in primis nostrae innocentiae testis

pleading with me to ask you — and I hope it's no trouble for you — that you share the speech that you gave to Eugenius this morning. I, too, am very desirous of hearing it, not only because I have heard, on the testimony of Ridolfo, a man thoroughly steeped in culture, that it was worthy of your wisdom and reputation for seriousness but also because I am eager to learn what you said about the rumor disseminated to the public against our innocence and about infamy. For yesterday evening   21 I was about to speak to my father about other matters and this topic in particular, in order to strengthen my knowledge. For his previous discourse about infamy was sufficient in view of the time but, I thought, not altogether so; from what you just said, I believe you hold the same view. Therefore if you will have the kindness to repeat your speech for us, you will be obliging not only my friend Niccolò here, but me as well.

Rinaldo. Is that also your view, Niccolò?   22

Niccolò. Indeed it is. For in view of the commendation of your eloquence that I hear each day from my father, I am gripped by an incredible eagerness to hear you. And so when I was walking to the town square just now and met Giannozzo Manetti, who, together with Francesco Soderini here was praising to the skies the discussion of the harms of exile that you and Palla conducted yesterday, and he invited me to come to hear — he and Soderini were hastening to you — they did not have to urge us at great length. Therefore I earnestly implore you to allow my longstanding wish to be fulfilled. For this will give me the greatest satisfaction of all.

Rinaldo. I would indeed oblige you, Niccolò, and our friend Ono-   23 frio as well, if I could supply what you have requested. But since I am a little bit upset by this undeserved turn of events, please bear with my silence. Moreover, I did not go with any preparation for speaking. For how could I have known that Eugenius, who was above all a witness of our innocence, would offer a

esset?), nec ea quae quasi Demades aliquis sum locutus vel orationis nomine digna sunt.

24 *Rhodulphus.* Sine, Rainalde, quaeso, exorari te. Mos gerendus est
adolescentibus tui, ut vides, studiosis. Quod si minus feceris,
ipse pro te gratiam inibo. Nam quae dixisti, commendavi ita ut
sum senex memoriae omnia diligenter.

Rainaldus. Recte, Rhodulphe, mones. Nam nec ego placeo mihi,
nec ex tempore ac tumultuarie locutus quae sum, satis memini.
Itaque ut gratiam istam omnem ineas, non modo non graviter
fero, sed etiam laetor.

25 *Rhodulphus.* Faciam equidem quod te velle animadverto, etsi pro-
nunciatio ipsa, quae vim maximam in dicendo habet, mihi non
eadem futura est qua tu unus omnium excellis maxime. Posteaquam Eugenius, perorata iam a Rainaldo communi optimatium
et honestissimorum civium causa, perhumane admodum multa
perbenigneque respondisset, subiunxissetque ad postremum
quod de rumore in nos per homines sacrilegos concitato inepti
quidam fabularentur, ita rursum Rainaldus exorsus est:

26   'Existimabam equidem, pater sanctissime, id nostris multis
ac maximis laboribus et vigiliis nos apud te iampridem assecutos, ut omnem optimatium vitam non secus ac solem et illustra-
tam haberes et patefactam. De quorum voluntate, studiis, institutis, moribus quid est quod aliud quisquam vel sentire vel
loqui possit quam et praeclara et summa omnia? Quae quidem
ipse tu, si aequus aestimator et iudex esse perrexeris, si tibi
quam nefarriis patriae proditoribus praebere aures malueris,
non solum me dicente recognosces, sed et capesses pro tua
dignitate causam nostram, et audaciae domesticorum hostium
non modo non cedes, sed ultro etiam pro tua iusticia et animi
magnitudine occurres, depelles impetus, furiosam temeritatem
27 compesces, insaniam comprimes. Nam quem alium hoc tempore

reply on the topic of infamy? What I said, like some Demades, is unworthy of the name "oration."[7]

Ridolfo. Please, Rinaldo, allow yourself to be persuaded. You should humor young men who, as you see, are your fervent partisans. But if you would not, I will undertake the favor on your behalf. For I committed all that you said to memory, insofar as my advanced age allowed.   24

Rinaldo. You rightly caution me, Ridolfo. I am neither satisfied with my performance nor do I sufficiently remember what I said on the spot and in some confusion. And so I am not only not offended but even glad for you to undertake that favor.

Ridolfo. I shall do so, since I see that is what you want, even if the delivery itself, which has the greatest power in oratory[8] and in which you above all excel, will not be the same. When Rinaldo had finished speaking about the common cause of the nobles and loyal citizens, and Eugenius had replied at length and with great affability and kindness and at the end added what some boors were saying against us on the basis of a rumor stirred up by unscrupulous persons, Rinaldo in his turn began as follows: 25

"I thought, holy father, that we had through our intense and alert efforts long ago achieved a place in your thinking such that you considered the entire life of the nobles to be as brilliant and visible as the sun. What else could anyone either think or say about their intentions, their pursuits, their customs, and their character than that they are all of utmost distinction and quality? If you continue to be a fair assessor and judge and to lend your ears to yourself rather than to wicked traitors to their homeland, you will not only recognize these points when I say them but you will even, in accord with your standing, adopt our cause and not only not yield to the criminality of domestic enemies but, in line with your justice and greatness of soul, take the initiative on your own, beat back their attacks, check their raging audacity, and squelch their madness. For at this time we   26   27

appellemus, obtestemur, imploremus, habemus neminem. Cum publicis enim legibus ac iudiciis reliqua nostra omnia perfugia, praesidia, subsidia, opes, consilia ceciderunt; quae ut releves ac tollas, tuae sapientiae et aequitatis est. Agitur de republica Florentina; at de ecclesiastica item agitur. Agitur de Florentino, de communi optimatium statu ac salute; at de tuo quoque et ecclesiastico principatu et incolumitate agitur. Agitur, inquam, agitur de spe omnium bonorum; quam si sustentare tuerique volueris, intelliges—mihi crede—intelliges profecto et tibiipsi et ecclesiae Romanae te salutifere et pro tua amplitudine prospexisse.

28   'Ais tu, summe pontifex Eugeni, increbuisse publicis rumoribus apud populum Florentinum, sensisse viros optimatis cum Philippo Maria et ei nostram rempublicam traditum ire cum Gerardo Landriano pontifice, illius ad te legato, constituisse; cuius quidem rei infamia non licere tibi pro tua dignitate studere causae nostrae. Magna profecto est conscientiae vis, magnum innocentiae robur, magna illesae mentis constantia. Neque fieri ullo pacto potest quin is qui cuipiam facinori sit obnoxius, vel vultu vel sermone, vel aliquo corporis motu ac gestu, latentem animi morbum exprimat, et reluctantem etiam excutiat. Nulla enim arte, nulla calliditate depravari omnino potest soler-

29   tia sagacitasque naturae. Itaque si me dicentem attenderis, si aut oris aut totius corporis motum atque habitum animadverteris, quantum rumorum vel vanitati vel perfidiae credendum sit, pro tua ista acutissima mentis acie divinaque sapientia facile perspicias. Qui recte sibi suaeque reipublicae consultum volunt, duo sibi proponere in primis solent: et honestum et utile. Nam quamquam utilitas ab honestate seiungi nequit, ipse tamen

have no other on whom to call, no one to appeal to or beseech. Along with the public laws and policies our entire refuge, our guard, our resources, and plans have fallen to the ground; to lift them up and revive them is the task of your wisdom and justice. The Republic of Florence hangs in the balance, but so does the Church. The common position and well-being of Florence and the nobles is at stake but also that the primacy of you and of the Church be kept intact. What is at issue, I say, is the hope of all sound citizens; if you are willing to support and guard it, you will understand — believe me — you will truly understand that, in accordance with your stature, you have looked out for yourself and the Church of Rome, with yourself as her safeguard.

"You say, Eugenius, supreme pontiff, that among the people   28
of Florence the public rumor is rife that the nobles conspired with Filippo Maria and had resolved with bishop Gerardo Landriano, his ambassador to you, to betray our Republic to him; in view of the infamy of this plan you may not, in view of your stature, support our cause. The force of conscience is great, great the strength of innocence, great the steadiness of an intact mind. It is quite impossible for anyone guilty of crime to avoid expressing, by facial appearance, speech, or some bodily movement, the mind's latent illness, thereby bringing it to light, however unwillingly. For nature's cleverness and keenness cannot be frustrated by any artifice or shrewdness. Therefore if you   29
pay close attention to me as I speak, if you take note of the movement and state of my face and my entire body, with your mental keenness and unparalleled wisdom you may easily perceive how much stock to place in the speciousness or treachery of rumors. Those who wish to take proper thought for themselves and their homeland tend to consider two points in particular: the honorable and the expedient. For although the expedient cannot be divorced from the honorable, I shall

seiungam verbo quae re omnino coniuncta sunt, ut anteaquam de rumoribus loquar, intelligas quam perperam ac perniciose et ad rem et ad dignitatem cum publice tum privatim nobis consuluissemus, si regi quam regere, si servi quam liberi ac domini esse maluissemus.

30 'Et ut de honestate prius disseram: huius tantam vim esse arbitror, ut cum nullis omnino neque commodis sit nec emolumentis comparanda. Quid enim est virtute pulchrius, quid maius, quid admirabilius, quid divinius? Videmus quottidie reliqua omnia quae corpori sunt fortunaeve tributa, omni brevi momento decorem suum omnem qui videbatur magnitudinemque amittere, et quae spectationi stuporique fuerant, et contemni et haberi pro nihilo. At virtutis decus in dies magis magisque efflorescit, pubescit vigor, maiestas[9] crescit in cumulum, et quam nulla vis externa potest eripere, sua bonitate diuturnitateque immortalis eos atque felices efficit quorum sit delectata 31 hospitio. Haec una profecto est, quae omnia conservet, alat, augeat, sustineat ac veluti sensu afficiat. Non aliunde virtus pendet, nulla petit subsidia, sed seipsa contenta est. Nullis adminiculis nititur, sed ita radicibus suis haeret ut neque impetum sciat neque necessitatem ullam pertimescat. Et qua ipsa non eget, opem omnibus pollicetur. Quare qui huius praesidiis utitur, nunquam in bonorum potest aut in malorum errore et ignoratione versari. Nam et superiora secum memoria repetit et praesentia perspicit, et multo ante quam facta sint, futura omnia providet. Ita praeterea sese accingit ut neque faciat cuiquam 32 nec vel in se vel in alterum patiatur iniuriam. Sed quoniam exploratum et firmum ducit, ubi pietas adversus Deum non sit, ibi neque fidem neque societatem hominum neque iustitiam esse posse, humanum omne atque divinum ius aeque observat ac veretur. In periculis vero atque laboribus ita est magno et

nonetheless in theory separate elements completely joined in fact,[9] so that before I speak about rumors you may understand how badly and destructively we would have consulted our own interests, both for the issue at hand and for our own status, both privately and publicly, had we preferred to be ruled rather than to rule, to be slaves rather than to be free men and masters.

"To begin with what is honorable: I think that this has such   30 great force that it may be compared with no advantages or material gains of any kind.[10] For what is more comely than virtue, what greater, more wonderful, more divine? Each day we see all the other qualities assigned to the body or to fortune lose in an instant all their seeming glory and grandeur, and we see qualities that had been looked at with stupefied wonder despised and held to be worthless. But the glory of virtue flourishes ever more with time, its vitality matures, its grandeur rises to completeness; no outside force can snatch it away; and by its goodness and long duration it immortalizes and blesses those with whom it is pleased to reside. This is the one quality that pre-   31 serves, nurtures, fosters, supports all things and as it were endows them with sense. Virtue depends on nothing else, seeks no support, is content with itself. It relies upon no aids but clings so fixedly by its own roots that it neither feels any attack nor fears any compulsion; and while requiring none herself, she avows aid to all. Therefore whoever takes advantage of virtue's protection can never be wrong or ignorant about goods and evils, recalls events of the past, has insight into present ones, and foresees all future ones before they occur. In addition, he so prepares himself that he neither inflicts harm on anyone nor allows harm to be inflicted on another. But since he considers it   32 a proven and reliable tenet that where piety toward God is lacking, there can be neither good faith nor fellowship nor justice among men, he equally keeps and reveres every human and divine law. In dangers and hardships he has such a great and

excelso animo, ita est fiduciae bonaeque spei plenus, ita et tole-
rantem sese et perseverantem praestat, ut non modo non terrea-
tur ullis aut belli aut doloris aut mortis etiam minis, sed vel
ultro adeat ac perferat. Cupiditates autem omnis et temerarias
animi concitationes atque insanos aestus ea gubernatione regit,
ea comitate retinet, eo pudore placat ac fingit, ut non modo non
posse, sed ne velle quidem obesse videantur. Et quis adeo mente
barbara sese truculentum saevumque praebuerit, ut in patriam,
33   ut in semetipsum armet libidinem suam? Quid enim, per immortalem Deum, turpius,[10] quid foedius, quid flagitiosius[11]
quam se ita prosternere atque abiicere ut nihil a languida quapiam et inerti pecude differre existimetur? Quid magis ab homine alienum quam qui ita sit natura et factus et constitutus ut
caeteris animantibus praesit atque dominetur, eum sic humilem
ignavumque videri, sic demitti ac frangi, ut multis etiam beluis
sit inferior? Quot enim animalia reperiantur quae non tam
mente ac ratione quam mentis et rationis imagine, pro quadam
infusa naturae vi, nullis blandiciis, nullis oblectationibus, nullis
artibus induci, nullis denique neque minis nec verberibus cogi
ad servitutem queant? Nam iniuriae sibi aut suis esse ne animantis quidem est.

34   'Atqui et fuerunt et sunt non nulli (et ii quidem admodum
detestabiles) qui regnandi gratia minus vituperarint iniuriam.
Itaque impios illos Euripidis versus,

Nam siquidem ius deseras, regni decet
causa relinquas, rebus in aliis pius,

crebro solent usurpare sermone, quippe qui fortis ac magna-
nimi esse dictitent imperare, non pati imperium. Quibus sane

elevated soul that he is full of confidence and good hope; he
shows himself so enduring and persevering that he is not only
undaunted by any threats of war, suffering, or death, but voluntarily undertakes and endures them. He rules the desires and
rash impulses and insane emotions of the mind with such mas-
tery, holds them back with such good humor, and appeases and
molds them with such modesty that they seem not only to be
unable but not even to want to cause mischief. Who has shown
himself so barbarous, so harsh and cruel as to arm his lust for
power against his homeland and against himself? By immortal
God, what is more disgraceful, foul, shameful than to lay onself
so low as to be thought to differ not at all from some sluggish
and lazy beast? What is more unlike a man than for him who
has been made and set in place by nature that he be at the head
of and exercise dominion over other living things to be seen to
be so lowly and craven, so downcast and broken, that he is inferior even to many beasts? For how many animals may be found
that, not so much by the mind's reason as by a false image of
the mind's reason, by dint of a certain inherent force of nature,
can be induced by no honeyed words, no treats, no arts, can finally be compelled by no threats or lashes to enter into slavery?
For it is not natural even for an animal to harm itself or its own
family.

"And yet there are and have been some (and utterly execrable
they are) who would withhold criticism of wrongdoing for the
sake of maintaining power. Hence they are frequently abusing
those notoriously wicked verses of Euripides,

If you abandon justice, it is fitting to do so
For the sake of rule; be god-fearing in other matters,[11]

since their constant refrain is that it is the part of the brave
and great-souled man to exercise power rather than be subject to rule. I would think that leadership should be conceded

concedendum putarem, si ab aspectu iusticiae — quo nihil est insatiabilius, nihil formosius, nihil praestantius — si a communi utilitate, si a dignitate publica non discederent. Sed qui sic habet mentem immanitate efferatam ut splendorem incolumitatemque reipublicae suis commodis metiatur, in eo nulla pietas,

35   nulla sanctitas, nulla relligio esse potest. At quem usque gentium tam delirum atque amentem unquam, tam suiipsius, tam animantis omnino dissimilem inveniri putem, qui suam et publicam libertatem cum servitute commutet? Et qui vel princeps in civitate vel inter principes sit, ipse sibi dominum constituat? Eninvero quonam pacto qui ex omnibus animalibus rationis et cogitationis particeps, providus, sagax, multiplex, acutus, memor (quid plura?), mentis et consilii plenus sit, se adeo mentis praestet atque sensus inopem, ut neque praeterita meminerit,

36   nec intelligat praesentia, nec futura cogitet? Quae nos capere unquam oblivio tanta potuisset ut non proxima solum, sed vetera etiam illa quae populo Florentino cum Insubribus fere semper Ligurumque principibus bella plurima et maxima fuere, minus meminissemus? Quis adeo amens sit, qui nolit planam et stabilem vitae viam praecipiti ac lubricae anteferre? Praesertim cum ignari nequaquam simus eum qui bona, constanti gravique ratione sit fraetus, fructum omnem habere propositum; qui vero temeritatis agatur ductu, aliud nihil nisi pestem, perniciem, exitium expectare debere.

37   'Et enim quanam causa impulsi, nostram rempublicam nobiscum perditum ire hac tempestate per nefarriam sceleris immanitatem voluissemus, praesertim belli et pacis domi ac foris rebus secundis nostris, qui antea semper non modo exceperimus lacessiti intrepidis atque maximis animis pro libertate publica, verum etiam ultro susceperimus saepe ingentem bellorum

to them if they do not deviate from the appearance of justice—
than which nothing tends to be more satisfying, nothing more
beautiful, nothing more excellent—from the common interest,
and from public standing. But in a man whose mind has been
so carried away in cruelty that he measures the glory and safety
of the republic by his own interests, there is no room for the
fear of God, holiness, or religion. And who among all peoples   35
am I to suppose is found to be such a raving lunatic, so unlike
himself and an animal that he would exchange his own and the
public liberty for slavery? And who that has been the leading
citizen or among the leaders in the state would set a master
over himself? For how could one who of all animals partakes in
reason and thought, who is endowed with foresight, shrewd,
versatile, clever, endowed with memory (why go on?), filled
with intelligence and good counsel,[12] show himself so bereft of
reason and intelligence as to forget the past, fail to understand
the present, and take no thought for the future? How could   36
such forgetfulness lay hold of us that we fail to remember not
only the recent wars but even those numerous ancient, large-
scale ones that raged between the Florentine people and the
Lombards and the princes of the Ligurians? Who is so insane
as not to prefer a level and solid path of life to a steep and slip-
pery one? Especially since we know full well that he who relies
on a sound, steady and weighty reasoning faculty has the prospect of enjoying every fruit, whereas he who is guided by impulse should expect nothing except calamity, ruin, and destruction.

 "Moreover, with what motive would we have wanted, with   37
monstrous wickedness, our republic to be destroyed at this time
along with us, especially when in the past, during our heyday, in
war and peace, at home and abroad, when provoked, we not
only accepted the enormous onslaught and toil of wars intrep-
idly and with keen courage on behalf of the liberty of the state

impetum ac molem, pro communi dignitate atque splendore, adversus eosdem principes? Nec solum de imperio dimicatum est, sed de salute et vita. Nam quam nobis spem ullam proponi posse putaremus, quid aut magnificentius aut optatius expectandum fuisset, amissa gloria, principatu, patria? At vide quam tibi, quam prudenti cuique ab istis quos in populum rumores dispersos ais dissentiendum sit. Ita mihi et reliquis optimatibus

38 ac caeteris bonis civibus aliquando contingat salva frui incolumique patria, ut esse neminem suspicor Florentini generis et nominis, non optimatem duntaxat et honestum virum, sed ne infimae quidem abiectaeque sortis hominem — Cosmum tamen Medicem semper excipi ac secerni velim cum reliquis posteris senioris illius Cosmi, qui (quod omnes norunt) patria Mucellensis tristibus luctuosisque temporibus receptus in civitatem fuerat per flagitiosam ac nefandam turpitudinis foeditatem — nullum, inquam, prorsus esse Florentinum suspicor qui exquisitissimis etiam ac maximis et inauditis propositis praemiis contra

39 patriam initurus consilium unquam sit. Viros autem optimatis, quos et animi et consilii et pietatis et constantiae magnitudine non Florentiae tantum sed — quod aliorum pace dictum velim — totius etiam Italiae ornamenta ac lumina et esse et iure habendos arbitror, quae tanta feritas, asperitas, inhumanitas, quae tanta immanitas, quae crudelitas tanta capere potuisset, ut se per tantam iniuriarum scelerumque licentiam et suiipsorum notari vellent et patriae proditores? An qui aliis continentiae semper fuerint atque innocentiae exemplo, eos effraenata adeo praecepsque libido aut ullum tantum flagitii precium aut oscoenae ingens quaepiam mercedis magnitudo ita depravasset corrupissetque, ut se neque optimatis nec civis nec homines esse meminissent?

40 'Sed quoniam de honestatis parte satis mihi dixisse videor, iam quae separatim ad utilitatem spectant paucis perstringam.

but even took it on spontaneously on behalf of the common dignity and glory against those same princes? We did not just fight for power, but for our security and survival. For what hope should we suppose has been offered us, what grander or more desirable prize were we to hope for once we had lost glory, social standing, and homeland? But consider how you and every wise man ought to be at variance with the rumors you say have been disseminated to the public. So may it befall me and 38 the rest of the nobles and all other sound citizens one day to have the enjoyment of our homeland safe and intact, as I suspect that no one of Florentine blood and nation, not merely a noble and honorable man but not even a man of a low and abject kind — I would always want Cosimo de' Medici excepted and set apart together with the remaining posterity of that elder Cosimo, who (as all know) through scandalous and disgraceful vice had been received into the city in sad and lamentable times — I suspect, I say, that there is no Florentine who, even if the choicest, largest and unheard-of rewards were on offer, would ever plot against his homeland. As to the nobles, I hold 39 that in greatness of soul, wisdom, piety, and constancy they are and rightly ought to be considered not only the ornaments and luminaries of Florence but — I should like this said with the permission of the rest — of the whole of Italy: what savagery, harshness, inhumanity, monstrousness, what cruelty of such scale could take hold of them that by allowing themselves to commit such criminal wrongs they would be willing to be branded as traitors to themselves and their homeland? Or has unbridled lust or some great reward for crime or the huge scale of an obscene payoff so ruined and corrupted men who always were an example of self-control and innocence that they forgot that they were nobles or citizens or human beings?

"But since I believe I have said enough concerning the side of 40 the honorable, I shall briefly touch individually on the points

Et sunt et fuerunt persaepe non nulli qui falsa quadam et inani
emolumenti specie se omni facinori, flagitio, probro, dedecori
addixerint. Neque opus est C. Verrem aut M. Crassum aut
alium ex antiquitate quempiam meminerimus. Satis nobis unus
superque[12] exemplo fuerit idem Cosmus iste Medices, Iohannis
filius, quem inveterata et exaestuans habendi aviditas quasi ieiu-
nam et famellicam Scyllam aliquam ad omne immane facinus
concitat, ac veluti voracissimam et inexplebilem Charybdin — ut
est in fabulis — ad omnem sordidi et nequissimi quaestus pas-
41   tum vocat ac rapit. Experti sunt saepe et quottidie experiuntur
non Galli et Britanni et Germani modo, sed Romani etiam ipsi
pontifices istius teterrimi monstri efferatam avariciam ac rabiem, qui per mensarias insidias non peregrinos opulentos solum spoliare consueverit, sed Iohannem pontificem maximum,
quo se grandi eius pecunia ingurgitaret, veneno interemerit. At
quem unquam e viris optimatibus, ex ordine nostro, e bonis et
honestis civibus aut videris aut audieris aut legeris ex omni hominum memoria, qui cuiusquam lucri cupiditate vel in summa
42   opportunitate ac licentia a decoro discesserit? Loquar equidem
de meipso fidenter ac vero, ut unius exemplo reliquorum optimatium vita atque integritas liquidius appareat. Eram publice
legatus et summa quidem cum potestate ad Ladislaum regem,
potentissimum ac maximum et nostrae reipublicae hostem acer-
rimum, qui opes Florentinas ita iam attriverat atque perfraege-
rat ut de deditione nobis, non de victoria, de hoste placando,
non de incolumitate nostra cogitandum foret. Venit ad me
noctu clam in cubiculum pater cuiusdam adolescentis, cuius rex
ille obsequio secus quam regalis dignitas et continentia postula-
ret utebatur, ubi amotis arbitris petivit primum liceretne sibi
per fidem et iusiurandum meum audacter tutoque loqui mecum

pertaining to expediency. There are and often have been persons who have, out of a false and empty pretext of gain, committed themselves to every crime, disgrace, outrage, and dishonor. We need not call to mind Gaius Verres or Marcus Crassus or anyone else from antiquity.[13] Let that same Cosimo de' Medici, son of Giovanni, suffice and more than suffice as an example, whom an inveterate and seething greed of gain spurs on like some lean and hungry Scylla to every monstrous crime and provokes him, like a voracious and insatiable Charybdis — a figure of mythology — to seize every opportunity to feed upon sordid and wicked profits. Not only the French, British, and 41 Germans have often felt and do daily feel the savage greed and madness of that foul monster, but so do the popes themselves: for by his deceitful banking he has been accustomed not only to defraud wealthy foreigners but he poisoned Pope John in order to gorge himself on his vast wealth. But which of the nobles, men of our class, from among the sound and honorable citizens, have you either seen or heard or read about in all recorded history who, even when given prime opportunity and freedom of action, deviated from the good? I shall speak with full confi- 42 dence and truly about my own case in order that by one man's example the unblemished life of the rest of the nobles may be clearly seen. I was dispatched as the state ambassador and plenipotentiary to King Ladislaus, a man of great power and stature and a fierce enemy of our republic[14] who had already ground down and broken the power of Florence to the point that we had to deliberate about surrender, not victory, about appeasing the enemy, not our safety. The father of a certain young man came to my bedchamber secretly by night, a young man whose obedience that monarch was using far differently than his royal rank and self-control demanded. When we were alone, he first asked whether he might by my sworn pledge speak his mind freely and in safety of matters bearing upon the

quae ad meum meaeque reipublicae emolumentum et amplitu-
dinem vellet. Cui cum licere affirmassem, multa primo invectus
in libidinem et turpitudinem regiam, ita deinde subiunxit: "Qui
sceleri favet, ipse plane scelestus est. Itaque ne alterius in me
sceleri favere videar, ulcisci cupio, modo id mihi ut sine vitae
periculo, ita etiam cum digno aliquo emolumento faciendi facultas detur. Veneno interimam regem per filium." Et id qua via
esset effecturus, edocuit. Quod quoniam tum re turpe, tum
verbo oscoenum est, silentio praetereundum censui. Quid multis est opus? Ita rem exposuit ut nihil facto facilius iudicarem.
Petebat autem sibi publicam fidem ut darem, meumque patrocinium ad se recipiendum in civem Florentinum liberaliterque
tractandum. Quod tametsi utrunque mihi facere licebat vide-
bamque futurum ut maximis periculis rempublicam liberarem,
tamen, quoniam id in alieno facinore per insidias facere videbar,
reieci ab me hominem illico monuique nullam omnino in me
spem reponeret, neque quoad publicam nec quoad privatam fidem. Nam neque patrii moris esse nec mei ullum, vel maximum, emolumentum parare dolo. Abiit ab me homo subtristis
ac turbatus. Quid autem postea egerit, quid perpetrarit, ipse
viderit. Illud certo scio: placuisse optimatibus omnibus consilium meum neque repertum quenquam in nostra civitate qui id
factum improbarit, praeter unum Iohannem Medicem atque
eius filios duos, istos Cosmum et Laurentium, qui simul cum
caeteris Medicibus pro innata improbitate inveteratoque flagitio, palam clamitarent noluisse Rainaldum Albizium publicae
saluti et incolumitati consulere. At ea mea sententia semper
fuit, nihil tandem conducturum, neque publice nec privatim,
quod fraude, quod vitio, quod scelere partum[13] esset; quare
spem omnem in relligione, in virtute, in Deo statui oportere.

benefit and standing of myself and my republic. When I gave 43
him leave, he first excoriated the king's disgraceful lust, then
added: 'Anyone who enables wickedness is himself wicked. And
so in order not to be seen to enable wickedness committed
against me, I am keen to avenge it provided that I be granted
the means to do so without risking my life and with some worthy reward. I shall use my son to poison the king.' And he apprised me of the means by which he would do so. Since this is
both disgraceful in fact and obscene to relate, I decided that it
should be passed over in silence. Why go on at length? He laid
out the plan in such a way that I thought nothing could be
done more easily. Moreover, he asked that I give him a public 44
pledge and my advocacy for his acceptance into the citizenry of
Florence and generous treatment. Although I had the power to
do both things and I saw that I would thereby be freeing the
republic of the greatest dangers, nonetheless, since I would be
seen to be acting treacherously through another man's crime, I
instantly spurned the man and warned him never to put his
hopes in me whatsoever, either regarding a public or a private
pledge; for it is neither my country's nor my practice to obtain
a benefit, even a very large one, by deceit. The man withdrew,
grim and upset. What he did in the sequel, what crime he per-
petrated, is his affair. This I know for certain: all the nobles 45
approved my policy nor was anyone found in our community to
disapprove this action except Giovanni de' Medici and his two
sons, Cosimo and Lorenzo. They, together with the rest of the
Medici, in line with their inborn wickedness and inveterate
criminality, raised a public outcry that Rinaldo degli Albizzi
refused to look after the safety and well-being of the state. But
it has always been my opinion that nothing is profitable either
in public or private policy that is gained by vice or wickedness;
therefore all our hope ought to be reposed in religion, virtue,
and God.

46 'Quod si difficillimis ac periculosissimis reipublicae temporibus id nullo modo in utilitatis ratione habendum esse iudicavi quod et libertatem et principatum nobis vel afferebat vel tuebatur, quinam tantus nos furor et insania invasisset ut laetis et omni ex parte secundissimis rebus nostris incolumem florentemque rempublicam alteri cuiquam tradere vel prodere potius quam ipsi uti fruique mallemus? Num ingens quaedam vis auri animos optimatium depravarit? An ignoramus ne totam quidem Italiam, quae ex universo terrarum orbe omnium gentium ac nationum pecuniosissima et opulentissima est, satis esse quae nummorum magnitudine cum nomine Florentino contendat? Ea est Florentinis argenti et auri copia, ut vel mensarii nostri in ultimas usque terras ad ferendam indigentibus opem ad hominum usum ac fructum dispersi dissaeminatique sint.

47 Qua vel una re factum est ut magni semper et praepotentes omnis ingruentium hostium terrores et insurgentis fortunae turbines non solum pertulerimus semper, verum etiam fuderimus, fraegerimus, oppresserimus. Nunquid voluptas aliqua aut delectatio ad id nos facinoris pellexerit? Primum haec sua natura eiusmodi sunt ut pecudum ducenda sint, non virorum, non civium honestorum, non optimatium. Deinde ubi usquam gentium cumulatior aut voluptas aut delectatio quam Florentiae parari queat? Quo uno in loco quaeque omnia vel ad animi vel ad corporis vel ad extraria sive bona sive commoda accedere dixerimus non modo affluunt, sed redundanter et peremniter

48 affluunt. Verum quid sim longior in re perspicua? Nulla in servitute, nulla in obscuritate, nulla in infamia utilitas unquam esse possit. Quapropter si ii sunt viri optimates, semperque fuere, qui et publicis et privatis in rebus quamrectissime sibi consultum censuerint,[14] si nihil sine honestate sibi, sine virtute, sine animi praestantia in bonis duxerint,[15] si laudem sibi ac gloriam maxime omnium adamarint, quid est, per immortalem Deum, quod de prodenda patria ab quoquam insimulentur,

"If in times of greatest difficulty and peril for the republic, I   46
held that what either brought or guarded our liberty and hege-
mony should by no means be considered an advantageous policy, what enormous madness and insanity has possessed us that
in happy and altogether prosperous times we prefer to hand
over or betray our safe and flourishing republic to another
rather than enjoy it and have the benefit of it ourselves? Has
some huge quantity of gold corrupted the nobles? Are we unaware that not even all Italy, which is the wealthiest and richest
of peoples and nations of the entire world, is able to compete
with the Florentine nation in the size of its holdings? The Florentines have such a supply of silver and gold that our bankers
have been scattered and dispersed to the remotest lands to
bring aid to the needy for men's use and enjoyment. This one   47
fact has entailed that we, great and powerful as we are, have always not merely endured all threats of advancing enemies and
raging whirlwinds of fortune but have even leveled, broken, and
overwhelmed them. Has pleasure or enjoyment lured us to that
crime? In the first place, these things are by their nature such
that they should be accounted proper to beasts, not men, not
honorable citizens, not nobles. Next, where in any land could a
more perfect pleasure or enjoyment be obtained than in Florence? In this one place, all goods or advantages which we call of
the mind, the body, or external not only flow but overflow and
do so unceasingly. But why go on when the matter is crystal   48
clear? There can never be any advantage in slavery, obscurity, or
infamy. Therefore if those men are and always have been the
nobles who have thought to follow the most correct possible
policy in both public and private affairs, if they have considered
nothing good except moral goodness, virtue, and intellectual
excellence, if they have most of all been dedicated to their good
name and glory, by immortal God, why should they be accused

praesertim non modo nulla utilitate proposita, sed cum omnium potius emolumentorum, in amittenda patria libertate, et commodorum ac iucunditatum amissione atque interitu?

49 'Quod si cum Philippo Maria sensisse arguamur, quid quantumve senserimus, ipse nosti. Non enim te latet, sanctissime et sapientissime pater, quid Gerardus idem Landrianus verbis sui principis temptarit,[16] quod nisi honestissimum iudicasses, nunquam certe probasses. Probasti enim, ut nosti, idque ut fieret et Venetos es et nos vaehementer hortatus. Nam cum ab hoc isto legato peteretur ut in hanc societatem Philippus etiam ipse reciperetur quae Venetis ac nobis tecum communis est—et id ea quidem lege, ut qui ex quattuor sociis quippiam in sociorum quenquam admisisset, tris reliquos haberet adversos atque hostis—iustissimam tibi petitionem videri continuo respondisti, eamque factum iri societatem suasisti verbis pluribus. Nos autem etsi tacitis animi iudiciis quae suaseras probaremus, existimavimus tamen nihil omnino de nostra sententia respondendum, ni prius e senatu Venetorum quid ipsi quoque sentirent

50 didicissemus. Itaque posteaquam sumus ab Venetis certiores facti sibi non placere quae petebantur, continuo etiam nos in eorum sententiam ivimus. Quod quidem factum non tibi solum, sed Christo optimo maximo, cuius vices in terris geris, visum est improbatum. Nam et ipse per id temporis palam aperteque subdidisti: "Qui aequas conditiones renuunt, iniquas saepe subeunt." Et non multo post nostri sociorumque exercitus proximis diebus quodam divino iudicio superati ad Immolam et capti sunt, cum summo et fortissimo imperatore nostro Nicolao Tholentinati ac reliquis multis et clarissimis ducibus. Cuius cladis magnitudo tanta est ut si hostiles copiae adversus hanc urbem ire perrexerint, non de pugna sit hostibus sed de praeda

51 cogitandum. Quid igitur nos quisquam insimulet aut sensisse

by anyone of betraying their homeland, especially when not only has no advantage been placed before them but, by the loss of their ancestral liberty, rather the loss of all gains and benefits and pleasures?

"If we stand accused of conspiring with Filippo Maria, you   49
yourself know why and to what extent. For, most wise and reverend father, unless you had judged this to be most honorable, you would never have granted your approval to what Gerardo Landriano attempted in his prince's name. For, as you know, you did grant approval and you earnestly urged both the Venetians and us that this policy should come to pass. For when that ambassador begged that Filippo be admitted to the alliance that joins the Venetians and us with you — and with the stipulation that if any of the four allies inflict any harm on any of the others, he would have the three others as his opponents and enemies — you immediately replied that the request seemed to you just, and you argued at length that the alliance be formed. Although we tacitly approved your argument, we thought nonetheless that we should make no formal reply without having first learned the view of the Venetian senate. Therefore after we   50
were apprised by the Venetians that they did not approve the petition, we, too, immediately went over to their view. This action seemed to have been disapproved not only by you but by Christ, Greatest and Best,[15] whose representative on earth you are. For at that time you yourself openly and publicly commented: 'Those who reject fair terms, often submit to unfair ones.' Not long afterward, in the next days, our armies and those of our allies were, by a kind of divine judgment, defeated and captured near Imola along with that peerless and courageous commander of ours, Niccolò da Tolentino[16] and many other distinguished leaders. Such is the scale of that disaster that if enemy forces proceeded against this city, the enemy would have to take thought not for battle but booty. How, then,   51

cum Philippo Maria, aut nostram illi rempublicam tradere voluisse?

'Nam de rumoribus, quod dicitur, facilis est solutio. Primum
rumor omnis eiusmodi est natura ut sine mendacio esse vix
possit. Est enim rumor sermo quidam incerto auctore dispersus. Nam quottidie usu venit ut qui nocere bonis aut prodesse
malis velit, multa maligne paret, multa moliatur inique. Itaque
diffundit ambiguas voces in vulgus, et in multitudinem imperitam diutius impie cogitata mira arte dispergit. Qui ut sunt cre-
duli ac leves huiusmodi homines vel obscurius auditis ultro in-
52   crementa afferunt. Quare fama, ut aptissime Maro cecinit,

    malum quo non aliud velocius ullum,
mobilitate viget viresque acquirit eundo,
parva metu primo, mox sese attollit in auras.
ingrediturque solo et caput inter nubila condit.

Nullius enim generis hominibus parcit famae improbitas, vaga-
turque temere apud omnes, quique tollendi sunt, deprimit, et
53   deprimendos extollit. Sed ut est magni et alti animi adversos
rumores contemnere atque despicere, ita moderati et verecundi
existimare prosperos nihil omnino ad se pertinere. Non enim in
futilium hominum opinione humana virtus locata est, sed aut
in quadam abdita et solerti mentis acie aut in actionis morisque
praestantia. Quare qui sibi vixerit, qui nihil aut egerit aut dixerit cuius non recte possit rationem reddere, quid aut lanistas aut
fartores aut Medices curet? Verum ne prudentis quidem viri
munus existimem huiusmodi nebulonum sussurationibus falli.

could anyone accuse us of either having conspired with Filippo Maria or of being willing to hand our republic over to him?

"As to the point about rumors, the solution is easy. First every rumor is by nature such that it can scarcely exist without being a lie. For a rumor is talk that spreads on no known authority. For it is a daily occurrence that a person wishing to harm the sound citizens or benefit scoundrels contrives many things with wicked intent, engineering many things unfairly. And so he disseminates ambiguous words to the masses and artfully scatters among the unwitting multitude products of his unholy imagination that have been contrived over a long period of time. Such people, being gullible and easily persuaded, on their own add further points to the unreliable information they have heard. Therefore rumor, as Vergil aptly put it, 52

> an evil than which no other is swifter,
> Thrives on mobility and gathers strength as it goes,
> At first small out of fear, soon it rises aloft
> And walks upon the earth and hides its head in the
>   clouds.[17]

For the wickedness of rumor spares people of no kind, and it ranges fearlessly among all people; it presses down those who ought to be raised up and lifts those who ought to be pressed down. But as it takes a great and lofty soul to despise and disregard hostile rumors, so it takes a man of measured and modest mind to judge that favorable rumors have no bearing on him at all. For human virtue does not reside in the opinions of frivolous human beings but either in a certain hidden and clever mental keenness or in excellent action and character. Therefore he who has lived for himself, who has done or said nothing for which he cannot give a proper accounting, why should he care about either the woolworkers or the poulterers or the Medici?[18] I also would not think that a wise man should be deceived by 53

Debet enim vir callidus ac sapiens illud plane intelligere, mentiri alios vanitate quadam, alios perfidia. An quisquam ignoret facile plebem ipsam in utranque partem impelli, laudareque eosdem quos modo vituperarit, et rursus quae prius vitio dederat, quasi mutatis flatibus tollere in altum solere? Quis enim mentis compos quid istiusmodi pecudes aut dicant aut non dicant pensitandum putet, in quibus nulla est auctoritas, nullum consilium, nulla fides? An esse cuiquam obscurum debet, solere Cosmum aucupari fatuos et inertis homines, quos omnia immani voluptate et libidine metientis non modo magnitudine poculorum et omni genere nequitiarum superet, sed violatis omnibus officii et humanitatis legibus pro facinorum et dedecorum omnium instrumentis habeat? Quid enim homo appotus et vinolentus atque omni[17] flagitio probroque delinitus non et dicat oscoenius et faciat turpius? Nunquid oblitus es, summe pontifex Eugeni, quos de tua integritate et sanctimonia idem nequam iste Cosmus rumores atque maledicta in populum Florentinum superiore tempore dissaeminarat, cum de te in urbem recipiendo agebamus in senatu? Nonne—ut reliqua eius abominabilis portenti convicia et contumelias conticescam—te et Gebellinum esse et Gebellinam fovere factionem petulantissime effutiebat? Qua una re factum est ut impedimento fuerit quo minus per id temporis optimatium pietatem experirere. Nam quo iniquo et infelici fato accidat nescio, accidit tamen ut quorum etiam nomina perinde[18] ac barbara fere[19] ignorantur, Gelphi et Gebellini, contrariis mentibus infestisque et discrepantibus animis Italiam omnem a Germanis[20] pervaserint. Quae quidem pestiferae factiones quot quamque perniciosissimas clades persaepe intulerint et quottidie inferant, cum aliae plaerae-

the whisperings of such tricksters. For a shrewd and wise man should know that some lie because of vainglory, others out of treachery. Who would be unaware that the masses themselves are easily manipulated in either direction and praise the same people they just now excoriated, and likewise the qualities they had previously accounted vices they are accustomed, as if by a change in the direction of the winds, to lift on high? What sane 54 man would think that he should take into account what such beasts say or do not say, who have no authority, no policy, no trustworthiness? Or should it be obscure to anyone that Cosimo is in the habit of hunting after foolish and lazy men, that he may not only excel those who measure all things by unbounded pleasure and lust not only in the size of his cups and in every category of wickedness, but upon violating all laws of duty and humanity use them as tools for all his crimes and outrages? Take a drunk and alcoholic man branded with every crime and disgrace: what obscene thing would he not say? What disgraceful deed would he not perform? Surely you have not forgotten, Pope Eugenius, the rumors and insults that that same worthless Cosimo spread among the Florentine people on an earlier occasion, when we were debating in the senate about receiving you into the city? Did he not — to veil in silence the 55 other taunts and insults of this execrable monster — insolently chatter that you were a Ghibelline and a supporter of the Ghibelline party? By this single act a roadblock was set up preventing you from experiencing the nobles' piety at that time. For I do not know by what cruel and unhappy fate it occurred, but occur it nonetheless did, that the Guelfs and Ghibellines, whose names were almost unknown, like those of barbarians, spread from the Germans over the whole of Italy with hostile and conflicting sentiments. Almost all cities, including our own, bear witness to how many and how destructive were the disasters that these deadly factions often inflicted and still inflict

56 que propemodum omnes, tum urbs nostra testis est. Itaque Gebellinis post maximas strages urbe iampridem extrusis, id quod vico Gebellino cognomentum ascivit, tota civitas — non Gelpha solum, sed tanquam Archigelpha, ut vocant — Gelphorum partis amplexa est adeo ut huiusmodi appellationem augustam ac veluti sacrosanctam arbitretur. Num tu igitur Gebellinus aut ullarum huiuscemodi partium vel fautor vel probator, quoniam hominum malignitas eos de te rumores diffudisset in populum? Qui vero Basiliensem vel conspirationem vel coniurationem hac tempestate fovent ad tuum et ecclesiae Romanae principatum funditus evertendum, quae adversus te scelera, quae flagitia, quas nequitias non moliuntur, non confingunt,

57 non subdole dispergunt in populos? Quippe qui persuasum habeant per huiusmodi famae notas se quamfacillime quod impie cogitarint assecuturos apud homines imperitos ac totius veritatis rudes. Tu vero, qui prudentia aeque atque sapientia reliquis mortalibus mirabiliter antecellis, inanibus inertissimorum hominum vocibus et balatibus cedas? Malisque falsam calumniam ut veram culpam admittere quam nostrae pietatis meminisse? Nec enim oblivio cepisse te debet quales in te viri optimates fuerint, cum alias semper, tum praesenti hoc anno, cum te per Romanam illam factionem ac tumultuariam turbam coniectum poene in carcerem, imo coniectum, ea indignitate (ut par fuerat) liberavimus ac nostra classe, praefecto Felice Brancacio, forti et strenuo viro, pulcherrime adveximus in nostram hanc urbem, qua nunc ipsi cum iniuste ac nefarrie, tum maxima cum ignominia contumeliosissime eiicimur atque exterminamur.

58 Non enim fortuna viri optimates agi soliti sunt, sed ordine potius duci, non temeritate sed veritate, non erratione sed ratione, non vanitate sed constantia. Itaque nullis neque calumniis nec rumoribus nec adversis de te sermonibus credere voluimus,

every day. Therefore when after huge massacres the Ghibellines   56
had long since been driven from the city (which gave the 'Ghibelline quarter' its name), the entire city — not merely 'Guelf,'
but as it were 'Archguelf,' as they say — embraced the Guelf
party so warmly that it regarded such a designation as august
and, as it were, hallowed. Now then you surely are not a Ghibelline or one who backs or approves of any such party because
men's maliciousness spread such rumors about you among the
people, are you? Those who at this time promote the conspiracy or cabal of Basel to completely overturn your primacy and
that of the Roman church, what crimes against you, what outrages, what wickedness do they not engineer, do they not in-
vent, do they not cunningly spread among the people? The   57
reason is that they are convinced that by such stigmatizing of
reputation they can most easily achieve their unholy goals with
men who are inexperienced and unaware of the truth. Would
you who marvelously excel all other mortals in foresight and
wisdom give way to the empty words and bleatings of worthless
men? Would you rather accept a false canard as genuine guilt
rather than remember our piety? You should not lapse into
forgetfulness of how the nobles behaved toward you on other
occasions and in this current year: when that party and disorderly mob at Rome had practically thrown, I mean had actually
thrown, you into prison, we freed you from that indignity (as
was only right) and with our fleet, commanded by Felice Brancacci, a courageous and energetic man,[19] bore you brilliantly to
this city of ours, from which we ourselves are now cast out and
banished, wickedly and unjustly and with utmost disgrace and
insult. For the nobles are not accustomed to being driven by   58
fortune but are guided by social rank, by truth rather than rashness, by reason, not error, by steadiness rather than vainglory.
So we refused to believe any of the slanders, rumors, or disparaging comments about you, although there were many who

cum permulti essent qui palam clamitarent fore ut nostra omnis
in Eugenium pietas permagno nos damno et detrimento affice-
ret, quippe qui per aliorum incommoda quamcommodissime
59   rebus suis providere consuevisset. Nos vero cum diligenter
etiam atque etiam inita subductaque ratione nihil melius, nihil
castius, nihil sanctius, nihil denique pietatis plenius arbitrare-
mur, quam si et pura et integra et incorrupta tum mente tum
voce te, quem saepimento virtutum omnium vallatum iudicaba-
mus, et coleremus et omnibus prosequeremur officiis, eam omnem orationem sprevimus, repudiavimus, contempsimus. Neque illorum maledicta quicquam omnino ponderis habere
voluimus qui—ut et sunt et fuerunt semper exitium ac lues
bonorum omnium—ira inflamati furentesque libidine in tuae
innocentiae et sanctitatis nomen tam inconsulte ac temere per
omnem impietatem debaccharentur.

60   'Quamobrem si tu item intelligis huiusmodi adversus nos
voces omnis paratas et confictas atque dispersas esse per inimicos, per sordidos, per impurissimos homines, quorum insimula-
tio laudi ducenda sit et diffamatio in secundis habenda rumoribus, si non modo non tradere nostram rempublicam (hoc est
uxores liberosque nostros ac nosmetipsos et vitam nostram
prodere Philippo Mariae), sed ne cum illo quidem ad nostra
quoque et publica commoda—vel te aliquando non probante
duntaxat, verum etiam vaehementer hortante—sentire unquam
(quod honeste facere licebat) instituimus, si nihil neque publicis
nec privatis in rebus usui futurum iudicavimus semper quod a
decoro et officio abhorreret, quid est, per immortalem Deum,
quod quisquam sanae mentis atque sui conscius fidem ullam ei
infamiae praestandam censeat, quam et perditissimorum latro-
num improbitas pepererit et stultorum ac futilium hominum
61   levitas nutrierit atque auxerit? Num putas, pater sanctissime,

raised a public cry that all of our reverence for Eugenius would bring us considerable loss and harm, since, they said, he had made a practice of looking out for his own interests most conveniently by procuring others' misfortunes. We, however, after 59 having undertaken and performed the calculation with care and repeatedly, judged nothing was better, more innocent, more holy, and finally more full of devotion than if with pure, intact, and innocent thought and speech we revered you and attended you with all duties since we believed you were a man shielded by a wall of all the virtues, and we spurned, rejected and held in contempt all that talk about you. We refused to give any weight at all to the slanders of those who — as they are and always have been the ruin and plague of all sound citizens — fired by anger and raging with lust so thoughtlessly and rashly, celebrated an orgy of disrespect against your reputation for innocence and holiness.

"Therefore if you understand as we do that all such rumors 60 against us have been contrived, invented, and broadcast by enemies, base, vile, corrupt men, whose accusation should be considered an encomium and whose defamation be counted among favorable reports; if we have not only not decided to hand over our republic, that is, to betray our wives and children and ourselves and our lives to Filippo Maria, but decided not even ever to take his side for the sake of our private and public interest (something that honor allowed), not even while you were not only approving but strongly urging us to do so; if we have always considered that nothing in public or private affairs would ever be beneficial that is at odds with virtue and duty, then why is it, by immortal God, that anyone of sound mind and good conscience would think that any credence should be lent to this infamy, which the wickedness of desperate cutthroats has given birth to and the frivolity of fools and nobodies has nurtured and fostered? Surely you do not think, holy 61

innocentiam dignitatemque nostram eorum testimonio niti
oportere, qui sic habent mentem immanitate efferatam ut naturae divinae nullam sibi suspicionem velint? Et quinam hominum testimonium in nos dicunt? Cosmus et Laurentius Medices. An alius quisquam? Averardus item Medices? Oh calamitas,
oh miseria temporum! Eorumne testimonio damnari quenquam
oportet, in quibus neque relligio ulla est, nec veritas, nec fides,
nec bonitas, nec verecundia? Nam quis est, proh Deum atque
hominum fidem, qui nesciat Averardum Medicem, existima-
tione iampridem et publico et communi quodam omnium
consensu damnatum, pro intemperanti sua et barbara inaudita-
que libidine eiusdem Francisci huius adolescentis et avum dici
et patrem? Nam Cosmi et Laurentii calumnia quanti faciunda
sit, cum immani totius vitae turpitudine, tum eo potissimum
argumento probari potest, quod et uxores communis habent et
filios communis. Insimulat Cosmus Medices viros optimatis;
negat Pallas Stroza. Insimulat Laurentius Medices; negat Rhodulphus Pyrucius. Insimulat Averardus Medices; negat Franciscus Luna; negat Iohannes Ianfiliacius; negat Felix Brancacius;
negat Nicolaus Barbadorus; negat Matthaeus Bardus; negat
Petrus Castellanus; negant, inquam, negant omnes boni et graves et innocentes cives. Utris ergo credendum sit? Medicibusne
et carbonariis et foeneratoribus et cauponibus et aleatoribus
cunctisque impudicis, an viris optimatibus et luminibus reipublicae?

63   'Quod si nullis neque argumentis nostris nec rationibus moveris, veritate ipsa moveare necesse est. Eum penes te habes
quicum de tradenda civitate convenisse insimulamur, Gerardum
ipsum Landrianum, cuius integritatem virtutemque tanti facere soles ut eum dignum esse persaepe affirmaris qui tibi ad
dignitatis gradum quamproxime accedat, id quod brevi per te

father, that our innocence and honor ought to depend upon the
testimony of those whose minds have been so brutalized by
cruelty that they deny themselves any suggestion of a divine
nature. And who of all people is testifying against us? Cosimo
and Lorenzo de' Medici. Anyone else? Averardo de' Medici.[20]
O, the disaster, O the wretchedness of the times! Should anyone be condemned by the testimony of those devoid of religion,
truth, credibility, goodness, or shame? Who is there — O for
the love of God and men! — who does not know that Averardo
de' Medici, who was long ago condemned by public opinion
and the common consensus of all for his immoderate, barbarous, and unheard-of lust, is now called both father and grandfather of the same adolescent, Francesco! How much value   62
should be attached to the false accusations of Cosimo and
Lorenzo can be shown not only from the boundless disgrace of
their entire lives but also in particular by the fact that they have
wives and children in common. Cosimo de' Medici accuses the
nobles; Palla Strozza denies the charge. Lorenzo de' Medici
makes accusation; Ridolfo Peruzzi denies the charge. Averdaro
de' Medici makes accusation; Francesco della Luna denies the
charge; Giovanni Gianfigliazzi denies the charge, Felice Brancacci, Niccolò Barbadori, Matteo Bardi, Pietro Castellani all
make denials;[21] all sound and serious and innocent citizens do
so. Which of the two sides should one believe? Physicians,[22]
charcoal dealers, usurers, shopkeepers, gamblers, and all shameful people, or the nobles, the shining lights of the republic?

"But if you are moved by no arguments or reasoning of ours,   63
the truth itself must move you. You have in your service the
man with whom we are accused of having met concerning the
betrayal of the state, Gerardo Landriano; you set such store by
his integrity and virtue that you often have declared him worthy of occupying the second rank to yourself, something which
you have clearly indicated will be effected by you in a short

futurum non obscure testatus es. Ex hoc uno tibi veritatis facultas in manu est vel perdiscendae vel, si opus facto censueris, excutiendae. Quam ubi prolatam patefactamque tenueris, siquidem nos hac nominis labe dignos esse cognoris, ut vel tuae censurae gladio percutias licet; sin autem tantam indignitatem indignos esse qui patiantur viros optimatis depraehenderis, ut et nos patriae et nobis patriam restituas, te per relligionem, per pietatem, per iusticiam et bonitatem tuam rogamus oramusque.

64   Non pecunias petimus, non exercitus poscimus. Nihil vi, nihil armis agendum est. Solo ac libero verbo et nobis omnibus et toti reipublicae pro tua dignitate consules. Siqua sola ab domesticis hostibus oppressi sumus infamia, nos apud deceptum populum levaris, et optimatis et universam civitatem molestia omni aerumnaque levaris. Nemo enim ex horum istorum numero quos versutia et loquacitas Cosmiana novis argutiis dolisque fefellit ac nobis infestos reddidit, nemo, inquam, futurus est qui minus sit eius de veritate sermonem tanquam divinum quoddam oraculum et accepturus et habiturus, quem alterum in terris Deum certo existimant ac sanctissime venerantur, colunt, admirantur.'

65   *Nicolaus.* Maximas certe gratias, Rhodulphe, tibi et agimus et habemus — non enim pro me solum, sed pro Honofrio quoque respondeo — quod divinam huius summi viri nobis orationem recitaveris, cuius vestigia sequi instituimus. Dii boni, quae vis dicendi, quae copia, qui ornatus; quanta in rebus gravitas, quanta in verbis subtilitas! Nam totius compositionis numerus et suavitas tanta est ut nihil unquam sonantius audierim, nec iucundius quicquam.

66   *Rhodulphus.* Longe istud magis et diceres et sentires, Nicolae, si vel eius nixius contendentis nunc obstrepentem, nunc intonantem vocem veluti tubam aliquam in praelio vel cum ad sermonem

time. From this man alone you have in hand the power either of discovering or, if you deem it necessary, investigating the truth. When the truth has been brought to light and revealed and you have possession of it, if you have ascertained that we are worthy of this stain to reputation, you may strike us with the sword of your censure; but if you find that the nobles are unworthy to suffer so great an indignity, we beg and beseech you by religion, piety, justice and your own goodness that you restore us to our homeland and our homeland to us. We ask for   64
no money, no armies. Nothing should be done by force of arms. In view of your standing, by free speech alone you will take into consideration both us and the entire republic. If we have been crushed by our domestic enemies only through infamy, you will relieve us of that before the deceived populace, and you will relieve both the nobles and the entire city of all their trouble and suffering. For no one from the number of those whom the glib wiles of Cosimo have deceived with new sophistries and tricks and have made enemies to us, there will be no one, I say, who fails to welcome and consider like some divine oracle the account of the truth given by that man whom they certainly think of as a second God on earth, whom they revere, love, and admire with utmost piety."

Niccolò. We give you the greatest thanks, Ridolfo — I reply not   65
only on my own behalf but also Onofrio's — because you have recited for us the divine speech of that outstanding man whose tracks we have begun to follow. Good gods, what power, what abundance, what embellishment, what great solemnity in subject matter, what subtlety of diction! The rhythm and charm of the whole composition is so great that I have never heard anything more sonorous or more pleasing.

Ridolfo. You would say and think this far more, Niccolò, if you   66
had in person heard his voice in the heat of impassioned argument, now thundering like a trumpet in battle, or when he

descenderet quasi receptui cecinisset, eiusdem item cygneos concentus coram audisses. Nunquam enim mea sententia aut Timotheum illum desyderasses, qui, dum Minervae qui dicitur modulum tibia perite et sonantius canit, Alexandrum regem e convivio quasi afflatum exilientem ad arma excitavit, rursusque mutato numero et sui compotem reddidit et sibi suisque restituit, aut Hyagnin[21] aut[22] eius filium Marsyam aut Olympum aut alium quenquam qui magis in musicis claruisset.

67   *Nicolaus.* Puto id equidem. Verum neque tibi modo recitanti quicquam defuit, quod vel in voce vel in vultu vel in gestu ac motu praestare oporteret. Ac tua ista omni dictione ita sum delectatus ut Ciceronem aut Demosthenem aliquem viderer audire. Nam quantum ad ea quae ad diluendam nominis notam pertinent, quoniam Honofrius hic meus hanc sibi partem suo quodam iure vendicavit, nihil est quod dicam, ne dum gravissimas Rainaldi sapientissimi viri sententias laudare voluero, existimer tacito animi iudicio improbare opinionem Honofrii mei.

68   *Rhodulphus.* Sed tu, Honofri, quid dicis? Non satis vel ab patre tibi vel ab Rainaldo probatum est infamiam omnem esse contemnendam, quippe quae neque mala sit, nec habenda in malis?

    Honofrius. At ego, Rhodulphe, sentio longe secus. Quid enim minus existimem infamiam ipsam et sua natura malam et habendam in malis, cum et vitii praemium quoddam sit et quasi aliquod venenum invidiae?

    Rhodulphus. Intelligo valentioribus quibusdam viribus quam meis opus esse ad te refellendum. Quare vel Rainaldus tibi respondeat necesse est, vel Pallas pater. Verum cave tu ne Dares aliquis Entellum in harenam voces.

69   *Honofrius.* Ego, Rhodulphe, doceri cupio. Et vix aliud quicquam est quod malim quam mihi vaehementer probatum iri adversos

descended to a conversational tone as if he had signaled a re-
treat, like a symphony of swans. You would never, in my opinion, have felt any need for that famous Timotheus, who, when
he skillfully and sonorously played the "melody of Minerva" on
the flute, roused King Alexander to leap up from the banquet as
if possessed and rush to arms, and again when the rhythm was
altered he brought him back to his senses and restored him to
himself and his companions; or Hyagnis or Marsyas his son or
Olympus or anyone of special distinction among musicians.[23]

Niccolò. I do indeed think so. But in your performance you lacked   67
nothing that needed to be furnished, either in voice, facial expression, gesture, or movement. I was so delighted by that entire speech of yours that I seemed to be listening to some Cicero or Demosthenes. As to the arguments that bear upon
mitigating a black mark against one's reputation, since my friend
Onofrio here has claimed this part for himself by a kind of
right of his own, I have nothing to say, lest in my desire to
praise the weighty opinions of wise Rinaldo I be thought to
tacitly disapprove of my friend's view.

Ridolfo. What do you say, Onofrio? Has it not been demonstrated   68
convincingly by your father or by Rinaldo that all infamy ought
to be despised since it is neither an evil nor to be numbered
among evils?

Onofrio. But I think quite otherwise, Rinaldo. Why should I not
think that infamy itself is both by its own nature an evil and
ought to be numbered among evils, since it is a reward for vice
and like a poison of envy?

Ridolfo. I realize that stronger powers than I possess are needed to
refute your claim. For this reason Rinaldo should reply to you,
or your father Palla. But beware lest you be some Dares sum-
moning Entellus into the arena.[24]

Onofrio. I want to learn, Ridolfo. There is hardly anything that I   69
would more desire than for it to be demonstrated to me that

rumores in malis duci non oportere. Nam quamquam et patrem heri de infamia disserentem audivi et modo ex oratione
Rainaldi eadem ipsa de re polite multa et eleganter apud Eugenium dicta animadverto, vereor tamen ne aut itidem mihi accidat ut iis solet qui aquam intercutem patientes—quo magis bi-
berint, magis sitiunt—aut tanta sit rei magnitudo ut et maiorem
aliquam et robustiorem disputationem exposcat. Non enim durum esse non potest ut quibus pro virtutis magnitudine illustris
quaedam fama lausque et gloria debeatur, hi et vulgo vituperen-
tur et obscuri sint et infames. Eninvero ut bonus rumor plurimum expetendus est, ita malus fugiendus maxime. Itaque non
absurde Lacaena mulier, cum filium audisset et servatum esse et
fugisse ex hostibus, ad eum ita scripsit: 'Mala de te fama diffusa
est. Aut hanc elue, aut morere.' Alia vero, et ipsa item Lacaena,
cum publicam pompam ageret, audivit fratrem multitudine vul-
nerum in acie victorem interisse. Quare haudquaquam coronam
deposuit, sed exultans potius gaudio ad proximas conversa inquit, 'Ut multo melius est, amicae, in acie victorem mori quam
Olympiorum superatorem vivere.' Atqui si mihi detur optio,
longe mortem infamiae praetulerim. Nam quid amarius esse
possit quam cuius omnis vita plena sit confertaque honestatis,
cui velut ingenerata optimorum operum nobilitas videri omnibus debeat, qui et dignitati servierit semper et reipublicae
consuluerit et officii, non alicuius privati commodi, rationem
habuerit et pro patria caritate pericula propria adierit, vulnera
exceperit, aliquando etiam mortem appetierit, et quantum in
se positum senserat, alacri et forti animo subierit, eum non
modo extorrem agi, sed per omnis coronas carpi, accusari omni

hostile rumors need not be classed among evils. For though I heard my father discussing infamy yesterday, and just now I perceived many things in this speech of Rinaldo on this very topic that were spoken with polish and eloquence to Eugenius, yet I am afraid that either it might turn out with me as it sometimes does with those who suffer from edema—the more they drink, the thirstier they are—or the topic is so great that it demands a lengthier and more vigorous discussion. For it cannot fail to be a harsh situation when those who have earned fame, commendation, and glory in return for their great virtue are criticized by the common folk and live in obscurity and infamy. For in fact, as a good reputation is greatly to be sought, 70 so a bad one is particularly to be shunned. Therefore when she had heard that her son had survived the battle by fleeing from the enemy, a Spartan woman, appropriately, wrote to him as follows: "A bad report has been spread about you: either expunge it, or die." When she was marching in a parade, another woman, likewise a Spartan, heard that her brother had, though victorious, died in battle from a great number of wounds. She did not on this account lay aside her laurel wreath but turned to the women next to her and beaming with joy said, "How much better it is, friends, to die as a victor in battle than to live as a champion of the Olympic games."[25] And if the choice were 71 given to me, I would far prefer death to infamy. For what could be more bitter than for the man whose entire life is filled and packed with virtue, the ingrained nobility of whose splendid achievements ought to be seen by all, who has always placed himself in the service of honorable standing and has shown concern for the republic and upheld his public duty, not for any private advantage, and has run risks because of his paternal affection, has received wounds and even courted death and did so, insofar as he could, with keenness and courage, for that man not only to be driven into exile, but to be criticized by everyone,

72 ignominia, omni contumelia affici? Quid enim aut acerbius aut tristius auditu quam quorum fides ac virtus in totius civitatis et bonorum omnium causa nunquam contremuerit, sed publicae amplitudinis et emolumenti se actores semper defensoresque praestiterint, hos ita nunc consilii aut ingenii expertes existimari ut vulgo dicantur coniurasse in patriam? Atqui vel arrogans ille mihi vel dissolutus videri solet qui et quid de se quisque loquatur contemnit, et negligit hominum iudicia. Quorum profecto superbiae alterum esse puto, alterum negligentiae. Non igitur possum non affligi, cum animadverto amisisse nos una cum patria dignitate tum bonam famam, tum laudem ac gloriam, quibus nihil humano generi neque melius datum puto nec bea-

73 tius quicquam. Cum enim bona fama custos sit praedicatrixque virtutum, quibus solis et laus continetur et gloria, infamia vero — quam 'malam famam' significare arbitror — eadem ratione vitiorum sibi patronatum vendicet, nonne iure optimo infelix ille ac miser dicendus fuerit qui, cum factorum omnium consiliorumque suorum rectam ab se habitam rationem norit, non famae sed infamiae nomen subeat?

Rhodulphus. Responde aliquid Honofrio nostro, Pallas. Aut responde tu, Rainalde. Respondete aliquid tandem. Non enim absurda videntur mihi quae acutus hic adolescens et subtiliter fidenterque disseruit.

74 *Rainaldus.* Fidenter quidem, Rhodulphe, et fortassis etiam non minus vere quam subtiliter. Quare Pallas ipse respondeat malim. Nam ego quidem defessus defatigatusque sum, vel ea ista oratione quam tu pro singulari tuo erga me studio longe gravius et elegantius recitasti modo quam ipse mane apud Eugenium habuerim. Accingere igitur, Pallas. Obsequere Honofrio ac nobis. Audimus enim te libenter.

accused of every disgrace, to be the target of every insult? For   72
what is more bitter or sadder to hear than that those whose
reliable virtue in the cause of the entire city and of all its sound
citizens never wavered but who always showed themselves pro-
ponents and defenders of the greatness and interests of the
state, for them now to be considered so bereft of wisdom or
ability that they are publically denounced for having conspired
against their homeland? That man has always seemed to me
arrogant or irresponsible who despises what each person says
about him and looks down upon people's judgments. I attribute
the former reaction to pride, the latter to carelessness. I cannot therefore fail to be upset when I notice that we have lost,
along with our inherited rank, good reputation, commendation,
and glory, than which I think nothing better or more blessed
has been given to the human race. For since good reputation   73
protects and proclaims the virtues, by which alone praise and
glory are retained, and infamy — which I believe signifies "bad
repute" — claims for herself by the same reasoning to be an advocate of the vices, should he not rightly be called unhappy and
wretched who, though he knows that he has given a correct accounting of all his deeds and policies, receives a label not of
fame but of infamy?

Ridolfo. Palla, give some reply to our Onofrio. Or you do so,
Rinaldo. [To both] Give some reply finally. What this clever
young man said with subtlety and sincerity seems to me plau-
sible.

Rinaldo. With sincerity indeed, Ridolfo, and perhaps no less truly   74
than subtly. Therefore I would prefer for Palla himself to make
reply. For I am tired out and exhausted by that speech that you,
because of your exceptional affection for me, just now performed with far greater weight and elegance than it had in my
own delivery this morning before Eugenius. So, Palla, prepare
yourself. Oblige Onofrio and us; we will gladly listen to you.

75 *Pallas.* Vellem equidem, Rainalde, dignus foret meus sermo et tua
et Rhodulphi auditione. Quando enim ista aut didici aut cu-
ravi? Eorum ista provincia est qui, Sophistae appellati, quasi
Gorgias quispiam ad omnia quacunque de re quaesieris vel nova
vel difficilia vel obscura audacter continuo expediteque respon-
deant. Verum ne videar fortasse inhumanior, dicam quod sentiam, ea tamen conditione, ne quid ab me dictum efferatur.

Rainaldus. Age tandem, si libet. Ipse tibi pro omnibus qui hic ad-
sunt bona fide recipio futurum, ne verbum quidem ullum hoc
ostium egrediatur, et id sane Florentino, non Lacedaemonico
more. Nonne idem facturus es, Poggi?

76 *Poggius.* Equidem, Rainalde. Lacedaemoniorum morem ignoro,
sed te demiror, qui tanquam mores civitatis ignores, existimes
quicquam diutius teneri arcanum posse. Non fallam, Pallas,
opinionem tuam. Nam nequis dolor laterum me torqueat, quidquid audiero, efflabo quamprimum. Deferam ad Cosmum omnia.

Pallas. Utere ingenio tuo, Poggi. Verum tu, Nicolae, quid ais?
Sentisne cum Honofrio, an id minus?

Nicolaus. Imo plane. Quid enim, Pallas, non sentiam, cum ille qui
bonis rumoribus utitur, felix est, secundum Pindarum.

77 *Pallas.* Num bonis rumoribus felicitatem, malis vero miseriam
constare putas?

Nicolaus. Certe. Qui enim secunda utitur fama et laudatur plurimum, is mihi per gloriae splendorem felicitatem summam adeptus videatur. Cuius quidem spe rei elatus Hector ait apud Homerum: 'Nunquam mea fama peribit.' Et alio loco sapientissimus
Graecorum ille apud eundem poetam: 'Caelum mea fama petivit.'

Palla. I would wish, Rinaldo, for my words to be worthy of your   75
and Ridolfo's hearing. When have I learned or given attention
to such matters? That is the sphere of those called "sophists,"
who, like some Gorgias, give a reply boldly, on the spot, and
directly to all queries on whatever subject, whether new or difficult or obscure.[26] But lest I seem lacking in humanity, I shall
say what I think but with the stipulation that what I say remains confidential.

Rinaldo. Proceed then, if you please. I personally promise you in
good faith, on behalf of all who are here present, that no word
should pass beyond this door, and that by Florentine, not Spartan custom.[27] Won't you do the same, Poggio?

Poggio. I am unfamiliar with the Spartans' custom, Rinaldo, but I   76
am surprised that you think that anything can be kept secret
for long, as if you were unacquainted with the city's customs. I
shall not disappoint your expectations, Palla. For unless some
pleurisy torments me, I will blab, as soon as possible, whatever
I hear. I will report it all to Cosimo!

Palla. Use your head, Poggio. But what do you say, Niccolò? Do
you agree with Onofrio or not?

Niccolò. Indeed I do. For why should I not agree, Palla, when, according to Pindar, he who enjoys good repute is happy.[28]

Palla. Do you think that happiness consists in good repute, misery   77
in bad?

Niccolò. Certainly. For he who enjoys good repute and is lavishly
praised seems to me to have attained the pinnacle of happiness
through the brilliance of glory, buoyed by the hope of which,
Hector says in Homer: "My reputation will never perish." And
in another passage that wisest of the Greeks says in the same
poet: "My reputation has risen to heaven."[29]

78 *Pallas.* Tua te plurimum, Nicolae,[23] fallit opinio. Nam vel cum Oreste Euripideo, 'Laus immodica molestia quoque afficit ad haec,' an ignoras laudem non esse perfecti boni sed medii?

Nicolaus. Ignoro equidem. Quid enim 'perfectum,' quid 'medium' vocas?

Pallas. Perfectum dico quod et optimum est et summum bonum. Id enim τὸ τελείον ἀγαθὸν Graeci nominant. Medium vero— hoc est commune bonum, quod illi appellant κοινὸν ἀγαθόν— eiusmodi esse bonum existimo quod via quaedam nobis sit cum eundi, tum perveniendi ad perfectum illud et ultimum bonorum omnium bonum. Tenesne quae dicuntur?

79 *Nicolaus.* Maxime. Verum quid est quur perfectum bonum laudandum non sit, si medium laudatur?

Pallas. Quoniam maius quiddam felicitas meretur quam laudem favoremque popularem.

Nicolaus. Et quidnam illud?

Pallas. Honorem, opinor, et quem Graeci μακαρισμόν, nostri 'beationem' vocant.

Nicolaus. Nomina intelligere mihi videor, sed vim differentiamque non videor. Quare ut et nomina ista et alia quae quidem ad id negocii pertinere ullo pacto censeas, et res item quarum causa istiusmodi nomina sunt inventa, in medium proferas, cupio et exopto. Idque ut facias, te maiorem in modum rogo.

80 *Pallas.* Uti igitur ab his quae modo dicebantur exordiar: aliud est *beatio,* aliud *laus,* aliud *praedicatio.* Sed praedicationem nunc voco quod a Graecis ἐγκώμιον dicitur. Est enim *praedicatio* operis singularum rerum quas vel speculamur vel agimus oratio praestantiam magnitudinemque demonstrans. At *laus* non singillatim sed generatim ac summatim idem quod praedicatio ipsa etiam praestat. *Beatio* vero quae vitae felicitati et beatitudini

Palla. Your opinion is much mistaken, Niccolò. Do you not know,   78
with the Euripidean Orestes, that "immoderate praise encum-
bers one with trouble"[30] or that praise belongs not to the absolute but the intermediate good?

Niccolò. I do not indeed. What do you mean by "absolute" and
"intermediate"?

Palla. I call absolute what is the best and highest good. The
Greeks call it *to teleion agathon* ("the complete good"). I deem
the intermediate — this is the common good, which they call
koinon agathon — a good of such sort that it is a kind of path for
us for going to and arriving at that perfect and final one of all
the goods.[31] Do you understand?

Niccolò. Indeed. But why is it that the absolute good is not to be   79
praised if the middle one is praised?

Palla. Because happiness deserves something greater than praise
and popular favor.

Niccolò. And what is that?

Palla. Honor, I believe, and what the Greeks call *makarismos*, what
our people call "blessing."

Niccolò. I think I understand the terms but not their force and
distinction. Therefore I desire and hope you may share these
terms and others you consider in any way relevant to this matter and likewise the things for the sake of which such terms
have been invented. I earnestly beg you to do this.

Palla. To begin, then, with these terms that were just now being   80
discussed. One is *blessing*, another *praise*, a third *proclaiming*
(*praedicatio*), but let me use the term *praedicatio* for what is called
by the Greeks *enkomion*. For the *praedicatio* of a work is speech
that demonstrates the excellence and greatness of separate elements that we are looking at or acting out. But *praise* lays out
the same information as *praedicatio* not point by point but in a
general and summary manner. A *blessing* is an end that is given

datur finis est. *Finem* autem voco qui ad aliud nihil, sed alia ad ipsum referuntur. Nec enim ii omnino recte fines mihi videntur dici qui supra se finem habent ad quem ipsi referantur omnes.

81 Quod si et hi quoque fines dicendi sint, non perfecti sed medii quidam existimentur. Ille autem perfectus, qui et ultimus est et optimus. Nam *fama* nomen Graecum est. Quo 'sermonem' significari verbum φημί, unde tractum est, satis liquido declarat. Itaque aliud nihil est quam quidam popularis sermo, qui siquidem auctorem unde proficiscatur ostenderit, famae sibi nomen vendicat; sin id minus, non *fama* sed *rumor* dici solet, quod ipsum tamen ab ῥῶ verbo (hoc est 'dico') deduci manifestum est. Hunc autem populi sermonem (id est famam) in utranque partem capi solere, et vituperationis et laudis, non obscure Virgilius docet, cum ait: 'Tam ficti pravique tenax quam nuncia veri.'

82 Quod si verum fateri licet, longe magis mendacio fama quam veritati favet. Itaque suapte vi quodammodo naturaque mala est, etiam si minus addatur 'mala,' sicuti *facinus* malum est, etiam si 'malum' haud addatur. Ut enim *facinorosus* semper in malo capitur, ita *famosus* in bono nunquam. Quare ut 'bonum facinus' dicimus aliud esse quam 'facinus,' ita 'bonam famam' aliud esse quam 'famam' fateamur necesse est. Nam gloria sine fama esse non potest. Est enim gloria alicuius clara ac celebris fama cum laude. Et 'gloriosos' quidem non minus eos dici mos est qui et inani et falsa quam qui et certa et vera ducuntur[24] gloria. Itaque et de milite glorioso legimus apud Plautum et eiusmodi quendam nebulonem Terentius Thrasonem inducit. Sed utcunque res habet, laus (quod modo dicebam) non est perfecti sed medii boni.

to happiness and a blessed state of life. I call an *end* what refers
to nothing else but is itself a point of reference for other things.
For those things do not all appear to me to be correctly called
ends that have an end beyond themselves to which they themselves refer. But if these things ought also to be called ends,   81
they should not be thought of as absolute but as intermediate.
An absolute end is one which is both complete and best. Now
fame (fama) is a Greek word. That it means "speech" is clearly
shown by the verb *phemi* ("I say"), from which it is derived.[32]
So it is nothing other than a kind of popular talk, which, if it
shows the authority from which it springs, lays claim to the
name of fame; otherwise it is usually called not fame but rumor, a term that is clearly derived from the Greek verb *rho*, that
is, "I say." Vergil clearly shows that this talk of the people, that
is, "fame," is usually conceived of in two ways, one of criticism,
the other of praise when he says, "[Fame] clings just as much to
something made up and distorted as it reports the truth."[33] But   82
if truth be told, *fama* is far likelier to promote a lie than the
truth. Therefore by its own force and nature it is, to some extent, an evil even if "bad" is not added, just as a crime *(facinus)*
is evil even if "bad" is not added.[34] For just as the word *facinero-
sus* ("criminal") is always used in a bad sense, so *famosus* is never
used in a good one. Therefore as we say that a good deed *(bonum facinus)* is different than a crime *(facinus)*, so we must admit
that good reputation *(bona fama)* is different than reputation
(fama). For glory cannot exist without reputation, since glory is
someone's distinguished and well-known reputation combined
with praise. It is customary for those persons to be called glorious who are led by empty and false glory no less than by true.
Therefore we read in Plautus about a braggart soldier, and Terence brings onstage Thraso, a scoundrel of this type.[35] However
that may be, praise, as I was just now saying, belongs not to the
absolute but the intermediate good.

83   *Nicolaus.* Existimabis me fortassis impudentem. Verum, Pallas, ig-
noscas velim desyderio meo. Nulla enim arrogantia moveor,
nulla insolentia. Sed quoniam omnes natura trahimur sciendi
cupiditate, non siqua sunt quae mihi scire fortasse videar, sed
quae cum nesciam, scire vaehementer cupio, vel forsitan im-
prudentius loquor. Memini legisse aliquando apud Aristotelem
laudem esse 'orationem quae virtutis magnitudinem declarat.'
Primum quid differat virtutis magnitudo a felicitate non satis
intelligo. Nam si cumulata virtus felicem hominem reddere nequeat, reddat profecto aliud nihil. Deinde siquidem ea est vis et
natura laudis ut virtutis magnitudinem declaret, quare id minus
sibi de felicitate vendicet, quae sola virtutis magnitudine felix ac
beata est?

84   *Pallas.* Non dubito, Nicolae, quin videaris tibi non modo aliquid
dixisse, sed ita dixisse ut contra validius dici nihil possit. At
falleris plurimum. Nam neque alicuius virtutis magnitudo felicitatem efficit — id quod tempestive, si ocium dabitur, cognosces — nec qualiscunque virtus laudatur. Nam cum sint in animo
tum habitus vel potentiae, tum agitationes (sic enim τὰς ἐνερ-
γείας non minus apte aliquando quam 'operationes' libet interpretari et 'motiones'), non ille mihi continuo laudandus videtur
cui in habitu vel in potentia maxima etiam et cumulatissima

85   virtus sit, agat autem nihil. Nam optimam cuiusque rei vel dis-
positionem vel habitum vel potentiam dicimus quoad usus eius
quidam est aut opus. Id autem ultimam volunt perfectionem
assecutum, cui ultimum suiipsius bonum contigit. Neque enim
si secus sentiamus, verum sit celebratum illud Graecorum pro-
verbium: 'Probos nihil praestare improbis in vitae dimidio.'
Nam cum somnus sit ociositas quaedam et quies animi, non
autem agitatio, patet et felices et miseros dissimilis non esse in

Niccolò. You will perhaps think me immodest, but please excuse   83
my wish, Palla, for I am moved by no arrogance or insolence.
But since we are all by nature drawn by a desire to know,[36] I
have a strong desire to know not what I think I know, but what
I do not know — or perhaps I am speaking out of turn. I recall
once having read in Aristotle that praise is "speech that discloses
the greatness of virtue."[37] In the first place I am unclear how
the greatness of virtue differs from happiness (*felicitas*). For if
amassed virtue cannot make a man happy (*felix*), surely nothing
else would. Second, if the force and nature of praise is such that
it discloses the greatness of virtue, why does virtue not enter
a claim for itself concerning happiness, which is happy and
blessed solely because of a great amount of virtue?

Palla. I do not doubt, Niccolò, but that you think that you not   84
only have made a point but have done so in such a way that no
stronger argument can be adduced in opposition. But you are
much mistaken. For neither does the size of some virtue create
happiness — a point that you will recognize in due course if leisure is available — nor is praise bestowed upon every virtue no
matter of what sort. For since the mind has on the one hand a
disposition and potentialities, on the other hand movements
(*agitationes*) (for so we can translate *tas energeias* no less aptly
than *operationes* or *motiones*),[38] that man does not seem to me
immediately to require praise who has in his disposition or in
his potential even a massive amount of virtue, but who does
nothing. For we say that the disposition or makeup or potenti-   85
ality of each thing is best insofar as there is a certain use or
work for it. They claim that it has attained its final perfection
when it has come into possession of its final good. If we think
otherwise, that famous proverb of the Greeks would not be
true: "Honest men are no better than wicked in half their
lives."[39] For since sleep is a kind of leisure and quiet of mind,
and not a movement of it, it is obvious that the happy and

somno, nisi quoad bonorum imaginationes meliores esse quam malorum solent, modo morbus quispiam aut membrorum[25] aliqua debilitas offensiove[26] impedimento non fuerit. Itaque siqua est alia animi pars, sicuti certe est nutritiva, huius sane vis totius virtutis pars esse non potest, quemadmodum neque vis corporis. In somno enim pars nutritiva magis perficit, sensitiva vero appetitivaque nequaquam in somno perfecta est. Et quoniam ita habet sensus ad corpus ut mens ad animum, dupliciter de virtute dicendum est. Nam aliae sunt corporis virtutes, aliae animi. Et corporis quidem quattuor sunt, quae quattuor item animi virtutibus comparantur ac veluti respondent: sensuum integritas, bona valitudo, vires et ad currendum et ad reliquos corporis motus, pulchritudo. Animi vero: prudentia, iusticia, fortitudo, temperantia. Et animi quidem bona — quae Plato in primo *De legibus* divina vocat — eo differre a bonis corporis, quod ad eorum laudem satis sit siquis recte habuerit ad proprium virtutis opus atque actionem. Sed in corporis bonis nequaquam id sufficit quod ad alicuius virtutis habitum bene quis habeat, ut ad palestram, ad cursum. Potest enim his quispiam uti et mali alicuius et boni causa. Propterea non temere Plato subdidit humana bona a divinis pendere, et qui maiora accepisset, facile etiam eum minora assecuturum; sin autem secus fiat, cariturum utrisque. Tantum igitur corporis virtutem laudamus, quantum ea ab animi virtute non dissenserit. Animi vero non ociosam et dormitantem, sed quae in actione opereque versetur. Et quoniam laus eorum est quorum bonitas refertur ad aliud, virtus autem est huiusmodi — refertur enim ad felicitatem;

wretched are not unlike in sleep except to the extent that the
dreams of good men are generally better than those of bad,
provided that no illness or weakness or failure of the limbs
stands in the way. And so if there is another part of the soul, as   86
there certainly is a nutritive part, its power cannot by any
means be a part of the whole of virtue, just as the power of the
body is not. For in sleep the nutritive part does its work, but
the sensitive and appetitive parts are not carried out in sleep.
Since the senses relate to the body just as the mind relates to
the soul, virtue should be spoken of in two ways, for some virtues belong to the body, others to the soul. Indeed, there are
four that belong to the body, and these four are compared to
and, as it were, correspond to those of the soul: the well-being
of the senses, good health, strength for running and other
bodily movements, beauty; of the soul: prudence, justice, courage, and temperance. And the goods of the soul, which Plato in   87
the first book *On the Laws* calls divine,[40] differ from those of the
body in that there are sufficient grounds for praising them if
someone possesses them correctly for the performance and exercise of virtue. But in the case of the bodily goods it is by no
means sufficient for someone to be well endowed for the exercise of some virtue, for instance for wrestling or running. For
anyone can use these qualities for both a good and a bad purpose. Hence Plato, with good reason, added that human goods
depend upon divine goods, and the person who had received
the greater goods would easily acquire the lesser ones; if it fell
out otherwise, he would lack both. We therefore praise the virtue of the body to the extent that it is not at odds with the
virtue of the soul. We praise a virtue of the soul, however, that
is not inactive and sleeping but is engaged in action and work.
And since praise concerns those things whose goodness is di-   88
rected toward something else, and virtue is the sort of thing
(for it is directed toward happiness, and happiness is the

felicitas vero est perfectum et summum bonum — cui aliquid laude melius praestantiusque debetur — id autem vel honos est, vel beatio, aut etiam admiratio, si fortasse quoniam in usum nondum satis venerit, beatio minus probetur — patet et virtutem laudandam esse et felicitatem honorandam admirandamque, praesertim cum id honorem quasi divina res aliqua mereatur quod bonorum principium sit et causa. Ut enim Deus principium est et causa totius bonitatis, ita felicitatem bonorum omnium humanorum principium ponimus. Nam quo felices 89 simus, agimus quaecumque agimus. Sed eorum quae aguntur appetunturve finis habet principii rationem. Ratio enim eorum quae ad finem spectant, a fine proficiscatur necesse est. Quibus sane rationibus satis ostendi arbitror felicitatem esse bonum quoddam honorabile atque admirabile. Quidquid enim vel inusitatum est vel perrarum ac idem et excellens et magnum, vulgo admirantur atque honorant. Huiusmodi autem esse felicitatem dubitat nemo.

90 *Manettus.* Non possum, Pallas, non probare quae subtiliter simul et quamverissime disseruisti de laude. Idque Orpheus etiam — quicunque is tandem, sive Crotoniates sive alius quispiam fuerit — in *Argonauticis* videtur sensisse. Ita enim antiquissimus ille vir ac idem eruditissimus incipiens ait:

O rex arquitenens, domitor Pythonis et alti
Parnasi qui saxa tenes summumque cacumen,
virtutem cano, Phoebe, tuam; quare, optime vates,
mi famam tu redde bonam.

91 *Pallas.* Apte quidem, Manette, ut semper, Orphei versus interpretaris. Quare si Nicolaus noster mihi non credit, saltem Orpheo credat, si placet. Vides enim, Nicolae, petere sibi Orpheum ab Apolline bonam famam, quoniam eius virtutem laudet?

absolute and highest good) that is owed something better and more excellent than praise (this is either honor, blessing, or even wonder, since, because it has not yet come to be used sufficiently, blessing is ruled out), it is clear that virtue is praiseworthy and happiness is to be honored and admired, especially since it deserves honor as a kind of divine thing since it is the origin and cause of good things. For as God is the origin and cause of all goodness, so we hold that happiness is the origin of all human goods. For whatever we do we do in order to be happy. But the end of those things that are done or desired takes account of its origin. The purpose of those things which aim at an end must arise from that end. I think it is sufficiently shown by this reasoning that happiness is an honorable and admirable good. The masses greatly admire and honor whatever is uncommon or rare and at the same time excellent and great. And no one doubts that happiness is a thing of this sort.

Manetti. I cannot but approve, Palla, of your subtle and true discourse about praise. And in the *Argonautica* Orpheus, too (whoever he was, whether the native of Croton or someone else), appears to have been of the same mind. For this is the way that most ancient and likewise learned man begins his song:

> O bow-bearing king, conqueror of Python, who possesses
> The rocks of high Parnassus and its summit,
> I sing your virtue, Phoebus; therefore, great poet,
> May you grant me a good reputation.[41]

Palla. You have, as always, aptly rendered these verses of Orpheus, Manetti. Hence if our friend Niccolò does not believe me, let him, if you please, at least believe Orpheus. For do you see, Niccolò, that Orpheus seeks a good reputation for himself from Apollo since he praises his virtue?

89

90

91

Nicolaus. Certe. Tibique vaehementer assentior laudem non esse perfecti sed medii boni, posteaquam non felicitatis eam sed virtutis esse docuisti. Verum quid honorem esse vis?

92 *Pallas.* Arbitror equidem honorem aliud nihil esse quam exhibitionem reverentiae in alicuius egregiae absolutaeque virtutis testimonium. Isque non in verbis solum, ut laus, sed etiam in factis positus est. Non enim honore verborum duntaxat aliquem reverenter prosequimur, verum etiam aliis quibusdam honorificentissimis factis, id quod intueri licet in thriumphantibus aut in maiestatis[27] solio constitutis.

Nicolaus. Ergo quantum intelligere videor, virtus est ea quae nobis et bonam famam et laudem et gloriam parit, quaeque tum felices nos reddit, tum etiam honorandos?

Pallas. Recte accipis.

93 *Nicolaus.* Vitium igitur nos facit infamis, nos dignos esse qui vituperemur ostendit, nos perpetua nominis caligine tenebrisque obscurat, nos denique sempiternae miseriae, nos contumeliae obiicit?

Pallas. Maxime.

Nicolaus. Effice igitur — nisi molestum est — ut quibus artibus infamiam fugere et bonam famam consequi possimus per te nobis discere liceat. Quod si feceris, non laudem modo atque gloriam assecuturos, sed felices quoque ac beatos nos aliquando fore spero. Nam ut ait illa Electra Sophoclea, 'Genitis honeste turpis est vitae rubor.'

94 *Pallas.* Paucis quod petis expediam, tametsi non is sum cuius verba pro oraculis sint habenda. Falli enim possum, utarque non tam veritate, quae soli sapienti perspecta est, quam verisimili quadam veritatis coniectura. Nam ulterius quo progrediar nihil habeo.

Nicolaus. Quod tibi minus perspectum fuerit, quis nostrum adeo demens fuerit qui id se perspicere posse speret? Itaque aperi

Niccolò. Certainly. I strongly agree with you that praise belongs
not to the absolute good but to an intermediate one, now that
you have taught that it does not concern happiness but virtue.
But what do you hold honor to be?

Palla. I think honor is indeed nothing other than a display of re-   92
spect for attesting to someone's extraordinary and absolute virtue. Therefore it does not consist in words alone, as does praise,
but also in deeds. For we do not treat someone with reverence
by mere verbal honor but also by some other highly honorific
deeds, as can be seen in the case of people who parade in triumph or are placed on a throne of majesty.

Niccolò. So as far as I understand, virtue is what supplies us with
a good reputation, praise, and glory and makes us happy as well
as deserving to be honored?

Palla. You understand correctly.

Niccolò. Therefore vice makes us infamous, shows that we deserve   93
reproach, shrouds us in a perpetual fog and shadow of infamy
and finally exposes us to endless unhappiness and scorn?

Palla. Exactly.

Niccolò. Therefore, if you please, allow us to learn from you how
we can flee infamy and acquire a good reputation. If you do
this, I hope that we will not only attain praise and glory but
will also one day be happy and blessed. For as Sophocles' Electra says, "To those honorably born a disgraceful life is shameful."[42]

Palla. I will handle your request briefly, though I am not one   94
whose words should be taken as oracular. As I am fallible, I will
not so much make use of the truth, which is known to the wise
man alone, but rather a sort of probable inference of truth. I
have no way of proceeding beyond that.

Niccolò. Which of us would be so mad as to hope to see what you
have not? So open the treasure-houses and hidden sources of

sapientiae tuae thesauros abditosque fontis, quo istinc quantum ingenii nostri et adolescentiae facultas tulerit hauriamus.

95 *Pallas.* Primum omnium illud vos scire cupio, bonis artibus vaenari oportere bonam famam. Quamobrem et quid bonum vocem et quas bonas artes vos, adolescentes, auditote. Puto enim operae precium fore si anteaquam longius progrediar, paucis complectar quidnam illustres gravissimique philosophi de bono ipso statuerint, et quidnam esset et quotuplex. Et quoniam Stoici magnum quiddam in philosophia mihi profiteri visi sunt, ii primi quid sentiant audiendi sunt, qui sequentes communis notiones bonum utilitatem esse definiunt, aut non aliud ab utilitate. Et utilitatem quidem virtutem dicunt bonamque actionem. Non aliud ab utilitate esse volunt bonum hominem et

96 amicum. Virtus enim, imperitantem rationis vim repraesentans quomodo[28] habeat, et bona actio, quae operatio quaedam sit secundum virtutem, manifesto prodest. Bonus autem homo atque amicus, qui et ipsi e numero bonorum sint, neque utilitas esse dicendi sunt, neque alii ab utilitate. Idque ob huiusmodi causam. Sectatores enim Stoicorum partem dicunt neque eandem esse cum toto nec aliam a toto, veluti pes neque idem est cum toto homine. Non enim totus homo est pes, nec alius a toto. Nam toto cum pede totus ipse homo intelligitur homo. Sic igitur quoniam boni hominis et amici pars est virtus, pars autem neque eadem esse cum toto possit nec alia a toto, dicebatur bonus homo et amicus non esse alius ab utilitate. Itaque omne bonum ea definitione compraehendi putant, sive continuo utilitas sit, sive non sit ab utilitate aliud.

97 Qua quidem ex re consequenter bonum tripliciter dicunt appellari. Nam uno modo id bonum dici ex quo aut a quo fit

your wisdom so that from them we may drink as much as the powers of our nature and our youth may allow.

Palla. First of all I want you to know that one must hunt after good reputation by means of good arts. Hear, then, young men, what I mean by the good and what I mean by good arts. I think it would be worthwhile if, before I proceed further, I briefly set out what views distinguished and authoritative philosophers have held about the good itself, both what it is and of how many parts.[43] Since the Stoics have, I think, raised great claims in philosophy, their views should be heard first. Following common notions, they define the good as a benefit or something not distinct from a benefit. They say that virtue and good action are a benefit. They claim that a good man and a friend is not distinct from a benefit. For virtue, which embodies the ruling power of reason, however it may be, and good action, which is an activity in accord with virtue, are manifestly beneficial. A good man and friend, who are themselves numbered among the goods, neither should be called a benefit nor are different from a benefit, and that for the following reason: the Stoics' followers assert that a part is neither identical with the whole nor is it different from the whole, as for instance a foot is not the same as an entire human being. For the entire human being is not a foot, not is a foot different from the whole. For the whole man himself is understood as a man, including the whole foot. So therefore because virtue is a part of a good man and part of a friend, yet this part cannot be the same as the whole nor different from the whole, it was said that a good man and friend are not different from a benefit. And so they think that every good is encompassed by this definition, whether it is something immediately beneficial or something not different from the beneficial.

Hence they assert that the good is spoken of in three ways. For in one sense that is called good from which or by which a

95

96

97

utilitas, quod certe principalissimum est et virtus. Ab hac enim tanquam a fonte quopiam omnis naturaliter manat utilitas. Secundo autem modo id per quod utilitas contingit. Sic enim non solum virtutes dicentur bona, sed etiam quae secundum virtutes actiones proficiscuntur, siquidem per hasce utilitas contingit. Ultimo vero modo bonum dicitur illud quod utilitatem afferre potest. Et haec quidem assignatio complectebatur tum virtutes, tum actiones secundum virtutes, tum amicos, tum probos viros, tum etiam et Deum et bonos angelos (interpretor enim 'bonos

98 angelos' quos gentilitas σπουδαίους δαίμονας vocabat). Atqui ob eam causam aliter atque aliter tum apud Platonem et Xenocratem, tum apud Stoicos bonum nominatur. Nam Academici cum dicunt aliter nominari bonum secundum speciem et aliter secundum participationem speciei, non quid sit bonum ostendunt, sed boni significata multis modis[29] exponere videntur, et quae invicem plurimum discrepent, nec habeant quicquam inter se commune, quemadmodum licet intueri in hac voce *ca-*

99 *nis.* Ut enim ex hac ipsa voce prolatio quidem significatur sub quam et 'animal latrabile' cadit et 'aquatile' et 'astrum,' nihil autem huiusmodi prolationes habent invicem commune, neque secunda prolatione prima continetur, nec tertia secundam complectitur, sic etiam cum dicitur bonum secundum ideam et bonum quod est particeps ideae, expositio quidem eorum bonorum est quae significantur, verum et separatorum et quibus nullum omnino huiusmodi bonum contineatur. Et hi quidem hoc pacto de bono locuti sunt. De quorum celebri subtilique sententia quod meum iudicium sit, non multo post, ut spero, disseram. Nam neque Stoicis neque ipsi Peripateticorum principi Aristoteli, maximo in philosophia et gravissimo viro, in iis assentior quae contra huiusmodi bonum subtiliter magis quam

100 vere disseruit. Sed ut redeam ad Stoicos: volunt ii quidem in ipsius boni appellatione secundum significatum complecti

benefit is created, which certainly is the major one, namely virtue. For from this as if from some fountain all benefit naturally flows. In the second sense that by which benefit accrues, for in this way not only will the virtues be called good but even the actions that proceed in accord with the virtues, since benefit accrues through these. In the final sense that is called good which can add benefit. This category embraced the virtues, actions according to the virtues, friends, good men, and even God and good angels (I render as "good angels" what the heathen called *spoudaios daimonas* ["good demons"]). And for this reason "good" is termed in one way by Plato and Xenocrates, in another way by the Stoics. For when the Academic philosophers say that good is defined in one way according to form and in another way according to its participation in form, they do not show what the good is, but they seem to set for the significations of the good in many ways: these in turn are in substantial disagreement and share nothing in common, as may be seen in the case of the word *dog*. For as by this word an expression is indicated which comprises both "an animal capable of barking," "a water animal" [dog fish], and "a star" [the dog star], but these expressions have nothing in common (neither is the first expression comprised in the second, nor does the third embrace the second), so also when the good is spoken of as according to the form and the good that is a participant in the form, it is an exposition of the goods that are signified, but of separate ones and ones in which nothing good at all is included. This is how they spoke concerning the good. I shall shortly, I hope, set out my view of their famous and intricate theory. For I concur neither with the Stoics nor with what that very prince of the Peripatetics, Aristotle, a supreme philosopher and man of great authority, argued in his criticism, subtle rather than true, of this kind of good. But to return to the Stoics: they claim that in the definition of the good the second definition contains the

98

99

100

primum et tertio quoque duo contineri. Fuerunt autem qui dicerent id esse bonum quod sit propter se expetendum; alii vero id esse bonum definiunt quod ad felicitatem adiuvat; aliqui vero quod felicitatem compleret bonum esse volebant. Felicitatem autem esse secundum Zenonis et Cleanthae et Chrysippi assignationem vitae facilem ac prosperum decursum.

101   Veruntamen quo bonum assignatur, genus est huiusmodi. Consueverunt autem non nulli, cum tripliciter dicatur bonum, continuo ad definitionem primi significati inquirere, quoad 'id quod dicitur bonum, est illud ex quo aut a quo utilitas proficiscitur,' ut 'si vero bonum est illud a quo utilitas fit, solam generalem virtutem dicere oporteat bonum esse. Ab hac enim sola utilitas fit. Excidit autem ab ea definitione quaeque virtus particularis, ut prudentia, ut temperantia reliquaeque virtutes. Nam a nulla ipsarum haec ista[30] utilitas proficiscitur. Sed a prudentia proficiscitur sapere et non — quod communius est — prodesse. Nam si hoc ipsum prodesse contingat, non erit secundum definitionem prudentia, sed generalis virtus. Et a temperantia quod de ipsa praedicatur, temperantem esse, non — quod commune

102   est — prodesse. Et eodem modo de reliquis dici potest.' Contra ii cupientes quam definitionem posuerant sustinere, ita respondent: 'Cum a nobis dicatur id esse bonum ab quo utilitas proficiscitur, idem est ac si dicatur bonum id esse ab quo ad aliquid eorum quae in vita sunt utilitas proficiscitur.' Sic enim quaelibet etiam particularis virtus bonum erit, quae quidem nequaquam communiter utilitatem afferat, sed eorum aliquid praebeat quibus utilitas fit. Harum enim virtutum alia ut sapiamus praestat, sicuti prudentia, alia ut temperantes simus, sicut temperantia. At hi quidem Stoici, cum volunt huiusmodi responsione

first and the other two are comprised by the third. There have
been those, however, who have said that the good is that which
is to be sought for its own sake. Others hold that that is good
which contributes to happiness. Others, however, have asserted
that the good is that which achieves full happiness. According
to the definition of Zeno, Cleanthes, and Chrysippus, happiness is a trouble-free and prosperous course of life.

But the category to which the good is assigned is as follows. 101
When the good is spoken of as threefold, some are inclined to
inquire immediately into the definition of the first signification,
that is, "what is called good is that from which or by which
benefit originates," stating that "if the good is truly that from
which benefit is derived, we would have to say that only general
virtue is good, for benefit is produced from it alone. Every specific virtue is then excluded from that definition, such as prudence, temperance, and all the other virtues; for this benefit
originates from none of them. But from prudence derives 'being wise,' not the more common 'being beneficial.' For if 'being
beneficial' would come about, it will, according to the definition, not be prudence but general virtue. And from temperance
comes about what is predicated of it, 'to be moderate,' not the
common 'be beneficial.' And the rest of the virtues can be spoken of the same way." On the other hand, there are those who, 102
desiring to support a definition they had offered, reply as follows: "When we say that the good is something from which
benefit springs, it is the same as saying that the good is that
from which benefit springs for any of the things that are present in life." So even any particular virtue will be good, though it
may not bring benefit in a common way but furnish any of
those things from which benefit is generated. For of these virtues one provides that we be wise, namely prudence, another
that we be temperate, namely temperance. But these Stoics,
while wishing by such a reply to evade the first charge, have

primum crimen effugere, in alterum sunt crimen devoluti. Si enim horum alterum est quod dicitur bonum id esse ab quo utilitas ad eorum aliquid proficiscitur quae in vita sunt, generalis virtus, quae bonum sit, sub definitionem minime cadet. Non enim ab ipsa utilitas ad eorum aliquid proficiscitur quae in vita sunt, quoniam una e particularibus fiet, sed simpliciter utilitas.

103 Et alia in hanc sententiam multo plura quae non versute minus quam acute inventa sunt, ab iis dici solent qui de verbo potius quam de re disceptare consuerunt. Nobis autem satis sit si ostendimus qui definit bonum id esse quod prodest, vel quod per se expetendum est, vel quod ad felicitatem comitetur aut huiusmodi aliam assignationem affert, eum non quid bonum sit docere, sed quod bono accidit declarare. Qui vero quod bono accidit ostendit, haud is mihi bonum ipsum videtur ostendere.

104 Continuo igitur quod et conducit bonum et quod expetendum est secundum quod bonum dicitur, videlicet bonum et quod felicitatis est effectivum, nemo est qui dissentiat. Verum si rursus quaeratur quid tandem est hoc prodesse et quod per se sit expetendum et quod felicitatem efficiat, non modo non consentient sed dissentient maxime.

Poggius. Et quamobrem ita dissentiant, Pallas, cum prius consenserint id esse bonum quod esset utile, et quod expetendum foret, et quod felicitatem efficeret?

105 *Pallas.* Quoniam, Poggi, de substantia quaeritur, non de accidente. Nam alii bonum dicent virtutem, alii indolentiam, alii voluptatem et eam quidem tum mentis bene compositae rectaeque rationis, tum — quam ipse tantopere persequeris — dissoluti sensus petulantisque appetitus, alii vero aliud quippiam vel simplex vel coniunctum. Quod si ex superioribus definitionibus patuisset quid esset bonum, haudquaquam dissentirent perinde[31]

fallen into a second one. For if the first charge is that it is claimed that the good is a thing from which a benefit derives for any of those things that are present in life, general virtue, which is a good, will hardly fall within the scope of the definition. For from general virtue a benefit does not originate for any of those things that are useful for whatever is present in life, because then it would become one of the specific virtues, but benefit in general. And against this view many other arguments 103 are usually advanced which have been thought up no less cagily than cleverly by them, who have made a habit of debating more about words than the subject matter. For us let it suffice if we demonstrate that he who defines the good as what is beneficial or what must be sought for its own sake or what is a concomitant of happiness or puts forward another definition of this sort is not teaching what is good but is showing the accidents of the good. But he who shows the accidents of the good does not seem to me to show the good itself. There is therefore no one 104 who would not readily agree that what is beneficial is good and also what ought to be pursued in accordance with what is called good, that is to say, what is productive of happiness is good. But they will not only fail to agree but will vigorously disagree if it is asked what finally is that "beneficial" and what ought to be sought for its own sake and what produces happiness.

Poggio. And why would they disagree this way, Palla, when they agreed before that what is beneficial is good and what ought to be sought and what creates happiness?

Palla. Because, Poggio, the question concerns the substance, not 105 an accident [of the good]. For some will say that virtue is the good, others freedom from pain, others pleasure, and a pleasure both of a well-ordered and reasonable mind and also the pleasure of undisciplined sense and unruly appetite (that you yourself so keenly pursue), others something else, whether simple or compound.[44] But if what is good had become clear from the

ut[32] ignorata natura boni. Non igitur eae definitiones quid sit bonum, sed quid bono accidat, omnes docent. Itaque non solum ob hanc causam reiiciendae sunt, verum etiam quia rem

106 quae esse nequeat videntur appetere. Nam qui aliquid eorum quae sunt ignorat, is neque illius accidens potest cognoscere,[33] uti[34] siquis ad eum qui quid sit equus ignoret dixerit 'equus est animal hinnibile,' is quod est equus minime docet. Nam qui equum ignorat, quid etiam sit hinnire, quod equo accidit, ignoret necesse est. Et qui audiat bovem esse 'animal mugibile' nec teneat quid sit bos, huic bos haud monstratur. Neque enim mugire, quod bovi accidit, is compraehendat qui bovem ignorarit.

107 *Poggius.* At ego profecto, Pallas, aliter bovem definirem, intelligererque ab omnibus.

Pallas. Quonam modo, Poggi? Dic, obsecro. Aiunt enim te non definiendi minus quam bibendi vim rationemque tenere.

Poggius. Bibendi, Pallas? Verum Nicolaus Nicolus me admodum bibendo superat, qui dum mihi propinat, antequam[35] poculum porrigat, ter et iterum ebibit.

Pallas. Sit sane ut vis, sed quid tandem bovem definis esse?

108 *Poggius.* Bos est Laurentius Medices. Num habes quicquam quod huic definitioni obiicias? Aspice Laurentii latera, aspice palearia, incessum consydera. Nonne cum loquitur, mugit? Os vide et linguam e naribus mucum lingentem. Caput cornibus totum insigne est. Ita, mediusfidius, bovem mihi videor aptissime definire esse Laurentium Medicem, ut et lupum Averardum et vulpem Cosmum. Nam et ille fur ac latro, et hic fallax et subdolus.

aforementioned definitions, they would not have disagreed, as if the nature of the good remained unknown. So all these definitions fail to teach what is good, but the accidents of the good. Not only for this reason should they be rejected, but also because they seem to desire to attain something that they cannot. For he who is ignorant of some entity cannot know its accident either; for instance, if someone should say to a man who does not know what a horse is, "A horse is an animal that can whinny," he is hardly teaching what a horse is. For he who does not know a horse must be ignorant of what whinnying is, which is an accident of a horse. And if a man who does not know what a cow is hears that a cow is an "animal that can moo," he has not been shown what a cow is, for a man who does not know a cow would not understand mooing, an accident of a cow.

106

Poggio. But, Palla, I would certainly define a cow differently and would be understood by all.

107

Palla. How so, Poggio? Please tell me. They say that you understand the force and method of definition no less than of drinking.

Poggio. Drinking, Palla? But Niccolò Niccoli quite surpasses me in drinking: when he toasts me, he drains his glass three times and more before offering it up.

Palla. Be that as you wish, but what do you define a cow to be?

Poggio. Lorenzo de' Medici is a cow. Do you make any objection to this definition? Look at Lorenzo's flanks, look at his jowls, consider his gait. Does he not moo when he speaks? Look at his face and his tongue licking the snot from his nostrils. His entire head is decked out with horns. So by the god of oaths I think I most aptly define a cow as Lorenzo de' Medici, just as I define the wolf as Averardo and the fox as Cosimo, for the former is a thief and bandit, the latter wily and deceitful.

108

Pallas. Etiamne in Cosmum tuum, Poggi, cavillaris? Quid si rescierit?

109 *Poggius.* At est mihi apud eum fides. Et quo magis mireris quam est nescius sui, libellos duos scripsi, quos nondum aedidi: alterum *De nobilitate*, alterum *De infelicitate principum*, quibus homo ineptus se laudari putat, cum vituperetur ab me maxime, quippe quem et ignobilem esse doceo et infelicem.

Pallas. Assentaris igitur Cosmo?

Poggius. Et quidnam aliud?

Pallas. Sed facis tu quidem iniuste?

110 *Poggius.* Minime omnium. Nam homini reddo quod suum est. Deposuit apud me loculos plaerosque assentationum plenos, ea lege ut ipse pro arbitrio uteretur et mihi quoque liceret uti cum vellem.

Manettus. Age, Pallas, si libet. Sine Poggium nugari in Cosmum, qui tametsi et ignobilitati est et infelicitati obnoxius, mirifice tamen laudatur cum per assentationes Poggianas vituperatur, praesertim cum quidquid scribit Poggius et ineptum est et insulsum. Redi, obsecro, unde digressus es.

Pallas. Quur in te, Poggi, tam saepe Manettus ludit?

111 *Poggius.* Hic est mos, Pallas, Sophistarum, qui cum nihil sciant, omnia scire existimari volunt. Vel heri quam multa et petulanter in me iocatus est et insolentissime debacchatus? Verum haec nunc missa faciamus. Repete iam orationis curriculum unde diverteras, et calcis aliquando memineris; teque oratorem malis quam philosophum tandem iudicemus.

Pallas. Revocemus igitur nostram orationem, unde nescio quo pacto defluxerat. Et id quod erat in manu resumamus absolvamusque breviter. Itidem igitur cui quid est ipsum bonum obscurum sit, ei frustra et inutiliter dixero bonum id esse quod expetendum est aut quod utilitatem affert. Nam primum quae

Palla. Are you even railing against your friend Cosimo, Poggio?
What if he gets wind of it?

Poggio. He trusts me. And to amaze you even more as to his lack   109
of self-awareness: I have written two pamphlets that I have not
yet published, one *On Nobility*, the other *On the Unhappiness of
Princes*, in which the fool fancies he is being praised when he is
being excoriated by me, since I teach that he is both ignoble and
unhappy.[45]

Palla. Are you, then, flattering Cosimo?

Poggio. What else?

Palla. But you are acting unjustly.

Poggio. By no means, for I am rendering to the man what is his   110
own.[46] He has left on deposit with me several strongboxes filled
with flatteries with the stipulation that he himself may use
them at will and I can also when I wish.

Manetti. Please continue, Palla. Let Poggio moo against Cosimo,
who is guilty of ignobility and unhappiness but is strangely
praised when he is being excoriated by Poggio's flatteries, especially since whatever Poggio writes is inept and tasteless. Please
return to the point from which you digressed.

Palla. Why, Poggio, does Manetti so often mock you?

Poggio. This, Palla, is the style of the sophists, who, though they   111
know nothing, want to be thought to know everything. Yesterday, for instance, what a bacchic orgy of mockery he celebrated
against me with his rude insolence! But let us drop the subject.
Take up the thread of the speech at the point from which you
digressed. Take thought for the goal, and may you prefer for us
to think of you as an orator rather than a philosopher.

Palla. Let us then recall our discourse, from which we somehow
diverged. Let me take up again and settle briefly what we had in
hand. Well then, it would be vain and useless for me to tell a
person to whom it is unclear what the good itself is that the
good is what should be sought or what produces a benefit. For

sit ipsius boni natura discendum est, deinde intelligendum quod
112   et expetendum est et felicitatem efficit. Natura vero ignorata
boni, huiusmodi definitiones quid bonum sit docere non possunt. Et de his quidem satis. Non enim longiores esse possumus. Ex his autem quae brevi oratione perstrinximus, quid
huiusmodi philosophi malum esse definiant, abunde patere censeo. Malum est enim ea ratione quod bono contrarium aut detrimentum affert aut non aliud a detrimento. Et detrimentum
quidem est quemadmodum vitium et mala actio, sed non aliud
a detrimento quemadmodum malus homo et inimicus. Inter
haec autem duo, bonum et malum, id esse Stoici volunt quod
ἀδιάφορον nominant, nos 'indifferens' recte appellemus. Id
autem est quod neutrum habet. Nam quod indifferens est, ne-
113   que in malis est nec in bonis numerandum. Quae enim Peripa-
thetici bona aut mala minima et perexigua esse volunt corporis
et fortunae, ea Stoici in bonis aut in malis non numerant neque
ducunt, sed tum 'indifferentia,' tum 'commoda vel incommoda,'
tum προηγμένα (hoc est 'praelata') vel ἀποπροηγμένα (id
est 'reiecta') vocant. Sed quoniam boni substantiam quaerimus
potius quam accidens quodpiam, illud omnium primum intelligi oportet, quo de bono sermo nobis habendus sit. Nam alia
bona sunt quae in hominis actionem non cadunt, alia vero
cadunt. Quaedam enim eorum quae sunt, ut nullam habent
cum motu communitatem, ita ne cum bonis quidem quae in
114   actionem cadunt. Et haec indubitato natura sunt optima. Quaedam vero habent cum motu communitatem, quare etiam cum
actione, sed nequaquam nostra, qui mortales sumus, verum eorum qui mortalitatem pati non possunt. Quae autem in humanam actionem cadunt, ea rursus duplicia sunt. Alia enim eiusmodi esse dicimus ut eorum gratia agamus, alia vero quae
propter haec in actionis participationem veniant: ut et bonam
valitudinem et divitias ponimus in eorum genere quae propter

first he should learn what the nature of the good itself is, then
understand what is to be sought and produces happiness. If the   112
nature of the good is not known, such definitions cannot teach
what the good is. Enough of these matters; we cannot go on at
excessive length. I think it abundantly clear from the points I
briefly touched on what such philosophers define as evil. By
this reasoning the evil is what is opposite to the good or what
brings harm or something not different from harm. A harmful
thing is something like a vice and a harmful action, just as a
harmful thing is something like a bad man and an enemy. The
Stoics claim that in between these two things, the good and the
bad, is what they call the *adiaphoron*, which we correctly call
"indifferent." It is what has neither; for what is indifferent
should be counted neither among evils nor goods. What the   113
Peripatetics claim to be small and trivial goods and evils of the
body and fortune the Stoics do not count among good or bad
things nor consider them as such, but call them now indifferents, now benefits or hindrances, now *proegmena*, that is, "preferred," or *apoproegmena*, that is, "rejected." But since we are investigating the substance of the good rather than any accident,
it is first of all necessary to understand about which good we
ought to carry on our discussion. There are some goods that do
not apply to human action, but others that do. For some of the
things that exist, since they have no relationship with motion,
therefore have no relationship either with the goods that apply
to action. And these are undoubtedly the best by nature. But   114
some do have a relationship with motion, hence also with action, but not action that is ours (we who are mortal), but of
those beings that cannot experience mortality. Moreover, those
things that apply to human action are of two kinds. We say
that some are such that we do them for their own sake, but
others come to participate in action for the sake of these [i.e.,
the first group]. For instance, we place good health and riches

se agantur, et ea quae ad bonam valitudinem pecuniasque pertinent, in iis numeramus quae non propter se, sed horum gratia
115   in actionem veniant. Quod cum ita sit, haud est obscurum felicitatem ex his omnibus bonis quae in hominum actionibus sita
sunt, et perfectum esse et optimum et summum bonum, ad
quod tamen qui pervenire per media quae dicimus bona instituerit, necesse fuerit ut cum illa etiam sibi proponat bona quae
in nostram actionem non cadunt sed immortalis cuiusdam naturae sunt, tum ad ea omnem mentis aciem intendat quae nulli
motui sunt obstricta,[36] sed natura incommutabilem stabilitatem
habent et sempiterna sunt et optima, ac ita certe optima, ut
nihil nobis sine illis non modo non optimum, sed ne minima
quidem ex parte bonum esse possit.[37]

116   *Manettus.* Profecto, Pallas, tuam istam bonorum distinctionem et
probo et laudo, qua et Aristotelem sequeris et a Platone non
discedis et Christianam philosophiam in primis imitaris. Sed
quid bonum esse definis?

Pallas. Istuc venio, Manette. Non enim ulla nos debet dubitatio
tenere aliud esse bonum quod et per sese bonum est et secura
sua tranquillitate ineffabilique praestantia gaudet, non modo
motionis omnis atque actionis expers quae aliunde motum accipiens non sua vi suaque natura et movetur et agitur, sed ita
omnino bonorum omnium quaeque sunt quaeque dicuntur et
fons est et causa, ut nihil quod eo vacet, bonum esse queat; et
aliud etiam quod aeterniore moderatioreque quam nostra est
117   actione utitur. Nam inferiorum nostrorumque bonorum quis
adeo amens sit qui nesciat longe magis atque magis illud bonum praestare cuius gratia caetera expetuntur, quam id quod
non propter se sed propter aliud expetendum sit? Sed quoniam
paulo ante dixeramus aliud esse bonum perfectum, aliud

in the category of things which are carried out for their own sake, and the things that are relevant to good health and wealth we classify among the things that are carried out not for their own sake but for the sake of these. This being so, it is clear 115 that, of all the goods that reside in human action, happiness is the perfect, highest, and best; yet he who has decided to reach this good via what we call intermediate goods must have as his goal not only those goods that do not apply to human action but are possessed of a sort of immortal nature, but must also direct all the sharpness of his mind to those things that are not bound to any motion but have by nature a constant stability and are eternal and best and are best to such an extent that without them nothing can be not only best, but not even in the slightest degree good.

Manetti. Certainly, Palla, I approve and praise your distinction of 116 goods, in which you follow Aristotle and do not depart from Plato, and most of all you take as your model Christian philosophy. But what do you define as the good?

Palla. I am coming to this, Manetti. For there should be no doubt that we maintain that there is one good that is good in and of itself and delights in its own secure tranquility and inexpressible excellence, which is not only immune from any motion and action which, receiving an impulse from elsewhere, not from its own force and nature, is both moved and driven, but is so entirely the source and cause of all things that are or are called good that nothing can be good which lacks it; and there is also another good that employs an action that is more eternal and measured than ours. For is anyone so insane that he does not 117 realize that, among our inferior goods, that good for the sake of which the others are sought is far superior to the one that is to be sought not for its own sake but for the sake of something else? But since we said a little while ago that an absolute good is one thing, an intermediate something else, we claim that the

medium, id interesse volumus felicitatem et virtutem, quod hominem et hominis partem, ut bonum hominis sit felicitas, bonum hominis partis sit virtus ipsa. Et quo facilius teneamus
hominis bonum in eo quo homo est, quid cuiusque rei sit bonum sciamus oportet. Nam et homo alia quadam perfectione
perfectus in eo dicitur, secundum quod homo est, et alia leo,
secundum quod leo. Atque bonum est cuiusque rei quando in
substantia et potentia (quam enim Graeci δύναμιν, nos modo
'vim,' modo 'potentiam,' nonnunquam etiam tum 'potestatem,'
tum 'virtutem'[38] dicimus) potest agere quaecunque sunt secundum naturam. Id autem in animalibus quibusque intueri licet.
Nam potentia, quae instrumentale bonum est, tempore antecedit operationem, at ratione sequitur. Si enim ad doctrinam referatur, operatio et prior est et nobis certior cognitu quam potentia quoad perfectionem. Alicuius enim rei perfectionem vel
potentia dicimus vel operatione. Nam huius gratia potentia est.
Id autem cuius gratia aliud est, prius hoc est quod esse constat
propter illud, et cuiusque rei finis tempore quidem posterior
est, ratione vero prior. Nam ratione finem proponimus, et ita
quae ad finem sunt quaerimus ac paramus. Omnia igitur primo
ex potentia procedunt ad operandum. Verbi causa ex saemine
generatur homo, qui tamen neque in quantitate instrumento-
rum nec in membris quae in ipsis sunt instrumentis continuo
perfectus est. Sed ubi membra parvam quandam acceperint
quantitatem, et quod humidius est, desiccatum fuerit, et qui
per membra spiritus diffluit, perseveranter constiterit, perficitur
paulatim in corpore ad corporalis operationes. Ac ita de puero
vir efficitur.

Idem quoque in animi potentiis tam notionis quam motionis—quae naturales sunt animi partes—esse animadvertitur.

118

119

120

difference between happiness and virtue is the same as between
a man and a part of a man, namely that happiness is the good
of a man and virtue itself the good of a part of a man. And in   118
order that we may more easily understand the good of a man
qua man, we must know what is the good of each thing.⁴⁷ For a
man is said to be perfect with a certain different perfection *qua*
man and lion with a different one *qua* lion. And the good of
each thing exists when in substance and potential (for what the
Greeks call *dynamis* we sometimes call "force," sometimes "potential," sometimes we also call it "power," sometimes "virtue") it
can carry out whatever things are according to its nature. This
can be seen in all animate beings. For potential, which is an
instrumental good, temporally precedes action but follows it
theoretically. To speak in terms of teaching, action is prior to
and easier for us to recognize than potential as regards perfection. For we speak of the perfection of anything in terms of its
potential or its action. For potential exists for the sake of this   119
[i.e., action]. Moreover, that for the sake of which another
thing exists is prior to that which is agreed to exist for its sake;
and the end of this thing [i.e., the thing for the sake of which
another exists] is temporally posterior but theoretically prior.
For by reason we propose an end and by reason we seek out
and prepare the things that contribute to the end. All things
therefore first advance from potential to action. For example,
though a man is generated from seed, he is not immediately
perfect in the number of his organs or in the members that are
in these organs. But when the members have gained a certain
small increase and what is moist has been dried out and the
spirit that flows through the members is established in a steady
pattern, the individual attains completion little by little in body
for bodily activities. And so a boy becomes a man.

The same also is noticed in the potentialities of the mind,   120
both of its conceptualization and motion (these are the natural

In ipsa enim hominis generatione[39] ea boni saemina sparsim hae virtutes accipiunt in quibus inchoatio quaedam ad humanum bonum accommodata sita est. Huiusmodi vero saemina experimento paulatim et tempore atque assuetudine coeunt perficiunturque, et ita quae secundum naturam sunt optima agere possunt. Non enim philosophus ille mihi vel habendus vel nominandus videtur, qui ignoret nullam esse potentiam quae ex se perfecta sit. Necesse enim est ut per habitum perfectionem 121 capiat ad agendum vel innatum vel partum. Nam — ut ipsam animi substantiam agitationemque mentis in aliud commodius tempus reiiciamus — tria in animo inesse quae operationum actionumque nostrarum principia sint, philosophi omnes consentiunt: potentiam, passionem, habitum; et potentiam quidem principium esse materiamque passionis, ut iracundiam, verecundiam; passionem vero insurgentem quandam potentiae motionem, ut iram, pudorem; at habitum esse partis irrationalis robur atque conatum assuetudine ingeneratum; et eum quidem si recte a ratione instituatur, virtutem fieri, sin autem prave, vi-122 tium. Quae autem loquimur de activorum potentiis, quae perfectione nunquam vacant, intelligenda non sunt. Quibus quidem rationibus sequitur ut bonum humanum sit, secundum hominis naturam perfecta posse optimaque perficere. Neque illud ignoremus oportet, id esse in partibus quoque accipiendum quod in toto sit. Nam sicut animus sua natura est corpore perfectior, ita animi partes corporis partibus longe praestant. Sic oculi visio, sic pedis incessus perfectio est. Itaque non ab re dicit 123 Aristoteles: 'Si oculus animal foret, eius animus visus foret.' Et ita aliud est hominis bonum secundum quod homo est, aliud secundum hominis partes: illud perfectum, hoc tanquam medium et imperfectum. Inde fit ut[40] aliud sit[41] cupiditatis bonum, aliud irae, aliud rationis, aliud intellectus, et mentis ipsius aliud. Quare cum de hominis bono quaeritur, secundum quod homo

parts of the mind). For in the process of man's generation, these powers receive the seeds of the good in a random manner; in them is located a certain initial impulse adapted to the human good. Such seeds gradually by experimentation and with time and habituation coalesce and ripen, and thus can do things that are best according to nature. For I should not consider or call that man a philosopher who is unaware that there is no potentiality that is perfected on its own. For it must attain perfection for acting by a condition that is either innate or acquired. For 121 all philosophers agree that there are in the mind — to postpone the substance and movement of the mind to another more convenient time — three starting points of our activities and actions: potential, passion, disposition. Potential is the starting point and material of passion, such as anger or modesty; passion is a kind of surging movement of potential, such as anger or shame; disposition is the mainstay of the irrational part and is produced by habituation; this, if it has been rightly instructed by reason, becomes virtue, if badly, vice. But what we 122 are saying should not be understood about the potentialities of the agents, which never lack perfection. For these reasons it follows that it is a human good to be able to achieve the perfect and best qualities according to the nature of man. Nor should we be unaware that the same should be understood in the parts as in the whole. For just as the mind is more perfect than the body, so the parts of the mind far excel the parts of the body. So vision is the perfection of the eye, walking that of the foot. Therefore Aristotle aptly says: "If the eye were an animal, sight would be its mind."[48] And thus a man's good is one thing ac- 123 cording to the fact that he is a man, but different according to a man's parts: the former is perfect, the latter as it were intermediate and imperfect. It follows that one thing is the good of desire, another that of anger, another of reason, another of intellect, and of the mind itself yet another. Therefore when one

est, ita est id bonum definiendum secundum quod est hominis bonum et secundum quod est partium eius. Ut enim felicitas est hominis bonum, ita virtus nequaquam hominis sed partis hominis bonum est.

124 *Manettus.* Quid singularum rerum bonum esse, Pallas, definias, quidque tum partis, tum etiam totius hominis bonum esse velis, satis liquido intelligere mihi videor, idque omnino admittendum esse arbitror. Verum si idem feceris de eo quod communiter — ut ita loquar[42] — bonum accipiatur, non erit fortassis hisce adolescentibus tuus hac etiam de re sermo vel intempestivus vel iniucundus. Nam mihi huiusmodi quoque boni cognitio pernecessaria videtur.

125 *Nicolaus.* Quinimo, Pallas, quod Manettus opportune subiecit, idem ut abs te peterem meus hic Honofrius hortabatur. Itaque nisi molestum est, nobis expone et quid id bonum quod rebus omnibus sit commune esse velis, et utrum per se aliquod bonum esse putes quod et primum ita sit ut ante id bonum aliquid nihil sit, ac idem in bonis omnibus boni causam esse pateat. Videmus enim secundum Platonem bonum id existimari quod a prima idea boni secundum boni formam proficiscatur.

Pallas. Hoc tu mihi honeris, Manette, imponis, qui dum Nicolao obsequeris, vires nostras minus metiare. Num enim ignoras quae petuntur esse in media philosophia recondita?

126 *Manettus.* Perge, Pallas, perge, obsecro. Redde nos bonos bonitate tua. Nam haud scio quantum postea futuri una simus.

Poggius. At ego te, Pallas, moneo ut, si sapis, sophisticam omnem istiusmodi garrulitatem omittas, et Epicuri nostri aliquando memineris, qui solus quid bonum esset intellexit.

inquires into a man's good according to the fact that he is a man, that good should be defined according to what is a man's good and according to what is the good of his parts. For as happiness is the good of a man, so virtue is by no means the good of a man but of a part of a man.

Manetti. I think I understand clearly, Palla, what you define as the good of individual things and what you claim to be the good of the part and also of the whole man, and I think that it should be altogether accepted. But if you were to do the same about what is commonly, so to speak, accepted as good, your discussion about this matter as well will perhaps not be untimely or unpleasant to these young men. For a knowledge of such good seems to me also quite necessary. 124

Niccolò. Indeed, Palla, my friend Onofrio here was urging that I ask you what Manetti opportunely added. So if you please, set out for us what you hold that good to be which is common to all things and whether you think that there is something good which likewise is first in the sense that no other good is before it and is clearly the cause of good in all good things. For we see that, according to Plato, that is thought to be good which proceeds from the first idea of the good according to the form of the good.[49] 125

Palla. You are imposing this burden on me, Manetti, since in humoring Niccolò you are failing to measure my strength. For you are surely not unaware, are you, that what you are asking about is hidden in the center of philosophy?

Manetti. Go on, Palla, go on, I beg you. Make us good by your own goodness, since I do not know how much we shall be together hereafter. 126

Poggio. But I warn you, Palla, if you are smart, to lay aside all such sophistic loquacity and take into consideration at long last our friend Epicurus, who alone understood what is good.

Pallas. Fortasse, Poggi, modo quam ille voluptatem posuisset tene-remus.

Rainaldus. Omitte, Pallas, Poggium nunc, si libet, cum esculentis et potulentis suis, et quae Manettus ac Nicolaus postulant, dili-genter explana. Non enim res parva est neque inutilis.

127 *Pallas.* Faciam ut iubes, Rainalde, posteaquam imprudenter adeo in huiusmodi sermonem delapsus sum. Faciam autem pro viri-bus. Quod enim non potero, non debebo. Principio igitur bo-num id utique statuo esse, cui ultima sui perfectio contigerit. Nam si bonum a fine ultimo suae bonitatis rationem capit, huiusmodi vero finis ubi accesserit, nihilo res eget, quippe quae nihil ad id cuius gratia singillatim sunt reliqua appetit sibi adiici. Non enim ultimum foret, siqua appeteretur adiectio. Id igitur bonum est, quod ultimum sit secundum naturam finem consecutum. Si id praeterea bonum non est cui vitium sit ad-mixtum, et cuicunque ultimum minus contigit, huic vitii quip-piam inhaeret (quantum autem habet vitii, tanta bonitate caret), quonam igitur pacto id bonum dici convenit quod ultimam suiipsius perfectionem consecutum nondum sit? Ad haec nihil cuique rei addi potest praeter huius ipsius rei bonum.

128 At bonitatis quattuor sunt causae: quae efficiat, quae mate-riam praestet, quae formam tradat, quae finem addat. Quare cum sola ipsius finis causa est quae, ad extremum accedens, rem perficiat, quis ambigat solam finalem causam esse illam ad quam accedere nihil potest? Si enim id perfectum est quod nulla re eget, eo fit ut is nihilo egeat cui quod ex finis causa fit, nihil addi possit. Igitur[43] id bonum esse perspicuum est, ad quod

Palla. Perhaps, Poggio, provided that we understand what he held pleasure to be.

Rinaldo. Forget about Poggio now, Palla, if you please, with his feasting and drinking, and explain carefully what Manetti and Niccolò are asking. For this is neither an insignificant matter nor a useless one.

Palla. I will do as you wish, Rinaldo, after having imprudently slipped into a discussion of such a trivial nature. I will do so as best I can; what I cannot do I ought not do.[50] In the first place I hold without qualification that the good is a thing's attainment of its own ultimate perfection. For if the good receives the reason for its goodness from the final end, when such an end is attained, the thing requires nothing, for it craves that nothing be added to itself in addition to that for the sake of which the rest individually exist. For if any additional thing were to be desired, this would not be its final stage. And so the good is something that has reached its final end according to its nature. Moreover, if whatever has any admixture of fault is not the good, and if some fault inheres in whatever has not attained its final end (to the extent that it possesses a fault, to that extent it lacks goodness), how is it appropriate, then, for something to be called good that has not yet reached the final state of perfection? Moreover, nothing can be added to anything but the good itself.

There are four causes of goodness: one that brings it about, one that supplies its matter, one that passes on its form, and one that adds its end. For this reason, since it is only the cause of the end itself which, arriving at the end, perfects a thing, would anyone doubt that the final cause is alone the one to which nothing can be added? For if that which lacks nothing is a perfect thing, it therefore turns out that a man would lack nothing to whom nothing could be added that came about from the cause of its end. It is therefore clear that the good is

127

128

ultimi finis perfectio accesserit. Rursus siquidam[44] id bonum esse asseverant ad quod omnium vel appetitus vel impetus fertur, hoc ultimum sit oportet. Nam nisi ultimum esset, aliud quiddam amplius appeteretur. Nunquam enim quiescit appetitus quoad eorum aliquid desit quae addi possunt. Aut igitur nihil est bonum, aut hoc est necessario solum bonum, cui ultima perfectio sit apposita. Insuper ens, verum et bonum secundum subiecta quidem convertuntur, at rationis nomine differunt. Id enim 'ens' dici putant quod quancunque demus[45] differentiam entitatis quodammodo assecutum sit, 'verum' autem quod per formam entis veritatem ratitudinemque acquisierit, quod ipsum tamen in virtute et operatione nonnunquam est imperfectum. Sed post 'ens' et 'verum' id etiam addatur oportet quod virtute et operatione perfectum est ultima suae perfectionis forma, ac ita continuo bonum est. Quo fit ut id non ab re bonum esse videatur quod ultimi finis accessione perfectum est. Hoc autem confirmemus exemplo. Eandem habet proportionem bonum et verum ad ens quam homo qui generare iam potest et puer cui nondum generandi facultas adest habet ad saemen ex quo generatur. Ut enim hominis saemen primo est in potentia tantum ut ex ipso generetur homo, neque sub forma saeminis adhuc aliquid est quod operatione hominis formam habeat, ita entis ratio propter suam transcendentiam atque communitatem nihil dicit definite. Dicit autem communem quandam rationem duntaxat, quae ad definita et perfecta entia potentiam habent. Atqui sicut homo, simulac e saemine generatus et ortus est, mollibus adhuc membris et instrumentis corporeis nondum sua quantitate perfectis, est verus homo (habet enim quaeque hominis principia interiora, ut animum mentis rationisque capacem; habet corporis secundum naturam

something to which the perfection of the final end has been
added. Again, if some assert that the good is that toward which
the desire and force of all is carried, this good must be final. For
if it were not final, something further would be desired. For the   129
appetite never rests as long as it lacks any of the things that can
be added. Therefore there is either no good, or necessarily there
is only a good to which ultimate perfection has been added. In
addition, being, true, and good are interchanged according to
the subject [sc. of which they are predicated] but differ in terms
of their definition. For people think that is called "being" which
somehow has attained whatever difference of being we attribute
to it, "true" that which has gained truth and solidity by the form
of its being, though it is itself sometimes imperfect in virtue
and action. But after "being" and "true" must be added that
which, perfect in power and action, is the ultimate form of its
own perfection and is thus instantly good. The result is that a   130
thing rightly seems to be good which is perfect by addition of
the final end. Let us confirm the point with the following example. The good and true have the same relation to being as a
man who already has generative power and a boy whose capacity for generating is not yet present have to the seed from which
generation occurs. As a man's seed is at first only potentially
present so that a man may be generated from it, and under the
form of the seed there is not yet anything that by activity may
have the form of a man, so the definition of being claims no
specificity because of its transcendence and commonality. It
merely claims a kind of general definition, namely beings that
have the potential to become precisely formed and perfect beings. And just as a man, as soon as he has been generated and   131
arisen from seed, though his members and bodily organs, still
soft, are not yet perfect in their quantity, he is a true man (for
he has all the inner principles of a man, such as a soul with the
capacity for mind and reason; he has bodily organs according to

273

instrumenta), neque tamen perfectus est. Non enim potest omnia operari quae humanae sunt perfectionis, ut generare similem sui. Nam ita quodque perfectum est, si tale quicquam efficere possit cuiusmodi ipsum est. Eodem igitur modo verum est quod iam attigit entis ratitudinem et perfectionem substantialem atque specificam. Quod ipsum tamen quoniam nondum ad virtutem perfectamque ac suam operationem pervenerit, necesse est his bonum addatur. Id enim secundum propriam rationem ita habet ut homo perfecta aetate, si aut cum eiusmodi puero aut cum saemine conferatur. Quapropter cum omnibus in rebus apparet bonum esse ab ultima perfectione — tunc enim quodque bonum est, cum ea optime potest absolvere quae secundum suam sunt naturam — cui obscurum videri debet, id esse bonum quod ita ab ultimo suae naturae fine perfectum sit, ut omnia pro absolutissima suae naturae bonitate perficere possit?

133 *Manettus.* Reliqua tibi, Pallas, assentior. Sed unum est quod requiram, et id quidem discendi gratia.

Poggius. Imo temptandi, Pallas; fallacias Manetti cave.

Manettus. Sit sane ut insimulat Poggius. Modo ex te aliquid discamus eorum quae multa ignoramus, me vel quaerendi vel temptandi causa locutum existimato.

Pallas. Age, Manette, quaere ut libet. Novi enim verecundiam et modestiam tuam.

134 *Manettus.* Quidquid est, in eo quod sit, bonum esse puto. Ac multa certe sunt quae licet[46] ultimam suae naturae perfectionem consecuta minime sint, bona tamen esse nemo neget. Et Aurelius Augustinus, summa eruditione et sapientia vir, non ab re ait: 'In quantum sumus, boni sumus.' Hoc igitur modo bonum ab ultima perfectione non differt.

nature), but he is not perfect. For he cannot do all the things which belong to human perfection, such as generating a child like himself. For each thing is perfect if it can create anything of its own kind. In the same way something is true that has already attained the solidity of being and a substantial and specific perfection. But all the same since it has not yet arrived at virtue and its own perfect functionality, the good must be added to these things. For this is the case according to its own definition, just as if a man of mature age is compared with a boy of his kind or with a seed. Since therefore in all things the good is seen to be derived from their final perfection — for then each thing is good when it can best accomplish the things that are according to its nature — to whom should it seem obscure that the good is that which is perfect from the final end of its own nature so that it can accomplish all things in accord with the most absolute goodness of its nature?

132

Manetti. I agree with you on the rest, Palla. But I would make one request, and that for the sake of learning.

133

Poggio. Rather for the sake of baiting, Palla; beware Manetti's traps!

Manetti. Let it be as Poggio accuses; provided that we learn from you some point of the many of which we are ignorant, you can suppose that I have spoken for the sake of inquiring or of baiting.

Palla. Come, Manetii, ask as you please; I am familiar with your reserve and modesty.

Manetti. Whatever exists, in that it exists, I hold to be good. And there are surely many things that no one would deny are good even though they have failed to attain the ultimate perfection of their nature. Augustine, a man of supreme learning and wisdom, said to the point: "Insofar as we exist we are good."[51] In this sense therefore the good does not differ from final perfection.

134

135   *Pallas.* Non equidem negabo quodque bonum esse in eo quod est. Quod enim simplicem entitatem habet, id in[47] inchoatione bonum habet. Entitas enim simplex in potentia est et in primis entis principiis. Quod si entitatis perfectionis veritatem per formam attingit, habet bonitatem ad essentiam in specie definitam. Sin autem entitatem per speciem habet in speciei forma et iis quae ad formam perfectam consequenter accedunt, tum bonitatem perfectam habet. Quaeque res enim in forma et iis quae deinceps ad formam ipsam accedunt, perfecta et terminata est. Nam quaecunque natura sunt perfecta, si modo virtus impedita non sit, secundum proprium et generalem habitum operantur. Quae vero consequuntur ad formam, quaque in specie sunt et virtus tum naturalis tum propria et operatio non impedita. Qua quidem re fit quidquid est, in eo quod sit, bonum esse. Habet

136   autem tantum bonitatis quantum essentiae. Itaque nihil est ex omni parte bonum, nisi quod ad ultimam sui perfectionem pervenerit. Et quoniam quid esset per se bonum quaerebatur, ante omnia intelligamus oportet 'per se' (ut Aristoteli videtur) dupliciter dici. Est enim 'per se' quod non est 'per accidens,' et est 'per se' quod non est 'per aliud.' Non igitur parum interest utrum quod dicitur per se bonum, sitne per substantiam et non per accidens, an sit per seipsum bonum et non per aliud. Eninvero inter omnia bona unum quippiam bonum necessario dandum est ab quo ipso[48] bona omnia tanquam a causa proficiscan-

137   tur. Nam si secus fiat, neque omnis multitudo ad unitatem reducatur, nec etiam omnis multiplicitas ad univocationem, nec id quod est per accidens queat ad id reduci quod per se sit. Quae quidem omnia philosophiae praeceptis contraria sunt. Esto igitur aliquid per se bonum, quod et substantialiter et non per aliud bonum sit. Praeterea quisnam dubitet in omnibus

Palla. I do not deny that any good is in what exists. For what has
simple being possesses the good in an incipient state. For simple
being is in potentiality and in the first beginnings of being. But
if it attains the truth of the perfection of its being through
form, it has goodness that is defined according to the essence in
a species. But if, on the other hand, it has being through a species in the form of a species and in those things that, in conse-
quence, reach perfect form, then it has perfect goodness. For
each thing that is in a form and in those things that in turn
reach the form itself is perfect and complete. For whatever
things are perfect by nature, provided that their power is not
impeded, act in accord with their proper and general disposition. But things that attain to form are in each species a power
that is both natural and proper to it and an action that is unim-
peded. In this way it results that whatever is, in that it is, is
good; and it has as much goodness as essence. Therefore there
is nothing good in every respect unless it has arrived at its own
final perfection. And since what is good *per se* has been a subject of inquiry, first we must understand that *per se* (in Aristotle's view) is said in two senses. For there is a *per se* that is not
by accident (*per accidens*) and there is a *per se* that is not through
something else (*per aliud*). It therefore makes no small difference
whether what is called good *per se* is so by its substance and not
by accident or is good *per se* and not through something else.
For among all good things some one good thing must necessarily be granted from which itself all good things arise as if from
a cause. For if it were otherwise, neither could the entire multitude be reduced to a unity, nor could the entire multiplicity be
reduced to a single designation, nor could that which is by accident be reduced to that which is *per se*. All these consequences
are contrary to the teachings of philosophy. Let there therefore
be something good *per se* which is good in its substance and not
through something else. Furthermore, who would doubt that in

135

136

137

participantibus eam esse naturam, ut aliquid necessario sit quod per se id habet quod participans habet per accidens, sicuti in visus disgregatione est ipsum videre quod homo albus per accidens habet? Neque per accidens id haberet, nisi quam participat albedo idem per se haberet. Cum igitur bonus vir habeat boni operationem participando, necessitate aliquid est quod eandem operationem per sese habeat. Hoc autem est quod dicimus per se bonum. Rursum quidquid est bonum aliud illud per quod hoc dicimus esse bonum, aut per se bonum est aut per aliud. Quod si per aliud est bonum, infinita erit progressio. Sin autem per se dixerimus esse bonum, tum aliquid est per se bonum cuius participatione quidquid participat bonum efficitur.

139   Unum igitur per se bonum est, per quod omnia bona efficiuntur, id quod huiusmodi rationibus, ut arbitror, Plato ductus et probavit et voluit. Cuius etiam auctoritate confirmatior factus eandem ipsam ego sententiam non solum sequor, sed etiam[49] facile ac libenter sequor, eamque veluti e divino quodam veritatis oraculo emanasse puto.

140   *Manettus.* Esse tamen quosdam, Pallas, existimo, qui tibi id non omnino concedant. Nam si ponatur unum aliquod bonum quod omnia quae bona sunt participative contineat, hoc sit unum necesse est aut individuo aut specie. Sed <quod>[50] individuo non est unum, ne specie quidem unum esse possit. Non enim bonorum omnium bonitates specie unum sunt. Nam equi bonitas ut est bene currere, bene sessorem vehere et bene hostem expectare eumque terrere, non eadem quae bovis est bonitas, non canis, non leonis neque alicuius huiusmodi quoad speciem. At ne genere quidem una est. Quotquot enim genera eorum quae sunt dixeris, tot singillatim bonitates reperias genere

138

all cases of participation their nature is such that there is necessarily something which has *per se* what the participant has by accident, as in the analysis of a visible form it is possible for one to see what a white man has by accident? Nor would he possess 138 it by accident unless the whiteness in which he participates had the same quality *per se*. Since therefore a good man has by participation the performance of good action, there is of necessity something that has the same performance *per se*. This is what we call the good *per se*. Again whatever that other good is through which we say this thing is good, it is good either *per se* or through another thing. But if it is good through another thing, then there will be an infinite regression. But if we say that it is good *per se*, then there is another thing good *per se* by participation in which whatever participates is made good. There is therefore one good *per se* by which all good things are 139 made good; led, I believe, by such arguments Plato both demonstrated and held this position. Strengthened by his authority, I not only follow the same view but do so readily and gladly and think it has emanated as if from a wondrous divine oracle of truth.

Manetti. I believe, however, that there are some, Palla, who would 140 not at all give ground to you. For if some one good is posited that encompasses all things that are good by means of participation, this must be one either individually or by species. But since it is not one individually, it could not be one by species either. For the goodnesses of all good things are not one by species. For since the goodness of a horse, to gallop well, to make a good mount, to do a good job of awaiting and terrifying the enemy, is not the same as the goodness of a cow, a dog, a lion, or of any such animal as far as the species is concerned. But not even in respect to genus is there a single goodness. For as many genera as there are of the things that you have discussed, so many goodnesses you will find that, one by one, differ in genus.

diversas. Itaque si neque individuo nec specie nec genere est unum bonum, videtur nullum esse primum bonum.

141 *Pallas.* Et acute, Manette, quae contradiceres invenisti, et non dilucide minus quam subtiliter explicasti. Verum ad ista omnia vel cum Aristotele facilis est responsio. Nam primum ad omnia sequentia relationem habet, et quo plus aliquid est, eo est relationibus multiplicius. Itaque dupliciter accipi 'primum' potest: proportione et natura. Quod autem aut generis aut specie aut individui natura nihil sit per se bonum, ab quo bona omnia dicantur, assentiendum arbitror. Sed esse proportione aliquid per se bonum quod neque per accidens bonum sit nec per aliud, ad quod quidem ipsum si respiciatur, per quandam similitudinem habitudinum bona omnia bona sunt, quis est qui dissentiat? Et eo bona vel meliora dici possunt vel optima, quo sunt boni[51] il-

142 lius[52] similiora. Eiusmodi vero bonum est primum bonum, quod substantia perfecta omnia perficit secundum proprias et — ut ita dixerim — connaturalis attributiones, et id quidem ad propriam operationem, modo impedita non sit. Ad illius enim proportionem quodque bonum et melius et optimum appellari licet. Hoc enim quod ita per se et non per accidens nec per aliud est, per se bonum esse dicimus.

Manettus. Qui intelligendum vis, cum ais non esse bonum per aliud? Scire enim cupio.

143 *Pallas.* Dico, inquam, Manette, non esse per aliud bonum vel tanquam per causam quae eiusmodi bonitatem efficiat, vel tanquam per suae bonitatis formam. Quo quidem utroque modo primum bonum esse per se bonum et dicimus et volumus. Nam neque causam habet quae suam bonitatem efficiat, nec etiam speciem ante se quam participet, cum et ipsum tamen sit omnis boni efficiens causa, et ad eius bonitatis rationem quae et in

Therefore since neither individually nor in species nor in genus
is there a single good, it seems that there is no first good.

Palla. Manetti, you have discovered your counterargument keenly   141
and have explained it with clarity and nuance. But to all those
points of yours there is a ready reply based on Aristotle. The
first has a relationship to all subsequent items, and the further
down the series something is, to that degree it is more manifold
in its relationships. Therefore "first" can be understood in two
senses: by proportion and by nature. But that there is either by
the nature of the genus or the species or the individual nothing
good *per se* from which all things are called good, ought I think
to be agreed. But who would disagree that there is something
good *per se* by proportion, which is good neither by accident
nor through something else, but if one were to look to the thing
itself, all good things are good by a certain similarity of dispositions? And goods can be called either better or best insofar as
the goods are more similar to it. The first good is a good of this   142
type, which perfects all perfect substances in accord with their
own proper and, so to speak, connatural attributes, and that for
their own activity, provided that it not be impeded. In relation
to the proportion of that good, each good can be called better
and best. We assert that this good which is *per se* and not by
accident or through something else is the good *per se*.

Manetti. How do you want it to be understood when you assert
that it is not good through another thing? I want to know.

Palla. To repeat, I assert, Manetti, that it is not good through an-   143
other thing or as if through a cause that produces such goodness or as if through the form of its own goodness. I both assert and claim that the first good is good in both ways. For
neither does it have a cause that produces its own goodness nor
a species prior to itself in which it participates, since it is itself
the efficient cause of everything good, and with reference to the
definition of its goodness, which is in itself and itself, every

ipso est et ipsum est, omne bonum proportione sit bonum.
Quod ipsum certe primum bonum ita primum esse censemus,
ut ante id nihil aliud boni sit, et cum aeque in aliis omnibus
bonum esse constet, tum bonitatis causa in bonis omnibus.
Nam primum quidquid esse in multis dixeris quod non aequivoce in illis sit, id in uno primo quopiam poni oportet quod
aliorum omnium causa sit. Sed cum bonum in multis invenia-
tur in quibus non est omnino aequivoce, id[53] in primo quodam
ponatur oportet quod aliis omnibus bonitatis sit causa. Non
enim aequivoce est in multis quod secundum proportionem ad
unum sit in omnibus. Haud[54] enim ad unum proportionem
habet aequivocatio. Nam proportio ad unum est habitudinum
similitudo ad unum quod diversa in specie et in una proportione participatur, veluti est navis ad gubernatorem et regni ad
regem gubernatio. Neque enim eisdem praeceptis navis gubernationem gubernator solet quibus regni gubernationem rex per-
sequitur. Nec idem specie est gubernatio navis et regni, cum
similitudo tamen habitudinum una sit in utroque. Cum huiusmodi ergo similitudinem in omnibus unam esse videamus, ut
unum sit primum bonum, ad cuius proportionem et similitudinem alia bona dicuntur bona, intelligere mihi videor esse unum
primum bonum, quod substantialiter bonum est et efficiens
causa cuiusque bonitatis. Cuius quidem boni forma proportio-
naliter servatur in omnibus. Deinde si omnis multiplicitas, ut
arithmetici docent, ad unum reducitur quod primum est totius
multiplicationis principium, cumque magnam adeo bonorum
multiplicitatem cognosci liceat ut propemodum ad infinitiem
tendat, id quod in omni et arte et doctrina vitandum est, huiusmodi scilicet infinities contrahatur oportet. Qui autem contrahi
quicquam possit, nisi ab uno proficiscatur referaturque ad

144

145

146

good thing is good by proportion. We hold that this first good
itself is surely first in the sense that there is no other good before it, and since it is agreed that there is equally good in all
other things, then it is the cause of goodness in all good things.
For that which one might call first in many things, if it be unequivocally present in them, ought to be posited in some one
first thing so that it may be the cause of all the others. For since   144
the good is found in many things in which its presence is quite
unequivocal, it should be posited in a certain first thing to be
the cause of goodness for all the others.[52] For what is present in
all according to proportion to the one is unequivocally present
in many things. For equivocation has no proportion in respect
to the one. For proportion in respect to the one is a similarity
of dispositions to the one that is participated in by different
species in a single proportion, like the steering of a ship to the
captain and the governing of a kingdom to the king. For the
captain generally carries out the steering of a ship by different
precepts than those by which a king carries out the governing
of his kingdom. The governing of a ship and a kingdom are not
the same in species even though there is a single similarity of
dispositions in both. Since therefore we see that there is one   145
similarity of this kind in all things such that there is a single
good with respect to the proportion and similarity of which
other things are called good, I think I understand that there is
a single first good that is good in its substance and the efficient
cause of each goodness. The form of this good thing is propor-
tionally preserved in all things. Then if, as mathematicians
teach, every multiplicity is reduced to one thing which is the
first principle of all multiplication, and since so great a multiplicity of goods can be known that it reaches almost to infinity—a thing that must be avoided in every art and teaching—
this kind of infinity must, of course, be contracted. But how   146
can anything be contracted unless it starts out from one and is

unum? Nam quod a pluribus est, non contrahitur, sed diffundi-
tur potius. Quamobrem primum quoddam bonum detur est
opus, ab quo similitudo ipsa substantialis boni in bona omnia
diffundatur. Ad haec omnis resolutio in uno est posita, sive
posterius resolvatur in prius, sive compositum in simplex, sive
effectum in causam efficientem. Sed cum multa bona esse videamus quae neque priora sunt nec simplicia, sed composita,
nec etiam causae efficientes sed effecta, ea necessario sunt in
unum resolvenda secundum omne resolutionis genus. Esto igitur resolutio in uno primo quod indubitato bonorum omnium
147 primum est. Ad postremum quod est in quovis ordine, vel primum est vel a primo. Itaque in eorum ordine quae bona sunt,
aut quodque bonum primum esse aut a primo concedendum
est. Et cum eorum quodque primum esse non possit, necessario
est a primo. Igitur[55] unum quoddam primum statuendum est
quod sit aliorum omnium causa.

   Manettus. Sinisne, Poggi — quod tua pace fiat — Pallantem aliquid
paululum rogem quo nulla nobis eorum quae doctissime simul
elegantissimeque disseruit dubietas relinquatur?

148 *Poggius.* Sino equidem, quanquam in tanta ista tot bonorum bonitate bonum aliud nihil animadverto praeter unum illud quod
semper iudicavi: totam philosophiam esse inanem quandam
vaenditationem ipsamque inutilem ac prorsus puerilem. Pro-
pera igitur. Adventat enim caenandi tempus.

   Manettus. Aiunt, Pallas, Peripatetici primum quod est consequentium causa, ita esse in consequentibus ut de eorundem esse[56]
ratione putandum sit. Nihil autem unum est quod de ratione
bonorum omnium (quae numero, specie ac genere differunt)
putari oporteat. Nam eorum quae genere differunt, nullo modo
una ratio esse potest. Quod si ita est — sicuti[57] certe est — fit ut

brought back to one? For what begins from several things is not contracted but rather diffused. Therefore a certain first good must be granted, by which the very likeness of the substantial good is spread to all goods. In addition, every resolution comes to one thing, either by resolving the latter into the former, the compound into the simple or the effect into the efficient cause. But since we see many goods that are neither prior nor simple but compound and are also not efficient causes but effects, these must necessarily be resolved into a single thing in accordance with the entire genus of resolution. Let the resolution therefore consist in one good thing which is undoubtedly the first of all goods. Finally what exists is in some kind of order, 147 whether it is the first thing or from the first thing. Therefore one must admit that in the order of those things which are good, each good thing is either first or from the first. Therefore a certain first one must be posited that is the cause of all others.

Manetti. Would you allow, Poggio — by your leave — for me to pose a brief question to Palla so that we may be left in no doubt about those matters that he has learnedly and elegantly discussed?

Poggio. I do allow it, albeit in such great goodness of so many 148 goods I notice no good except that one that I have always held: all philosophy is a sort of pointless salesmanship, and it is useless and quite childish. So make haste. Dinnertime is approaching!

Manetti. The Peripatetics say, Palla, that the first that is the cause of consequents exists in the consequents in the sense that it must be thought to exist from the definition of those same things. But there is no one thing that must be thought to exist on the basis of the definition of all the goods (which differ in number, species, and genus). For there can by no means be a single definition of those things that differ by genus. If that is

aliquid primum bonum esse non possit quod aliorum omnium causa sit et ratio.

149 *Pallas.* At Stoici, Manette, qui nulla re sunt quam Peripatetici obtusiores,[58] ut solent omnia diligenter partiuntur primum dupliciter, tum principii, tum generis ratione. Sed quod esse dixeris secundum generis rationem, id quidem et de consequentium omnium ratione et eorum esse causam dicas necesse est. Nam inde suae essentiae principium capiunt. At primum quod est secundum principii rationem, nulla fit necessitate ut de eius vel essentia vel substantia quicquam sit. Ut enim punctus est lineae principium, neque tamen quicquam est nec de essentia nec de substantia lineae, quo substantia scilicet est subiectum, sed eiusmodi principium esse constat in quo ponatur lineae inchoatio, quanvis huiusmodi inchoatio neque ad essentiam lineae nec ad subiectum terminata sit, eodem etiam modo in alia quaque natura usu venit ut principium id sit quod est de illius generis

150 essentia. Hoc autem vocamus genus, ac rursus principium sit, quod simplex est formae inchoatio, et ea quidem neque ad essentiam nec ad subiectum terminata. Hoc vero principium dicimus, non genus. Quare hoc modo qui posuerit unum principium esse bonorum, haud errarit. Et id quidem genus neque in genus nec in speciem cum bonorum quopiam queat incidere. Atque sub hoc huiusmodi bono reliqua bona omnia continentur communitate principii, non generis.

151 Quod ipsum unum ac primum et simplex et separatum et sua natura bonum immensum, sempiternum, nulli motui, nulli actioni subiectum, qui sibi proponere sequique voluerit, non

so — as it assuredly is — the result is that there could be no first good that is the cause and definition of all the others.

Palla. But the Stoics, Manetti, who are by no means more obtuse   149 than the Peripatetics, as is their custom, first divide everything in two parts, namely by means of a thing's principle and its genus. But what you said exists according to the definition of its genus you must say exists on the basis of the definition of all its consequents and is their cause. For they derive the beginning of their essence from it. But there is no necessity for the first, which exists in accord with the definition of its principle, to be anything that is derived from either its essence or substance. For just as the point is the principle of a line but nonetheless is not anything derived from the essence or substance of a line by which its substance is a subject [of predication], but it is agreed to be a principle of the kind in which the beginning of the line is posited although such a beginning is terminated neither by the essence of the line nor as the subject of a line in predication, in the same way also in every other nature it is a matter of common experience that the principle is that which is derived from the essence of that genus. But this latter we call a genus, and   150 again let it be the principle that is the simple beginning of a form, and let this beginning be terminated neither in the essence of a thing nor as a subject of predication. We call this a principle, not a genus. Therefore in this way he who posited that there is a single principle of good things was scarcely in error. And this genus can share neither a genus nor a species with any of the goods. And moreover, all the rest of the goods are subsumed under a good of this type by the sharing of a principle, not of a genus.

Whoever may wish to set as his goal and pursue a thing that   151 is by its own nature good, which is one and first and simple and separate, unbounded, eternal, subject to no motion and no action, will understand that he is himself good not only by the

solum bono medio quod in triplici illa virtute intellectus et rationis morisque situm est, sed perfecto etiam bono quod bonorum omnium summum est se bonum intelliget. Neque dubitabit quid potius sibi expetendum sit, honestumne an utile, vel nunquid id magis voluptatis ratio praescribat. Nam praestantissimo illo ineffabilique bono et haec omnia absolutissime continentur, et quaecunque alia vel dici vel excogitari bona possint. Id autem nusquam est, si in mente divina non esse dixerimus. Est id, inquam, in divina mente divinaque sapientia, et in ea quidem sapientia quae non multiplicitate sed unitate dicenda sapientia est, cum ipsa tamen infinitos bonorum thesauros complectatur. Aliud autem bonum esse quod alio bono dicatur bonum, aliud vero quod seipso bonum sit, puto esse perspicuum. Et hoc, mediusfidius, bonum solum est, simplex, incommutabile, proptereaque[59] et aeternum et immortale, et ita summum ac perfectum ut eo nihil superius esse possit, nihil perfectius. Nanque aliud illud imperfectum est idemque commutabile et mortale. Caetera enim bona omnia sunt a Deo quidem, sed de Deo certe non sunt. Nam si de Deo ea esse dixerimus, necessario fateamur idem esse quod Deum. Non autem quod ab Deo factum est, idem esse quod Deum dicendum est. Itaque si solus Deus et incommutabile ac simplex est bonum, quaecunque ab eo bona facta sunt—quoniam ex nihilo facta esse constat, hoc est ex eo quod modo non esset—mutabilia certe sunt et non simplicia. Facta enim sunt, non genita. Nam quod de simplici bono genitum esset, etiam simplex esset, idemque omnino quod illud est de quo sit genitum. Quare siquidem totius hominis bonum felicitatem esse volumus, hanc autem aliud nihil esse quam Deum, felicitatem vero assequi posse neminem, nisi— quod per medium bonum fieri dicimus—virtutis ad eam iter et eundi et perveniendi ante didicerit, virtus certe omnis tenenda est atque exercenda. Est autem virtus habitus rectae mentis.

152

153

154

intermediate good that resides in that triple virtue of intellect and reason and behavior, but also by the perfect good, which is the highest of all. Nor will he hesitate over which is rather to be sought, the honorable or the expedient, or whether the principle of pleasure rather dictates the latter. For all these things are completely comprised in that most excellent and ineffable good. This, however, exists nowhere if we deny that it exists in the divine mind.[53] It exists, I affirm, in the divine mind and divine wisdom and in that wisdom that must be called wisdom not by multiplicity but unity, since it contains infinite treasures of goods. I think it is clear that one thing is good because it is said   152 to be good for another thing, another thing is said to be good because it is good by itself. And the latter alone, as God is my witness, is simple, unchangeable, and therefore both eternal and immortal and so supreme and perfect that nothing can be higher or more perfect. For the other is imperfect and likewise changeable and mortal. All the other goods are from God but certainly not derived from God. For if we were to assert that they are derived from God, we would have to admit that they are the same as God. But what has been made by God need not be said to be the same as God. Therefore if only God is an   153 unchangeable and simple good, whatever goods have been made by him—since it is agreed that they have been made out of nothing, that is, from what was just now nonexistent—are certainly changeable and not simple. For they have been made, not generated. For what would be generated from a simple good would also be simple, and is quite the same as that from which it was generated. Therefore if we claim that the good of the entire person is happiness and that the latter is nothing other than God, but that no one can attain happiness unless he has first learned the route for traveling to and arriving at it, which we assert happens through an intermediate good, all virtue must certainly be held fast and exercised. Virtue, however, is a   154

Menti autem intellectum quasi videndi aciem et rationem, quam
veluti aspectum ponebamus, hesterno sermone tribuimus. Alia
est igitur virtus intellectualis, qua speculamur, ut scientia atque
sapientia; alia rationalis, qua in actione versamur, ut calliditas et
prudentia; alia rursum virtus est moris, quem irrationalis partis
animi qualitatem esse statuimus, ut iusticia, fortitudo, temperantia, liberalitas reliquaque huiusmodi.

155 *Manettus.* Contine aliquantisper, Pallas, si videtur, cursum orationis tuae. Est enim paululum aliquid reliquum quod requiram.

Pallas. Loquere, Manette, tuo arbitratu.

Manettus. Constituebas heri superiorem inferioremque rationem,
quarum alteram circa aeternorum et incommutabilium contemplationem versari, alteram in temporalium mutabiliumque rerum actione positam esse censebas. Nunc autem non duplicem
rationem, sed rationem modo intellectumque complecteris.
Quid ista[60] differre inter se vis?

Pallas. Et nihil et multum.

Manettus. Quonam modo? Nunquid idem intellectus est quod
ratio?

156 *Pallas.* Meministine quid intellectum esse definivimus?

Manettus. Quid tandem?

Pallas. Est, inquam, intellectus transitio quaedam ex propositionibus in conclusiones, et ea quidem ratiocinatione utens[61] ad rem
eam quae intelligitur compraehendendam.

Manettus. Quid postea?

Pallas. Per ea enim quae certiora sunt, obscuriora concludimus, et
ita ratiocinando quae intelligere volumus, deinceps comprae-
hendimus. Num quicquam aliud praestat ratio?

Manettus. Imo id istud. Verum idem ego interesse arbitrabar quodammodo intellectum et rationem quod aeternitatem et tempus.

disposition of the right mind. In yesterday's conversation we assigned intellect to the mind as a kind of acuity of vision and reasoning, which we held to be like vision. Therefore one virtue is intellectual, by which we contemplate, as, for instance, science and wisdom; another is rational, by which we engage in action, as, for instance, cleverness and prudence; a third virtue is that of character, which we have held to be a quality of the irrational part of the soul, as, for instance, justice, courage, temperance, generosity, and other such qualities.

Manetti. Restrain a bit, if you please, Palla, the course of your 155 speech. For a small point remains for me to ask about.

Palla. Speak, Manetti, at your discretion.

Manetti. Yesterday you established that there is a higher and lower reasoning, about which you held that the one deals in the contemplation of things eternal and unchanging, the other resides in the doing of temporal and changing things. Now, however, you do not embrace a twofold reasoning but only reasoning and intellect. In what respect do you claim that they differ?

Palla. Both not at all and a great deal.

Manetti. How so? Is not the intellect the same as reason?

Palla. Do you remember what we defined intellect to be? 156

Manetti. What, then?

Palla. Intellect, I repeat, is a certain transition from propositions to conclusions and one that uses inference to grasp what is understood.[54]

Manetti. What comes next?

Palla. Through the things that are more certain we draw conclusions about the more obscure and thus by inferring what we wish to understand, finally we achieve understanding. Surely reasoning does not perform anything else, does it?

Manetti. No, that is it. But I thought that the difference between intellect and reason is the same as between eternity and time.

157 *Pallas.* Et recte tu quidem arbitrabaris. Sed istam omnem differentiam non rationis intellectusque natura efficit, sed obiecta. Nam intellectus et ratio eadem virtus sunt, sed officiis distinguuntur. Ut enim eadem videndi virtute et album videmus et nigrum, ita eadem vi mentis inferiora superioraque cognoscimus. Itaque easdem virtutes modo intellectualis, modo rationalis dicimus. Nonnunquam etiam uno 'mentis' nomine rationem intellectumque complectentes 'mentalis' appellamus. Qua ductus sententia, eandem heri vocabam rationem superiorem quam intelligentiae nomine hodie complector.

Manettus. At idemne intelligentiam quod intellectum nominas?

Pallas. Maxime; id quod maiores etiam nostros, quotquot Latine ac docte locuti sunt, consuesse animadverto. Quod si doctrinae gratia ea quandoque invicem interesse quippiam velimus, dicemus intellectum eam esse animi vim quae invisibilia percipiat, ut angelos, ut daemonas, ut animos, ut omnem denique crea-

158 tum spiritum. Intelligentia vero erit ea vis animi quae continuo supponitur Deo. Cernit, inquam, nullo medio summum ipsum verum ac vero incommutabile. Ita enim animus hominum et sensu corpora et imaginatione similitudines corporum et ratione corporum naturas percipere dicitur. Sed intellectu creatum, at intelligentia increatum spiritum compraehendit. Et ut reliqua omittam, quoniam de ratione nobis et intellectu atque intelligentia sermo erat, ratio, cuius sunt visibilium rationes definitionesque et investigationes invisibilium, iuvatur inferius,[62] sed intellectus atque intelligentia, quorum est spiritualia et divina compraehendere atque contemplari, superius iuvantur.

159 Nam tum rationalis spiritus, quoniam ex dono creationis facultatem habet et cognoscendi veri et diligendi boni, nisi radio interioris lucis fuerit illustratus caloreque succensus, sapientiae

Palla. And you rightly thought so. But the nature of reason and   157
   intellect does not make that entire difference, but their objects.
   For the power of intellect and reason is the same, but they are
   distinguished by their functions. For as we see white and black
   by the same power of seeing, so by the same power of the mind
   we recognize lower and higher things. Therefore we say that the
   same virtues are now intellectual, now rational. Sometimes we
   even call them by a single word "mind" embracing reason and
   intellect as "mental." Led by this idea, yesterday I called "higher
   reason" the same thing I encompass today with the word "intelligence."

Manetti. But are you calling "intelligence" the same as intellect?

Palla. Indeed so; I see that this was the practice of our ancestors
   insofar as they spoke learnedly in Latin. But if we ever for purposes of teaching should wish for there to be some difference,
   we say that intellect is the power of the soul that distinguishes
   invisible things, such as angels, demons, souls, finally every created spirit, whereas intelligence will be that power of the soul   158
   which is immediately below God: it sees, I say, with no intermediary the true and unchangeable itself. Thus men's soul is
   said to perceive both by bodily sense and by imagination the
   likenesses of bodies and by reason the natures of bodies. By
   intellect it grasps the created, by intelligence the uncreated
   spirit. To set other points aside, since our discussion has been
   about reason and intellect and intelligence, reason is useful at
   the lower level, since explanations of visible things and definitions and investigations of invisible things are proper to it,
   whereas intellect and intelligence, whose province is to compre-
   hend and contemplate things spiritual and divine, are useful at
   the higher level. Now the rational spirit, since it has as a gift of   159
   creation the capacity to know the truth and love the good, unless it has been illuminated by the beam and kindled by the
   heat of an inner light, will never attain a disposition of wisdom

nunquam caritatisve affectum consequetur, tum Deus (qui et
ignis et lux esse dicitur) lucis splendorem quem in se retinet ex
sese emittens intelligentiam ad veritatis cognitionem illuminat,
ignis vero de se calorem emittens, sed non amittens, ad virtutis
amorem inflamat affectum. Et quemadmodum sol ab oculo non
videtur nisi in solis lumine, ita verum illud atque divinum lumen aliter atque in ipsius lumine ab intelligentia videri nullo
pacto poterit. Quare propheta inquit: 'Domine, in lumine tuo
videbimus lumen.'

160   *Manettus*. Et istis omnibus quae dicis assentior, et singula e veritatis sinu prodisse puto. Verum satis mirari non possum quid vel
scientiam contemplationis esse velis quam hesterna disputatione
actionis posueris, vel calliditatem inter virtutes numeres, cum
sint qui dicant calliditatem in virum bonum non cadere.

Pallas. At Fabium illum Maximum, qui 'cunctando,' ut inquit Ennius, 'restituit rem,' et Cyrum Persarum regem, et C. Iulium
Caesarem ac reliquos omnis strenuos et summos imperatores
eosdemque prudentissimos callidos vocant. Calliditas sane
(quam σύνεσιν Graeci nominant) actionis est virtus, in iis-
161   demque versatur in quibus prudentiam volunt. Quare *callidus*,
quem eundem fere quem prudentem dicimus, is est appellatus
cuius animus usu ut[63] manus opera *concalluit*. Sed de hisce fortasse postea. Nam de scientia quod requiris, nihil est quod du-
bites. Alia enim ratione quadam scientiam heri actionis esse
statuebam, et alia nunc speculationis. Nonne prudentia ipsa,
quae in agendo et primaria est et princeps, nonnunquam specu-
lativa inducitur? Temperantiam vero, quae moralium virtutum
una sit, sunt qui velint generis locum sibi in agendo defendere.
Multo sunt plura quae sentire intelligereque possimus quam

and love; on the other hand, God (who is said to be both fire
and light), by emitting the brilliant light that He holds within
Himself, illuminates intelligence for the knowledge of truth,
while a fire emitting heat from itself but not losing it, sets
aflame the recipient for the love of virtue. And just as the sun is
not seen by the eye except in the sun's light, so that true and
divine light will by no means be able to be seen by the intelligence except in His own light. Therefore the prophet said:
"Lord, in Thy light we shall see light."⁵⁵

Manetti. I agree with all the things you are saying, and I believe   160
each one of them has come forth from the heart of truth. But I
am quite amazed that you claim that knowledge is a matter of
contemplation, though yesterday you said it belongs to action
or that you count cleverness among the virtues although there
are those who deny that it is suitable for a good man.

Palla. But they call the renowned Fabius Maximus, who, as Ennius said, "restored the state by delay,"⁵⁶ and Cyrus, King of
Persia, and C. Julius Caesar and all other energetic and outstanding commanders both most prudent and clever. Cleverness (which the Greeks call *synesis*) is a virtue of action; they
claim that it is active in the same men in whom prudence is.
Therefore he is called "clever" (*callidus*), whom we say is in gen-   161
eral the same as the prudent man, whose mind has become
"calloused" (*concalluit*) by experience and work.⁵⁷ But perhaps
we shall discuss these matters afterward. As to your question
about knowledge, there is no reason for you to be in doubt. For
yesterday I had one reason for relating knowledge to action,
another one now for relating it to speculation. Is not prudence
itself, which is the major and first virtue in action, sometimes
introduced for purposes of speculation? There are those who
claim that temperance, which is one of the moral virtues, de-
fends a place for itself in the sphere of action. There are many
more things that we can think and understand than express in

quae propriis ac suis verbis exprimere. Quo fit ut eodem etiam
162 verbo diversis in rebus plaerunque nos uti oporteat. Verum si-
quando singillatim ac fuse quae nunc summatim generatimque
libamus tetigerimus, singulas istiusmodi differentias minutatim
digeremus. Sed iam, ne Poggio molestiores simus, ad infamiam
redeamus.

Poggius. Ita, Pallas, obsecro. Abit enim caenandi hora. Et ego
iamdudum siti conficior. Quod te etiam pati eo magis consenta-
neum est, quo prolyxiore es usus oratione.

Pallas. Dicebam equidem bonis artibus vaenari bonam famam
oportere. Bonas autem artis virtutes appello, quibus solis viri
boni et redduntur et nominantur. Et quo praestantior virtus
163 fuerit, eo viri bonitas existimabitur cumulatior. Qui enim ita
sese instituerit, ut nihil erret in moribus, nihil per animi perturbationem aut gesserit aut cogitarit, utaturque omnibus in rebus
ratione duce cuius edicta semper in omni actione tueatur, intel-
ligatque nihil esse prorsus humanum bonum quod Deo vacet—ad quem unum et universam mentem et quidquid menti
obtemperat ac paret referre debeat—quid huic aberit quo minus dicendus sit bonus, non media solum, sed perfecta etiam
bonitate? Huiusmodi autem vir, seipso contentus, quid de se
caeteri loquantur aut non loquantur, non requiret. Permagna
illa mihi et perillustris virtus videri solet quae suae conscientiae
potius quam alieno testimonio contenta sit. Ut enim vero et
sapienter inquit Augustinus: 'Decus latet, dedecus patet; quod
malum geritur, omnis convocat spectatores, quod boni geri dicitur, vix invenit auditores, tanquam honesta erubescenda sint et
inhonesta glorianda.'

their own proper words. The result is that we must often use
the same word in regard to many various things. But if we will   162
ever deal individually and expansively on the points we now dip
into in summary and general form, we will minutely distinguish
individual differences of this type. But now, so as not to annoy
Poggio, let us return to the topic of infamy.

Poggio. Do so, Palla, I beg you. For dinner hour has already
passed, and I have for a long time now been tormented by
thirst. You are probably suffering this even more since you have
spoken at such length.

Palla. I was saying that one must seek a good reputation with
good arts.[58] I call the virtues good arts, by which alone men are
made and called good. And the more outstanding the virtue,
the more abundant the man's virtue will be reputed. He who   163
has equipped himself in such a way that he commits no mis-
takes in behavior, neither does nor thinks anything in a state of
emotion, uses reason as his guide in all matters, and always
guards its decrees in every action, and understands that there is
no human good apart from God (to whom alone he must attribute his entire mind and whatever conforms to and obeys the
mind), what will he lack that would prevent him from being
called good, not merely in respect of an intermediate good, but
even of perfect goodness? A man of this sort, content with
himself, will not inquire what others say, or do not say, about
himself. I have always thought that virtue to be grand in scale
and distinction that is content with the testimony of its own
conscience rather than of others. As Augustine truly and wisely
remarked, "Glory is in hiding, disgrace is on view; if a wicked
act is being performed, it convenes all spectators; if a good deed
is said to be taking place, it scarcely finds people willing to listen, as if honorable actions were to be blushed at and dishonorable ones matter for boasting of."[59]

164 *Nicolaus.* Nunquid igitur quae de nobis alii dicunt contemnenda omnino sunt?

Pallas. Nequaquam. Non enim frustra, Nicolae, inquit apostolus: 'Providemus bona non solum coram Deo, sed etiam coram hominibus.' Ad haec idem etiam scribit: 'Placete omnibus per omnia, sicut et ego omnibus per omnia placeo, non quaerens quod mihi utile est, sed quod multis, ut salvi fiant.' Subditque: 'De caetero, fratres, quaecunque sunt vera, quaecunque sancta, quaecunque iusta, quaecunque casta, quaecunque carissima, quaecunque bonae famae: siqua virtus, siqua laus, haec cogitate

165 quae didicistis et accepistis et vidistis in me.' Quid pluribus? Virtute nobis, sed bona fama aliorum saluti consulimus. Praestat etiam bona fama non obscurum argumentum vel magnitudinis vel parvitatis animi nostri. Nam hisce rumoribus qui superbius efferuntur, siquidem vera audiunt, humili mihi tamen atque abiecto animo videntur. Sin autem falsa, illud secum memoria repetant quod scriptum est: 'Qui confidit in falsis, ipse pascit ventos.' Et recte id quidem. Fit enim esca spiritibus ma-

166 lis. Quem autem nulla aura movet neque secundus quisquam ventus[64] extollit, hunc ego magno et invicto animo virum iudico planeque sapientem. Mala vero fama non modo probamur, celsone simus an demisso animo, verum etiam utrum eos ipsos inimicos per quos eiusmodi calumniam subeamus, sicuti par est diligamus. Sed ii mihi ridendi plurimum videri solent, qui cum male vivunt, tamen laudibus delectantur, minime cogitantes neque malam conscientiam sanari laudantis praedicatione, nec

167 bonam vitiantis obprobrio vulnerari. Fuerunt praeterea (et hodie sunt) non nulli qui vel per facinora famosi esse quam ignorari maluerint. Et ut Medices omnis reliquaque istiusmodi prodigia sileamus: memoriae proditum est Pausaniam adolescentem,

Niccolò. Should we then altogether despise what others say 164
about us?

Palla. By no means. For, Niccolò, the apostle did not say in vain,
"Let us lay up goods not only in the sight of God but also of
men." In addition, he also writes: "Satisfy all people by all
means, as I satisfy all people by all means, not seeking what is
expedient for me but what is so for many, that they may be
saved." And he adds: "Furthermore, brothers, whatever things
are true, whatever are holy, whatever are just, whatever are pure,
whatever are lovable, whatever are of good repute; if there is
any virtue or praise, think on what you have learned and received and seen in me."[60] Why go on? By virtue we take our- 165
selves into consideration, by good reputation, the salvation of
others. For good reputation provides a clear proof of the greatness or smallness of our soul. For those who are puffed up by
these rumors, even if they are true, seem to me to possess a
base and wretched soul. But if the rumors are false, let them
remember what has been written: "He who places his trust in
falsehoods is feeding on the winds"[61] — and rightly so, for he
becomes bait for evil spirits. The one, however, who is moved 166
by no breeze, whom no favorable wind lifts up, I judge him to
be of great and invincible soul and perfectly wise. We are tested
by bad reputation not only as to whether we are of lofty or
humble soul but also whether we love, as we should, those very
enemies at whose hands we suffer such calumny. I tend to mock
the people who, while living a discreditable life, nonetheless
take pleasure in praise, since they fail to consider that neither
can a bad conscience be healed by an encomiast's proclamation
nor can a good one be wounded by a faultfinder's censure.
Moreover, there have been (and still are today) some who 167
would prefer to be notorious by their crimes than to remain
anonymous. To veil in silence all the Medici and other monsters
of their ilk, it is recorded that when young Pausanias heard

ubi ex Hermocle audisset alia nulla expeditiore via se nominis celebritatem consequi posse quam si virum illustrem aliquem occidisset, continuo Philippum regem interemisse. Quo quidem facinore factum est ut is Philippi gloria illico gloriosus efficeretur. Sed hunc vel dolor iniuriae vel alia quaepiam privata causa movere fortasse potuit. At est inventus qui Ephesiae Dianae templum, toto orbe conspicuum atque admirabile, incendere non dubitaret, quo per consumptionem praeclari operis nomen suum clarissimum redderet. Is enim improborum mos est, ut, modo eorum nomen longe lateque per orbem terrarum pervagetur, quem bonis aut nequeunt aut nolunt, vel malis artibus aditum moliantur ad famam. Mea autem sententia semper fuit bene vivendum esse et omnia quotquot mortalibus bona contingere possint, in virtutis praestantia atque in Deo sita existimare oportere. Nam ita virtutem fama ut umbra corpus sequi consuevit. Itaque turpissimum est quam ancillulam[65] et paedisecam debet, famam sibi virtus dominam heramque constituat. Quemadmodum vero virtutem fama, eodem modo infamia vitium sequatur necesse est.

169 *Honofrius.* At illos infamis fieri, pater, qui male vixerint, qui nihil nisi per libidinem, per animi impotentiam, per nequitiam egerint, nemo est qui repraehendat. Sed qui propter eximiam atque singularem morum excellentiam vitaeque sanctimoniam splendidissimis laudibus et uno et exuberanti omnium ore celebrari meruerint, eos publice carpi et omni convicio, omni obprobrio palam lacerari, non potest non durum esse atque permolestum. Nam quantum splendor patriae splendorem virtuti afferat, declarat dictum illud Atheniensis Themistoclis in nequam hominem natum Seriphi. Hic enim, cum illum non sua sed Athenarum gloria nominis splendorem assecutum diceret, apte Themistocles prudenterque respondit: 'Verum neque ipse

from Hermocles that he could gain fame by no quicker route than by killing some distinguished man, he immediately assassinated King Philip. The result of this crime was that he immediately became famous through Philip's fame. Perhaps outrage over a wrong or some other private motive moved Pausanias,[62] but a man was found who did not hesitate to incinerate the temple of Diana of Ephesus, an structure admired throughout the world, in order to make his name famous by the destruction of an outstanding building.[63] For such is the   168 habit of scoundrels that, provided that their name travel far and wide through the world, they pave a way to fame even by wicked arts if they cannot or will not do so by good ones. But my view has always been that one should live according to moral principles and one must believe that all goods, as many as can fall to the lot of mortals, depend upon outstanding virtue and on God.[64] For in general reputation follows virtue as a shadow does a body. Therefore it is shameful for virtue to set up reputation, which ought to be her handmaiden and follower, as her mistress. Just as reputation follows virtue, so must infamy vice.

Onofrio. But, father, no one would dispute that those persons who   169 have led an immoral life, who have never acted without being guided by lust, lack of self-control, and wickedness, suffer infamy. But those who because of their extraordinary and unparalleled excellence of character and integrity of life have deserved to be celebrated with the most distinguished praises and the enthusiastic cheers of all, for them to be publicly criticized and excoriated with abuse and opprobrium of all sorts cannot but be harsh and grievous. For the famous reply of Themistocles of Athens against a worthless nobody born at Seriphus shows how much luster the homeland adds to virtue. When the latter said that it was not by his own glory but that of Athens that he had achieved an eminent reputation, Themistocles replied aptly

170   si Seriphius forem, clarus essem, nec tu si Atheniensis.' Quare
et in amittenda patria patrium quoque splendorem amittimus,
et quos uno omnium testimonio laudatissime decantari pientissimum[66] sit, vulgo vituperamur censemurque infames.

     Pallas. Miror quid tamdiu, fili, tacueris, neque obieceris quicquam
ad ea quae de hac re multa minusque usitata dicebantur.

     Honofrius. Pararam enim, mi pater, Nicolaum mihi, qui pugnam
non solum iniret, sed etiam conficeret. Verum posteaquam rem
ad triarios rediisse animadverto, succenturiatus accedo.

171   *Pallas.* Fuit sane, fili, Themistocles magnus quidam vir, sed non is
sapiens, qui sua omnia in se posita esse duceret; quem tamen
propriae virtutis, non patriae existimatio, non patriae modo sed
universae quoque Graeciae gloriosissimum effecit. Sola, mihi
crede, virtus est quae hominem magnum ac praeclarum reddat.
Et huiusmodi quidem vir ubiubi tandem sit, et magnus certe
futurus est et victurus in gloria. Tarquinius ille Priscus non
Corinthi, non Tarquiniorum gloria claruit, sed animi magnitudine ingeniique praestantia eum sibi splendorem peperit, ut et
peregrinus et exulis filius Romae regnaret. Servii Tullii nomen
est obscurum nemini, qui et servus et ex serva natus Prisco

172   successit in regnum. Possem huiusmodi innumerabilis meminisse, qui nullo patriae splendore maximi splendidissimique
fuere. Quinam apostolis ipsis clariores? Qui nulla patriae luce,
nullo nomine dum virtutem veritatemque sequuntur, non huius
nostri crepusculi duntaxat, sed multo magis fulgentissimae illius atque immensae lucis splendidissimam claritatem assecuti
sunt. Quod autem durum et permolestum putas invidia laborare

and shrewdly: "Neither would I be famous if I were a Seriphian, nor would you if you were an Athenian."[65] Therefore in losing 170 our homeland we also lose our ancestral luster, we, who would fitly have our praises sung in highest tribute by the testimony of all, are commonly censured and held to be infamous.

Palla. I am surprised, son, that you were silent and raised no objection to the many unusual arguments made on this topic.

Onofrio. That is because, father, I had prepared Niccolò not only to begin the battle for me but also to complete it. But since I see that the matter afterward reverted to the reserves, I am joining in as a replacement.[66]

Palla. Themistocles was indeed a great man, son, but not a wise 171 man, who would hold that all his goods are in himself; it was, however, the regard for his own virtue, not for his homeland and not his homeland alone but even of all Greece that lent him such great glory. Believe me, it is virtue alone that makes a man great and distinguished. And a man of such quality, wherever he may be, will assuredly be great and will live in glory. The renowned Tarquinius Priscus was distinguished neither by the glory of Corinth nor by that of the Tarquins; yet by his greatness of soul and the excellence of his natural gifts he endowed himself with such renown that, though a foreigner and the son of an exile, he ruled over Rome. The name of Servius Tullius is obscure to no one, who, though a slave and the son of a slave woman, succeeded Priscus in the kingship. I could call to mind 172 countless men of this kind who were great and distinguished even though their homeland lacked distinction. Who, I ask you, are more famous than the apostles? Without the illumination of a homeland, without a name, in pursuing virtue and truth they attained the most radiant distinction not merely of this twilight of ours but of that blazing and boundless light. As to the fact that you hold it to be harsh and grievous for those persons to

qui pulcherrimis titulis digni sint, primum qui iusti bonique sunt, infames esse non possunt, praesertim[67] apud bonos et sapientis viros, qui non iniquitatis sed iusticiae oculis veritatem cernunt. Mali autem erubescant necesse est, cum seipsos et eos quos vituperant expenderint. Quo fit ut eam omnem adversus probos et sanctos viros infamiam, quoniam nullis radicibus nixa est, ita brevi languere interireque oporteat, ut 'vera gloria' — quod prudentissime inquit Cicero — 'radices agit atque etiam propagatur.' Quod si ea futura sit temporum calamitas, ut dispersi rumores nixius diutiusque perdurent, ea sit sapienti proposita consolatio, quod apud immortalem et sempiternum Deum (qui omnia videt, metitur, disquirit, iudicat) suae innocentiae testimonium ac praemium, quod apud improbos non potuerit, locupletissimum et longe pulcherrimum atque optimum consequetur. Scriptum est enim: 'Gaudete et exultate. Merces enim vestra multa est in caelis.' Interim vero vos moneo, adolescentes, ut animi bono studeatis malitisque boni esse quam videri. Et quod de Aristide legitur, vobiscum assidue cogitate. Cum enim versus illi recitarentur in theatro quos Aeschylus in Amphiaraum scripserat:

> Nam vult vir esse, non videri, hic optimus,
> qui mentis altae fructifer sulcans segetem
> consulta callens germinat gravissima,

in Aristidem oculos cuncti qui spectaculo aderant continuo convertere.

Poggius. Iam satis, Pallas, superque dictum. Iam, obsecro, mitte nos. Expector enim ad aedes Bertheldinas. Familiare mihi convivium est.

Soderinus. At ego, Pallas, ni te putarem iam defessum, aliud quiddam occurrebat quod peterem. Non enim infamia mihi tam

labor under envy who are worthy of the fairest titles, first, those
who are just and good cannot suffer infamy, especially in the
eyes of good and wise men, who see the truth with the eyes not
of prejudice but of justice. The wicked ought to blush when
they weigh on the scales themselves and those whom they lam-
baste. The result is that all ill-repute directed at men who are   173
upstanding and have integrity, since it is supported by no roots,
must quickly fade and die, just as "true glory" — as Cicero wisely
says — "takes root and even spreads."[67] But if the disaster of the
times is going to be so great that the scattered rumors endure
with greater stubbornness and longevity, let this consolation be
held out to the wise man, that he will obtain a testimony of and
reward for his innocence, though he could not in the eyes of
scoundrels, before immortal and eternal God (who sees, measures, inquires into, and judges all things) — a reward that is
most opulent, by far the most fair, and best. For it has been
written: "Rejoice and exult; for an abundant reward is yours in
heaven."[68] Meanwhile I caution you, young men, that you pur-   174
sue the good of the mind and prefer to be good rather than
merely to seem good. And consider carefully what is said about
Aristides. For when those famous verses were recited in the
theater that Aeschylus had written about Amphiaraus:

> For he wishes to be the best man, not to seem,
> Who fruitfully plowing the crop of his lofty mind
> Through his experience grows profound counsels,[69]

immediately all who were attending the performance turned
their eyes toward Aristides.

Poggio. Palla, enough and more than enough has now been said. I
beg you now release us. I am awaited at the house of the
Berteldi.[70] Some friends are holding a banquet for me.

Soderini. But as for me, Palla, another thing occurred to me that   175
I would ask if I did not think you already tired. For it is not

videtur metuenda quam paupertas, cuius etiam metu torqueor, formidanda.

Pallas. Modo Poggius velit, pete, Soderine, ut libet.

Poggius. Novam hic te cantionem aggredi cupit, quam in diem posterum serves licet. Quare vale et tace.

Pallas. Abit Poggius, Soderine, ut vides. Itaque, si videtur, postridie quod de paupertate metuis inter nos commentabimur.

infamy that seems to me so dreadful but poverty, fear of which torments me.

Palla. Provided Poggio is willing, feel free to ask, Soderini.

Poggio. He is keen for you to attack a new song, which you can keep for tomorrow. Therefore farewell and no more discussion.

Palla. Poggio, as you see, is leaving, Soderini. Therefore, if it is agreeable, tomorrow we will discuss among ourselves your fears concerning poverty.

LIBER TERTIUS

De Paupertate

COLLOCUTORES

Leonardus
Rainaldus
Pallas
Rhodulphus
Poggius
Manettus
Soderinus
Honofrius
Nicolaus

1 Croesus, rex Lydorum, Vitaliane Borrhomaee, quoniam propter ingentes illos innumerabilisque thesauros felicissimum sese iudicaret, existimasset — ut mea fert opinio — et G. Fabricium et Thebanum illum Epaminondam reliquosque huiusmodi idcirco infelices admodum ac miseros, quia essent pauperrimi. Nam opinabatur ille fortasse felicem atque beatam vitam iis in rebus et sitam esse et collocatam, quae tantisper sunt in nostra potestate, dum fortunae livor — ut ita dicam — nondum excanduerit. Sed eam Croesi regis sententiam non solum a Solone, uno e septem illis sapientibus quos Graecia summis laudibus tollit ad caelum, verum etiam ab extremis luctuosissimi exitus aerumnis reprobatam damnatamque

2 audimus. Et profecto non mediocris mihi stulticia videri solet quod ob id se quisquam felicem putet, quod singulis temporum momentis ob varios rerum eventus et inopinatos casus potest amittere. Nostra enim felicitas, siquidem velimus quod Apollinis praecepto monebatur, nosipsos nosse, haud extrinsecus petenda

BOOK THREE

On Poverty

SPEAKERS

Leonardo Bruni
Rinaldo degli Albizzi
Palla Strozzi
Ridolfo Peruzzi
Poggio Bracciolini
Giannozzo Manetti
Francesco Soderini
Onofrio Strozzi
Niccolò della Luna

Croesus, King of Lydia, judged himself most fortunate, Vitaliano   1
Borromeo, because of his vast wealth; he would have thought — in
my opinion — both Gaius Fabricius and the famous Epaminondas
of Thebes and others of this type unhappy and wretched because
they were very poor. For he perhaps believed that a fortunate and
happy life depends upon those things that are in our power, so
long as the envy of fortune — so to speak — has not yet become
inflamed. But we hear that this view of Croesus was not only disapproved and condemned by Solon, one of those seven wise men
whom Greece praised to the skies, but also by the extreme misery
of his lamentable end.[1] It generally seems to be a measure of one's   2
great stupidity for anyone to think himself fortunate on account of
a thing which he can lose at any moment because of various out-
comes of events and unforeseen disasters. If we would wish to
know ourselves, as was recommended by Apollo's teaching,[2] our
happiness should hardly be sought from outside, since it resides in

est, quippe quae in nobis sit posita, et ita posita ut in omni rerum humanarum statu felices esse possimus. Nam si hominem scimus non animum esse, non corpus, sed tertium quiddam, quod et animo constet et corpore, immortali mortalique natura, nequaquam ambigere nos oportet ita virtutes corporis animi virtutibus 3 ut corpus animo esse subiiciendum. Quare si animus est ea pars quae tum movet corpus, tum regit imperio, et omnia fortunae bona, quaecunque tandem vel esse vel dici queant, non animi sed corporis causa habentur in precio, liquido intelligi potest quam haec inferiora sint et minimi faciunda omnino si ad animi praestantiam conferantur. Quod cum ita sit, nolim tamen ita in pistrinum divitias dedere, ut reiiciendae prorsus contemnendaeque videantur, praesertim eae quae honestati se comites addiderunt.

4 Nam sunt nonnunquam maximo emolumento et nobis et nostris, universaeque reipublicae, quemadmodum saepe vidimus tuo exemplo, Vitaliane, contingere, qui ut es vir magnificus et illustris, habens cum istis pluribus tuis egregiisque virtutibus divitias maximas honestissimasque coniunctas, quantas unusquisque inter Italos habet nemo, quammaximo persaepe usui accedis, non tuis tecum duntaxat, verum etiam Philippo Mariae Anglo, unico lumini atque splendori et nominis et gloriae Latinorum. Ut enim silentio praeteream ingentia illa opportunaque subsidia quae princeps excellentissimus in turbulentissimis belli tempestatibus abs te accipit, quanto sis[1] ei ornamento inter pacis etiam quietem atque ocia vel 5 montes ipsi campique loquuntur. Nam quotusquisque est, qui aut Mediolanum divertens aut per Insubres iter faciens non afficiatur abs te vel eximiis commodis vel honore aliquo non vulgari? Tu publicum et munificentissimum hospitium quoddam es omnium eruditorum, omnium bonorum, relligiosorum, nobilium, principum, imperatorum, regum summorumque pontificum, eo ore ac vultu, et tanta cum alacritate et elegantia quadam ingenua, ut non

ourselves and in such a way that we can be happy in any state of human events. Now since we know that man is not soul, not body, but a certain third thing, which consists of soul and body, immortal and mortal nature, we should by no means be in doubt that as the body must be subordinated to the soul, so the virtues of the body should be subordinated to those of the soul. Therefore if the soul is that part that sometimes moves the body, sometimes rules it by command, and all the goods of fortune, whatever they may be or be called are valued for the sake not of the soul but the body, it can be clearly understood how these things are lower and to be rated at minimum value if they are compared with the preeminence of the soul. Although this is so, I would nonetheless not wish to disparage riches in such a way that it seems they must be rejected and despised, especially those riches that are joined as companions to moral goodness. For sometimes they have been of great benefit both to us and to our friends and to the entire republic, as we have often seen happen in your case, Vitaliano: as you are an excellent and distinguished man, possessing in combination with your many outstanding virtues vast and most honorable wealth such as no other Italian has, you make extensive use of it, not only for your own relations but also for Filippo Maria Visconti, the unrivaled light and luster and glory of the nation of the Latins. For to pass over in silence that huge and timely financial support that the excellent prince received from you in troubled times of war, even the very mountains and the plains declare how great a blessing you are for him during the quiet and leisure of peace. For how few there are who, spending the night at Milan or traveling through Lombardy, have not been treated by you with exceptional kindnesses or some uncommon honor? You play the part of a kind of public and most generous host of all the learned, all the sound citizens, all the religious, the nobles, princes, generals, kings, popes, with such a countenance and expression and with such great attentiveness and a certain native elegance that you

3

4

5

conferre sed accipere beneficium videaris. Itaque si humanae divitiae in istiusmodi et tanta virtute viros se velut aliquod in asylum et tutissimum portum vel profugientes vel reduces tanquam ab improborum insectatione procellisque receperint, reiiciendae certe non sunt, sed benigne potius excipiendae atque hospitaliter.

6   Atqui paupertas illa quae violenta non sit et gravis, sed et levis et voluntaria, nullo pacto damnanda est prudenti iudicio. Non enim in eo genere posita est, quo vel minor homo sit vel deterior censendus, quandoquidem praestantissimos videamus et clarissimos quosdam viros, Paulum Aemylium,[2] Scipionem Africanum posteriorem, qui neque patris esset nec avi dissimilis, aliosque permultos, qui cum facile possent et sine ulla infamiae nota affluentissime abundare fragilibus istis fucatisque divitiis, nunquam voluerunt.

7   Democritus Abderites et Crates Thebanus, et alii item philosophi pene infiniti graves ac nobiles, cum essent admodum divites, paupertatem mirabili studio adamarunt. Certe satis is dives est, cui nihil deest. Quid autem huic deesse possit, qui habet appetitionem rationi obtemperantem? Nam effraenati appetitus nullo auro, nullo argento, nullis Persarum gazis expleantur. Habendi cupiditas nullis finibus continetur. Quo plus possidet, plura quaerit; adeptaque aeque ac prius contenta est, et eo fortasse minus quo magis in dies magisque inflamatur, idem quodammodo patiens quod ii solent qui aquae intercuti sunt obnoxii. Nam sitis in ita affectis bibendo augescit. At paupertas nemini esse gravis potest qui et suo et quod adest contentus sit. Non caritudo pecuniarum sed rationis atque consilii paupertatem efficit.

8   Quo fit ut et pauper dives et dives pauper nonnunquam dicendus sit in primisque iudicandus. Sed haec hactenus. Nam in hoc tertio libro *Commentationum Florentinarum* ea disseruntur quae de paupertate graviter ac docte disputata audieram, et ab eisdem viris qui pridie huius diei de infamia sunt locuti, et a doctissimo et eloquentissimo viro

seem not to be granting but receiving a kindness. Therefore if human riches have taken refuge in men of such quality and such great virtue as if in an asylum and safe haven, they surely ought not to be rejected but rather received with kindness and hospitality.

Indeed a prudent judge should by no means condemn that condition of poverty that is not cruel and severe but light and voluntary. For it is not in the category of things on account of which a man should be thought lesser or inferior, since we have seen some excellent and distinguished men, Aemilius Paulus, Scipio Africanus the Younger, who was like both his father and grandfather, and many others, who, although they could easily, without any taint of infamy, enjoy a great abundance of those perishable and seductive riches, always refused them. Though they were quite wealthy, Democritus of Abdera and Crates of Thebes, and likewise other profound and illustrious philosophers practically infinite in number, embraced poverty with a remarkable enthusiasm. Certainly the man who lacks nothing is sufficiently wealthy; and what can that man lack whose appetite is obedient to reason? For unbridled appetite is satisfied by no gold, no silver, no treasures of the Persians. The desire for possession is confined by no bounds. The more it possesses the more it seeks; once it has gained its object, it is as content as before or perhaps even less so in that it is inflamed more and more, day by day; it somehow undergoes the same experience as those suffering from dehydration: their thirst is increased by drinking.[3] But poverty cannot be oppressive to anyone who is content with his own present possessions. For the cause of poverty is not lack of money but of reason and planning. The result is that sometimes we should call and judge a poor man rich and vice versa. But I draw a line under this. For this third book of *Florentine Discussions* consists of a discourse about poverty that I heard conducted with learning and authority and by the same men who spoke the day before about infamy, with the

6

7

8

Leonardo Arretino, familiari nostro. Par est enim talium virorum auctoritatem longe plus apud te valere quam ullam Philelfi amicitiam.

Nam Leonardus, qui posito tandem parumper metu quem ex impunitate et audacia impiorum non mediocrem animo conceperat, ad Rainaldum venerat Pallantemque salutatum, ubi utrunque animadvertit de suo adventu occultius quiddam animis volutare et colloqui clanculum, ita ad Rainaldum conversus silentium rumpit.

9 *Leonardus.* Quantum assequor coniectura, mirari te video, Rainalde, quid tam sero eam ad vos in hac praesertim mutabilitate fortunae, quae non magis vobis quam et mihi et bonis omnibus acerba videri debet et permolesta. Sed certe nihil est quod te mirari oporteat, siquidem non mea me voluntas, sed ratio temporis retardavit.

Rainaldus. Equidem miratus sum, Leonarde, nec te tua fallit opinio. Id enim loquebar ad Pallantem, qui etiam ipse miraretur quid minus statim venisses ad tuos vel consilii vel consolationis gratia.

10 *Leonardus.* Nunquid meo vobis consilio opus est, hominibus prudentissimis? An ullo consolationis genere viris gravissimis planeque sapientibus?

Rainaldus. Homines sumus, Leonarde, non dii. Praeterea ea est rerum perturbatio ac fluctus, ut ad tantae navis gubernacula nullus sit adeo peritissimus gubernator qui sibi satis omnino constet. Verum quae nunc te causa magis adduxit?

11 *Leonardus.* Distuleram tantisper adventum meum in hoc totius civitatis tumultu ac turbine, dum viderem quo se tandem reciperet effraenata haec perditissimorum hominum praecepsque insania, quo certi aliquid afferrem ad vos vel de spe vel de interitu reipublicae. Nunc autem intellectis inimicorum insidiis, quibus

addition of my friend Leonardo Bruni, a most learned and eloquent man. It is only right for the authority of such men to have
far greater weight with you than any friendship with Filelfo.

When he had finally for a while laid aside the considerable fear
he harbored in view of the impunity and boldness of the criminals, Leonardo had gone to greet Rinaldo and Palla. When he
noticed that they both were secretively pondering some question
concerning his arrival and speaking in a clandestine manner, he
turned toward Rinaldo and broke his silence.

Leonardo. As far as I can infer, Rinaldo, I see that you are sur-   9
prised that I come to you so late, particularly in this precarious
set of circumstances that must look every bit as bitter and
grievous to me and to all sound citizens as it does to you. But
surely there is no reason for you to be surprised, since it was
not my own wish but a calculation of the timing that held me
back.

Rinaldo. I was indeed surprised, Leonardo, and your thought was
not mistaken. This is what I was saying to Palla, who was also
surprised that you had not come immediately to your friends,
whether to provide counsel or offer consolation.

Leonardo. Surely you, men of great foresight, have no need of my   10
advice, do you? Or do men who possess authority and complete
wisdom stand in need of any type of consolation?

Rinaldo. We are men, Leonardo, not gods. Moreover, the disturbing shifts of events are such that no one is so skilled that he is
a self-sufficient pilot at the rudder of so great a ship. But what
cause has now brought you to us?

Leonardo. Amid this swirling commotion of the entire state I post-   11
poned my arrival until I could see where the unbridled and
headlong madness of the desperate citizens would come to rest,
so that I could bring you some news about the hope or the ex-
tinction of the republic. Now, however, since I have learned of

viros optimatis perditum ire cogitant, eundum existimavi ad
vos, quo facti per me de huiusmodi dolis certiores consulatis in
rem quamoptime. Nam Cosmiani omnes, ut sunt homines impurissimi, per omne flagitium atque[3] turpitudinem nummos
cogunt, quibus infimae plebis animos et omnem inopum turbam sibi concilient ac muneribus trahant in partes suas. Huiusmodi autem hominum quanta sit multitudo, nemo est qui nesciat.

12 *Rainaldus.* At cum bonis, Leonarde, et optimatibus vincere nos
oportet, non cum multis et civitatis faece. Verum ex quibus
gurgustiis Medices nummos eruunt?

Leonardus. Sane e gurgustiis, Rainalde. Nam quidquid alea permultos iam annos in arcam condidit, quidquid monasterium illud quod Medicium vocant ex omnibus sordibus congestum
habet aeris, partim precario, partim precio, quod privatim
cuiusque aut aleatoris aut lenonis aut prostibulae peculium restat, emungitur. Grandis pecunia conflatur adversus optimates,
ac variis artibus datur opera ut nos ad inopiam agant. Arbitrantur enim ubi nos careamus auro, ipsi autem abundent, facile
futurum ut zonarios omnis ac lanarios et huiusmodi lucriones
asciscant sibi adiutores contra principes civitatis. Quae ipsa
omnis in nos indignitas eo mihi videtur indignior, quo ab in-
13 dignissimis omnium infertur. Itaque nostrum fuerit, Rainalde,
si sapimus, adversus abiectam illam et debilitatam manum prius
consulere quam ex omni perditorum hominum genere viribus
comparatis magis magisque invalescat. Nam eiusmodi hominum colluvio neminem amat, nisi quem in se viderit largiorem.
Quare qui plus pecuniae habuerit quod largiatur in plebem, ille
mea sententia ex hac tristi et obscura contentione victor est
evasurus.

the intrigues by which our enemies think to destroy the nobles, I realized I had to come to you so that I could inform you about these plots and you could form the best possible counterplan. For since all of Cosimo's party are utterly base, they are gathering money by every crime and vice so that with it they can win over the sentiments of the base commoners and the entire crowd of the poor and draw them to their side. Everyone knows how vast is the number of men of this sort.

Rinaldo. But we must win with the sound citizens and the nobles, 12 not with the many and the dregs of the city. But from what dens of vice are the Medici deriving their funds?

Leonardo. From dens of vice indeed, Rinaldo. For whatever proceeds from dicing over many years has been stored up in their strongbox, whatever that monastery that they call the "Medicean Monastery" has gathered from all unsavory enterprises, partly as a tip, partly as a price, whatever pocket money remains to any gambler, pimp, or prostitute, is gained through fraud.[4] A vast sum of money is being gathered against the nobles, and in various ways they are exerting themselves to drive us into destitution. They think that if we are without gold but they have a great deal of it, it will be easy to enroll all the girdle makers and wool makers and profiteers as allies against the leading citizens. This disrespect for us seems even more outrageous because it is being inflicted by the most unworthy citizens of all. Hence it 13 should be our task, Rinaldo, if we are smart, to form our plans against that wretched and enervated band before it gains more and more power with the combined forces of all sorts of worthless men. For such a collection of human refuse loves only a man it has seen play the benefactor to itself. And so whoever may have more money to lavish on the commons will in my opinion emerge victorious from this sad and underhanded contest.

Rainaldus. At ego te miror, virum eruditum planeque philosophum, qui plus roboris ponas in fragilitate divitiarum quam in
solida meraque virtute. Nam vel laudare divitias nefas est.

14 *Leonardus.* Nequaquam tu quidem sentis cum Crantore, qui philosophus non ignobilis in theatro Graecorum omnium ita Divitias loquentes inducat: 'Nos quidem, o Graeci universi,[4] ornamentum omnibus praebemus hominibus. A nobis vestiuntur
calcianturque ac reliquum fructum capiunt. Usui sumus et vali-
tudinariis et valentibus. Atque in pace quidem delectamus, in
bellis vero nervi sumus rerum gerendarum.' Praeterea si paupertas est inimica philosopho, ut videtur Aristoteli, duci divitias in
amicis manifestum est. Itaque dicit Aristoteles tum incipere
animum studiis libero dignis homine dare operam, cum omnibus ad necessitatem voluptatemque affluentibus rebus sollicitudine liber est.

15 *Rainaldus.* Velim tu mihi, Pallas, patronus accedas ad defenden-
dam paupertatem contra divitias, quibus tantum tribuit Leonardus, ut sine iis et manca sit virtus et inermis philosophia, ob
eam arbitror causam, quod et ipse dives est ad sexagintamilia
aureum, et apud te loquitur, cui gratificari putat, quippe qui
adeo sis locuples ut ad trecentamillia aureum aut etiam[5] amplius aedes tui fundique ascendant. Sed noli, obsecro, plus ipse
divitiis quam veritati tribuere. Hic mihi Graecis testimoniis
probat quae dicit. Quare tu, qui Graeci sermonis doctissimus es
interpres, paupertatis causam capesse, facitoque Leonardus intelligat non plus posse divitias quam virtutem.[6]

16 *Leonardus.* Tanquam istud ab me dictum sit, Rainalde, quod virtuti putem divitias inimicas, et non in eo genere positas quod a
Graecis ἀδιάφορον, a nostris 'indifferens' dicitur. Nonne ita
est, Pallas?

Rinaldo. Well I am surprised that you, a man of learning and a perfect philosopher, assign greater power to riches, unstable as they are, than to solid and genuine virtue. For even praising riches is committing a wrong.

Leonardo. You disagree entirely then with Crantor, a distinguished 14 philosopher, who in a pan-Hellenic assembly brings Wealth onstage speaking as follows: "Greeks, we provide an embellishment for all men. We give them their clothes and shoes and all their other benefits. We are useful to the sickly and the strong. In peacetime we give delight, in time of war we are the basis for exploits."[5] Moreover, if poverty is the philosopher's enemy, as Aristotle thought, it is clear that wealth must be counted among his friends. Thus Aristotle says that the mind begins to devote attention to the studies worthy of a free man when he is free of worry, with all things for necessity and pleasure provided in abundance.[6]

Rinaldo. Palla, I would like you to join me as an advocate for de- 15 fending poverty against wealth, to which Leonardo attaches such great importance that, without it, virtue is defective and philosophy unarmed; I think it is for the reason that he is wealthy himself, to the extent of 60,000 florins,[7] and he is speaking before you, whom he thinks to please because you are so rich that your house and estates amount to 300,000 florins or even more. But do not, I beg you, give greater importance to wealth than to truth. He is demonstrating his points to me based on Greek sources. Thus, since you are a highly learned interpreter of the Greek language, take hold of poverty's case, make Leonardo understand that wealth has no greater power than virtue.

Leonardo. You say that, Rinaldo, as if I had said that I thought 16 wealth inimical to virtue and not placed it in the category that the Greeks call *adiaphoron* and we call "indifferent." Isn't that so, Palla?

Pallas. Ita sane, ut ais, Leonarde, siquidem non Academicos et Peripateticos sequi, sed Stoicos malimus.

Rhodulphus. Nunquid etiam, Pallas, philosophi vestri in suis disciplinis ita dissentiunt ut Florentini in reipublicae gubernaculis?

Pallas. Dissentiunt, Rhodulphe, illi quidem, at non pro evertendo, ut nostri, sed pro constituendo statu felicis vitae.

Rhodulphus. Quid tandem aiunt utrique? Expone, si videtur. Non te impediam. Nam de republica sehorsum postea commentabimur inter nos, siquid remedii in tantis aerumnis afferri queat.

17   *Pallas.* Haec provincia Leonardi fuerit, qui ut est vir doctus et eruditus, in istiusmodi sermonem non tam incidit quam devenit. Hic enim, Rhodulphe, tibi ac item nobis cumulatissime satisfaciet, docebitque non solum quid dissentiant ii philosophi, sed etiam quid consentiant.

Leonardus. Age, age, Pallas, si libet. Tua enim provincia ista omnis futura est, qui Academicorum, Peripateticorum Stoicorumque meministi, et duobus proximis his diebus tum summatim de incommodis exilii, tum de infamia gravissime simul[7] es disertissimeque locutus.

18   *Pallas.* Inepte sane multa, Leonarde, locuti sumus. Verum ineptum me iudicatum iri malui quam morosum. Quare eo[8] mihi magis venia danda est quo inepte multa disserui. Itaque ne tu aeque morositatis ac ego ineptitudinis nomen subeas, gratificare nobis omnibus in primisque hisce adolescentibus, qui, ut vides, oculos habent in te conversos incredibili desyderio audiendi tui.

Leonardus. Ne ipse quoque tanquam Poggius hic noster morositatis nomini fiam obnoxius, faciam, Pallas, quod te velle intelligo, modo siquid defuerit ipse subvenias, ne iure ipse ineptus iudicer.

Palla. It is as you say, Leonardo, if we prefer to follow the Stoics rather than the Academics and Peripatetics.

Ridolfo. Surely, Palla, your philosophers do not quarrel in their schools as the Florentines do over the governance of the republic, do they?

Palla. Quarrel they do, Ridolfo, but not about overturning the basis for a happy life, as our people do, but about creating one.

Ridolfo. What are the arguments of either party? Set them out if you please. I shall pose no obstacle. Afterward we'll discuss the republic separately among ourselves to see if some cure can be applied amid such woes.

Palla. This will be Leonardo's area of expertise; since he is a   17
learned and erudite man, he does not so much fall into such discussions as seek them out. He will give perfect satisfaction to you and to us, Ridolfo, and will teach us not only on what points those philosophers differ but also on what they agree.

Leonardo. Come, come, Palla, if you please. That entire job will be yours since you are the one who has called to mind the Academics, Peripatetics, and Stoics, and in these last two days you have held forth both on the disadvantages of exile in summary form and also on infamy, with great authority and eloquence.

Palla. Indeed, Leonardo, I spoke many things ineptly. But I pre-   18
ferred to be judged inept rather than contentious. Therefore I should rather be pardoned for the fact that I discoursed ineptly on many matters. So then to avoid earning a reputation for belligerence as I did for ineptness, humor all of us and especially these young men, who, as you see, have trained their eyes on you with an unbelievable yearning to hear you.

Leonardo. So as not, like our friend Poggio here, to incur a reputation for contentiousness, I shall, Palla, do what I know you want, provided that, if something is missing, you yourself will come to my aid, lest I myself be rightly condemned as inept.

19 *Poggius.* Aggredere tandem, Leonarde, ne qui me vocas, te morosum ostendas. Nam siquid opus fuerit, ego pro te praestabo.
Intelligesque non omnia posse Graecos, qui ne 'inepti' quidem
habeant nomen.

Leonardus. At ego, Poggi, non modo tibi, Graecarum litterarum
imperito, id non assentior, sed ne Ciceroni quidem, ipsi Latinae
eloquentiae principi, qui ut Latinos in verborum etiam copia
(quod ridere nonnunquam soleo) Graecis illis locupletissimis
anteponeret, haud est quandoque veritus, homo doctissimus,
vero mendacium anteponere. Nam quam nostri 'ineptitudinem,'
illi ἀσχημοσύνην nominant, et 'ineptum' ἀσχήμονα. Eodem
modo quod nos 'apte' dictum factumve narramus, Graeci id
proferunt εὐσχημόνως; et 'aptitudinem' dicunt εὐσχημοσύ-
νην. Haec et alia plaeraque cum non ignoraret Cicero Graecis
esse, his tamen carere illos insimulabat, quo sua Latinis redderet cariora.

20 *Rainaldus.* Leonarde, de ista re satis, si videtur. Itaque omissis
grammaticis ac Poggio ad philosophos redi. Et quam sapientissimus Pallas noster disserendi provinciam tibi delegavit, eam
pro tua humanitate liberaliter suscipe ac gere. Nam te omnes
audire vaehementer cupimus.

Leonardus. Posteaquam intelligo, Rainalde, accidisse mihi praeter
institutum et consuetudinem meam ut de rebus gravissimis
eisdemque pulcherrimis omnino sit disputandum, tibi tandem
meoque Pallanti obtemperabo. Verum nolite grandius mihi honus imponere quam humeri ferre possint.

Rainaldus. Nihil maius nobis praestabis quam quod soles omnia et
sapienter et pulchre.

21 *Leonardus.* Qui magis inter Ionicae sapientiae philosophos claruc-
runt, tum veteres Academici, tum etiam Peripatetici — nam de
Stoicis iniiciam paulo post — cum certo quodam disciplinae ordine atque modo procedere voluerunt, huiusmodi quadam in

Poggio. Get on with it, Leonardo, lest you who call me contentious   19
show yourself to be the same. If necessary, I shall stand in for
you; and you will learn that the Greeks cannot do everything,
since they do not even have a word for "inept."

Leonardo. Well, Poggio, I not only disagree with you, an ignoramus in Greek literature, on this point, but even Cicero, the
prince of Latin eloquence, who, in order to place the Latins
ahead of those superbly endowed Greeks in richness of vocabu-
lary (a fact that sometimes makes me laugh), felt no scruple,
learned man though he was, in preferring a lie over the truth.
For what our countrymen call "ineptitude," they call *aschemo-
syne,* and "inept," *aschemon.* Likewise what we say was "aptly"
said or done, the Greeks express as *euschemonos,* and they call
"aptitude" *euschemosyne.* Although Cicero was not unaware that
the Greeks had these and many other such words, he nonetheless accused them of lacking them in order to enhance the esteem the Latins felt for his works.[8]

Rinaldo. Leonardo, enough about this topic, if you please. Let us   20
leave grammatical matters and Poggio aside and return to the
philosophers. Our friend Palla, wisest of men, has turned the
floor over to you; be so kind and generous as to take up the
task. For we are all very eager indeed to hear you.

Leonardo. Since I know, Rinaldo, that it has fallen to my lot, contrary to my practice and custom, to discourse on the weightiest
and at the same time fairest of topics, I shall oblige you and my
friend Palla. But please do not impose a greater burden upon
me than my shoulders can bear.

Rinaldo. You will be providing us with nothing greater than what
you usually do with wisdom and eloquence.

Leonardo. Those who were distinguished among the Ionian phi-   21
losophers, then those of the Old Academy and also the Peripatetics — for I will speak about the Stoics a little later —
when they wanted to proceed in a certain order and method of

docendo partitione sunt usi. Volunt enim bona esse alia in nobis, alia extra nos. Et quae in nobis alia animi, alia corporis appellari. Atque animi quidem bona iusticiam dicunt et prudentiam et fortitudinem et temperantiam reliquasque huiusmodi
virtutes. Corporis vero pulchritudinem, habitudinem, bonam
valitudinem, vires ac caetera talia. Sed extraria bona amicos
duci, incolumitatem patriae, divitias et quaeque extra nos posita
secundis populi rumoribus celebrantur. Quare secundum hanc
partitionem in bonis etiam divitiae, Rainalde, non in malis nu-
merantur.

22   *Rainaldus.* Intelligo, Leonarde, etsi partitionem istam non probo.
Nam isto pacto paupertas in genere malorum videatur reposita,
quam, si ita sit, non absurde Soderinus heri vel absentem pertimescere videbatur.

Leonardus. De paupertate non multo post quaeri poterit. Impraes-
sentiarum quod propositum est persequamur. Vituperaras[9]
enim divitias, quas prima hac partitione non modo non esse
vitio dandas, sed laudandas etiam concedas oportet. Sunt autem
qui inter eosdem Academicos ac Peripateticos eodem ipsi modo
quo Stoici partiantur, quanquam et a superioribus et inter seip-

23   sos verbo magis videntur mihi quam re differre. Nam aliqua
bona dici sed minima (quoniam et extra animum et extra corpus sint posita), aliqua vero quae corpori tribuantur, non
maxima ut animi, sed mediocria quaedam esse, eadem ipsa
utraque atque haec videntur mihi, in quibus a Stoicis selectio
relinquitur. Dicunt enim illi eorum quae sunt — sic enim τὰ
ὄντα quandoque interpretari malo quam 'entia,' quanquam ita
etiam utar, si videbitur — alia esse bona, alia mala, et alia esse

learning, used this kind of division in their teaching. They claim that some goods are in us, others outside of us. Of those that are in us, some are called those of the mind, others of the body. The goods of the mind they call justice and wisdom and courage and temperance and the remaining virtues of this type; of the body, beauty, condition, good health, strength and others like them. Friends are held to be among the external goods, as are the security of one's homeland, wealth, and favorable reports circulated by popular rumor. Therefore, according to this division, riches are counted among the goods, Rinaldo, not the evils.

Rinaldo. I know, Leonardo, though I do not approve of that division. For in that way poverty would seem to be placed in the category of evils, poverty that Soderini yesterday plausibly, if that were the case, seemed to dread even when it is not present.   22

Leonardo. We will presently investigate about poverty. For now let us pursue the topic that has been proposed. Now you criticized wealth, which you must admit, according to this first division, is not only not to be held a fault, but even to be commended. There are those who, intermediate between the Academics and Peripatetics, make a division in the same way as the Stoics, although they seem to differ from their predecessors and among themselves in wording rather than in matter. For some things   23 are called goods but very small ones (since they are located outside both the soul and the body), others that are assigned to the body are not the greatest goods, as are those of the mind, but middling goods: both of these seem to me to be the same ones the Stoics leave to choice. For they say that "of those things that exist" — for I prefer to render *onta* in this fashion rather than as *entia,* although I will use the latter, if it seems appropriate — some are goods, others evils, and that there are certain others in

quaedam inter haec quae nec bona sint nec mala censenda, quae
quidem ipsa 'indifferentia' nominant.

Verum ex his vir gravissimus Xenocrates utens singularis
numeri casibus ita dicere consuevit: 'Omne quod est, aut bonum est aut malum, aut nec bonum nec malum, quod ipsum
etiam est indifferens; separatum scilicet quoddam genus, quod
neque in bonorum nec in malorum sit ratione reponendum.'
Quam quidem rerum partitionem etsi veteres illi omnes videntur amplexi, omnesque consentiunt rerum differentiam esse in
tris partes distributam, nihilo tamen minus in contentionem
prodeunt cum dicant definitionem ab universali parum differre,
quippe quae idem sit potestate. Nam qui dicit verbi causa 'orator est' — ut Cato definiebat — 'vir bonus dicendo peritus,' hic vi
plane idem dicit quod ille quicunque ita definiat, 'siquid est
orator, id est vir bonus dicendi peritus,' sed differentiam facit in
voce, idque sophistice. Quamobrem quod etiam ita dicitur, 'eorum quae sunt, alia sunt bona, alia mala, alia neque bona neque
mala,' id tale secundum Chrysippum universale vi est, ac si dicatur, 'siqua sunt entia, ea vel bona sunt vel mala vel indifferentia.' Atqui huiusmodi universale mendacio subiacet, quandocunque mendacium ullum subiunctum habet. Nam subiectis
duabus rebus — alia bona, alia mala; aut alia quidem bona, alia
indifferenti, vel mala[10] etiam et indifferenti — siquidem dixeris
'hoc est entium bonorum,' verum sit; quod si dicas 'haec sunt
bona,' sit mendacium. Non enim sunt bona, sed hoc quidem est
bonum, hoc autem malum. Et eodem modo, si dicas 'haec sunt
mala,' falsum sit. Nam mala certe non sunt, sed ipsorum alterum. Idem quoque de indifferentibus accidat. Falsum est enim
'haec sunt indifferentia,' quemadmodum de bonis malisque ostendimus.

Margin: 24, 25

between them that should be thought neither good nor evil which they call "indifferent."⁹

Among them Xenocrates, a man of great authority, using the singular number, used to say: "Everything that is is either good or evil, or neither good nor evil. The latter is itself indifferent, a certain separate class that is to be included in the reckoning neither of the goods nor of the evils." Although those ancients seem to have embraced this entire division of things, and all agree on a categorization of things into three parts, nonetheless they enter into conflict when they assert that the definition scarcely differs from the universal, since it is the same in signification. For he who says, for example, "an orator is"—as Cato defined—"a good man skilled in speaking,"¹⁰ is clearly making the same assertion in terms of signification as someone might in defining it thus, "if an orator is anything, it is a good man skilled in speaking," but he makes a verbal distinction and does so in a sophistical manner. Therefore the statement "of those things which are, some are goods, others evils, others neither goods nor evils" is, according to Chrysippus, universal in signification, as if it were said, "If there are any existing things, they are either good or bad or indifferent." But such a universal would be reduced to a falsehood whenever it possesses any subordinate falsehood. For if two things are subordinate—one good, the other evil; or the one good, the other indifferent or evil and indifferent—if you would say "this is made of good entities," it would be true; but if you would say "these are goods," it would be a falsehood. For they are not goods, but this is good, this evil. And in the same way, if you would say "these are evil," it would be false. For they are certainly not evils, but one of them is. The same happens also concerning the indifferent. For "these are indifferents" is false, just as we showed concerning goods and evils.

24

25

26 *Manettus.* At mihi, Leonarde, videtur Xenocrates in sua illa partitione prudentior, qui singularis numeri usus sit casibus. Nam si
pluralibus casibus esset usus, eius omnis partitio monstratis
diversi generis rebus necessario mentiretur.

Leonardus. Mones tu quidem, Manette, subtiliter ac docte.

Manettus. Ad haec cum omnis sana generis partitio ea sit quae
propinquas dividit atque coniunctas species, nonne siquis ita
partiatur, 'homines alii sunt Latini, alii Scythae, alii Turci, alii
Aegyptii, alii Persae,' idcirco is erret, quoniam aliarum propin-
quarum specierum non coniunctam et propinquam speciem
diiungit,[11] sed huius speciei species?

27 *Leonardus.* Certe, Manette, ut dicis. Itaque rectior ea fuerit partitio, id quod te video intelligere, cum dicitur 'homines alii sunt
Latini, alii barbari,' et per subdivisionem, 'barbari quoque alii
sunt Scythae, alii Turci, alii Aegyptii, alii Persae.' Idem rursus
dicendum fuerat in eorum quae sunt partitione. Nam quaecunque bona et mala sunt, differentiam apud nos habent. Quaecunque vero inter bona malaque sunt, non differunt quoad nos.
Itaque longe subtilius partiamur si dixerimus 'eorum quae sunt,
alia non differunt, alia differunt; et differentium quidem alia
sunt bona, alia mala.' Talis enim partitio eius partitionis est similis qua modo dicebatur: 'homines alii sunt Latini, alii barbari;
at barbari alii Scythae sunt, alii Turci, alii Aegyptii, alii Persae.'

28 *Manettus.* Tuum[12] istum partiendi modum non possum equidem
non probare, quem ab illis item perpulchre video observatum
qui dixerunt bona esse alia in nobis, alia extra nos. Et rursus
quae in nobis essent, alia esse animi, alia corporis. Nam cum
divisio fieri multipliciter soleat, ut cum genus in species

Manetti. But, Leonardo, I think Xenocrates was more prudent in   26
his division since he used the singular number. For if he had
used the plural, once things of different kinds were being re-
ferred to, his entire division would have been false.

Leonardo. You are cautioning us with acuity and learning, Manetti.

Manetti. Furthermore, since every sound division of a class is such
that it divides neighboring and conjoined species, if someone were to divide thus, "some men are Latins, others Scythians, others Turks, others Egyptians, others Persians," would he
therefore be mistaken, since he does not separate out a neighboring and overlapping species of other neighboring species,
but a species of this species?

Leonardo. It is surely as you say, Manetti. Therefore, as I see you   27
know, the more correct division would be: "some men are Latins, others barbarians," and by subdivision "some barbarians are
Scythians, others Turks, others Egyptians, others Persians."
The same ought to have been said in the division of existing
things. For whatever things are good and bad have a difference
for us; but whatever things are between the bad and good do
not differ as far as we are concerned. Therefore we make a far
finer division if we say "of existing entities some do not differ,
others do; and of those that differ, some are good, others bad."
Such a division is similar to the division by which it was just
now said: "some men are Latins, others barbarians; but some
barbarians are Scythians, others Turks, others Egyptians, others Persians."

Manetti. I cannot but approve that method of division of yours,   28
which I see has been finely maintained by those who have said
that some goods are in us, others outside of us; and again of the
ones that are in us, some are of the mind, others of the body.[11]
For although a division is usually made in a number of ways, as
when we divide a genus into species and apportion the whole

partimur, et cum totum in proprias distribuimus partes, et cum vocem plura significantem in significationes proprias secamus — praeterea cum secundum accidens tripliciter dirimentes aut subiectum in accidentia separamus, aut accidens in subiecta dividimus, aut in accidentia accidentia partimur — ea sane divisio et princeps est et reliquis divisionibus antecellit, qua genus in suas species distribuitur. Verum non ab re intelligere abs te cupio quot modis verbum hoc substantivum 'est' accipiendum putes apud philosophos.

29 *Leonardus.* Non inepte, Manette, rogas. Falluntur enim non nulli persaepe, vim verbi istius et consuetudinem ignorantes. 'Est' autem duo significat, et id primo quod verbi substantivi proprium ducitur, 'existit' — ex quo 'dies *est*' dicimus, hoc est 'existit' — et item 'apparet,' secundum quod dicunt aliqui mathematici nonnunquam 'inter duo quaedam astra intervallum *est* ulnae,' quod non pro eo accipiunt omnino quod 'est' substantivum verbum significat, sed quod 'apparet,' cum id intervalli quod tum propter altitudinem, tum propter aspectus distantiam ulnae spacio videtur circumscribi, ad centum fortassis stadia aut etiam amplius terminetur. Cum igitur 'est' particula duplex significatum recipiat, cum speculando dicimus 'eorum quae *sunt*, alia sunt bona, alia mala, alia nec bona nec mala,' 'sunt' hoc loci non 30 substantive ponimus, sed ut 'apparent.' Nam de bonorum ac malorum neutrorumque subsistentia ad naturam cum iis disceptandum est qui certis quibusdam suisque decretis addicti sunt. Hos Graeci vocant δογματικούς. Sed horum quodque secundum id scilicet quod 'apparet' appellare consuevimus, aut bonum aut malum aut indifferens. Qua sententia, ut existimo, ductus Timo ille Phliasius ita scripsit in *Sillis:*

into its proper parts and when we divide a word that has several senses into its proper senses — moreover when classifying in a threefold manner according to the accident, we either separate the subject into accidents, or divide the accident into subjects, or divide the accidents into accidents — this division is first and precedes the rest of the divisions by which a genus is apportioned into its own species.[12] But I want to know from you the answer to a relevant question: how many ways you think the substantive verb "is" (*est*) is to be understood in the philosophers?

Leonardo. Your question is pertinent, Manetti. For some people often fall into error by mistaking the sense and usage of that verb. "Is" signifies two things, the first what is held to be proper to the substantive verb, "exists" — hence we say "it is day," that is "is present" — and likewise "appears," according to which some mathematicians sometimes say "between two stars there is an interval of an arm's length," which they do not at all understand in the sense that *est* signifies the substantive verb but that it "appears," since that interval which seems to be circumscribed by an arm's length both as to height and as to viewing distance may be bounded by 100 stades[13] or even more. Since therefore the word "is" admits a dual signification, when we say in theorizing "of the things that *are*, some are goods, others evils, others neither goods nor evils," we are not using "are" in this passage as a substantive but as "appear." For a debate about the status in the natural order of things good, evil, and neither must be conducted with those who are committed to certain fixed tenets of their own. The Greeks call them *dogmatikoi* ("dogmatists"). But we have grown used to naming each thing according to what it "appears" to be, either good or evil or indifferent. Guided, I believe, by this view, the renowned Timon of Phlius wrote as follows in his *Silloi*:

29

30

Vera loquor, nam vera mihi mea dicta videntur.
Ordo mihi rectus, regula recta mihi[13] est.
Quod manet ipsa dei semper natura bonique
inconcussa quibus fit sua vita viro.

31   *Manettus.* Verum, Leonarde, 'videri' et 'apparere' differuntne invicem an idem significant?

Leonardus. Differunt sane, sed ita differunt ut pro eodem saepe accipiantur. Nam 'apparere' ad sensus, 'videri' autem ad mentis iudicium opinionemve refertur. Ut igitur tandem redeam ad rem ipsam, qua de sermo haberi coeperat, non minus quam Stoici Academici veteres et Peripatetici triplici illa entium partitione sunt usi, ut et virtutem et quae pro virtute actio sit animi bonum appellarint; contra autem et vitium et vitiosam actionem mali nomen habere voluerint. Quidquid vero praeter animi aut virtutem fuerit aut vitium, id neque bonum nec[14] malum, sed indifferens nominarunt.

32   *Manettus.* At indifferentium estne ulla differentia?

Leonardus. Certe, Manette, si ad veritatem quam ad contentionem dicere malimus. Quis enim corporis commoda fortunae commodis non admodum anteponat, ut divitiis bonam valitudinem, generis claritudini formae praestantiam? Quinetiam ipsa inter se vel corporis vel fortunae commoda plurimum differunt. Nam quotusquisque sit qui bonam valitudinem bonitati formae non praeferat? Qui non se nobilem quam divitem malit?

33   *Rainaldus.* Iocaris nobiscum, Leonarde, quasi nescias Cosmum et Laurentium Medices non modo nobilitati at[15] virtuti etiam ipsi sine ulla disceptatione divitias anteferre.

Leonardus. At iocari mihi potius, Rainalde, tu videris, qui putes febrientes habere gustus,[16] iudicium aut discrimen. De viris ingenuis atque Florentinis mihi habetur sermo, non de Mucellensibus et servilibus beluis, qui ut obscurissime sunt et nati et

I speak truth, for my words seem to me true.
    To me the order is right, the standard is right
Since the nature of god and the good remain,
    By which a man's life becomes unshakeable.[14]

Manetti. But, Leonardo, do "seem" and "appear" differ or mean the   31
    same thing?

Leonardo. They do differ but in such a way that they are often
    understood as the same. For "appear" is oriented toward the
    judgment of the sense, "seem" to the judgment or opinion of the
    mind. To return to the very topic concerning which the conver-
    sation began, the Old Academics and Peripatetics no less than
    the Stoics used that triple division of beings in order to call
    virtue and action on behalf of virtue a good of the mind and
    contrariwise claim that vice and related action has the name of
    evil. Whatever there was apart from the virtue or vice of the
    mind, they called neither good nor evil but indifferent.

Manetti. But is there any distinction among the indifferents?   32

Leonardo. Certainly, Manetti, if we prefer to speak for the sake of
    truth rather than disputatiousness. For who would not place
    the advantages of the body above those of fortune, for instance,
    good health above riches, beauty before distinguished lineage?
    Indeed, the advantages of the body and of fortune differ a good
    deal. For how few are there who would not prefer good health
    to good fortune? Who would not prefer to be well born rather
    than rich?

Rinaldo. You are joking with us, Leonardo, as if you are unaware   33
    that Cosimo and Lorenzo de' Medici have no qualms putting
    wealth not only before nobility, but also before virtue.

Leonardo. But I think you are rather joking with me, Rinaldo,
    since you think that people suffering from fever have taste,
    judgment, or discrimination. I am talking about freeborn men
    and Florentines, not natives of the Mugello and tame beasts

alti et educati, nunquam sciant in media luce versari. At ipse tu, qui splendorem generis virtutemque prae te fers, num te Cosmum — Laurentium enim omitto ut fatuum — quam Rainaldum malis?

34   *Rainaldus.* Afficis me tu quidem contumelia, Leonarde, qui Cosmo nescio cui homini flagitioso et nequam aut ulli Medici Rainaldum Albizium comparandum existimes, aeri aurum, solem tenebris. Iuvat enim de me nunc neque loqui nec sentire humilius quicquam.

   Leonardus. At nequaquam de te[17] mihi, Rainalde, habetur impraesentiarum oratio, viro clarissimo atque[18] optimo, sed de nobilitate ac virtute, quam utranque in medium protulisses et Cosmiano foenori quodammodo[19] subiecisses.

35   *Rainaldus.* Eninvero malim me nunquam natum quam impurissimum Cosmum istum vel esse vel haberi, cuius etiam nomen cum audio, stomachor ad nauseam. Tanta est turpissimae[20] eius[21] vitae sordes ac sentina. Sed quam vim tamen habeant divitiae, videmus in huiusmodi homine, qui et ignobilis et nullius pravitatis expers viros optimates eiicit patria.

   Leonardus. Num idcirco pluris quenquam facias, quia interdum plus possit, non rationis consilio sed temeritate fortunae?

   Rainaldus. Minime. Sed apud plebem divitiae valent plurimum.

   Leonardus. Et apud sicarios sicae, et venenum apud veneficos.

36   *Rainaldus.* Esto sane, ut vis. Sed quid nobilitatem fortunae subiicis, quae sine virtute esse non possit?

   Leonardus. At habet[22] nobilitas admixtas virtuti divitias. Nam virtus diuturna, peremniter in posteros cum divitiis propagata, et conflat nobilitatem et perficit. Sed divitiis fortuna ipsa

who, since they were born, reared, and educated in obscurity never know how to act in broad daylight. But you who make the luster of your family and its virtue a point of pride, surely you would not prefer to be Cosimo — I set Lorenzo aside, fool that he is — than Rinaldo, would you?

Rinaldo. You insult me, Leonardo, in thinking that Rinaldo degli 34 Albizzi ought to be compared to some Cosimo, some worthless criminal, or to any of the Medici, gold to bronze, the sun to shadows. It would be helpful at this moment if you would neither say nor listen to demeaning remarks about me.

Leonardo. But my present speech is by no means about you, Rinaldo, a distinguished and excellent man, but about nobility and virtue, both of which you put forward for discussion and somehow connected with Cosimo's profiteering.

Rinaldo. I would prefer never to have been born than to be, or be 35 thought to be, that defiled Cosimo; even when I hear his name I feel sick to my stomach, such is the squalor and filth of his disgraceful life. But we see the power that wealth has in the case of such a man, who, though of lowly birth and partaking of every kind of wickedness, expels the nobles from their homeland.

Leonardo. Surely you would not attach greater importance to any man because he sometimes has greater power, not by rational planning, but by the randomness of fortune?

Rinaldo. No, but wealth has a great deal of influence with the common people.

Leonardo. And so do daggers with cutthroats and poison with poisoners.

Rinaldo. Let it be as you say. But why do you make nobility de- 36 pend upon fortune, though it cannot exist without virtue?

Leonardo. Yet nobility has wealth combined with virtue. For long-lasting virtue, constantly bequeathed to posterity along with wealth, both creates and perfects nobility. But fortune itself is

dominatur. Nam quanquam secundum Iuvenalem, 'nobilitas sola est atque unica virtus,' non de vera illa et sapientis[23] nobilitate loquimur, sed de hac vulgari et nostra, qua populi favoribus nobiles iudicamur.

37 *Rainaldus.* Quantum intelligo, iudicio sapientum sola virtute illustris quaedam nobilitas esse queat, quae nulli fortunae subiaceat.

Leonardus. Recte, Rainalde. Nam ut idem poeta cecinit:

> Paulus vel Cossus vel Drusus moribus esto.
> Hos ante effigies maiorum pone tuorum.
> Praecedant ipsas illi te consule virgas.

Itaque subdidit non absurde:

> Prima mihi debes animi bona: sanctus haberi
> iusticiaeque tenax factis dictisque mereris?
> Agnosco procerem.

38 *Rainaldus.* Sitne ulla nobilitas, Leonarde, quae virtutis inops versetur in laude?

Leonardus. Minime omnium, nisi ea fortasse qua et latrones nobilis et nobilis nonnunquam dicimus meretrices, quorum facinora ac flagitia in obscuro non sint, sed in omnium ore versentur.

Rainaldus. Verum cum in istiusmodi tum corporis tum fortunae, si ea tandem ulla sit, vel commodis vel incommodis tanta differentia sit, quid ea nunc vocas indifferentia?

39 *Leonardus.* Quoniam quod modo dicebatur, non differunt quoad nos. Nam sine ullo discrimine his singulis et recte licet et prave uti. Id autem illustretur exemplis. Grandis est pecunia Cosmi Medicis. Grandis Vitaliani Borrhomaei. Hic omne vivum, omne

the master of wealth. For although, according to Juvenal, "nobility is the sole and singular virtue,"[15] we are not speaking of that true nobility of the wise man but about this common nobility that belongs to us, by which we are judged noble by granting favors to the people.

Rinaldo. As far as I understand, in the opinion of wise men, a   37
distinguished nobility subject to no fortune can exist by virtue alone.

Leonardo. Well said, Rinaldo, for as the same poet wrote,

> In character be a Paulus or Cossus or Drusus.
> Place them ahead of the likenesses of your ancestors.
> When you are consul let them precede the rods themselves.

And he aptly adds:

> You owe me first the goods of the mind. Have you deserved
> By deed and word to be held blameless and steadfast in
>   justice?
> Then I grant it: you are a noble man.[16]

Rinaldo. Would there be, Leonardo, any nobility lacking virtue   38
that is worthy of praise?

Leonardo. None at all, unless perhaps in that sense in which we sometimes speak of noble thieves or noble prostitutes, whose disgraceful deeds are not obscure but circulate on everyone's lips.

Rinaldo. But if there is so great a difference in the advantages or disadvantages of the body and of fortune, if there is any such thing, why do you now call them indifferents?

Leonardo. Since, as was just said, they make no difference as per-   39
tains to us. For one may without any difference use these both rightly and badly. Let me illustrate with examples. Cosimo de' Medici is a very wealthy man; so is Vitaliano Borromeo. The one has his whole livelihood, his whole profit, in usury.

lucrum habet in foenore. At Vitalianus quidquid habet, bonis omnibus habet. Hic noster ad avariciam refert omnia, ille ad liberalitatem ac beneficentiam. Hic habet patriam[24] vaenalem. Ille se splendidissimo suo principi vaenalem praestat ad incolumitatem dignitatemque reipublicae. Utitur Cosmus ad omnem turpitudinis foeditatem nummis suis. At ille suis ad honestatis decus ac lumen. Itaque nihil in divitiis boni est, nihil mali, sed instrumenta quaedam esse possint et bonae actionis et malae, pro ingeniis moribusque utentium.

40 *Soderinus.* Suadet sane tua oratio, Leonarde. Sed quod tua pace dictum velim, minime persuadet, praesertim mihi, qui—quod heri dicebam—paupertatem admodum formidandam putem, cum omnibus, tum exulibus. Quos ea carere non posse docet M. Anneus Seneca, cum ait in persona Thyestae:[25]

> Fugiat trepidi comes exilii
> tristis egestas.

41 *Leonardus.* Quod tibi non persuadeo, Soderine, miror, homini modesto et nobili, qui quod in teipso expertus sis et in aliis animadverteris exemplo, id nunc subdubites. Te in omni Florentina vel adolescentia vel iuventute nemo nec adolescens est habitus nec pulchrior iuvenis. Deformior Laurentio Medice item nemo. Te omnes vidimus et probum adolescentem et pudicum iuvenem. Laurentium vero per omne improbitatis intemperantiaeque flagitium quamnequissime volutatum, nemo est qui nesciat. Nec te formositas a bonis actionibus retardavit, nec a malis illum deformitas. Possumus enim, si volumus, et incommodis quae dicuntur uti commode, et commodis rursus incommode. Vel gravissima omnia quae videntur, ea si ratione moderemur, levissima fiant. At levia quaeque reddantur gravia

But whatever Vitaliano has he has for the benefit of all good men. Our Cosimo makes greed his guiding principle, Vitaliano generosity and the bestowing of benefits. Cosimo considers his homeland up for sale; Vitaliano makes himself available to his distinguished prince for the well-being and standing of the republic. Cosimo uses his funds for every shameful act, Vitaliano his for the glory and luster of good deeds. Therefore in wealth there is neither good nor evil, but it can be, as it were, an instrument of both good and bad action in the hands of people who use it in accord with their own nature and character.

Soderini. Your words make a case, Leonardo. But, with your per- 40
mission, they fail to persuade, particularly me, since — as I said
yesterday — I think that all persons should dread poverty, but
exiles in particular. That they cannot get rid of it is shown by
M. Annaeus Seneca, when he says in the person of Thyestes:

> May sad poverty flee,
> The companion of the anxious exile.[17]

Leonardo. I am surprised, Soderini, that I fail to persuade you, a 41
moderate and noble man, since you now harbor covert doubts
about what you have experienced in your own case and noticed
by example in that of others. Among all the young people of
Florence, none has been regarded as more handsome than you.
By the same token, no one is uglier than Lorenzo de' Medici.
We have likewise all seen you to be a decent young man and
a modest youth. But there is no one who is unaware that
Lorenzo was so shamefully involved in every wicked and immoderate crime. Neither did your good looks hold you back
from good actions, nor did his ugliness keep him from bad acts.
For we can, if we wish, use the so-called disadvantages advantageously and again the advantages disadvantageously. All the
circumstances that seem most burdensome, if we govern them
with reason, turn out to be very easy. But easy circumstances

temeritate duce. Nam quod egestas exilium comitetur, non modo Sycharbae uxor Elissa Dido nequaquam assentiatur, sed ne Demaratus quidem ille Corinthius, aliique permulti quos[26] operosum sit numerare.

42 *Soderinus.* Paupertas tamen in malis est numeranda.

Leonardus. Minime, Soderine. Est[27] enim ex indifferentium genere.

Soderinus. At ista indifferentia quae abs te commodis et incommodis definiuntur, mala quaedam bonaque continent, si non maxima illa quae tu animi esse describis, vel mediocria saltem vel minima. Sit igitur paupertas minimum malum aliquod, quoniam non inter corporis sed inter fortunae reponis incommoda. Malum est tamen ea ratione, quod nihil omnino est quod egere iis velit quibus servatur ac gaudet. At divitiae non solum res necessarias[28] sed voluptarias[29] etiam parant ac prae-

43 bent mortalibus. Itaque rectissime, quod paulo ante memineras, et Crantorem locutum[30] arbitror et Aristotelem. Nam qua tranquillitate incipiat unquam animus ingenuis quibusquam[31] studiis accingi, ubi earum rerum inopia sit quibus necessariis vitae commodis honestaeque voluptati consulamus? Animus enim aut sollicitus aut aeger nihil recte queat nec intelligere nec agere. Quantum autem ornamentum, quantum fructum et in bona et in adversa valitudine e divitiis capiamus sentimus quottidie. Nam et belli et pacis eas nobis in omnes partes esse commodissimas, neminem esse puto quem lateat. Haec autem paupertas praestare qui[32] possit, cuius etiam nomen odiosum est? Quis

44 pauperem sibi vel amicum asciscat vel socium? An sumus fortasse nescii in omne facinus paupertate homines impelli solere? Hinc furta, hinc peculatus, hinc sacrilegia, veneficia, circunscriptiones, expilationes, latrocinia, neces proficiscuntur. Mentiri,

are made burdensome if rashness is our guide. For by no means would Elissa Dido, the wife of Sycharbas, or even the renowned Demaratus of Corinth, or many others whom it would be tiresome to enumerate, agree that penury is the companion of exile.[18]

Soderini. But poverty must be counted among the evils.   42

Leonardo. No, Soderini. It belongs to the class of indifferents.

Soderini. But those indifferents that are defined by you in terms of advantages and disadvantages include certain evils and goods — if not the very great ones that you define as belonging to the mind, then at least the middling or smallest ones. Let poverty, then, be some minimal evil since you place it among the disadvantages, not of the body, but of fortune. It is, however, an evil for the reason that there is nothing whatsoever that is willing to be deprived of the things by which it is sustained and flourishes. But wealth provides mortals not only with necessary but also with pleasurable things. Therefore I think that Crantor   43 and Aristotle spoke quite rightly, as you recalled a little while ago. For with what peace could a mind ever begin to equip itself with the studies of a freeborn man if there is a dearth of the things by which we provide for the necessary benefits of life and for honest enjoyment?[19] For a troubled or ailing mind could neither understand nor do anything properly. Each day we are aware how much benefit, how much enjoyment we derive from wealth in good and adverse health. Indeed, I think it escapes no one that wealth is most beneficial to us in all facets of war and peace. How could poverty provide these benefits, poverty whose very name is odious? Who would enroll a poor   44 man as his friend or ally? Are we perhaps unaware that men generally are driven to all sorts of crime by poverty? This is the source from which theft, embezzlement, sacrilege, poisoning, brigandage, plundering, theft, murder arise. Poverty is not

fallere, fraudare[33] paupertas non erubescit. Qua ipsa ductus opinione sapientissimus ille Ulysses ait apud Homerum:

Odero semper enim qui paupertatis ob ipsum
fallere pergit honus.

Quare nemini absurdum videri debet quid[34] pauper habeatur suspectus testis. Nam quam inopia auctoritatem adimit iuraturo, eam afferunt divitiae. Quo fit ut et divitem eodem nomine quod est 'locuples,' quippe qui *locis* abundet pluribus et auctoritatis *plenum* appellemus. Quid non aufert paupertas? Divitiae quid non afferunt? Nero quandiu pecuniis abundavit, et imperator est dictus et patriae pater. Pereuntibus nummis ipse etiam periit. Demarati illius Corinthii filius ex homine Graeco et Lucumone, non solum L. Tarquinius Priscus nominari apud Romanos meruit vi nummorum, sed haberi quoque et esse rex Romanorum. Et ne dicendo vel prolyxior iudicer vel ineptior, quanquam divitiae ducuntur ex eo indifferentium genere quod inter bona ac mala tanquam medium locum tenet, dignae mihi tamen videntur quae vel mediocribus bonis omnibus non mediocriter antecellant.

46 *Leonardus.* At idem Crantor, Soderine, hoc abs te plurimum dissentit, qui ubi Divitias in illo universo ac publico Graecorum spectaculo cum maximo omnium consensu pro se causam egisse introduxisset, ita rursus Voluptatem in medium procedentem facit causam contra Divitias pro se dicere, ut probet se iure optimo Divitiis praeferendam, quippe quae nec firmae sint nec diuturnae, nec etiam propter sese ab hominibus[35] expetantur, sed propter illum qui ex iis[36] fructus ac voluptas sequitur. Itaque suffragiis Graecorum omnium a Voluptate Divitiae

ashamed to lie, deceive, defraud. Guided by this view, the wise Ulysses says in Homer:

> I shall always hate the man who proceeds to practice
> deception
> On grounds of the burden of poverty.[20]

Therefore no one should think it absurd that a poor man is held to be a suspect witness. For wealth adds the credibility that penury takes away. Hence we call *wealthy* (*dives*) and *rich*   45 (*locuples*) by the same name, since he abounds in many *places* (*loci*) and is filled (*plenus*) with authority.[21] What does poverty not take away? What does wealth not bring? As long as he had ample money, Nero was called emperor and father of his country.[22] When his wealth failed, he, too, perished. It was through the power of his money that the son of the renowned Demaratus of Corinth deserved not only to acquire the name L. Tarquinius Priscus among the Romans, in place of "the Greek Lucumo," but to be considered and to be king of the Romans.[23] And lest my speech be judged too long-winded or silly, although wealth is considered among the class of indifferents that holds as it were the intermediate position between goods and evils, nonetheless it seems to me worthy in no small degree to surpass all the middling goods.

Leonardo. But even Crantor, Soderini, disagrees with you in this   46 regard, since when by universal consent he brought Wealth onstage in that public pan-Hellenic spectacle to plead her case, so again he has Pleasure advance to center stage and plead the case against Wealth to prove that she is quite rightly to be preferred to Wealth, since the latter is neither strong nor long lasting nor sought by men for her own sake, but because of the enjoyment and pleasure that follows from her. Therefore by the votes of all the Greeks Wealth was defeated by Pleasure and not by Pleasure alone but also by Good Health. For when

convincuntur, nec a Voluptate solum, verum etiam a Bona Valitudine. Nam cum esset Voluptas iam palmam reportatura,
continuo Bona Valitudo cum magna omnium de se expecta-
tione progreditur, docetque neque Divitias nec Voluptatem usui
47   cuiquam[37] esse posse ubi ipsa[38] defuerit. Quod Graeci rursus
audientes non inviti in sententiam eunt Bonae Valitudinis. Monemur igitur a gravissimo Crantore vel inter ipsa indifferentia
commodorum atque incommodorum non mediocre faciundum
esse discrimen, et quod non modo inter minima, sed etiam inter mediocria maximum divitias bonum ducis, esse omnino
minimorum minimum, et ita bonum si non ad improbos eae
diverterint, sed ad probos et innocentes viros, qualis est Pallas
noster, qualis Vitalianus is Borrhomaeus, qui modo nobis versabatur in ore. Nam siquem perditum atque impurum hominem
et Cosmum aliquem Medicem divitiae nactae sint, in summis
censeo numerandas malis, utpote quod ad malorum omnium et
causam et effectum instrumenta sese et[39] adiutrices praebeant.

48   Nam paupertatem habendam in malis eo tibi pacto conces-
sero, si hominibus improbis comitem se addiderit, qui certe
longissime se praestarent ad omnem improbitatem ac nefas
promptiores, si divitiarum comitatu uterentur. Nec facit paupertas ut iis egeas quibus serveris et gaudeas, modo paucis sis
contentus. Nam si naturam sequi vivendi ducem quam effrae-
natas animi libidines malimus, nunquam simus ita pauperes ut
non pluribus abundemus ad necessitatem cultumque naturae.
Quot enim terra ipsa per sese nullo labore nostro liberalissime
nobis profusissimeque largitur, quibus animus bene institutus
49   tranquillus laetusque sit? Quinimo, si rem iudicare sine invidia
velimus, animus hominis qui divitiis obruatur, quietus esse vix
unquam possit. Ea est enim natura divitiarum, ut quo sunt

Pleasure was about to carry home the victory, suddenly Good Health comes forward, provoking great expectations about herself, teaching that neither Wealth nor Pleasure can be of use to anyone when she herself is missing. When the Greeks heard   47
this they readily cast their vote for Good Health.[24] We are therefore warned by Crantor, a man of great authority, that one must make a strong distinction of advantageous and disadvantageous things among the indifferents. As for the fact that you consider wealth not merely the greatest good among the smallest, but even among the middling goods, it is altogether the smallest of the smallest — and a good only insofar as wicked men have no recourse to it, but upright and blameless men such as our friend Palla and Vitaliano Borromeo, whom we were just discussing. For if wealth falls into the hands of a desperate and foul man, some Cosimo de' Medici or other, I think it should be counted among the worst evils, since it offers itself as an instrument and means of assistance for causing and carrying out all evils.

I shall grant you that poverty should be included among the   48
evils with this proviso: if it joins scoundrels as a companion, who certainly lend themselves far more readily to every base and criminal act if they enjoy the companionship of wealth. Poverty does not cause you to lack the things you need to survive and flourish, provided you are content with a few possessions. For if we prefer to follow nature as a guide for living rather than the mind's unbridled lusts, we would never be so poor that we fail to have an abundance of things for natural needs and ways of life. How many things does the earth, on its own and without our effort, generously and profusely bestow on us, by which the mind is trained to be calm and happy? What is more, if we should be willing to judge the matter with-   49
out envy, the mind of a man overwhelmed by wealth could scarcely ever be quiet. For such is the nature of wealth that the

grandiores cumulatioresque, eo magis animum sollicitent ac torqueant neque consistere usquam sinant. Quare summi philosophi pauperes vivere quam divites maluerunt.

Poggius. Vixerunt sane illi pauperes, Leonarde, quoniam divites esse non possent.

50 *Leonardus.* Si litterarum potius quam lectorum monimentis, Poggi, delectarere, vel sentires aliter vel loquereris. Audi, si videtur, Diogenem. Dicam enim Latine, quoniam Graece si tecum loqui velim, mortuo loquar. Sic enim scribit ad Cratetem Thebanum:

> Diogenes Cyon Crateti salutem. Accepi te omne patrimonium detulisse in concionem ac id patriae cessisse, in medioque stantem proclamasse: 'Crates Cratetem a Cratete liberum mittit.' Et ea quidem largitione cives omnis laetatos esse, nobisque delectatos, qui tales homines faciamus. Voluisse quoque ob hanc rem accersere nos Athenis. Verum te, qui nostrum iudicium scires, impedimento eis fuisse. Hic igitur laudo sententiam tuam. Afficior etiam voluptate quod patrimonium tradideris, quoniam citius quam expectaram hominum opiniones bonitate superasti. Sed quamprimum redeas velim. Nam tibi ad alia exercitatione etiam opus est. Nec praeterea tibi securum est ibi diutius tempus terere, ubi similes tui non sunt.

51 Erat Democritus quingentorum talentum dives, quae dum negligit ac despicit, ultro fit pauper. Xenocrates ille gravissimus quae ab Alexandro rege talenta quinquaginta dono ad se data intueretur, minime accepit, iis inquiens sibi opus non esse. Thales Milesius cum paupertatem probro dari tum sibi tum caeteris

more ample and abundant it is, the more it troubles and torments the mind and does not allow it to come to rest anywhere.
For that reason the leading philosophers preferred to live as
poor rather than wealthy men.

Poggio. Doubtless they lived as poor men, Leonardo, because they
could not be rich.

Leonardo. If, Poggio, you took greater pleasure in the masterpieces   50
of literature than tales from the bedroom, you would think or
speak differently. Listen to Diogenes, if you please. I shall say it
in Latin since, if I were to speak in Greek, I would be address-
ing a corpse. This is the way he writes to Crates of Thebes:

> Diogenes the Dog sends greetings to Crates. I have heard
> that you brought your entire patrimony to a public assem-
> bly and turned it over to your homeland, and standing in the
> midst of them you proclaimed: "Crates frees Crates from
> Crates"; and that all your fellow citizens were delighted by
> that largesse, and they delighted me since I made a man of
> such quality. For this reason, they wanted to summon me to
> Athens too. But you, who know my opinion, were an obsta-
> cle to them. Therefore I praise your idea. I feel pleasure that
> you handed over your patrimony because, more quickly than
> I had expected, you surpassed people's opinions with your
> goodness. But I would like you to return as soon as possible,
> for you need experience for other things. Besides, it is not
> safe for you to spend time in a place where there are no
> people similar to you.[25]

Democritus was wealthy with a property worth 500 talents;   51
neglecting and despising these, he became a pauper voluntarily.[26] When Xenocrates, a man of great authority, looked at the
five hundred talents given him as a gift by King Alexander, he
did not receive them, saying he had no need of them.[27] When
Thales of Miletus heard that he himself and other philosophers

philosophis audiret, quam esset sapienti facile ditari, cum vellet, ostendit exemplo suo. Cum enim maximam olei fore copiam multo ante prospexisset, olearias omnis officinas admirantibus caeteris conduxit. Quo tempestive factum est ut grandem argenti vim prudentissimus vir colligeret. Sic enim docuit aliud nihil esse in causa sapientum paupertatis quam quod negligerent contemnerentque divitias. His enim abundamus quorum nos delectat studium. At philosophos ob eam rem divitiae non delectant, quod eas sapientiae studiis admodum adversari intelligant. Nunquam enim animus liber sit, quem noctes ac dies cogitare oportet de quaerenda servandave pecunia.

Poggius. Verum unde sibi suisque studiis res necessarias suppeditabit vir sapiens, si nummis caruerit?

Leonardus. Num etiam verbis careat, qui nummis caret? Nunquid huic interdictum sit quo minus a possidentibus quaerat?

Poggius. At petere, Leonarde, sapientem fortasse pudeat? Id enim servile est ac turpe.

Leonardus. Respondeat tibi sapientissimus idem Diogenes, Antisthenis auditor:

> Diogenes Cyon Metrocli salutem. Non stola solum et nomine ac victu, Metrocles, tibi audendum est, sed ut ea etiam quae salutaria sunt ab hominibus petas. Non enim id turpe est. Nam et reges et principes petunt a subditis pecunias, milites, navis, cibum. Et aegrotantes a medicis medicamenta, et ea quidem non modo febris, sed horroris etiam ac famis. Et amatores ab amatis pueris suavia et attrectationes. Herculem vero aiunt vires etiam ab stultis capere solitum. Non enim quae sunt secundum naturam gratis petis ab hominibus aut deteriore commutatione, sed

were reproached for poverty, he showed by his example how easy it is for a wise man to become wealthy when he wants to. Since he had far in advance foreseen that there would be a huge supply of oil, to the surprise of all others, he rented all the oil presses. By this timely move it came about that this very shrewd man garnered a great quantity of silver.[28] In this way he taught 52 that the only reason wise men are poor is that they make light of and despise wealth. For we have an abundance of the things that we enjoy pursuing. But philosophers take no pleasure in riches because they understand that riches conflict with the pursuit of wisdom. A mind would never be free that has to think night and day about seeking and preserving money.

Poggio. But from what source will the wise man supply the things necessary for himself and his studies if he should lack funds?

Leonardo. Surely he who lacks funds would not also lack for words, would he? Surely he would not be prohibited from seeking them from those who have them?

Poggio. But, Leonardo, perhaps a wise man would be ashamed to ask; for to do so is slavish and base.

Leonardo. Let the same wise Diogenes, student of Antisthenes, 53 reply to you:

> Diogenes Cyon sends greetings to Metrocles. You should be bold, Metrocles, not only in dress and reputation and way of life, but also in asking from men for the things that will sustain you; it is no disgrace. For kings and princes ask for money, soldiers, ships, and food from their subjects. The sick ask their physicians for medicines, and not only for fevers but even for chills and hunger. Lovers ask the boys they love for kisses and embraces. They say that Hercules made it his practice to take strength even from fools. For you are not asking men for naturally free goods or things acquired in exchange for an inferior item, but for things that benefit ev-

ad omnium salutem, et ut eadem facias quae Iovis filius
Hercules consuevit, referasque multo meliora quam ipse
accipis. Quaenam haec sunt ? Ne adversus veritatem, cum
haec agis, praelium capias, sed potius adversus gloriam.
Cum hac omnino tibi pugnandum est, quanvis nihil te
lacessierit. Nam adversus res huiusmodi pulcherrimum
esse bellum consuevit. Socrates autem dicebat bonos viros
non petere, sed exigere. Ipsorum enim aeque omnia atque
deorum esse. Et hoc ipsum ex eo concludere nitebatur,
quod dii essent rerum omnium domini, sed res amicorum
esse communes. At virum bonum dei amicum esse. Itaque
res proprias petes.

Poggius. Valeret fortassis istiusmodi sententia et syllogismus, Leonarde, apud stultorum turbam, qui rerum ignari atque imperiti,
ut fatuae quaedam mulierculae solent, mirantur dicta magnifica.
Nam vir gnarus[40] et callidus rem longe malit quam verba consyderare.

Leonardus. Audi, Poggi, rursum ante Diogenem, deinde ad gnarum istum et callidum quem ignoras orationem vertam.

Diogenes Cyon Crateti salutem. Statuas etiam ipsas quae
in foro sunt adi atque farinam pete. Nam huiusmodi quoque meditatio pulchra est. Incides enim in homines qui
minus sentiant quam statuae. Et cum Gallis ac mollibus
magis quam tibi impartiant, non mireris. Nam quisque
proximum honorat. Gallis enim multitudo magis quam
philosophis delectatur.

eryone; and you are asking so that you may do the same as
Jupiter's son Hercules was accustomed to do and return
much better things than you yourself receive. What are these   54
things? When you do these things, may you take up arms,
not against truth, but against glory. You must fight with the
latter even though it has not provoked you. For war against
things of this type has tended to be beautiful. Moreover,
Socrates used to say that good men do not beg but demand.
For all things belong to them and to the gods. And from this
he strove to solve [this syllogism]: since the gods are the
masters of all things, and the property of friends is held in
common, but the good man is a friend of god, you are therefore asking for your own property [when you ask help from
a good man].²⁹

Poggio. Perhaps, Leonardo, a pronouncement and syllogism of this
type may carry weight before a throng of fools who, ignorant
and lacking experience of the world, as foolish women usually
do, they marvel at grandiloquent speeches. A knowledgeable
and skilled man far prefers to consider the subject matter rather
than the words.

Leonardo. First listen to Diogenes once again, Poggio, then I shall   55
turn my discussion to that knowledgeable and skilled man,
whom you do not know.

> Diogenes Cyon sends greetings to Crates. Go to the stat-
> ues that are in the marketplace and ask for some grain. A
> thought experiment of this kind is also a fine thing. For you
> will run into men who have less feeling than statues. Do not
> be surprised when they give to priests and effeminates rather
> than to you. For each man honors the next. The crowd takes
> greater delight in priests than in philosophers.³⁰

56 Iubet Diogenes, Poggi, ut vides, esse petendum sapienti etiam ab stultis, ea credo ratione ductus, ut insipientibus causa detur resipiscendi aliquando. Nam nihil debet esse nobis commune cum improbis. Cyrus tamen ille maior suos monebat sermonem conserendum esse cum omnibus, sed utendum bonis duntaxat. Itaque vir sapiens ab omnibus petet res necessarias, ut communes a probis, ab improbis vero ut suas, quanquam etiam sunt qui ab improbis nihil petendum existiment, ne illa quoque quae nostra ducimus e contubernio improborum ullam improbitatis labem contraxerint. Praeterea turpe est (indignumque in primis) ut vitae subsidia aut ullum adminiculum a flagitiosis ho-
57 minibus suscipere videamur. In quam quidem sententiam ita Crates Thebanus scripsit ad socios.

> Crates sociis salutem. Nolite ab omnibus res necessarias petere. Nec ab omnibus quae dantur accipite. Haud enim fas est a malis hominibus virtutem ali. Licebit autem vobis ut etiam soli a solis peritis philosophiae propria exigatis, nec aliena petere existimate.

Ut vides, Poggi, uterque petendum censet et Diogenes et Crates, sed alter ab omnibus, alter a bonis tantum. Ille quae sua sint, exigenda putat vel ab improbis. Hic nullum sibi cum improbis commercium esse vult, ne ii fortasse laudem aliquam sibi comparent ex ea quam simulant familiaritate bonorum, id quod
58 Phalarin facere solitum audimus. Non enim mediocri sibi laudi ascribebat quod Epicharmus, Stesichorus, Pythagoras sua usi beneficentia dicerentur. At Abaris, Cratete longe antiquior, a Phalaride quamhumanissime invitatus non modo neglexit

As you see, Poggio, Diogenes commands that the wise man   56
even beg from fools, guided, I believe, by the principle that
fools should be given a reason finally to return to their senses.
For we should have nothing in common with scoundrels. Cyrus
the Elder warned his relations that they must engage in conversation with all, but only be friends with the good.[31] Therefore
the wise man will ask for necessities from the good as common
property, from the base as his own, though there are those who
think one should ask for nothing from the base, lest those
things that we consider ours should acquire any taint of base-
ness from their contact with scoundrels. Moreover, it is a disgrace (and particularly unworthy) for us to be seen to receive
sustenance or any aid whatsoever from reprobates. To this ef-   57
fect Crates of Thebes wrote as follows to his friends:

> Crates sends greetings to his friends. Do not ask for necessi-
> ties from all; and do not accept the things given by all. For it
> is hardly right for virtue to be supported by bad men. It will,
> however, be open to you, as single individuals, to demand
> your own property from single individuals experienced in
> philosophy, and do not think that you are asking for the
> property of others.[32]

As you see, Poggio, both Diogenes and Crates think one should
seek support from others — the former from all, the latter only
from the good. The former believes one should demand the
things that are one's own even from the base. The latter wants
for himself no dealings with scoundrels, lest they perhaps gain
some credit for themselves from their pretended friendship
with the good, a thing we have heard Phalaris used to do. For it   58
added mightily to his reputation that Epicharmus, Stesichorus,
and Pythagoras were said to have enjoyed his beneficence. But
Abaris, far older than Crates, though invited in very cordial
terms by Phalaris, not only spurned all his kindness, perhaps

omnem eius benignitatem, forsitan usus Cratetis sententia, sed hominem plane contempsit amarissimisque conviciis laceravit.

Verum quem tu istum vocas gnarum et callidum? Certe non Themistoclem, non Agesilaum, non Fabium Maximum, non M. Catonem, non Philippum Mariam Anglum, hostem etiam nostrum, qui omnem prope antiquitatem consilio et prudentia mirabiliter superat. Nam apud huiusmodi viros ratio illa omnis et iudicium sapientis plurimum valeret.

59 *Poggius.* At apud Cosmum Medicem, Leonarde, minime omnium valeat qui rem malit quam verba expendere. Huius divitiae sunt amplissimae, nec eas tamen consumit in umbras. Non enim te fugit quam saepe multi istiusmodi Diogenes et Cratetes eius aedes frequentant, ut aliquid implorent, aliquid petant. Quos facile semper audit, exaudit nunquam. Nam in iis nullam nec publicam videt nec privatam utilitatem esse repositam, praeter impudentiam singularem, sed in eos se liberalem praestat qui vel sibi possint vel reipublicae esse usui. Quibus artibus factum vides ut se magnum potentemque reddiderit et cunctis gentibus atque aetatibus admirandum.

60 *Leonardus.* Admirandum sane, Poggi, ut dicis, quippe qui, ut est et plebeius et humilis et abiectus latro, infimo atque sordidissimo sterquilinio civitatis, flagitii foeditatisque commercio se vallarit, omnes sibi egestatis mendicitatisque consortes asciverit, quoscunque spargendi veneni sicaeque vibrandae artifices novit, contubernio sodalicioque suo dignatus sit, cunctos facinorosos ac nequam ad sese non tam muneribus ullis quam ingenti spe tur-
61 pitudinis ac nequitiarum pollicitationibusque contraxerit. Nam facile imperita egentium et desidiosa inertium atque perditorum manus a versuto et usque per omnem impuritatem artibus malis exercitato Cosmo Medice concitatur, et eius lingua vino

on the basis of Crates' view, but clearly despised the man and savaged him with the bitterest abuse.[33]

But whom are you calling knowledgeable and skilled? Surely not Themistocles, Agesilaus, Fabius Maximus, Marcus Cato, nor Filippo Maria Visconti, who is also our public enemy, who marvelously surpasses practically all of antiquity in counsel and wisdom. For with a man of this kind that entire line of reasoning and the judgment of a wise man would carry the greatest weight.

Poggio. But Leonardo, in the eyes of Cosimo de' Medici, the man 59 who prefers to weigh the subject matter rather than the words would carry least weight of all. Cosimo's riches are vast, and he does not spend them on illusions. You have not failed to notice how many a Diogenes and Crates and suchlike haunt his house to beg or ask for something. He hears them readily but complies with none. For he sees that no public or private advantage lies in them except for an unparalleled brazenness, but he shows himself generous to those who could be of use to himself or to the republic. By this policy you see that he has made himself great and powerful and an object of wonder for all clans and age-groups.

Leonardo. An object of wonder indeed, Poggio, as you say, seeing 60 that he is a vulgar, lowborn, miserable thief who has entrenched himself using the city's lowest and filthiest manure — a vile and shameful sort of trade —; who has enrolled on his side all the destitute and the beggars; who has held worthy of his intimate society whomever he knows to have mastered the arts of sprinkling poison and brandishing a dagger;[34] and who has drawn to himself all worthless criminals, not so much by gifts as by boundless hope and his promises of base wickedness. The inex- 61 perienced and lazy band of impoverished and forsaken weaklings is easily stirred up by Cosimo de' Medici, a man practiced in evil ways through all sorts of tainted activity; and by his

etiam crassa ac fracta quasi quodam seditionis discordiarumque flabello ventilatur. Quibus rebus qui magnum illum, qui potentem, qui admirandum putat, stultus sit. Nam quanti duci oporteat huiusmodi hominum colluvionem, nemo est qui nesciat. Scitis enim quanta ii animi mobilitate levitateque ad omnem aurae flatum novis rebus semper student.

Poggius. At locupletem esse Cosmum et admodum pecuniosum nunquam, Leonarde, neges.

62   *Leonardus.* Fortassis id verum. Sed ne tu quidem, Poggi, negare audeas[41] et mensarium hominem esse Cosmum et eundem meritorium et sordidissimum foeneratorem, quique unus plane omnium ex omni hominum memoria sit avarissimus. Quo certe vitio nullum est tetrius, nullum capitalius, nullum ab invicto et excelso animo magis alienum. Nonne et quottidiano et communi et pervulgato et uno atque eodem omnium sermone dicitur usuque comprobatur malle avarum vita quam pecunia se privari? Malit profecto Cosmus et siti sese atque inedia confectum iri quam quaestuarios suos loculos foeneratoriosque sacculos vel minima ex parte exhaustum iri. Quis igitur miretur si viri sapientes et graves frustra eius aedes frequentant, frustra

63   aliquid implorant, aliquid petunt? Hos vero dici abs te, Poggi, impudentis, qui pudorem iandiu omnem cum pudicicia perdidisti, rideat sane Aristippus, qui admiranti cuipiam istiusmodi Cosmiones et tanquam turpes divitias honestae paupertati anteponenti ob idque dicenti videre se philosophos semper apud divitum ianuas, respondisse traditur: 'Et enim medici quoque aegrotorum ianuas frequentant, neque idcirco aegrotum se quisquam malit quam medicum.' Idemque Dionysio interroganti cur divitum philosophi nec philosophorum divites peterent ia-nuas, respondit: 'Quoniam quibus egeant philosophi sciunt, at

64   divites quorum indigeant ipsi nesciunt.' Si nosset, inquam, tuus

tongue, thick and broken by wine, as it were like a fan stirring up sedition and civil strife.[35] The man who on account of these facts thinks him great, powerful, or admirable would be a dunce. There is no one who is unaware how much value should be attached to such an impure mixture of men. You know the magnitude of their fickleness and frivolity, how at every puff of air they are always eager for revolution.

Poggio. But you would never deny, Leonardo, that Cosimo is wealthy and quite rich.

Leonardo. Perhaps that is true, Poggio, but see that you do not   62
dare to deny that Cosimo is a banker, a hireling and a filthy usurer, the single greediest man in all of recorded history. No other vice is more loathsome, more worthy of punishment, none more at odds with an invincible and lofty soul than this. Is it not said in everyday conversation everywhere by all persons without distinction, as well as proven by experience, that a greedy man would rather be deprived of his life than his money? Cosimo would rather die of hunger and thirst than have his cash boxes, filled with the profits of usury, drained even to the slightest degree. Who, then, should be surprised that wise and serious men throng his house in vain, beg and petition in vain? Aristippus would surely laugh that you call   63
these men brazen, Poggio—you who long ago lost all sense of shame along with your chastity. Aristippus is said to have replied to someone who admired such Cosimos, who preferred tainted wealth to honorable poverty and who said for that reason that he often saw philosophers at the doors of the rich: "And indeed physicians throng the doors of the sick, but no one would on that account prefer to be a sick man rather than a physician."[36] He likewise replied to Dionysius, who asked why philosophers seek out the homes of the wealthy but not vice versa: "Because philosophers know what they need, but the wealthy do not."[37] If your friend Cosimo knew in what a large   64

iste Cosmus quanto in errore versatur, quam est mentis atque sensus inops, non modo huiusmodi viris se facilem praestaret et liberalem aut implorantibus aut petentibus, sed ultro anteverteret et totum se hisce dederet, quo immanibus animi morbis horum curatione liberatus ad sanitatem cuius maxime indiget redire tandem inciperet.

Poggius. Ita loqueris ac si nihil prorsus eroget Cosmus et ad ornanda divina templa et ad maritalem puellarum pudorem.

65 *Leonardus.* Ad puellarum sane pudorem, Poggi, prostituendum, quasi omnium unus ignores ea conditione nummorum aliquid mendicis quibusdam humillimisque parentibus Cosmum tuum praebere solitum, ut virginum filiarum florem delibet primus. Nam quod de templis simulas, ridiculum dictu est, cum Florentino sit inauditum nemini, Iohannem pontificem qui Baldasar dicebatur idcirco tam grandem pecuniam legasse istius prodigiosi hominis patri, Iohanni Medici, ut divorum et Laurentii et Marci templa, quae iam vetustate delabebantur, repararet atque reficeret, et ea pulcherrimis bibliothecis aedificiisque ornaret. Alterum iandiu coeptum adhuc pendet. De divi autem Marci

66 templo verbum nullum. Quinimo cum viri relligiosissimi qui ab ipso usque constitutae aedis initio templi curam semper habuerunt habentque assidue, quamsaepissime pro suo munere Cosmum monuerint ne patiatur diutius pientissimi illius pontificis memoriam obliterari per tam feram conficiendi operis cunctationem, interminatus his dicitur propediem curaturum sese ut inde eiiciantur. Non enim instituisse nec velle se quicquam de summa dimminuere, sed quod de summa provenerit, in eiusmodi nugas consumere. Et nominas tu mihi Cosmum, hominem corrupto depravatoque ingenio, cui nihil in vita praeter nummos sit dulce, proinde[42] atque non eum esse Cosmum intelligas qui nulla ratione adduci possit ut siquid, non dicam de

error he is involved, how deprived he is of intelligence and sense, not only would he show himself agreeable and generous to such men when they beg or petition him, but he would take the initiative and turn himself over to them completely so that he might be freed by their treatment from the raging diseases of his mind and begin finally to return to the sanity that he so greatly needs.

Poggio. You speak as though Cosimo spends nothing to equip churches and to provide dowries for young girls.

Leonardo. He provides prostitution for young girls, Poggio! — as if   65 you were the only one who doesn't know that Cosimo makes a practice of furnishing money to certain poor and humble parents on condition that he be the first to pluck the flowers of their virgin daughters! Your claim about churches is ridiculous, since no Florentine has failed to hear that it was Pope John, whose given name was Baldassare,[38] who bequeathed a huge sum of money to that monster's father, Giovanni de' Medici, so that he would repair and refurbish the churches of San Lorenzo and San Marco, which had fallen into decay, and equip them with the finest libraries and buildings. The one project, begun long ago, is still in progress; there is no word about the Church of San Marco. What is more, when the men of religion who   66 from the very first founding of the church always have had and still have charge of it cautioned Cosimo, in accordance with their obligations, that he not allow the memory of that pious pope to be effaced by such high-handed delays in finishing the work, he is said to have threatened to have them expelled immediately from the premises, as he had resolved not to reduce the capital but to spend the interest on trifling changes. And you cite Cosimo to me, a man of corrupt and depraved character, who savors nothing in life except money! As if you didn't know that Cosimo can't be brought by any means to reckon

67 vivo, sed de lucro dimminutum sit, non vitam existimet sibi dimminutam. Nam quam is aliam ob rem instituisset foedissime bonos omnis crudelissimeque vexare et omnibus qui pace et concordia uti vellent bellum facesque inferre, nisi ut vim argenteam extorqueret? Quare a nemine unquam nobis vel infestissimo saevissimoque hoste tantum mali optatum est quantum efficere impurissimus Cosmus nititur. Nam quo facilius posset omnes argenti aurique gurgites et exhaurire et exorbere, concordiam omnem civium ac benivolentiam — qua una re firmissimus reipublicae status conservari solet — quantum in se fuit e medio sustulit pacemque peremit.

68 Huiusmodi tu hominem, Poggi, et gnarum vocas et callidum, et non plane stultum atque insanum, qui, ut est rerum bonarum omnium imperitus, nullam de aequo et bono, nullam de decoro, nullam de honestate rationem habeat, sed cum veneficis atque impudicis et dies versetur et noctes. Quibus sane et facinoribus et flagitiis obrui non tam facile posset si nummorum inopia premeretur. Cum enim in perditissimorum hominum potestatem ii concesserint, instrumenta se praestant et adminicula ad malorum omnium officinam. Et volumus divitias numerandas in bonis, quasi non ea sit natura boni, ut illos etiam bonos reddat in quorum domicilium se receperit. Nec etiam fieri potest ut bonum ullum cum malo conveniat, aut eius 69 familiaritate uti velit. Sed in divitiis nullum videmus esse discrimen. Non enim malorum minus quam bonorum hospitio delectantur. Quod ipsum Homerus cogitans non imprudenter ait:

Iupiter ut libuit, tribuit mortalibus aeque,
sive probis sublimis opes, seu mente profanis.

that his life hasn't suffered a loss when his profit—I don't say
his capital—has suffered a loss! For what other reason would   67
he have resolved to harass all sound citizens in so vile and cruel
a fashion, and to set fire and bring war on all those who wanted
to enjoy peace and harmony, except in order to extort a large
amount of silver? No enemy, however hostile and cruel, has
ever wished on us an evil so great as that which Cosimo, that
horrible man, is striving to bring about. For in order that he
could more readily draw off and soak up every fountain of silver
and gold, he has, to the extent that he could, made away with
all concord and goodwill among the citizens—by which alone
the stability of the republic has traditionally been preserved—
and has destroyed the peace.

That's the sort of man, Poggio, you are calling knowledge-   68
able and clever rather than stupid and insane. Since he is ignorant of all good arts and takes no account of what is just and
good, what is appropriate, and what morally good, he spends
his days and nights in the company of assassins and corrupt
persons. He could not be so easily overwhelmed by shameful
crimes if he were pressured by lack of money. When money has
passed into the power of the reprobate, they present themselves
as instruments and aids for the manufacture of all evils. And we
claim that riches should be counted among the goods, as if this
were not the nature of the good, to make those persons good
with whom it has gone to dwell! It cannot come about that any
good is on good terms with a wicked man or wishes to be his
friend. But we see that wealth makes no discrimination: it takes   69
pleasure in the hospitality of the wicked no less than that of the
good. In view of this Homer shrewdly said:

As he pleases, Jupiter gives ennobling wealth
Equally to mortals, just or wicked.[39]

Nam quod rerum affluentia ad necessitatem voluptatemque humanam liberet animum sollicitudine—id quod et ipse modo ex Aristotelis sententia non tam veritatis quam disserendi gratia intulissem, et Soderinus noster non invitus amplexus sit—non solum veteres Stoici omnes et alii plures nobilissimi philosophi, sed quotquot se Christi optimi maximi imitatores voluerint, 70 indubitato negent. Nam huiusmodi affluentia in omnem perturbationem animum iniiciat, qua qui sit affectus, secum habitare nunquam possit. At vir sapiens, cum nihilo careat, semper in omnem fortunae mutabilitatem non tranquillus esse non valeat. Itaque vel nudus (ut de gymnosophistis Indorum traditur) et intelliget omnia agetque pro virtute. Nec scio an plus dedecoris ac detrimenti quam ornamenti et fructus ab auro atque ar- 71 gento generi hominum importetur. Nemo ut sit pauper litem movet aut testamenta supponit aut circunscribit aut peculatur. Turbandae pacis et excitandi belli divitiae sunt in causa. Nec tam raptus Helenae (qui fingitur ab Homero) quam habendi cupiditas Graeciam armavit adversus Troiam, ut Thucydides meminit. Praeterea quam sit paupertas tutior quam divitiae, Sycharbae nex docet Arionisque delphinus. Nam Aristippus, prudentius sibi consulens, cum navigans advertisset quanto in discrimine versaretur, qui grande aurum in praedonum navigio secum veheret, mox id omne deiecit in mare, 'Huius iactura, 72 inquiens, saluti mihi futura est.' Itaque Flaccus Horatius, non ignorans quantum in divitiis sit periculum, quanta calamitas, ita cecinit:

Aurum ire per medios satellites
et perrumpere amat saxa, potentius
ictu fulmineo; concidit auguris

Not only all the Old Stoics and many other famous philosophers, but all who have claimed to be imitators of Christ, Best and Greatest, unhesitatingly deny that an abundance of things providing for necessity and pleasure frees the mind of care — a point which I myself introduced just now on the basis of Aristotle's view, not so much for the sake of truth as of argument; and our friend Soderini readily embraced this view.[40] For such abundance exposes the mind to every emotion; and he who is so afflicted can never live with himself. But since he lacks nothing, the wise man cannot but always be serene in the face of every vicissitude of fortune. Therefore even if naked (as is recorded of the Indian gymnosophists), he will both understand all things and act in accordance with virtue. I rather think that more disgrace and harm than embellishment and profit have been brought to the human race by gold and silver. No one initiates a lawsuit or forges wills or practices fraud or embezzlement in order to be a poor man. It is wealth that stands accused of disturbing the peace and stirring up war. It was not so much the abduction of Helen (as was invented by Homer) as the greed of gain that armed Greece against Troy, as Thucydides records.[41] The murder of Sycharbas and the story of Arion's dolphin teach us that poverty is safer than wealth.[42] Aristippus took canny provision for his own safety: when during a voyage he noticed in what great danger he was, since he was transporting a great amount of gold with him in a pirates' vessel, he right away jettisoned the whole thing with the words, "The casting away of this treasure will be my salvation."[43] And so Horace, knowing what great risk and misfortune are found in riches, wrote as follows:

70

71

72

> Gold is wont to go through the midst of armed guards
> And break rocks apart more powerfully
> Than a lightning bolt; the home of the Argive augur

Argivi domus ob lucrum
dimersa exitio; diffindit urbium
portas vir Macedo, surruit aemulos
reges muneribus; munera navium
saevos inlaqueant duces.

73   Quare apte Virgilius atque sapienter:

Quid non mortalia pectora cogis,
auri sacra fames?

At quod paupertas facit:

Cantabit vacuus coram latrone viator.

74   Quod si paupertatis nomen esset tantopere odiosum — ut modo
dicebat Soderinus — nunquam ea a philosophis Christianis, qui
veram callent philosophiam, inter virtutes reponeretur. Nam
quod pauper quispiam vel mentiatur vel occidat, non tam paupertas est in causa quam animi vitium. Nec pauper ullus qui
probus sit, habetur suspectus a legibus, nec dives improbus non
suspectus. Quod enim locupletis nomine et divitem appellemus
et gravem, non magis mihi divitias id commendet quam Cosmus Medices, qui cum sit locupletissimus, et levissimus tamen
est et nullius auctoritatis apud innocentis et sanctos viros. Praeterea aliud est a cetariis et fartoribus stultaque multitudine,
75   aliud a bonis et sapientibus laudari. Itaque non iniuria qui ab
assentatoribus suique similibus sit pater patriae appellatus
quandiu pecuniis abundabat, pereuntibus nummis ipse etiam
periit. Nec magis L. Tarquinium divitiae quam Numam Pom-
pilium paupertas ad Romani imperii fastigium sustulit. Sed
hunc altitudo animi atque prudentia, illum aequabilitas atque

Because of gain fell,
Collapsing into ruin; the Macedonian
Parted the doors of cities and undermined
Pretenders by gifts; gifts ensnare
    Fierce admirals.⁴⁴

Hence Vergil wrote aptly and wisely: 73

Accursed hunger for gold,
To what crimes do you not drive mortal hearts?⁴⁵

But poverty achieves this, that

The empty-handed traveler will sing in the face of the
    bandit.⁴⁶

But if the name of poverty is so odious—as Soderini was just   74
now saying⁴⁷—it would never have been classed among the virtues by Christian philosophers who are skilled in the true philosophy. For if some poor man tells a lie or commits murder,
the fault lies not in poverty, but in a vicious mind. Any poor
man who is honest is not held in suspicion by the laws, neither
is a wicked, rich man free of suspicion. As to the fact that we
designate both a rich man and a man of authority by the word
"wealthy" (locuples), this does not make wealth any more acceptable in my eyes than Cosimo de' Medici, who, although he is
very wealthy, is nonetheless very petty, and carries no authority
in the eyes of blameless and holy men. Moreover, it is one thing
to be commended by fishmongers and poulterers and the stupid
crowd, another by good and wise judges. Therefore he who was   75
named father of his country by flatterers and others like him
while he was endowed with copious wealth, when the funds ran
out, he too perished, and rightly so.⁴⁸ Wealth no more carried
Lucius Tarquinius to the pinnacle of Roman power than did
poverty Numa Pompilius. But loftiness of soul and foresight

integritas, utrunque privatum et peregrinum illustres utraeque
praestantesque virtutes evexerunt ad regnum. Nec ob divitias
Archelaus, probatissimus ille Macedonum rex, ad se accersebat
vel Socratem vel Euripidem, nec Artaxerxes Hippocratem, nec
Platonem Aristippumque Dionysius, nec Aristotelem Philippus, nec Alexander ac Perdicca Antipaterque Diogenem, nec
Ptolemaeus Soter Demetrium Phalereum, nec alii item alios
76 potentes imbecillos, opulenti inopes. Sola profecto animi bonitas ingeniique praestantia nos et praesentibus commendat et
posteris. Neque paupertate deteriores, nec divitiis meliores effi-
cimur. Et quanquam talis est quisque qualem se esse vult, nescio tamen an multo etiam magis ad animi virtutes paupertas sit
quam divitiae accomodatior. Itaque ad Lesbonacta[43] scribens
Apollonius Tyaneus ait: 'Pauperem quidem esse ut virum oportet, divitem vero ut hominem.' Tantum autem homini virum
antecellere arbitror quantum corpori animum. Quare qui se
hominem malit quam virum, divitias sibi comites asciscat. Sed
qui virum homini putat anteferendum, is omni ope atque opera,
si sapit, paupertatem sectetur amplectaturque.

77 *Poggius.* Sed tuum istum pauperem, Leonarde—quod paulo ante
dicebatur a Soderino—quis sibi compos mentis vel amicum vel
socium velit?

Leonardus. Certe boni omnes et graves viri. Quinetiam tui similes
laetari videantur consuetudine eruditi sapientisque pauperis,
quo egregiam de se aliquam apud alios opinionem concitent.

Poggius. Videantur sane, sed minime laetentur, cum intelligant nihil inde utilitatis praeter inane probitatis nomen ad sese perventurum. At 'probitas,' ut ille ait, 'laudatur et alget.' Non doctrina,

raised the one, fairness and integrity the other—both excellent
and celebrated virtues—to the kingship, though each man was
a private citizen and foreign-born. And it was not on account of
wealth that Archelaus, that upright king of Macedonia, summoned Socrates or Euripides to his presence, or Artaxerxes
Hippocrates; or Dionysius Plato and Aristippus; or Philip Aristotle; or Alexander and Perdiccas and Antipater Diogenes; or
Ptolemy Soter Demetrius of Phalerum, nor other powerful
men weak ones, or wealthy men those lacking in resources. It is 76
surely only the goodness of our mind and the excellence of our
nature that commends us to our coevals and to posterity. We
are made neither worse by poverty nor better by wealth. And
although each of us is such as he wishes to be, I rather think
that poverty is much better adapted to the virtues of the mind
than is wealth. Therefore Apollonius of Tyana said in a letter to
Lesbonax: "One must be poor as a man (*vir*), but wealthy as a
human being (*homo*)."[49] I think that a man excels a human being by as much as the mind does the body. Therefore let the
one who would prefer to be a human being rather than a man
enroll wealth as his companion. But let the one who thinks that
a man is to be preferred to a human being pursue and embrace
poverty with every resource and effort, if he is wise.

Poggio. But what sane man, Leonardo, would want that poor man 77
of yours as a friend or companion, as Soderini said a bit earlier.[50]

Leonardo. Surely all good and serious men. What is more, people
like you appear to enjoy the company of a learned and wise
pauper in order to provoke in others a fine opinion of themselves.

Poggio. They do indeed appear to, but they do not enjoy it, since
they know that no advantage will accrue to them from it except
an empty reputation for virtue; but "virtue," as he said, "is commended and left in the cold."[51] Not learning, not virtue, but

non virtus, sed soli nummi dignitatem afferunt. Quare non falso Naso locutus est inquiens:

Ipse licet venias Musis comitatus, Homere,
    si nihil attuleris, ibis, Homere, foras.

78 *Leonardus.* Tu mihi, Poggi, de amoris corruptela atque levitate e poetis, non e philosophis de seriis rebusque gravissimis dicta depromis, ignarus tu quidem, ut videris, eam esse naturam sapientis, ut quoniam sit natus ad communem omnium utilitatem ac decus, nunquam existimet suam vel auctoritatem vel dignitatem ex alio quopiam quam ex sese ipso (id est virtute Deoque) pendere. Quod ut dilucidius intelligas, probetur exemplo. Fuit Apollonius, qui modo nobis versabatur in ore, vir Pythagoreus et pauper. Is a Lacedaemoniis accersitus est per legatos Lacedaemona.[44] Quas legati litteras a republica reddidissent, non

79 invitus legit, et item exemplum publice facti de se decreti. Litterae autem erant huiusmodi:

Lacedaemonii Apollonio salutem. Decretum honorem tibi misimus, exemplum hoc gemma publica signantes, ut videas. Decretum autem erat tale. 'Quemadmodum senatores consuluerunt Tindaro, qui magistratus docuit, decretum est et a magistratibus et a populo Apollonium Pythagoreum esse civem habereque et vinum et aedium possessionem. Statuimus autem insignem imaginem pictam atque aeneam virtutis gratia. Sic enim maiores etiam nostri viros bonos honoravere, quippe qui putarent esse Lycurgi filios, quicunque vitam cum diis convenientem[45] elegissent.'

only money brings public standing. Therefore Ovid was right in saying:

> Though Homer might come in person, escorted by the Muses,
>> If you have brought no gift, out the door with you, Homer![52]

Leonardo. You are citing words about corrupt and frivolous love 78
from the poets, not words from the philosophers about serious and weighty matters, since you are evidently unaware that the nature of the wise man is such that, since he has been born for the common benefit and glory of all, he would never reckon that his own authority or worth depends on anyone other than himself (that is, on his virtue and on God). Let me show this by an example so that you may understand it more clearly. Apollonius, whom we just now mentioned, was a Pythagorean and a poor man. He was summoned by the Spartans through ambassadors to come to Sparta. He gladly read the letter which the ambassadors brought from the republic and likewise a copy of the public decree about himself. The letter was as follows: 79

> The Spartans send greetings to Apollonius. We have sent you an honorific decree, sealing the copy with this state seal, as you may see. The decree is as follows: "Whereas the senators have consulted Tindarus, who instructed the magistrates, it has been decreed by the magistrates and the people that Apollonius the Pythagorean is a citizen and has possession of both wine and a house. We have moreover decreed a splendid painted bronze statue of him because of his virtue. For our ancestors also honored good men in this fashion, since they held whoever had chosen a life in conformity with the gods to be sons of Lycurgus."[53]

Nunquid propter divitias ab Lacedaemoniis Apollonius an propter virtutem, Poggi, et civitate donatus est et tam pulcher-
80   rime honoratus? Sed audi, obsecro, ingenti animo philosophum. Nam lectis litteris intellectoque decreto nec exhilaratus est laudibus nec elatus honoribus, ut ad gratiam magis quam ad veritatem responderet. Quinimo legatos intuens qui nihil prisci, nihil Laconici moris prae se ferrent, iis huiuscemodi litteras et ad ephoros et ad Lacedaemonios dedit:

> Apollonius ephoris et Lacedaemoniis salutem. Viros vestros aspexi qui superioris labri pilos non haberent, femoribus ac cruribus et laevibus essent et albis, induti sagulis mollibus ac tenuibus, anulis multis pulchrisque circundati, calceum Ionicum calciati. Itaque legatos qui dicebantur non agnovi. At epistola Lacedaemonios dicebat.

81   *Soderinus.* Durum est tamen, Leonarde, ac plane triste contemptui haberi, quod paupertas facit.

    Leonardus. De contemptu, Soderine, alius sermo est, et olim advesperascit. Sed ubinam facit contemptum paupertas?

    Soderinus. Cum in aliis locis honorificis, tum in publicis et consessibus et conviviis.

82   *Leonardus.* Ridiculum profecto, quod e stultorum iudicio pendere sapientis honorem putes. Aristippus Cyrenaicus, cum intempestive petenti ex philosophia quippiam gratificari Dionysio aliquando noluisset, ob idque iussu indignati Dionysii ultimus inter convivas discubuisset, conversus ad tyrannum, 'Voluisti,' inquit, 'tu quidem, Dionysi, facere locum hunc illustriorem.' Et Damonidas Lacedaemonius, positus in ultimum chori locum[46]

Was it on account of riches or virtue, Poggio, that Apollonius was granted citizenship and so splendidly honored by the Spartans? But pay heed, I beg you, to the great-souled philosopher. 80 For upon reading the letter and understanding the decree, he was neither so overjoyed by the praises nor so puffed up by the honors as to make a polite rather than sincere reply. Rather, gazing upon the ambassadors, who gave no sign of the ancient manner, no sign of the Spartan custom, he gave them this letter for the ephors and the other Spartans:

> Apollonius sends greetings to the ephors and the Spartans. I looked at your men, who had no hair on the upper lip, had thighs and legs that were smooth and white, were dressed in soft and thin little cloaks, wore many beautiful rings, and were wearing Ionian shoes. Therefore I failed to recognize the so-called ambassadors. But the letter said they were Spartans.[54]

Soderini. It is nonetheless harsh and distressing, Leonardo, to be 81 held in contempt, which is what poverty produces.

Leonardo. Contempt, Soderini, is a topic for another conversation, and it started to grow dark some while ago. But where does poverty cause contempt?

Soderini. Not only in other honorable places but also in public meetings and gatherings.

Leonardo. It is ridiculous for you to think that a wise man's honor 82 depends upon the judgment of fools. Once when Aristippus of Cyrene declined to humor Dionysius on an occasion when the latter asked, out of season, for something philosophical — and on that account, at the enraged Dionysius' order, was seated last in precedence among the diners — he turned to the tyrant and said, "You wished, Dionysius, to make this seat more distinguished."[55] Damonidas of Sparta, deployed by the producer in

ab illo qui chorum statuerat, coniectis in eum oculis, 'Bene,' inquit, 'invenisti, qui etiam locus ipse honoratus fieret.'

83 *Poggius.* At mihi de loco, Leonarde, nulla sit cura—et maxime in conviviis—modo eadem esculenta potulentaque apponantur. Sed vereor ne illud accidat quod apte ac vero poeta cavillatus est:

> Virroni murena datur, quae maxima venit
> littore de Siculo. . . (et)
> nos anguilla manet, longae cognata colubrae.

Nam vinum fugiens plaerunque et ius hesternum iis apponi qui ultimum insident mensae locum, ipse etiam interdum sum expertus.

84 *Leonardus.* Et tu tamen, Poggi, neque pauper es nec philosophus esse vis. Quod si philosophis audire velles, nihil profecto tale patereris.

Poggius. Et quonam pacto, Leonarde?

Leonardus. Audi Cratetem eundem, qui paulo ante loquebatur.

> Crates iuvenibus salutem. Assuescite vesci massa et aquam bibere. Piscem autem ac vinum nolite gustare. Haec enim et senectutem efferant, tanquam venena Circes, et iuventutem effaeminant.

85 *Poggius.* Obscura ista et iniucunda vivendi victitandique institutio quam ab Antisthene profectam, a Diogene auctam, a Cratete confirmatam video, est ferarum et earum quidem immanium, non urbanorum hominum.

Leonardus. Respondeat tibi idem Crates, ea quam Eumolpo scripsit epistola.

the last place in the chorus, looked at him and said, "You have found a good way of lending honor to this very place."[56]

Poggio. But, Leonardo, I have no concern about seating—espe-   83
cially at dinner parties—provided that the same food and drink are served. My fear is that what the poet aptly and truly satirized will happen to me:

> A huge moray fish is served to Virro, as big as they come
> From the Sicilian shore

and

> A common eel awaits us, a relation of the long garden
> snake.[57]

For I have myself, from time to time, experienced how wine that is reaching the dregs and yesterday's sauce is served to those who occupy last place at table.

Leonardo. But Poggio, you are neither a poor man nor claim to be   84
a philosopher. But if you were willing to give ear to the philosophers, you would endure nothing of the kind.

Poggio. How so, Leonardo?

Leonardo. Listen to the same Crates who was speaking a little while ago.

> Crates sends greetings to the young men. Get used to eating bread and drinking water; refuse to consume fish and wine. For, like Circe's poisons, they produce old age and emasculate youth.[58]

Poggio. That obscure and joyless teaching for living and dining   85
which, I see, originated with Antisthenes, was augmented by Diogenes, and reinforced by Crates, is proper to beasts, and savage ones at that, not to refined human beings.

Leonardo. Let the same Crates reply to you in the letter he wrote to Eumolpus:

Crates Eumolpo salutem. Tolerantia Diogenea obscura est
at secura, qua qui utitur, ditior his est qui stolis Carthagi-
nensibus induuntur. Et victus quidem est tenuis, sed ad
bonam valitudinem quam Persicus accomodatior. Et institutio est laboriosa, sed quam Sardanapali liberior. Quare
si et melior est ea tolerantia quam Carthaginensis stola, et
bona valitudo quam splendidus victus, et libertas quam
probrosa consuetudo, etiam quae haec facit philosophia
praestat omnibus, etsi minus aliorum philosophia, at Diogenis, qui compendiariam invenit ad felicitatem viam.

86   Magnus item Basilius, vir omni sanctimonia doctrinaque illustris, ad Gregorium Nazianzenum scribens iubet panem et
aquam his qui bene valeant satis esse. Nam leguminibus et ho-
leribus valitudinarios uti oportere. Consuetudine fiunt omnia
non solum levia sed etiam dulcia. Cibus ac potus et fame
condiuntur et siti. Quare Socratem quaerenti quid ad vesperum
usque contentius ambularet, respondisse tradunt se hoc pacto
obsonare famem. Et Darius, ab Alexandro superatus, cum inter
fugiendum siti confectus bibisset aquam et turbidam et cadave-
rum cruore inquinatam, negavit unquam suavius bibisse. At
Alexander Adae, reginae Carum, quae delectaretur quottidie ad
se mittere obsonia et crustulas per artifices et coquos magnifice
exquisitissimeque paratas, dixit longe meliores sibi esse obsona-
tores: ad prandium quidem nocturnum iter, ad caenam vero
87   prandii paucitatem. Artaxerxes, cognomento Memor, Cyri iu-
nioris frater, cum in fuga, sibi ereptis impedimentis, ficis siccis
et pane cibario vesceretur, 'Cuiusmodi,' ait, 'voluptatis eram imperitus?' In constituenda Lacedaemoniis republica permagnam
Lycurgus adhibuit diligentiam ut divitias e medio tolleret parsi-
moniamque induceret. Nam ut illas instrumenta quaedam esse

Crates sends greetings to Eumolpus. Diogenes' habit of ascetic behavior is strange but free of care: he who uses it is wealthier than those who clothe themselves in Punic robes. And the sustenance is meager but better adapted to good health than a Carthaginian diet. The regimen is toilsome but freer than that of Sardanapalus. Therefore if asceticism is better than a Carthaginian robe and good health than a splendid feast and freedom than a reprehensible habit, philosophy that produces these things is better than all, though not others' philosophy, but rather that of Diogenes, who discovered a shortcut to happiness.[59]

Likewise Basil the Great, a man distinguished for piety and learning, writing to Gregory Nazianzen advised him that bread and water are enough for those who are in good health. For sick persons should eat legumes and lettuce.[60] All things become not only easy but even pleasant by habit. Food and drink are seasoned by hunger and thirst. Thus they say that, to a man who asked why he walked contentedly until evening, Socrates replied that in this fashion he took care of his hunger.[61] Following his defeat by Alexander, Darius was parched by thirst during his flight and had drunk water that was murky and fouled with gore, yet claimed he had never drunk sweeter.[62] To Ada, the queen of Caria, who enjoyed sending him provisions and cakes sumptuously and exquisitely prepared by leading chefs, Alexander said that he had far better provisioners: for breakfast a night march, for dinner a small lunch.[63] When during his flight Artaxerxes, surnamed Memor, brother of the younger Cyrus, had his baggage seized and ate dried figs and coarse bread, he remarked, "What pleasure I have been missing!" In founding the Spartans' republic Lycurgus was careful to eliminate wealth and introduce parsimony. For as he thought wealth the tool for all the seductions and crimes that debase both the

86

87

arbitrabatur ad omnis illecebras et flagitia quibus et animus depravatur et corpus, ita parsimoniam ad utriusque virtutem esse tanquam iter expeditissimum. Quare convivia quae ad vitae continentiam publica esse voluit, non tam ab amicicia quam ab ipsa parsimonia 'phiditia' nominavit. Cum igitur atrum ius quod dicitur apud Spartiatas mirifice probaretur, adeo ut videri in summis illis quibus exercebantur laboribus suavius nihil posset, id regem Persarum Dionysiumque tyrannum ac caeteros omnis qui oscitantes eo atque inter ocia vesci vellent, ita vel gustatum offendebat ut nihil insipidius, nihil insuavius iudicarent. Itaque assuescendum est, Poggi, si volumus omnia nobis istiusmodi quae tu censes et iniucunda et dura, non modo videri nobis sed etiam esse tum facillima toleratu, tum iucundissima. Nam ut est apud Euripidem:

> Quem malorum gustus insuetum repperit,
> fert is quidem, sed colla cum subdit[47] iugo,
> riget dolore, sitque felicior obitu quam vivus.

89 *Honofrius.* Loqueris tu quidem, Leonarde, et vere omnia et sapienter. Sed aliud est esse pauperem, aliud fieri.

Leonardus. Mirabar equidem, Honofri, quid tam diu tacuisses, quem duobus proximis diebus permulta disseruisse audiebam. Num huic fortasse Poggio tuas partis mandare voluisti?

Honofrius. Minime, Leonarde. Sed tua sum oratione gravissima mirum in modum delectatus. Quare quandiu te dicentem animadvertebam, mihi audiendum, non dicendum existimavi. Nunc vero, cum video Poggium veluti herbam dare, non tibi ingratum fore sum arbitratus ut discendi gratia quid mihi se obtulisset efferrem. Nam modice iis ferendam paupertatem, qui nunquam divitias sint experti, facile tibi concedendum

mind and body, so he thought parsimony was the quickest route, as it were, to excellence in both mind and body. Thus he named the banquets — which, to promote self-restraint, he wanted to be public — *phiditia*, not after friendship but after parsimony itself.[64] Now the so-called black sauce met with 88 such wondrous approbation among the Spartans that it seemed nothing could be more delicious amid the rigorous training they undertook; but when it was consumed by the king of the Persians and the tyrant Dionysius and all others who wanted to enjoy it in their languid leisure, just a small sample gave such offense that they judged nothing more tasteless, nothing more unpleasant.[65] Therefore we must grow used to it, Poggio, if we want all things of the kind that you think are unpleasant and harsh, not only to seem to us, but even to be easy to tolerate and pleasant. For as Euripides says,

> He who is unused to a mere taste of evils
> Bears them, but when he places his neck beneath the yoke,
> It grows stiff with pain, and he would be happier dead than
>   alive.[66]

Onofrio. All that you say, Leonardo, is true and wise. But it is one 89 thing to be a poor man, another to become one.

Leonardo. I was surprised, Onofrio, that you held silent for so long, though I heard you discoursing at length the last two days. Did you perhaps wish to assign your role to Poggio here?

Onofrio. No, Leonardo. But I was wondrously pleased by your profound speech. So as long as I saw you speaking, I thought I should listen, not speak. Now, however, when I see Poggio, as it were, raising the white flag,[67] I thought it would not displease you for me to bring forward for the sake of learning what had occurred to me. For I suppose that you would readily concede that people should bear poverty moderately who have never

putem. Sed e divitibus pauperes fieri non potest non videri difficillimum toleratu. Nam ut ait Polyxena Euripidea, 'Vita turpis magnus est certe dolor.'

90 *Leonardus.* Et tu, Nicolae, quid ad ista sentis quae Honofrius est locutus?

Nicolaus. Equidem, Leonarde, idem illud, quod meus Honofrius. Ut enim ait apud eundem Euripidem Polynices, 'Pecuniae sunt maximo hominibus in precio.' Quibus sane qui caret, non turpiter vivere mea sententia non potest.

91 *Leonardus.* An ignoratis, adolescentes, nec paupertate turpitudinem nec honestatem divitiis, sed hanc virtute, illam vitio definiri?[48] Sed vos fortassis elegantiam laudatis; non hanc quae ingenii dici solet quaeque in repraehensione non est, sed eam potius quae ad lautiorem quendam et amoeniorem cultum victumque refertur. Istiusmodi autem elegantiam vitio dari ostendit Cato in eo libro cui titulus est *Carmen de moribus.* Ait enim: 'Avariciam omnia vitia habere putabant: sumptuosus, cupidus, elegans, vitiosus, irritus qui habebatur, is laudabatur.' Et recte quidem Cato. Laus enim virtutis est, non rerum inanium ac levium. De cibo ac potu satis multa locuti sumus. De cultu

92 corporis apparatuque domestico eadem est ratio. Non enim aut corporis cultus aut domesticae supellectilis famulatusque elegantia, sed eximius ac rarus virtutis ornatus reddit hominem admirandum cunctisque venerabilem. Qua sententia Homerus ductus, Ulyssem fingit, cum in Corcyram e naufragio et solus evasisset et nudus, Nausicaham[49] Alcinoi regis filiam primum, deinde Phaeacas[50] omnis in admirationem sui mirabiliter concitasse, et adeo concitasse ut nemo esset inter Phaeacas[51] qui, si optio data sit, non se Ulyssem et naufragum et nudum et solum

experienced riches. But to become poor instead of rich cannot but seem very difficult to bear. For as Euripides' Polyxena says, "A disgraceful life is assuredly a great distress."[68]

Leonardo. Niccolò, what do you think, in view of what Onofrio 90 has said?

Niccolò. Leonardo, I think the same as my friend Onofrio. For as Polynices likewise says in Euripides, "Money is the thing men value most."[69] Those who lack it can, in my view, only lead a disgraceful life.

Leonardo. Are you unaware, young men, that disgrace is not de- 91 fined by poverty nor honorable status by wealth, but the latter is defined by virtue, the former by vice? But perhaps you are commending elegance — not the elegance that is usually called "wit" and is not subject to censure, but rather the elegance that is oriented toward a luxurious and pleasant lifestyle. Cato, however, showed that such elegance is a vice in the book entitled *Poem about Morals.* For he says: "They supposed that avarice contains all vices: he who was considered addicted to luxury, greedy, elegant, corrupt, and feckless was commended."[70] And Cato was right. For commendation belongs to virtue, not to empty and trivial things. We have said enough about food and drink. The same reasoning applies to grooming and domestic 92 furnishings. For it is not the grooming of the body or the elegance of domestic furnishings and staff but the outstanding and rare embellishment of virtue that renders a man admirable and revered in the eyes of all. Influenced by this view, Homer depicts Ulysses when he escaped from a shipwreck alone and naked to Corcyra: he wondrously provoked first Nausicaa, daughter of King Alcinous, then all the Phaeacians to admire him, and did so to such an extent that there was no one among the Phaeacians who, if he had the choice, would not have preferred to be Ulysses, a shipwreck, naked, alone, and a foreigner,

et peregrinum mallet quam illis omnibus et fortunae quae dicitur et corporis frui commodis quibus felicitatem metiebantur.

93   Satis is certe dives videri debet qui (quod Stoici dicebant) 'et caelo potest et terra frui.' At ille plane ditissimus, qui Deo fruitur. Non enim nummis constare veras divitias arbitramur. Nam qui veris abundat, divitias alias non desyderat. Desyderent autem illi omnes necesse est qui id divitiarum genus amplectuntur, quod in evangelio Dominus 'Mammona iniquitatis' appellans, alterum quoddam esse mammona significat. Hoc autem genere divitias eas intelligimus non quibus exterior fucatur, sed quibus interior homo et ornatur et illustratur. Nam qui divitias ullas vel dicamus vel iudicemus, quae non modo non auferunt, sed afferunt etiam egestatem? Non enim nummosus[52] homo idcirco dives putandus est, quod millia nummum permulta possideat. Si enim eo plus cupit, quo plura possidet, fit sane ut tanto sit pauperior quanto nummosior. Recte igitur Diogenes eo se rege Persarum ditiorem esse dicebat quo pauciorum quam ille ad vitam indigeret.

95   Et Christus Iesus, qui totius mundi sit dominus, nihil possidebat in terris. Et cum excessisset e vivis, non suis sepellitur, sed alienis impendiis, ultro is quidem paupertatem quo nos divites redderet egestatemque secutus. Quare non absurde in eos dictum videmus qui se Christi voluerunt imitatores, regnum caelorum non esse divitum sed pauperum. Ait enim: 'Beati pauperes spiritu, quoniam ipsorum est regnum caelorum.' Quod si ita est, sicuti certe est,[53] quis ambigat infernum esse divitibus destinatum, ubi non Lazarus mendicus sed dives sepultus est?[54] Atqui operae precium est ut nostro nos spiritu pauperes, sed Dei spiritu divites simus, ubi veram consequi beatitudinem velimus. Decet nos, inquam, pauperes esse iis rebus omnibus

rather than to enjoy all those advantages of so-called fortune and of the body by which they measured happiness.[71]

That man, surely, should seem sufficiently wealthy who (as the Stoics used to say) "can enjoy the sky and the earth."[72] But he is clearly the richest who has enjoyment of God. For we think that true wealth does not consist in money. For he who has an abundance of true wealth feels no need for any other. But all those persons must feel such a need who embrace that form of wealth that in the Gospel Our Lord, calling it the "mammon of iniquity," indicates is a different sort of mammon.[73] By this means we understand that wealth is not that with which the outer man is adorned but by which the inner man is equipped and embellished. For how are we to call or judge anything "wealth" which not only does not remove need but even adds to it? For a moneyed man should not be thought wealthy because he has many thousands. For if the more he possesses the more he desires, the result is that the more money he has, the poorer he is. So Diogenes rightly said that he was wealthier than the king of Persia since he required fewer things for living.[74]

Jesus Christ, who is the Lord of the entire world, possessed nothing on earth; and when he departed from the living, He was buried not at his own but at others' expense, since he voluntarily followed a poverty and destitution by which he made us rich. Thus we see that it is justly said against those who claim to be imitators of Christ that the kingdom of heaven belongs not to the rich but to the poor; for He says: "Blessed are the poor in spirit because the kingdom of heaven is theirs."[75] But if this is so, as it assuredly is, who would doubt that hell is destined for the rich, where a rich man is buried, not the beggar Lazarus?[76] It is worthwhile for us to be poor in our spirit but rich in the Spirit of God if we should wish to achieve true blessedness. It is appropriate for us to be poor in all those

93

94

95

96

quibus in pestiferas animi permotiones quasi efferatas corporis beluas irritamur. In eis autem esse mundi[55] divitias nemo dubitat, quippe quae homines cum in alios improbae appetitionis morbos, tum maxime in superbiam trahunt. Istiusmodi enim divitibus superbe sapiendum non esse imperat apostolus Paulus.

97 Superbia vero invidentiam parit, qua primus ille ingratus[56] angelus per omnem impietatem immanitatemque raptus, simul atque creatus est caelesti se patria exterminavit et sempiterno tenebrarum addixit exilio. Contra autem paupertas ut nihil insolentius vel faciamus vel dicamus hortatur. Stultus enim sit qui suae humilitatis, quam debet paupertas efficere, conscius quicquam supra sese vel aggrediatur vel sentiat. Sed qui in eorum sit numero quos dicit apostolus, 'tanquam nihil habentes et omnia possidentes,' mihi certe videatur ditissimus, non auri et argenti, quod Petrus sibi quasi vile et humile esse negat, sed virtutis et Dei, cuius testimonium paupertatis professio sequi

98 debet. Et Dei quidem paupertas non in loculis ac sacculis duntaxat, sed in ipso est animo. Videmus enim non nullos qui scientiae paupertatis nomen atque studium profitentur in cute, cum intus sint rapacissimi quidam lupi.[57]

Nam quod non multo ante dicebat Honofrius, aliud sibi videri pauperem esse, aliud fieri, quasi qui nunquam divitias sint experti, paupertatem non ferant graviter, secus vero iis accidat qui cum essent divites, tandem redditi sunt pauperes, iocari mecum adolescentem existimo. Quod enim praesens malum non est, qui possit impendens malum esse? Permolestum etiam

99 sit quenquam fieri bonum virum cum sit malus. Verum ubi sese ipse collegerit et suae vitae turpitudinem inspexerit, libentissime ad virtutem et alacri animo convertatur. Hoc vero, quanquam initio propter inveteratum animi errorem videtur

matters by which we are provoked to destructive emotions, which are like savage beasts in the body. No one doubts that the riches of the world are among them, since they draw people into other diseases of base appetite, but especially into pride. The apostle Paul commands that we must not put on airs because of such riches.[77] Haughtiness breeds envy, by which that 97 first ungrateful angel, as soon as he was created, was taken over by all sorts of monstrous impiety, banished himself from his celestial homeland, and bound himself over to the darkness of eternal exile. On the other hand, poverty urges us not to do or say anything insolent. Let him be accounted stupid who, though conscious of his own humble status — a consciousness poverty ought to produce — attempts or thinks anything above himself. But those who are among those whom the apostle calls "as if having nothing and possessing all," would certainly seem to me wealthy indeed, not in the gold or silver that Peter denied himself as vile and low, but in virtue and God, whose testimony a vow of poverty ought to follow.[78] God's poverty is not merely in 98 strongboxes and sacks but in the soul itself. We see some who outwardly profess the reputation and pursue the science of poverty, while inwardly they are the most rapacious of wolves.

As to the point raised a little while ago by Onofrio, that he thinks it is one thing to be poor, something else to become poor — as if those who have never experienced riches are not heavily burdened by poverty, but that it happens otherwise for those who were once rich but have been reduced to poverty — I think the young man is joking with me. For how could what is not an evil now become an impending evil? Granted it is highly problematic for someone to become a good man when he is bad. But when he has pulled himself together and looked 99 closely at his shameful life, he may willingly and eagerly turn to virtue. Although this seems more difficult at the beginning because of the mind's deep-seated error, soon, when you have

difficilius, mox tamen, ubi velle coeperis, non modo facile iudices, sed iucundissimum ac pulcherrimum. Atqui siquid interdum boni divitiae in se[58] habeant, tunc sane habent — quod non multo ante dicebatur — cum se[59] (quod rarissime solent) apud virum gravem sapientemque receperint. Possunt enim et amicis et reipublicae esse usui. Quod si stultorum contubernio utantur, se malorum omnium atque maximorum et comites praestent et adiutrices. At paupertas id plaerunque efficit, ut et resipiscant insipientes et boni seipsis contenti sint. Nam philosophum quam debeat delectare paupertas, hac epistola Vespasianus Caesar ad hunc illum Apollonium Tyaneum ostendit:

> Imperator Vespasianus Apollonio philosopho salutem. Si ita omnes ut tu philosophari, Apolloni, vellent, agerent admodum feliciter et philosophia et paupertas. Nam philosophia quidem[60] incorrupte haberet, paupertas autem non invite.[61] Vale.

101 Et certe ita res habet, modo paupertas sit non invita: non modo nihil habet in se mali, sed plurimorum est bonorum causa. Itaque demus operam quo nihil huiusmodi nobis esse molestum possit, ut velimus esse pauperes. Qualis autem quisque vult, talis esse potest.

Pallas. Quaeque, Leonarde, et docte disseruisti et eloquenter, reliqua tibi assentior omnia. Sed quod iam secundum abs te usurpari video, an omnino sit verum, sane subdubito. Dixisti enim semel et iterum talis nos esse posse quales volumus. Nunquid si volumus, etiam optimi esse possimus?

102 *Leonardus.* Quid mirum si vir philosophus disquirit omnia diligenter? Fateor equidem, Pallas, licere mortali nemini esse optimo[62] vel volenti. Id enim divinae cuiusdam naturae est, non humanae. Quo enim pacto simus animo optimi, cum ne corpore

begun to want to make the change, you might decide it is not only easy, but an extremely pleasant and beautiful undertaking. Yet if wealth occasionally has some intrinsic good in it, surely it is at that moment — as was said a short while ago — when it has gone to dwell with a serious and wise man (a most rare occurrence).[79] For it can be beneficial both to friends and the republic. But if it dwells with fools, it makes itself the companion and enabler of all the greatest evils. But poverty for the most part causes fools to come to their senses and the good to rest content with themselves. For Vespasian shows in this letter to Apollonius of Tyana how the philosopher should take pleasure in poverty:

> The Emperor Vespasian greets the philosopher Apollonius. If all persons were willing to lead a philosophical life like you, Apollonius, both philosophy and poverty would be in a happy state. For philosophy would be free of corruption, and a life of poverty embraced without reluctance. Farewell.[80]

Surely this is so, provided that poverty is not involuntary: not only does it contain nothing evil, but it is the cause of a great many goods. Therefore let us strive that nothing of this sort be burdensome to us, so that we would wish to be poor. For each individual can be the kind of person he wants.

Palla. As to the rest of your learned and eloquent discourse, Leonardo, I agree with you. But I am in some doubt about whether the second point just made by you is true. For you've said time and again that we can be the kind of person we wish. Is it really possible that we can even possess the best character, if we [just] wish it?

Leonardo. Why should it be surprising if a philosopher investigates everything with care? I admit, Palla, that it is open to no mortal to be the best, even though he might wish it. For that belongs to the divine, not human nature. How may we be best

quidem liceat? Habeas sane omnem corporis diligentiam, non eo tamen corpus sit tibi omnium optimum. Nam diligentia satis esse nunquam possit, nisi etiam natura sit corpus et pulchrum et bonum. Praestabit igitur diligentia ut meliore sis corpore, sed omnium optimo nequaquam. Idem de animo quoque existimandum est. Non enim qui elegerit esse optimus, unquam possit, nisi natura ipsa, quae artem omnem diligentiamque exuperat, et existat et faveat.[63] Verum nos loquimur more nostro, qui omnis[64] optimos appellemus[65] in quibus praestantiora quaedam atque expressiora simulachra probitatis appareant. Nam si emendatissime loqui volumus, non modo optimum non dicemus quenquam e numero viventium, sed ne bonum quidem. Altius est enim atque admirabilius bonitatis lumen quam visis humanae mentis consequi valeat. Sed modo adsit voluntas, quae omnem probat ac reprobat actionem, quamproxime liceat pro divina benignitate ad bonum ipsum accedere.

104 *Manettus.* Ita est profecto, Leonarde, ut dicis. Nihil enim recte fieri potest si fiat invite. Quare nisi dies iam propemodum advesperascens dissuaderet, esset fortasse minime alienum a praesenti vestra omni commentatione, ut vel abs te vel ab hoc Pallante de ultroneo aliquid et de invito quoque dissereretur.

Leonardus. Imo sane, Manette, a Pallante, qui et diu iam tacet et consuevit de istiusmodi praeceptis philosophiae acute simul presseque disserere. Nec diei tempus impedimento esse possit, modo breviter Pallas, ut solet, rem perstringat.

105 *Pallas.* Leonarde, fuerit tuae humanitatis ne decurso iam poene stadio ad calcem deficias.

Rainaldus. Age, age, Pallas, si libet, obsequere Leonardo, qui et multa adhuc dixit et audiendi tui ostendit se cupidum.

103

in mind when we cannot even be so in body? You may surely care for body in every way without your body being, by that means, the best of all. Care could never be sufficient unless our body is by nature beautiful and good. Care will produce a better body but by no means the best of all. We must suppose the same about the mind. For he who has chosen to be best can never be so unless nature herself, which excels all art and care, rises up and bestows her favor. But we are speaking in accordance with our custom when we who label all persons "best" in whom some outstanding quality and more obvious likeness of goodness appears.[81] If we wish to speak in the most precise way, we will not call anyone numbered among the living "best" or even "good." For there is a higher and more admirable light of goodness than can be attained by the sight of the human mind. But provided that the will gives assistance, which approves and disapproves every action, one may, in accord with divine grace, approach as close as possible to the good itself.

Manetti. It is surely as you say, Leonardo. Nothing can be done correctly if it is done unwillingly. Therefore were not dusk closing in, it would perhaps be germane to your entire present argument for either you or Palla here to discuss voluntary and involuntary action.

Leonardo. Surely you should ask Palla, since he has kept silent for some time now and is in the habit of holding forth on such philosophical teachings with acuity and concision. The time of day should present no obstacle provided that Palla, as is his custom, summarize the topic with brevity.

Palla. Leonardo, it would be characteristic of your kindness, now that the race is almost complete, for you not to lose heart at the finish line.

Rinaldo. Come, come, Palla, please oblige Leonardo, who has already said a good deal and shows that he is eager to listen to you.

103

104

105

387

Pallas. Faciam, Rainalde, quod iubes, et id quidem ut tuae gravitati obtemperem, cui negare quicquam neque possum nec debeo. Sed faciam equidem verecundius aeque ac brevius, idque non modo pro[66] ingenio meo, sed propter Leonardum, quo praesente quicquam supra vires attingere non debeo non vereri.

106   *Poggius.* At brevitatis quaeso, Pallas, maxime omnium memineris, ne caenandi tempus praetereat.

Pallas. Faciam, Poggi, ne metuas tantum accingere non minus ad audiendum aliquid et dicendum quam ad caenandum. Quo igitur certo quodam ordine ad rem veniam, pauca mihi sunt praemittenda, quibus veluti iactis fundamentis omnis de ultro-
107   neo invitoque ratio expeditius in fastigium surgat. Virtutem esse quandam perturbationum mediocritatem video concedi ab omnibus. Quo fit ut is qui probatis moribus esse velit, cuiusque perturbationis mediocritatem necessario observet. Itaque non potest esse non difficile quandoquidem in qualibet perturbatione medium capere nos oportet.[67] Non enim eadem facilitate capias medium circuli qua circulum pinxeris. Facile et verecundamur et irascimur. Sed in his mediocriter habere non facile possumus. Et ne sim longior quam par sit, in omni perturbatione intueri licet facile id esse, quo medium continetur, sed medium ipsum quod laudem nobis affert, esse admodum difficile. Qua ipsa re fit ut bonum non possit esse non rarum.

108   *Manettus.* Prudenter tu quidem, Pallas, ac vero praesertim si ea Socratis sententia vera est, qui diceret in nobis non esse ut vel boni essemus vel mali.

Pallas. Loquere, Manette, si placet, istam Socratis sententiam, quo aut nos refellere aut illum subtilius queas.

Manettus. Siquis, inquit, quenquam interrogarit utrum esse velit iustus vel[68] iniustus, nullus dicat iniusticiam; eodem modo de fortitudine ac timiditate, et de aliis virtutibus semper identidem

Palla. I shall do as you bid, Rinaldo, in order to comply with your authority—you, to whom I neither can nor should deny anything. But I shall do so modestly and briefly, not only because of my limited talent, but because of Leonardo: with him present I must fear taking up something beyond my powers.

Poggio. But please, Palla, most of all keep brevity in mind, so that 106 dinner time does not pass us by!

Palla. I shall do so, Poggio, to allay your fear that you are girding yourself to listen and speak as much as to dine.[82] In order to approach the topic in a certain fixed order, I must preface a few remarks; once these have been laid down like foundations, the entire argument about the voluntary and involuntary will quickly be built up to the pediment.[83] I see that it is agreed by 107 all that virtue is a kind of middle range of emotion.[84] It follows that he who would wish to be of excellent character must observe the mean in every emotion. This poses a difficulty, since in each emotion we must find the mean. One may not find the middle of a circle with the same ease with which one may draw the circle. It is easy for us to grow ashamed and angry, but while experiencing these emotions we cannot easily sustain a middle state. To make a long story short, in the case of every emotion it is easy to see that by which the middle is delimited, but to find the praiseworthy middle itself is quite difficult. Hence the good can only be rare.

Manetti. You have spoken wisely and truly, Palla, especially if the 108 opinion of Socrates is true, who said that it is not up to us whether we are good or bad.[85]

Palla. Please, Manetti, tell us that opinion of Socrates so that you can subtly refute either us or him.

Manetti. He says that if anyone should ask someone whether he would want to be just or unjust, no one would say "unjust"; likewise, it is obviously the same with respect to courage and cowardice and the other virtues: if any persons are wicked, they

patet, siqui sunt mali, eos non ultro esse malos. Itaque perspicuum est nec ultro esse bonos.

109 *Pallas.* Si vel tua ista vel Socratis ratio vera esset, nunquam legum latores et mala atque turpia prohiberent et bona honestaque iuberent. At eos omnis mulctandos censent qui vel egerint mali quippiam, vel quod honestum sit agere neglexerint. Et cui ridiculus videri non debeat is legum lator qui ea iubeat quae ipsi agere non possimus? Sed recte ii quidem iubent, quippe qui norint in nobis esse ut et boni simus et mali. Quod si secus esset, nunquam ob virtutem laudaremur vituperaremurque propter vitium. At nemo laudatur unquam vituperaturve siquid invitus egerit. Itaque licet nobis ut aut boni simus aut mali.

110 *Manettus.* Cur ergo nemo illos vituperat qui aut aegrotent aut sint deformes?

Pallas. Et istud quoque Socratis est, Manette. Quod ipsum tamen esse falsum vel eo patet, quod huiusmodi homines etiam vituperamus, quoscunque in causa esse iudicemus suae malae valitudinis aut deformitatis, rursusque laudamus qui sua sibi opera atque diligentia et valitudinis bonitatem et formae dignitatem pepererunt, quasi hoc ultroneum de quo loquimur in his omnibus reperiatur.

Manettus. Dilucidius de hisce, Pallas, si videtur.

111 *Pallas.* Faciam equidem, ut potero sciamque. Quod substantiae omnes sint naturaliter principia quaedam, nosse vos omnes puto. Itaque natura omnis potest substantias tales gignere qualis est ipsa, ut homo homines, et quod animal sit omnino animalia, et planta itidem gignit plantam. Utraque enim haec ad gignendum vim habent, et eam quidem ex principiis, ut arbor ex saeminibus. Hoc enim principium quoddam est, et connubium actionum etiam quarundam est principium solis animantibus. Nam ex aliis agere nihil dicimus. Sed quod principia sequitur, ita habet. Nam quemadmodum habeant principia, sic
112 etiam quae sunt ex principiis habere necesse est. Quare primum

are not so voluntarily. Thus it is clear also that they are not good voluntarily.[86]

Palla. If that reasoning of yours, or of Socrates, were true, legisla- 109
tors would never prohibit wicked and shameful deeds and require good and honorable ones. But they decree that all persons who have done anything wicked or who have omitted to do what is right must be punished. Who wouldn't think the legislator foolish who commands us to do what we cannot do ourselves? But their requirements are correct, since they know that it is in our power to be good or wicked. If it were otherwise, we would never be commended for virtue and upbraided for vice. But no one is ever commended or upbraided for acting involuntarily. Therefore it is open to us to be either good or wicked.

Manetti. Why, then, does no one upbraid those who are sick 110
or ugly?

Palla. That point of yours was also made by Socrates, Manetti. That it is wrong is clear from the fact that we upbraid those men whom we judge to be responsible for their bad health or ugliness, while on the other hand we commend those who by their efforts and care have achieved good health or attractive looks, as though we assumed that the voluntary action we are discussing is found in all these cases.

Manetti. Please elucidate, Palla.

Palla. I shall, to the best of my ability and knowledge. I believe 111
that you all know that all substances are by nature principles in a sense.[87] Thus every nature can generate substances like itself, as a person generates people, and as what is animate generates animate things, and a plant likewise generates a plant. For each of these has the power to generate and has it from its principle, as a tree is generated from seeds. This is a kind of principle, and sexual union is a principle only for animate things. For we say that nothing derives from anything else, but what follows its principle is disposed in that way. For the things that derive 112

dicuntur motiones esse necessariae, et hae iure in primis a quibus secus fieri non potest, quandoquidem Deus, a quo manant
reliqua omnia, quaeque sunt quaeque futura sunt, est princeps.
Sed in principiis immobilibus,[69] ut in mathematicis, etsi per similitudinem dicitur, necessarium tamen ipsum nequaquam est.
Hic enim moto principio mutentur omnia maxime, quae de-
monstrantur, sed ipsa minime mutantur per sese, ubi alterum
ab altero sit sublatum, nisi causam[70] tollant per quam[71] de-
113 monstrent. At homo principium est cuiusdam motionis. Nam
actio est motio. Sed quoniam, ut in aliis quoque principium[72]
eorum est causa quae propter ipsum vel sunt vel fiunt, intelligendum hoc arbitror ut in geometricis demonstrationibus solet;
ubi quia sumuntur principia quaedam, quemadmodum habeant
ipsa principia, sic etiam habent quae sunt post principia, ut si
triangulus duobus rectis aequales habet, quadrangulus necessario habet quattuor, quod si triangulus mutetur,[73] quadrangulus
simul mutatur,[74] ut si trianguli tres fuerint, anguli sint sex oportet. Sic trianguli quattuor angulos octo sint habituri. Respondet
enim triangulo quadrangulus. Eodem modo si quadrangulus
non habeat quattuor rectis aequales, nec etiam triangulus duobus rectis aequales sit habiturus.

114   Quemadmodum igitur in his videmus, ita etiam in homine
usu venit. Homo enim quoniam vim habeat gignendae substantiae ex quibusdam principiis, eodem quoque modo actionum
quas agit gignendarum vim habet. Nam cum nec inanimatum
quicquam agere dicamus, nec aliud item ex animatis quam hominem, quis ambigat huic ipsi gignendae actionis natura vim

from principles must be disposed in the same way as the principles are disposed. Hence, in the first place, motions are said to be necessary, and rightly so, principally in the case of those motions deriving from things that cannot be otherwise, since God, from whom all else flows, both things that are and things that will be, is their first principle. But this is by no means a necessary condition in the case of immobile principles, as in mathematics, though we use this expression by way of analogy. In the case of mathematics, if the principle is moved, all things, especially those that are proven from it, are changed, but these things are not changed by themselves, as one thing has been removed by another, unless they remove the cause by which they make the proof. But man is the principle of a certain mo- 113
tion, for an action is a motion. Because just as in other things the principle is the cause of things that either exist or come into being because of it, I think this must be understood as it commonly is in geometrical proofs. In them, because certain principles are postulated, the things that follow from the principles are disposed like the principles themselves; for example, if a triangle equals two right angles, a square necessarily equals four, but if the triangle is changed, the square is simultaneously changed, so that if there were three triangles, there must be six angles. Thus four triangles will have eight angles. For the square corresponds to the triangle. By the same token, if the square were not to have four right angles, neither would a triangle possess two right angles.

So the same usage we observe in these instances occurs also 114
in the case of man.[88] Because he has the power of generating substance from certain principles, in the same way man also has the power of generating the actions that he carries out. Since we cannot say that something inanimate carries out actions, nor do animate things other than man carry them out, who would doubt that man himself has by nature the power of generating

esse? Quorumcunque autem agendorum homo et principium
est et causa, possunt ea fieri et non possunt, et in ipso est ut
haec quae sintne an minus sint, idem ipse in causa est, aut fiant,
aut non fiant. Sed quidquid fuerit in seipso vel facere vel non
facere, huius quoque ipse est auctor. At cuiuscunque ipse sit

115 causa,[75] hoc item in ipso esse crediderim. Sed quoniam philosophi omnes consentiunt virtutem ac vitium quaeque ab his opera
manant, alia in laude, alia in vituperatione versari — laudamur
enim vituperamurve nequaquam ob ea quae vel necessitate sunt
vel fortuna vel natura, at ob haec ipsa potius, quorum causa sit
in nobis; nam cuius alius sit in causa, id illi sane, non nobis affert aut vituperationem aut laudem — eo fit ut ipsam omnem et
virtutem et vitium in his ponamus quorum causa et agendi
principium sit in nobis. Quarum autem actionum et causam et

116 principium nobis dari conveniat, paucis expediam. Et ut certo
ordine progrediatur oratio, quoniam virtutem ac vitium esse
omnes volunt ex genere ultroneorum, quid ultroneum sit primo
definiamus idque simpliciter. Est enim ultroneum quod agimus
non coacti. Quod autem coacti agimus, id invitum dicere oportet. Quaecunque vero ultronea sint aut secundum electionem
cuiusque, eorum ipse est auctor. Sed eorum quaeque invita sint,
auctor ipse non est. Nam quisque eorum est causa, quaecunque
elegerit atque ultro egerit. Cum virtus ergo et vitium definiatur
ultroneo et invito, id utrunque primum se nobis offert considera-
randum, quippe quod in virtute ac vitio primum teneat locum.

117 Ultroneum igitur quiddam unum videtur esse ex hisce tribus:
aut secundum appetitionem aut secundum electionem aut secundum ratiocinationem. Et ut secundum horum aliquod videatur ultroneum, ita praeter aliquod horum sit invitum. Sed
appetitio distribuitur in tris[76] partes: voluntatem, iram, cupiditatem. Ut autem ab actione quae sit secundum cupiditatem
incipiamus: quidquid est secundum cupiditatem, videtur esse

action? Yet of whatever actions man is the source and cause, they can happen or not, and it is in his power, and he himself is responsible for their happening or not happening; and he himself is the author of whatever was in his power to do or not to do. I would think that he is the cause of whatever is in his power.[89] But since all philosophers agree that virtue and vice and the effects that spring from them receive sometimes praise, at other times blame — for we are never praised or criticized for those things that arise by necessity or fortune or nature, but rather on account of the very things of which we are the cause; for if responsibility belongs with another person, it surely brings no praise or blame to us — we thus assign all the virtue and vice to those things whose cause and origin of action is in our hands. Let me explain briefly which actions are those whose cause and origin is appropriately ascribed to us. So that my discourse may proceed methodically, since all claim that virtue and vice belong to the category of voluntary actions, let us first give a simple definition of what is voluntary. What we do under no constraint is voluntary. We must call involuntary what we do under constraint. The agent is the author of whatever things are voluntary or according to someone's choice, but he is not the author of involuntary actions. For each person is the cause of those things which he has chosen and chosen of his own accord. Since, then, virtue and vice are defined by the terms voluntary and involuntary, both of these offer themselves to us first for consideration, since they hold the first place in virtue and vice. Therefore some one condition of the following three appears to be voluntary: either according to appetency or according to choice or according to reasoning. As a voluntary act would appear to be according to some one of these, so an involuntary one would be contrary to one of these. But appetency is divided into three parts: will, anger, desire. To begin with action that is in accord with desire: whatever is according to

115

116

117

ultroneum. Nam quidquid non ultro agimus patimurve, coacti
118 facimus aut patimur, et invitum omne est violentum. Quod
vero violentum, idem etiam triste perinde[77] atque necessarium
omne afferat natura aegritudinem. Quo fit ut et violentum sit
quidquid est triste, et triste rursum quidquid est violentum. Et
cum aegritudo id sequitur quodcunque agimus praeter cupiditatem, voluptas quidquid agimus secundum cupiditatem necessario sequatur. Esse enim cupiditatem volunt e genere voluptatis. Quare violentum omne sit etiam invitum. Itaque hoc pacto
quidquid agas secundum cupiditatem, id[78] non invitum sed ultroneum est dicendum.

119 Sed rursus alia quaedam ratio hisce adversetur, ea quae de
incontinentia est. Nemo enim existimatur agere sponte quae
mala sunt, si ea quidem intelligat esse mala. At incontinens et
cognoscit haec esse mala et agit tamen, et agit is quidem secundum cupiditatem. Non ergo agit ultro, sed coactus. Itaque idem
secundum cupiditatem et ultroneum sit et invitum. Nam quidquid aliquis agit sponte, agit etiam volens, et quod vult, agit
sponte. Vult autem nemo quod malum esse arbitretur. At agens
incontinenter, non ea facit quae vult, quippe qui propter cupiditatem praeter id agat quod actu existimat esse optimum. Quare
idem simul ultro aget et invite, quod quidem fieri nullo pacto
120 potest. Sed quod etiam incontinens agit ultro, ratio alia potest
afferri. Agentes enim iniuste, sponte iniuste agunt. Sed incontinentes iniusti sunt et iniuste agunt. Incontinentes igitur agunt
iniuste, quae sunt secundum incontinentiam. Ad haec ratio alia
adversatur qua probatur non esse ultroneum. Continens enim
sponte agit, quae secundum continentiam sunt. Quod ni ita

desire appears to be voluntary. For whatever we do not do or suffer voluntarily we do or suffer under constraint, and everything done through violence is involuntary. What is done 118 through violence is also harsh, just as though everything that is by nature necessary brings suffering. Hence whatever is harsh is done through violence and whatever is done through violence is harsh. Since suffering follows whatever we do apart from desire, pleasure necessarily follows whatever we do according to desire. For they claim that desire comes from the genus of pleasure. In this way whatever you do according to pleasure should be called not involuntary but voluntary.

But there is again another theory that conflicts with these 119 points, namely the one about incontinence. For no one is thought to do of his own accord what is evil if he knows that it is evil. But the incontinent person both knows that this is evil and nonetheless does it and he does so in accordance with desire. Therefore he is not acting voluntarily but under constraint. Therefore the same thing is according to desire both voluntary and involuntary. For whatever someone does of his own accord, he does willingly, and whatever he wants to do, he does of his own accord. For no one wishes for what he thinks to be evil. But the person acting incontinently does not do what he wants, since on account of desire he does something contrary to what he thinks it best to do. Therefore he will act both voluntarily and involuntarily, which is impossible. But another argument 120 can be adduced that the incontinent person acts voluntarily.[90] Those who act unjustly do so of their own accord. But incontinent persons are unjust and act unjustly. Incontinent persons therefore carry out unjustly acts that are in accordance with their own incontinence. Another line of argument is opposed to this one, which proves [continence] to be involuntary. A continent person carries out of his own accord acts in accordance with his own continence. If it were not so, he would never be

esset, nunquam laudaretur. Sed propter spontanea homines
laudantur. Quod si est id spontaneum quod est[79] secundum
cupiditatem, quis dubitet id esse invitum quod sit praeter cupiditatem? Quo fit ut continens non ultro sit continens. Sed ne
id quidem quod praeter hoc sit, quod est secundum cupiditatem, videtur[80] esse ultroneum. Praeterea continens iuste agit
magis etiam quam incontinentia. Nam continentia virtus est.
At virtus iustiores facit. Utitur autem continentia, cum agit secundum ratiocinationem praeter cupiditatem. Quamobrem si
iuste agere est ultroneum, sicuti etiam iniuste agere — quoniam[81]
haec ambo videantur esse ultronea, necesseque sit ubi alterum
fuerit ultroneum, alterum quoque ultroneum esse, quod autem
sit praeter cupiditatem, ultroneum videri, simul igitur idem
quis agat sponte et invite — eaedem autem rationes etiam de ira
afferri possunt. Incontinentia enim et continentia non secus irae
videtur esse quam cupiditatis. Sed quod sit praeter iram, aegritudinem affert, atque[82] eius correptio violenta est. Quare si
violentum quod sit, idem quoque invitum est, sequitur id omne
esse ultroneum, quidquid fuerit secundum iram. Itaque Heraclitus eius vires impetumque consyderans, 'Difficile est,' inquit,
'pugnare adversus iram, quippe quae prosit animo.' Intelligebat
enim vir sapientissimus iram prohiberi sine aegritudine haud
facile posse.

121

Relinquitur tertia quaedam appetitionis species, quam esse
voluntatem proposuimus. Hanc itidem transigamus. Nam si
fieri non potest ut idem simul et sponte agatur et invite, quod
secundum eandem rem fuerit, fit sane ut id magis spontaneum
videatur quod est secundum voluntatem quam quod esse vel
secundum cupiditatem vel secundum iram asseratur. Agimus
enim sponte multa sine ira et cupiditate. Itaque non fuerit absurdum si nobiscum ipsi consyderemus an idem existimari

122

praised. But men are praised for voluntary acts. But if that is
voluntary which is according to desire, who would doubt that
what is contrary to desire is involuntary? Hence the continent
person is not continent voluntarily. But what is contrary to that
which is according to desire does not seem to be voluntary either. Moreover, the continent man acts justly more than incon-   121
tinence does.[91] For continence is a virtue, and virtue makes
people more just. A person exercises continence when he acts
according to reason, contrary to desire. Therefore if just action
is voluntary, so also is unjust action; since both of these would
seem to be voluntary, it would be necessary, if one of them were
voluntary, for the other one also to be voluntary, and for what is
contrary to desire to appear to be voluntary;[92] therefore someone acts at the same time both voluntarily and unwillingly. The
same arguments can be adduced concerning anger. Continence
and incontinence seem to be no less a case of anger than of desire. But what is contrary to anger brings on unhappiness, and
to be seized by anger is to be constrained by violence. Therefore
if whatever is done under constraint of violence is involuntary,
it follows that whatever is done according to anger is voluntary.
Thus, in view of its strength and violent onset, Heraclitus said,
"It is difficult to fight against anger since it benefits the mind."[93]
For that very wise man understood that anger cannot easily be
prevented without suffering.

The third species of appetency remains, namely what we   122
held to be the will. Let us likewise deal with it.[94] For if it is
impossible for the same act, in accordance with the same motive
[i.e., anger or desire], to be done both voluntarily and involuntarily at the same time, it follows that what is done according to
the will rather than what is claimed to be done either according
to desire or according to anger would appear more voluntary.
For we do many things willingly without anger and desire.
Therefore it would not be out of place for us to consider

oporteat voluntarium et spontaneum. Nam spontaneum idem

123 esse quod ultroneum Latinus et litteratus dubitat nemo.[83] Incontinentes enim ea volunt quae agunt, cum agunt scilicet. Agunt igitur mala voluntarie. Sed ultro nemo agit mala quae mala esse intelligat. At incontinentes et agunt quae mala sint, mala esse non ignorantes, et agunt ea quidem pro voluntate. Cum ergo non agant ultro, voluntas ultronea esse qui potest? Quae quidem ratio et incontinentiam tollit et incontinentem. Quod enim ultro non agitur, id certe vituperandum non est. At incontinens vituperatur. Ultro igitur agit. Quare voluntas ultronea sit oportet. Itaque de ultroneo explicatius est dicendum, quandoquidem rationes quaedam contrariae afferuntur. De vi igitur ac necessitate ante[84] dicendum est. Nam vim in rebus etiam inanimatis esse dicimus. Singulis enim rebus inanimatis proprius quidam locus tributus est, ut igni quidem qui sursum

124 est, terrae vero qui dehorsum est locus. Licet etiam vim equo afferre, ut si currentem illum appraehendas avertasque, et lapidem sursum et ignem dehorsum violenter coacteque ferri dicimus. Quibuscunque igitur causa sit extrinseca, ut aliquid vel praeter naturam vel praeter voluntatem faciant, dicimus eos vi facere quae faciunt. Sed in quibus causa ipsis est, hos ea vi facere nequaquam dicimus. Quod si secus foret, non fortassis absurde incontinens dixerit se malum non esse, quippe qui non ultro agat mala, sed quoniam vi cupiditatis repugnare nequeat. Violentum vero ita definiamus: violentum est cuius externa causa ea est quae nobis agendi vim infert. Nam cuius causa et

whether the voluntary and willed should be considered the same. For no one who is knowledgeable in Latin and well read would deny that the willing act (*spontaneum*) is the same as the act of one's free will (*ultroneum*). Incontinent persons want what they do when they do it. Therefore they voluntarily do evil things. But no one willingly does evil things that he knows to be evil. But incontinent persons both do things that are evil, though they are aware that they are evil, and do them willingly. Since therefore they do not act of their own accord, how can the will be voluntary? This argument eliminates both incontinence and the incontinent person. What is not done of one's own accord is certainly not to be criticized. But the incontinent person is criticized. Therefore he acts of his own accord. Therefore the will must be voluntary. And so we must give a lengthier account of the voluntary since conflicting arguments are being adduced. Therefore we must first speak about force and compulsion. For we say that there is force even in inanimate things. For a certain place of their own has been assigned to individual inanimate things, as, for instance, to fire, which is above, and to earth a place which is below. Force can be applied to a horse, as, for instance, if you catch it when it is galloping and redirect it, and we say that rock is violently pushed up and fire carried violently downward by force [e.g., a volcano].[95] For in the case of everything that has an external cause, whenever they act either contrary to nature or contrary to will, we say that they do what they do by force or violence. But in the case of those motions where the cause is within the agents, we don't say that they do them by force. If it were otherwise, the incontinent person would plausibly claim that he is not evil because he is not doing evil deeds voluntarily, but because he cannot resist the force of desire. Let us define the act compelled by violence thus: an act compelled by violence is one for which there is an external cause that forces us to act. For we neither call nor consider an

123

124

125 intrinsica est et in ipso, id violentum nec dicimus nec existimamus. De necessitate rursus necessarioque loquentes putamus nec esse omnino necessarium, nec item in omni re poni oportere, ut siqua voluptatis gratia egerimus. Nam siquis dicat eo a se amici uxorem vitiatam, quod a[85] voluptate coactus sit, ridiculus mihi quispiam videatur. Non enim necessarium in omni re dici convenit, sed maxime in externis, ut siquis idcirco in agrum contentius incedat, ne si serius eo pervenerit, messis pereat. Cum ex tribus autem illis partibus in quarum una quadam spontaneum ponebamus iam unam non tam accurate quam breviter (appetitionem, et ipsam quidem tripartitam) absolverimus, partes reliquae duae sunt: electio et ratiocinatio, quas ipsas paucis percurramus, ne Poggio huic nostro molestiores simus prolyxiore oratione.

126 *Poggius.* Tu ista, Pallas, ut libet cum hoc Rainaldo. Nam ego percurro ad aedes Bertheldinas, ubi caena et prolyxa parata est et lauta. Ibi ratiocinatio mihi est omnis et electio omnis.

Rainaldus. Si maluisses, Poggi,[86] te Socratis quam Epicuri similem, eruditum hunc Pallantis nostri prudentemque sermonem reliquis tuis omnibus deliciis facile anteferendum existimares. Sed tu omnia voluptate definis, non ea quae est animi et quam vel Epicurus fortasse sensit, sed corporis potius ea, qua sensus
127 laeviter demollitus et tanquam soporatus moveri solet. Verum, Pallas, non propter Poggium, cuius in patinis ac poculis semper est animus, sed propter hunc Leonardum potius, cuius omni opera in senatu semper est opus, quod reliquum est huiusce commentationis in posterum diem reiice, ubi non solum poteris de electione et ratiocinatione diligentissime persequi, sed etiam quod die tertio cum incommoda exilii velut enumerans

act to be compelled by violence when the cause of the act is in-
ternal and within the agent. Speaking of necessity and the nec-   125
essary, on the other hand, we think an action is not at all necessary, and likewise that necessity need not be posited in every
case, for example when we act because of pleasure. If someone
were to say that he had seduced a friend's wife because he had
been forced by desire, I would see that as ridiculous. For it is
not proper for something to be called necessary in every case,
but especially in external matters, as when someone hastens to
a field lest, if he arrive there too late, the crop be spoiled. Since
we have now completed — not so much carefully as briefly —
one of the three parts in one of which we classed the voluntary
(appetency, itself being tripartite), two parts remain, choice and
reasoning: let us briefly skim over these lest we annoy our
friend Poggio with this prolix discourse of ours.

Poggio. Do as you wish with Rinaldo here, Palla, for I am hurry-   126
ing to the Berteldi house,[96] where a banquet both prolix and
elegant is in readiness. That is where all my reasoning and
choice resides.

Rinaldo. Had you preferred, Poggio, to be like Socrates rather
than Epicurus, you would have judged this learned and wise
discourse of our friend Palla far preferable to all the rest of your
delicacies. But you define everything by the standard of pleasure — not that of the mind, which perhaps even Epicurus recognized, but rather that of the body, by which the senses,
gently soothed and as it were lulled to sleep, are customarily
moved. But Palla, not for the sake of Poggio, whose mind is   127
always on dishes and cups, but rather for the sake of Leonardo
here, whose work is always needed in the senate,[97] postpone
what remains of the present argument till tomorrow, when you
will not only be able to follow up with great care on the subject
of choice and reasoning, but when you will also instruct us, if
you please, with your usual learning and eloquence, on what

complectereris, de servitute memineras ex Honofrii filii sermone, docebis tu, si videbitur, et erudite, ut soles, et eloquenter.[87]

128 *Leonardus.* Quinpotius, Rainalde, exorandus est Pallas ut, posteaquam nunc abest omnis Poggiana molestia, et adhuc satis est diei ad id quod restat huius laudatissimi muneris, quae de rationandi eligendoque proposuit, diligenter absolvat. Delectat me profecto, Pallas, tua omnis oratio, et haec in primis quam ex praestantissimis philosophorum disciplinis nobis exponis. Semper ego te certe opinatus sum magnum quendam et sapientem virum. Sed quod ea quae acutissimi philosophi magno ocio magnisque laboribus invenerunt, ita copiose perdocteque teneres, ut tibi verum fatear, non arbitrabar.

129 *Pallas.* At noli mirari, Leonarde. Num es oblitus quod dicere solitum tradunt Philolaum: esse quosdam sermones nobis meliores? Non enim de prophetis et Sibyllis hominibusque afflatis modo intelligi id arbitror oportere, sed de iis omnibus qui quemadmodum ego apud vos gravissimos eruditissimosque viros loquuntur aliquid supra se. Sermo hic profecto meus non est, sed maximi illius sapientissimique viri, quo tu et ego doctore olim amicoque usi sumus, Manuelis Chrysolorae, cuius neptem Theodoram, modestam et pudicam adolescentulam, Iohannis Chrysolorae filiam, Franciscus Philelfus hic noster uxorem ha-

130 bet. Cum enim per id temporis quo illustris ille summusque philosophus Graecam sapientiam Florentiae doceret, et nostra haec urbs et universa prope Tuscia pestilentiali morbo laboraret, institui mutandi aeris gratia ruri tantisper agere, donec illa caeli inclaementia mitior Florentiae redderetur. Itaque invitatus a me Manuel, ut erat vir omni humanitate humanior, rus una mecum profectus est, ubi quandiu Florentiam pernicies illa

you were recalling about slavery from the conversation of your son Onofrio just two days ago, when you summarily dealt with the disadvantages of exile.

Leonardo. On the contrary, Rinaldo, since that nuisance Poggio is 128 gone and there is still enough daylight for the remnant of this commendable task that he held in prospect about reasoning and choice, we should beg Palla carefully to complete it. Your entire discourse pleases me, Palla, and in particular the part where you expounded for us doctrines from the outstanding philosophical schools. I have certainly always thought you a great and wise man. But, to tell you the truth, I did not suppose that you had mastered in such detail, and with such learning, what the most penetrating philosophers discovered with their great leisure and enormous efforts.

Palla. Do not be surprised, Leonardo. Have you forgotten what 129 Philolaus is reported to have said: some discourses are better than we are?[98] I think this must be understood not only about prophets and Sibyls and inspired men, but also about all those who say something over their heads, as I just did in your presence, you who are the most serious and erudite of men. You see, this discourse is not mine but that of a very great and wise man whom you and I once had as a teacher and a friend, Manuel Chrysoloras, whose grandniece Theodora, a modest and chaste young woman, daughter of John Chrysoloras, our friend Francisco Filelfo here has as his wife.[99] For at the time when that 130 distinguished and supreme philosopher was teaching Greek wisdom in Florence, and this city of ours and practically all Tuscany was suffering from plague, I decided for the sake of a change of air to spend time in the countryside until the rigors of the climate softened in Florence. Therefore, on my invitation, Manuel, being a man more humane than all humanity, set out with me for the countryside, where he remained constantly for as long as the plague was attacking Florence, for the air was

vexavit, mansit assidue. Nam ruri quod est mihi in Casentino,[88]
131   erat aer saluberrimus. Et quoniam ad quietem veneramus, non
ad laborem, ocio magis quam negocio studebam, idque ob eam
maxime rationem, ut viro illi quem ego, ut nosti, plurimum
venerabar, iucunditati essem in ea calamitate temporum, non
molestiae. Tum ille postridie ex quo eo loci perveneramus, circi-
ter meridiem, cum amota mensa simul sederemus in porticu,
magno cum silentio, ad me conversus: 'Cur non nostri, o Pallas,'
inquit, 'similes sumus?' Ad quod ego dictum veluti excitatus
132   non sine pudore subdidi: 'Cur istud, o Manuel?' Tum ille: 'Scis
enim agere proprium esse hominis. Nam caetera animalia, quoniam ratione carent, agere non dicuntur, quemadmodum ne
pueri quidem ob tenerae aetatis imbecillitatem, nec etiam ii qui
sanae mentis non sunt. Solos agere dicimus, qui rationis ductu
id faciunt. Nam appetitio nobis est communis cum beluis, quae
mentis inopes ad sensum omnia referunt.' Et ita vir ille doctissimus et optimus nihil omisit quod ad totius hominis vitam,
quod ad bene beateque vivendum pertineret. Quare non ipse
meum quicquam locutus sum, sed quae ex Manuele Chrysolora
audisse memini.

133 *Leonardus.* Recte quidem mones, o Pallas. Didicisti quae loqueris
ex illo viro qui et eloquentiam tot saecula iam sepultam et poli-
tiores omnes ingenii disciplinas apud Latinos tanquam ab inferis in lucem revocavit. Itaque prosequere quae coepisti, quaeque
ad humanam actionem omnino pertinent ratiocinationis praecepta nobis electionisque ostende.

Pallas. Ego tibi, Leonarde, nihil ostendam. Quis enim te nostra
aetate aut eloquentior aut doctior? Sed posteaquam eo res est
adducta ut minus cautus in me fuerim, malo vos imprudentiae
meae testes quam pervicaciae, modo intelligatis omnes me non
vobiscum sed cum his duobus adolescentibus habere sermo-
134   nem. Videmus non minus consuetudine fieri quam natura ut in

very salubrious at my estate in the Casentino. And since we had   131
come for rest, not for work, I was eager for leisure rather than
business, especially because I wished to be at that calamitous
time a source of pleasure rather than a burden to that man,
whom, as you know, I deeply venerated. Then, the day after our
arrival, around midday, after dinner, we were seated together
in the portico. Amid the deep silence he turned to me and
said, "Why, Palla, are we not like ourselves?" Stimulated by
this question, I replied, not without embarrassment: "How so,
Manuel?" He replied: "You know that action is proper to man.   132
For other animals, lacking reason, are not said to act, just as
children are not, by reason of the weakness of their tender
years, or the insane. We only say that they act who do it under
the guidance of reason. For we have appetency in common with
beasts, who, being devoid of mind, relate everything to the
senses." And thus that most learned and best man omitted
nothing relevant to the life of the whole man, to living well and
blessedly. Therefore I did not say anything of my own, but
what I remember hearing from Manuel Chrysoloras.

Leonardo. You are right to remind me, Palla. You have learned   133
what you are saying from that man by whom eloquence, buried
already for so many centuries, was called back among the Latins
as if from the underworld to the light, and so too were all the
cultivated disciplines of the mind.[100] Therefore continue what
you have begun, and show the precepts regarding reasoning and
choice that are relevant to human action.

Palla. I shall show *you* nothing, Leonardo. For what man of our
time is more eloquent or more learned than you? But now that
things have come to the point where I've abandoned caution, I'd
rather have you as witnesses of my imprudence than of my
stubbornness, provided that you understand that I am conduct-
ing a conversation, not with you, but with these two young
men. We see that it happens no less by habit than by nature   134

omni consultatione deliberationeve antequam aut agendum quicquam aut non agendum eligamus, intellectu atque ratione etiam atque etiam inquiramus quid sit factu optimum. Quam ipsam Virgilius sententiam secutus, ut mihi videtur:

Tuus, inquit, o regina, quid optes
explorare labor, mihi iussa capessere fas est.

Quasi dicere voluerit poeta prudentissimus: inquirere quid eligas, quod est rationis proprium, tui laboris sit, at mei quae iusseris efficere. Agimus enim secundum electionem, sed consultando rationandoque eligimus. Itaque ut de ratiocinatione — quoniam de appetitione antea percucurrimus — quod videtur esse consequens percurramus, ultroneum in nulla appetitionis specie esse constat. Ultroneum vero est invito contrarium. Eodem etiam modo qui faciens quid cognoscit aut hominem cui faciat aut qua ratione aut cuius rei gratia, is est invito contrarius. Quotiens enim accidit ut quempiam cognoscamus amemusque cui cupientes benefacere secus per imprudentiam faciamus? Dedit Lucretio poetae amica veneni quippiam, credens id esse philtrum quo ille in amorem sui magis accenderetur. Lucretius eo poculo insanivit. Non ultro fecisse id mulier existimanda est, sed imprudenter, ob idque invite, quoniam nihil huiusmodi secum ante mente versasset. Et filiae Peliae a Medea falso persuasae patrem, quem servare voluerant, perdiderunt, et id quidem invite quoque, quoniam ignoranter.

136   Quidquid enim aut necessitate facimus aut vi aut per imprudentiam, id invitum dicendum est. Nullo certe pacto ultroneum esse potest, quod sine intellectu et ratiocinatione sit factum.

that in every consultation and deliberation, before we choose what we should do or not do, we inquire repeatedly by intellect and reasoning what it is best to do. In line with this idea, I believe, Vergil says:

> It is your task, your majesty, to discover
> What you wish, it is right for me to carry out your
>   orders,[101]

as if the wisest poet meant to say: let your task be to inquire what to choose, which is proper to reason, but mine to carry out what you have ordered. For we act according to choice but choose by deliberating and reasoning. Therefore, to touch on what seems to be the next topic, reasoning — as we've already touched on appetency — it is agreed that voluntary behavior is not found in any species of appetency.[102] The voluntary is indeed opposite to the unwilling. By the same token, the person who in acting knows either the person for whom he does it, or for what reason or for what motive he does it — that person is the opposite of unwilling. For how often does it happen that we know and love people and want to benefit them, but harm them instead because of imprudence? A girlfriend gave some poison to the poet Lucretius in the belief that it was a philter for inciting him to greater love for her. By drinking it Lucretius was driven insane.[103] The woman should not be thought to have done this voluntarily but inadvertently and therefore unwillingly, since she had in mind nothing of the sort. And the daughters of Pelias, fraudulently persuaded by Medea, killed their father whom they had wanted to save, and this act, too, they did unwillingly, since it was done in ignorance.

Whatever we do by necessity or force or through lack of foresight must be called involuntary.[104] What is done without knowledge and reasoning can by no means be voluntary.

135

136

Mulierem Aristoteles refert dedisse cuipiam amatorium poculum, quo ille accepto animam efflavit; at mulierem in Ariopagum cum fugisset, idcirco esse ab Ariopagitis poena liberatam, quoniam id facinoris per imprudentiam perpetrasset. Dederat enim id poculi genus non ad mortem, sed ad amorem. Nam si de morte quicquam esset praemeditata, non dedisset. Haec igitur rationis intellectusque inquisitio et praemeditatio diligens tantam vim habet ut ultroneum secus esse non possit. Quidquid ergo in nobis fuerit non agere, et agimus tamen, et id quidem scienter ac propter ipsum, hoc necessario et dici ultroneum et haberi convenit. Quaecunque vero imprudenter agimus, etiam si nulla necessitas sit, si nulla vis, hoc ipso quod ignoramus, ea sunt invita. His vero tempestive admoneor, ut ne illud quoque praetereundum sit, scire et cognoscere dici duobus modis: uno cum habemus scientiam, altero cum utimur scientia quam habemus. Nam qui ea quam scientiam tenet minus utatur, interdum etiam sine iniuria dici potest ignorans, cum id scilicet recto quodam consilio fecerit, interdum vero non potest, ut si negligentia in causa fuerit ut ea minus sit usus. Itidemque siquis scientia careat, ita se facit vituperationi obnoxium si aut propter negligentiam aut propter voluptatem aut propter aliam animi perturbationem eo careat quod vel facile scitu vel necessarium vel pulcherrimum sit. Et ne sim prolyxior quam oportet: quoniam ex ante dictis videtur ultroneum ratione potissimum intellectuque definiri, reliquum est ut eadem brevitate de electione commentemur. Verum nescio quid Manettus secum clam loquitur. Nunquid est quicquam, Manette, quod improbes? Dic, obsecro. Malo enim discere quam docere, praesertim a te,

137

138

Aristotle reports that a woman gave a man a love potion; when he took it, he died. But when she stood trial at the Areopagus, she was acquitted by the jurors because she had done this through lack of foresight: she had given him that type of potion not for murder but for love. If it had been a premeditated murder, she wouldn't have given it to him. Therefore the investigation of reason and intellect and careful planning have such force that the voluntary cannot exist otherwise. Hence whatever it   137
was possible for us not to do, but we did nonetheless with knowledge and for its own sake, it is fitting to call and think of as voluntary.[105] Whatever we do from lack of foresight, even if no necessity is involved and no force applied, are involuntary for the very reason that we are in a state of ignorance. By these examples I am reminded in timely fashion that the following point should not be passed by: to know and understand are understood in two senses: in one sense when we have knowledge, in another when we use the knowledge that we have. For he who fails to use the knowledge he possesses can sometimes rightly be called ignorant; but when he has done this with a certain kind of correct planning, he sometimes cannot be excused as ignorant. For example, if negligence were responsible for his failure to use his knowledge. Likewise if someone lacks knowledge, he exposes himself to criticism, for example if through negligence or on account of pleasure or another emotion he should be lacking in what is easily known or necessary to know or most excellent to know. And so—not to go on   138
longer than necessary—since from the previous arguments the voluntary seems to be defined above all by reasoning and understanding, it remains for us to discuss choice with the same concision. But I rather think that Manetti is muttering to himself. Surely, Manetti, there is nothing that you disapprove, is there? Please tell me. I would rather learn than teach, especially

quem et acerrimo ingenio esse novi et cum doctrina, tum diligentia non vulgari. Nam quid loquar de Leonardo, quo praesente vel os aperire non possum non erubescere?

139 *Leonardus.* Perge, Pallas, secundis avibus. Et perfice nobis munus quod es aggressus. Nam si esculentis istiusmodi me referseris, nulla mihi alia caena[89] opus sit. Oratio mihi tua nectare omni suavior est et ambrosia omni iucundior.

Manettus. Et ego quoque nihil est quod impraesentiarum velim abs te requirere. Cras fortasse quaedam me docebis, si volueris.

Pallas. Ego te docebo, Manette?

140 *Manettus.* Docebis tu, inquam, Pallas, et erudite et facile. Potes id enim tu unus omnium quampulcherrime. Aliud tamen erat quod mecum nunc ipse meditabar. Et id certe nequaquam reticescam. In ea sciendi tua et cognoscendi partitione atque differentia—quae mihi profecto probatur plurimum visaque est tota Aristotelica, tota philosophica—dixisti et illum qui scientiam aliquam cognitu dignam ob suam vel negligentiam vel improbam ullam animi perturbationem non haberet, et illum quoque qui scientiam habens ea ob easdem causas non uteretur, esse

141 vituperandum. Itaque mecum ipse nescio quid de Karolo Arretino commentabar. Is enim et Graecam et Latinam eloquentiam profitetur. At Graece ne verbum quidem suo accentu, sua voce pronunciet; Latine vero ita inepte loquitur ut omnium ineptitudine videatur ineptior. Unde id, Pallas, putas accidere? Nunquid doctrina hominem an usu putas inferiorem?

Pallas. Respondeat tibi conterraneus eius Leonardus. Nam ego non ita familiariter isto homine unquam sum usus ut de ipso quicquam aut possim aut velim iudicare.

142 *Leonardus.* Non patiar me rogari, et hoc sane ob eam rem maxime, ne quod de electione restat in alterum diem reiciatur. Video

from you; I know you to be a man of the sharpest intellect and of no ordinary learning and care. Indeed, what should I say of Leonardo, in whose presence I can only blush just to open my mouth.

Leonardo. Carry on, Palla, with good omens. Finish for us the task   139
you have set yourself. Once you have filled me with morsels like these, I need no other dinner. To me your words are sweeter than any nectar and more savory than any ambrosia.

Manetti. I, too, would ask nothing else from you for the moment; perhaps tomorrow you will teach me something, if you would be willing.

Palla. I shall teach *you*, Manetti?

Manetti. I say you will, Palla, and with both learning and ease.   140
Indeed, you are the only one who can do so with consummate style. But there is another matter I was reflecting on just now, and I'm not going to keep quiet about it. In your division and differentiation of knowledge and understanding—of which I highly approve, and it appears completely Aristotelian and philosophical[106]—you said that criticism is incurred both by him who lacks worthy knowledge because of his own negligence or some shameful emotion, and by him who has knowledge but for the same reasons fails to use it. This made me think about   141
Carlo Marsuppini. He claims expertise in both Greek and Latin eloquence, but in Greek he pronounces not a word with its proper accent or sound, and he speaks Latin so awkwardly that he seems more inept than anyone.[107] How, Palla, do you think that this has come about? Do you think the man deficient in learning or in application?

Palla. Let his countryman Leonardo give you a reply. I've never been so close a friend of that fellow that I could or would wish to pass judgment upon him.

Leonardo. I don't care to be asked, mostly so that what remains to   142
be discussed about choice is not postponed to another day; I

enim solem iam inclinare. Karolus multa legit, multa audivit. Sed quoniam neque in doctoribus neque in libris ullo discrimine usus est, ita habet confusa omnia inter seque repugnantia ut neque sese ipse intelligat nec intelligatur ab aliis. Quod autem inepte loquitur, ingenii tarditas est in causa. Qua ipsa re fit ut et parum admodum scribat et siquid tandem aliquando scribit, id omne aridum durumque sit. Non enim homo vel in scientiae cognitione vel in eius usu accusandus mihi videtur, sed tum natura, tum fortuna, quarum altera doctores obtulit Karolo indoctos et indisertos, altera effinxit[90] hominem ingenio hebeti ac saxeo.

143 *Rainaldus.* Perhumane, Pallas, facit Leonardus, qui conterranei sui flagitia fortunae vitio naturaeque occultat. Nam neque negligentiam Karoli meminit, non dico circa quaestum et foenus, cui unus omnium diligentissime studet, sed circa laudatissimas disciplinas, nec meminit incontinentiam nec invidentiam in bonos omnis atque doctos viros, qua ita dies noctesque maceratur ut sui compos esse non possit. Sed quid, Manette, sentis de tuo Poggio, qui cum praestantiorem disciplinam teneat prorsus nullam, etsi lingua crassa est et voce rauca atque rancidula, ita tamen scribit ut laudetur a multis?

144 *Manettus.* Et a quibus laudatur Poggius, Rainalde? A cerdonibus sane et pistoribus, ab imperitis, ab impudicis omnibus. Nam quid egregium aut admirabile prae se ferre queat oratio quae nullis firmioris scientiae radicibus haereat, nullis sententiarum luminibus illustretur? Quis enim aut qualis sit usus qui a nulla scientia proficiscitur?

Leonardus. Longe utilius fuerit, ut mea fert opinio, si Karolo Poggioque omissis de electione Pallas quod recepit absolvat. Perge, Pallas, quaeso, quid de electione sentias perfice.

see that the sun is already setting. Carlo has read and heard a great deal, but since he has used no discrimination in regard to teachers or books, he has his knowledge all jumbled together and self-contradictory so that he neither understands it himself nor is understood by others. His slow intelligence is responsible for his clumsy speech. The result is that he writes little,[108] and what he writes is dry and harsh. It seems to me that the man should not be criticized either for his knowledge or for his lack of application. Nature and fortune should rather be blamed: the latter exposed him to teachers who lacked learning and eloquence; the former gave him a dull and inflexible mind.

Rinaldo. Leonardo is behaving very politely, Palla, in concealing his   143
countryman's sins beneath the fault of fortune and nature. He forgets about Carlo's negligence, not with respect to profit-making and usury, which he pursues more energetically than anyone, but with respect to the most highly prized disciplines, and he forgets his lack of self-control and envy toward all the good and learned men, which so consumes him day and night that he couldn't be in his right mind. But, Manetti, what do you think about your friend Poggio, who, though he is master of no outstanding discipline and has a coarse tongue and a hoarse and foul voice, nonetheless writes in a way that many find commendable?

Manetti. But who commends Poggio, Rinaldo? Artisans, bakers,   144
philistines, every shameless person. Can a discourse display any remarkable or admirable qualities when it is not rooted in solid knowledge and is embellished by no brilliant ideas? What kind of experience is it that derives from utter ignorance?

Leonardo. It would be far more useful, in my opinion, if we set Carlo and Poggio aside and Palla would conclude the discourse he undertook about choice. Please carry on, Palla, and finish discussing your ideas about choice.

145 *Pallas.* Faciam, Leonarde, quod petis. Verum nihil a me volo ex-
pectetis quod nesciam. Philosophorum enim et doctissimorum
hominum est huiusmodi commentatio, non Pallantis. Primum
igitur mihi dicendum videtur electio quid non sit, deinde quid
sit. Amotis enim tenebris mendacii, veritatis lux et clarius patet
et gratius. Electionem alii ultroneum, alii eam quae a ratiocinatione manat opinionem, plaerique appetitionem esse existima-
runt. Et appetitionem quidem in tris partes antea distribuimus:
voluntatem, iram, cupiditatem. Sed ira et cupiditas cum nobis
sit cum beluis quoque communis, qui electio habeatur, quae
146 cum sit cum ratione, solius est hominis? Quinetiam longe magis et irascuntur et cupiunt quae animalia ratione carent quam
ipsi nos, qui imperio ducimur rationis. Atqui sine ira et cupiditate multa eligimus. Illis vero vaehementius agitati non eligimus, sed constantiae inservimus. Praeterea cupiditas et ira sine
molestia animi nunquam sunt, sed electio sine molestia etiam
esse potest. Et Paris cum rapiebat Helenam, et Tydeus cum in
caput Menalippi[91] dentibus saeviebat, non electione, sed hic ira,
ille cupiditate ducebatur. Ut enim claemens et continens non
pro ira et cupiditate claementer agit et continenter, sed pro electione, ita incontinens et iracundus contempta electione iracunde
147 agit atque incontinenter, cupiditati iraeque obtemperans. Cum
igitur nec ira nec cupiditas electio sit, nunquid esset voluntas?
Non nulli enim idem esse voluerunt electionem et voluntatem.
Sed secus est. Nam voluntas eorum est etiam quae esse non
possunt, ut si velimus aut volatu per aera ipsum vehi aut fieri
immortales. At quicquam huiusmodi nisi qui mentis sit inops
eligat nemo. Ea enim eligimus quae per nos agi posse arbitramur. Nam siquid etiam posset agi quod a nobis tamen non
possit, frustra de eo futura sit nostra omnis electio, ut si

Palla. I shall do as you ask, Leonardo. But I want you not to ex-   145
pect anything from me that I don't know. This sort of treatment belongs to philosophers and learned men, not to Palla.
First, then, I think I must tell what choice is not, then what it
is,[109] for once the shadows of falsehood have been removed, the
light of truth is revealed and is more brilliant and welcome.
Some think that choice is voluntary, others an opinion flowing
from reasoning, many that it is appetency. And we previously
divided appetency into three parts: will, anger, desire.[110] But
since we have anger and desire in common with beasts, how is
choice possessed, which belongs to man alone, since it involves
reason? Furthermore, animals that lack reason grow angry and   146
desire far more than we who are led by the command of reason.
Indeed, we make many choices without anger and desire. When
we are violently stirred by these emotions, we do not choose,
but subject ourselves to self-control. Moreover, desire and anger
always disturb the mind, but choice can be free of mental dis-
turbances. When Paris abducted Helen and Tydeus savaged
Menalippus' head with his teeth, they were guided not by
choice, but the one by anger, the other by desire.[111] Just as a
mild and continent man does not act mildly and continently
out of anger or desire but out of choice, so the incontinent and
angry man, throwing choice to the winds, acts angrily and incontinently in compliance with desire and anger. Since, then,   147
neither anger nor desire is choice, is the will choice? Some indeed have claimed that choice and will are the same, but it is
not so. For we can also will impossible things, for instance, if
we were to wish to fly through the air or become immortal. But
no one except a mentally defective person would make such a
choice. We choose things we think we can do. If something
could be done that nonetheless could not be done by us, any
choice we might make concerning it would be in vain—for ex-

Poggium velimus sobrium aut non maledicum. Quo fit ut eligibile sit eorum aliquid quae sunt in nobis.

148   Ad haec electio non est finis, sed eorum quae ad finem referuntur. Voluntas autem finis est. Volumus enim bene valere, sed
quod ad bonam valitudinem refertur, eligimus: equitare, currere, luctari, eodemque modo stare, sedere, quiescere, et aut hoc
aut alio cibo uti. Volumus omnes felices esse. Eligimus vero quo
felices simus: alii sapientiam, alii divitias, alii aliud, ut quisque
sibi felicitatem definierit. Sed quoniam videmus voluntatem et
electionem non idem esse, inquirendum puto, opinione sit.
Nam cum eligere sit aliquid quasi melius ex aliis propositis
legere, altero scilicet alteri praelato tanquam meliore deteriori,
cumque id sine intellectu et meditatione fieri nequeat, eo fit
saepe ut ea opinemur quae ipsi praestare non possumus, ut siquis aut vires Gangaridarum opinetur aut diametrum et latus
mensuram admittere aut circulum transire in quadrangulum
149   posse. Eorum est enim electio, quae nostrae sunt potestatis, et
non aeterna, cum opinio aeternorum etiam esse queat. Praeterea bonum malumve eligimus. At opinio veri est aut falsi. Et
quod opinio ipsa non facit, per electionem aut bonis sumus aut
malis moribus. Facitque opinio ut quid ipsa res sit aut non sit,
conducatne an id minus aut aliquid huiusmodi nosse videamur,
at electio ut vel sequamur vel aspernemur. Magisque laudatur
electio, quoniam novit quid expediat quam quid sit rectum.
150   Opinio vero veritatis laudatur. Acciditque nonnunquam ut melius opinantes quod deterius fuerit victi perturbatione eligamus,
id quod Ovidius Naso minime ignorans ita Medeam loquentem
facit:

ample, if we willed that Poggio be sober and not given to slander. Hence the power of choice refers to things within our power.

In addition, choice is not an end but chooses things related 148 to an end.[112] But the will *is* an end. For we wish to enjoy good health, but we choose what is related to good health: to ride horses, run, wrestle, and by the same token to stand, sit, rest, and eat this or that. We all wish to be happy. But we choose that by which we may be happy: some wisdom, some wealth, others something else as each person has defined his own happiness. But since we see that will and choice are not the same, I think we ought to ask whether choice comes about through opinion. Since choosing is as it were to select the better among different options, with one thing preferred to the other, like preferring better to worse, and since this is impossible without understanding and thought, often the result is that we hold opinions about things that we ourselves cannot demonstrate; for example, if someone has an opinion about the strength of the Ganges-dwellers,[113] or that a diameter and a side allow for measurement, or that a circle can be squared. For choice is of 149 things that are within our power and not eternal, although opinion can also be about eternal things.[114] Moreover, we choose good or evil. But opinion is about true or false. By choice we are either of good or bad character, something that opinion by itself does not bring about. Opinion enables us to seem to know what a thing is or is not, whether it is in our interest or not or anything of this kind, but choice enables us to pursue or reject something. Choice is commended because it knows what is expedient rather than what is correct. Holding a true opinion 150 is commendable. It sometimes comes to pass that, though holding a better opinion, we are overcome by emotion and choose what is worse, a thing which Ovid makes Medea say:

Video meliora proboque,
deteriora sequor.

Haec enim propter amoris intemperantiam maluit Iasonis adul-
teri quam patriae patrisque salutem. Et cum eorum proprie sit
electio quae maxime novimus bona esse, interdum opinamur
quippiam esse bonum quod non admodum novimus. Insuper
quod opinioni est voluntatique commune, opinamur finem. Eligimus ea quae sunt ad finem, ut integritatem sensuum nemo
eligit, sed ea quibus sit sensibus integris. Semperque omnino
declarat qui eligit, et quid eligat et cuius gratia. Est certe illud
aliud quod facit ut aliquid eligamus, et hoc item aliud quod
propter illud eligimus. Cum igitur velle et opinari maxime sint
finis, eligere vero eorum quae ad finem referuntur, quid dicemus
electionem esse? Ultroneumne fortassis? Hoc enim reliquum
est ex iis quae modo proposuimus. An id etiam non dicemus?
Non enim viri atque prudentis ultroneum magis est quam cum
omnis aetatis et omnis sexus, tum etiam omnium animantium.
Et quod repente inconsyderateque fit, ultro certe fit, at non secundum electionem, quae sine ratiocinatione et intellectu esse
non potest. Quare cum electio nec ultroneum sit nec opinio nec
etiam appetitio, quid ea est tandem? Frustra enim sit opus nostrum, quod quid electio non sit ostendimus, nisi quid etiam ea
est intelligamus. Et ut nostra oratio tempestive ad ultroneum,
quo de antea dicere coeperamus, revertatur: id duplex est. Nam
aliud est ultroneum, quod nobis est commune cum reliquis
animantibus omnibus (et id quidem sine ratiocinatione), aliud
vero proprium nostrum, quod est secundum intellectum, quoniam intellectum a ratione nihil nunc differre volumus. Nam et

151

152

153

I see and approve the better course
But follow the worse.[115]

For because of the unruly passion of love she preferred the safety of the adulterer Jason to that of her homeland and father. Though properly choice is of things that we particularly know to be good, sometimes we hold the opinion that something is good but do not really know that. Furthermore — a feature that is common to opinion and will — we hold opinions about an end. We choose things that lead to an end; for instance, no one chooses the soundness of the senses but the things by which the senses possess soundness.[116] The person who makes a choice always shows both what he is choosing and the reason why. Certainly it is one thing that causes us to choose something and another thing for us to choose because of that thing. Since, then, to wish and opine belong to a goal but choice is of things that are oriented toward a goal, what shall we assert choice to be? Something voluntary perhaps? This is what remains of the options we just now set out. Or shall we say that it is not even this? For voluntary action [as such] belongs no more to a prudent man than it does to persons of any age or sex, or even to all living things. And what happens suddenly and without consideration certainly occurs voluntarily, but not according to choice, which cannot exist without reasoning and understanding. Therefore, since choice is neither the voluntary nor opinion nor appetency, what is it, then? Our effort showing what choice *is not* would be in vain unless we also understand what it *is*. So to bring our discourse back in timely fashion to the voluntary, which we began to discuss earlier: it is twofold. One [genus] of the voluntary we have in common with all the other living things (one that occurs without a reasoning process); the other is proper to us and is related to intellect, since our present claim is that intellect is no different from reason. For when we say

151

152

153

cum dicimus 'rationem superiorem,' aliud nihil quam intellectum significamus, et intellectum item pro ratione ponimus cum circa res inferiores humanasque versatur actiones. Cum igitur 'ratiocinationem' dico, eam non magis pro rationis quam pro intellectus inquisitione accipi volo. Ponimus, inquam, electionem in eo ultronei genere quod est secundum intellectum, et id quidem ita ut intelligamus non esse id eligibile quidquid est ultroneum, sed id solum quod venerit antea in consultationem. Est enim electio cum ratiocinatione, qua quidem re fit ut neque puerorum sit electio nec omnis hominis. Nam neque stulti neque mulieres eo sunt rationis usu ut recte quicquam possint eligere.

154   Sed hac de re apertius, ne nostra nimis protrahatur oratio. Electio est eorum quae — ut paulo ante dicebatur — sunt ad finem, quaeque possunt esse et non esse, et ipsa quidem talia ut de iis nobis consultatio haberi queat. Nam quaedam in consultationem non veniunt. Quaecunque enim possunt esse, ea non possunt et esse et non esse. Horum sane generatio potestatis nostrae non est, cum alia sint naturae vi, alia per alias causas fiant. Sed in ea cadit electio, quae non modo et esse possunt et non esse, sed etiam de quibus sit nobis potestas consultandi.

155   Haec vero sunt omnia quae ipsi agere possumus vel non agere. Itaque de rebus Hyperboreis minime consultamus, neque quo modo circulus fiat triangulus. Nam et res Hyperboreae in nostra potestate non sunt, et circulus fieri triangulus omnino non potest. At neque de his omnibus consultamus quae agere ipsi possumus. Nam sine ulla consultatione et sedemus et surgimus et alia permulta huiusmodi facimus. Nec item obscurum videri debet electionem non esse opinionem, cum et ad finem haec referatur, et eorum esse possit quae in nobis non sunt.

"higher reason," we mean nothing else than intellect, and we likewise posit intellect instead of reason when treating lesser affairs and human actions. When therefore I speak of "a process of reasoning," I wish it to be understood as much in the sense of "an investigation by the intellect" as in the sense of reason. We assign, I repeat, choice to the [second] genus of the voluntary related to intellect, and indeed in such a way that we understand that the act of choice does not relate to all voluntary acts whatever, but only to those that come under prior deliberative review. For choice occurs together with reasoning, which is why choice is not characteristic of children or of all human beings. For neither fools nor women have the use of reason in such a way that they can make correct choices in all cases.

To describe the matter more accessibly (and to keep the discussion within bounds)[117] choice relates to those matters — as I said a little while ago — that aim at a goal, that are contingent, and that can be subject to our deliberation. Certain things are not subject to deliberation; and whatever is contingent cannot both exist and not exist. The generation of these things is not in our power, since some come about by the force of nature, others by other causes. But choice falls within the scope of those things that not only are contingent but also subject to our deliberation. These are all the things that are contingent upon our power. Therefore we do not deliberate about the Hyperboreans' affairs nor how a circle may become a triangle. For the Hyperboreans' affairs are not in our power,[118] and a circle cannot become a triangle. But neither do we deliberate about all matters within our power. For we sit down and stand up and do many other such things without deliberation. And it should likewise be clear that choice is not opinion, since the latter is related to an end and can be held of things that are not in our power.

154

155

156 *Manettus.* Verum dic, Pallas, quaeso, quid tandem medici de iis consultant quorum scientiam ipsi teneant? At grammatici non consultant?

Pallas. Huius rei causa est, Manette, quod cum duobus modis erretur, aut rationando aut secundum sensum, in medicina quidem utroque modo errari potest, in grammatica vero secundum sensum et actionem. Nemo enim consultat qui sit scribendum Ciceronis nomen. Itaque erratum non sit in ipso intellectu—id quod in scientiis solet accidere—sed in actione scribendi. Et enim ea deliberatione non egent in quibus intellectus non erat, sed haec potius errato subiacent, in quibus quod opus sit, inde-

157 finitum est. At sensus et actionis consyderatio nunquam finem sit habitura. Cum ergo neque opinio electio sit neque voluntas (hoc est nec ratiocinatio nec appetitio), quid eam tandem esse volumus? Electio profecto est, ut mihi videtur, non hae ambae, sed tanquam utrunque harum. Quis enim repente eligit quod esset voluntatis? At quia nobis videtur quid agendum, idcirco agere hoc volumus. Sic igitur fit ut voluntatem opinio antecedat. Et quanquam videmus ambas existere homini eligenti, et opinionem et voluntatem, non tamen ambas electionem esse dicimus, sed utrunque harum.

158 Quod ut sit facilius cognitu, declaretur exemplo. Animal et animo constat et corpore, nec tamen animal dicitur esse corpus secundum seipsum, nec animus solus, sed quiddam animo corporeque compositum. Quanquam igitur ambo animali existunt animusque et corpus, haud tamen ambo haec animal esse dicimus, sed tanquam utrunque horum, ita habet electio ad ratiocinationem quae forma sit et appetitionem quae materiae locum teneat. Quod autem opinione constet atque voluntate electio, eo argumento probari potest quod eligendi munere tunc utimur, cum verbi gratia e duobus propositis alterum alteri

Manetti. But please tell me, Palla: why do physicians deliberate   156
about matters they have knowledge of, but grammarians do not
deliberate?

Palla. The cause of this, Manetti, is that, since error arises in two
ways, either by reasoning or because of the senses, in medicine
error arises in both ways, but in grammar because of sense and
action. No one deliberates over how Cicero's name should be
spelled.[119] Thus there would be no error in the understanding
itself — as generally happens in the sciences — but in the act of
writing. For where the intellect is not involved there is no need
for deliberation; error rather arises in matters where what is
needful remains undefined. But deliberation over sensation and   157
action is never going to come to an end. Since therefore choice
is neither opinion nor will (that is, neither a process of reasoning nor appetency), what do we claim that it is? Choice is
surely, I think, not *both* of these but, as it were, *each* of them.
For who instantly chooses what is within the purview of his
will? Rather, we will to do something because it [already] appears to us to be something we must do. In the final analysis,
opinion precedes will. And though we see both of them, opinion and will, in the man who is making a choice, we nonetheless
do not say that choice is both of them, but each of them [acting
in sequence].

    Let this be illustrated by an example to make it easier to   158
understand. A living thing consists of mind and body. A body
by itself is not called a living thing, nor a mind alone, but the
living thing is a certain compound of mind and body.[120] Therefore, though both mind and body are present in a living thing,
we do not say that a living thing is *both* of these but that it has
each of these. Thus, in the case of choice, the process of reasoning takes the place of form, and appetency the place of matter.
That choice consists of opinion and can be proven by the argument that we use the faculty of choosing when, for example, we

159 anteponimus. Quod sine consyderatione et consilio fieri qui potest? Opinio enim quasi animi iudicium antecedit electionem. Nam necesse est ante iudicemus quam eligamus, iudicare autem ante consultationem haudquaquam possumus. Inde fit ut ex opinione consultativa sit electio. Non autem de fine quem veluti calcem sagittario proponi nobis oportet, sed de iis consultamus quae ad finem tendunt, hocne an hoc expediat, aut si id visum fuerit, de modo consultamus, utrum hic modus servandus sit an ille, quod tam diu facimus donec generationis principium quod vocant ad nos ipsos reduxerimus. Si igitur perspicuum est ex ante dictis electionem eorum bonorum esse quae ad finem referuntur, et non ipsius finis, et eorum quidem quae tum agi a nobis possunt, tum controversiam afferunt hocne an illud sit eligendum, de his omnium primum est opus, ut intellectu quamdiligentissime inquiramus consultemusque; deinde ubi nobis re etiam atque etiam inquisita quid melius visum fuerit, ita quaedam agendi appetitio exuscitatur, quod tandem

160 cum agimus, ex electione agimus. Electio igitur est consultativa appetitio cum intellectu eorum quae agere ipsi possumus. Nam omnes quae eligimus, prius ratiocinando consultamus. Nec omnia quae consultamus, eadem eligimus. Dicitur autem consultativa, quoniam eius principium et causa consultatio sit, et propter consultationem appetitio fit. Quare consultatione quidquid caret, electione etiam careat necesse est. Atqui opinari quidem faciendumne aliquid sit an id minus, vel pluribus potest existere. At quod ex ratiocinatione proficiscitur, non potest. Nam id quo causam aliquam inspicimus, est animi consultativum. Si

prefer one plan to another. How could this happen without thought and planning? Opinion, as it were a judgment of the mind, precedes choice. For we must pass a judgment before choosing, and we can scarcely pass a judgment prior to deliberation. It follows that choice derives from deliberative opinion. We do not, however, deliberate about a goal that must be placed before us like a mark for an archer, but about those matters that look toward a goal, whether this or that is in our interest, or if this point is settled, we deliberate about the method, whether this method should be followed or that, which we continue to do until we have restored the so-called principle of generation to ourselves. If, then, it is clear from our previous discussion that a choice is made of those goods that look to a goal and not of the goal itself, and of those things that can be done by us, then they bring up a debate as to whether this or that should be chosen. We must first of all inquire and deliberate with our intellect as carefully as possible about these things; then, after we have investigated again and again what would be better, a certain desire to act is aroused, since when we finally act we do so by choice. Choice is therefore deliberative appetency with an understanding of those things that we ourselves can do. For all the things that we choose, we first deliberate beforehand by reasoning; but we do not choose all the things we deliberate over. It is called deliberative because deliberation is its origin and cause, and appetency arises because of deliberation. Thus an action that lacks deliberation also must be without choice. Thinking about whether something should be done or not can arise in several ways, but what originates from reasoning cannot. For the deliberative faculty of the mind is that by which we examine some cause. If there is one cause "for the

159

160

enim cuius gratia una est causa (quoniam quare causam dicunt, cuius gratia quid aut est aut fit), hoc in causa esse dicimus, ut si idcirco me dicam metuere patriae libertati, quia boni cives urbe eiiciuntur. Non ergo illos consultativos esse existimabimus qui nullam sibi calcem ad quam respiciant proposuerint.

161 Ut igitur eo redeamus unde non multo ante digressi sumus: quoniam quod est in nobis ipsis, vel agere vel non agere, siquis id egerit aut minus egerit propter id ipsum et non propter imprudentiam, hic ultro vel egisse vel non egisse putandus est; cumque permulta huiusmodi agimus nulla consultatione usi, nulla praemeditatione, eo fit necessario ut omne eligibile sit ultroneum, at ultroneum quod sit, id nequaquam esse eligibile. Et omnia quae sint secundum electionem esse ultronea, at ultronea

162 non omnia esse secundum electionem. Quod autem electio neque simpliciter voluntas sit neque opinio, sed quod et opinione et appetitione constat, quando ex habita consultatione ambae inter se[92] uno fine convenerint, quoniam puto satis esse dilucidum, reliquum est ut non modo nobis paupertas metuenda non sit, sed eligenda potius tanquam expeditissima quaedam itineris comes ad felicitatem. Nam quo minus occupati impeditique fuerimus auro et argento, eo facilior nobis futurus sit aditus et

163 ad virtutem et ad Deum. Tibi autem, Leonarde, habemus gratias maximas. Non enim solum pro me loquor, sed pro omnibus viris optimatibus, qui nulla mutabilitate fortunae amiciciae munus deserueris. Verum quoniam te Florentiae esse malumus quam exulem, cave, obsecro, ne istiusmodi tuum erga nos vel gratitudinis vel humanitatis officium sit tibi quicquam vel detrimenti vel molestiae allaturum.

164 *Leonardus.* At nihil est, Pallas, quod minus metuam quam me vobiscum, viris optimis et clarissimis, exulem fore, et id non modo quod sapiens ubiubi est, vel in patria est vel liber, quam

sake of which"¹²¹ (for they say there is a cause "for the sake of which" something either is or comes to be), we say that this is responsible. For example, I should say that I fear for my country's freedom because the sound citizens are being expelled from the city. We will not therefore reckon them to be men of deliberation who have set themselves no goal as a point of reference.

Now let us return to the point from which we digressed not long ago. Since action or inaction is what is in our power, if someone has done something or not because of that very thing and not through oversight, the agent must be thought to have acted, or not acted, voluntarily; and since we do many such things without thought or premeditation, it necessarily follows that any act based upon choice is voluntary, but what is voluntary is by no means an act based upon choice. All things that are according to choice are voluntary, but not all voluntary things are according to choice. I think it is sufficiently clear that choice is not simply will or opinion but something that consists of opinion and appetency together when, after consultation, both agree on a single goal. It remains not only that we need not fear poverty but that we should choose it as the least encumbering of companions for the journey to happiness. For the less occupied and hindered we are by gold and silver, the easier will be our access to virtue and to God. We thank you very warmly, Leonardo — indeed, I speak not only for myself but for all the nobles, since in no vicissitude of fortune have you abandoned the duty of friendship. But since we prefer for you to be at Florence rather than an exile, please be on guard lest your duty of gratitude or humanity toward us bring you some harm or trouble.

Leonardo. But there is nothing, Palla, that I fear less than becoming an exile along with you, the best and most distinguished gentlemen. That is not only because wherever a wise man is, he

161

162

163

164

ut orationis gladios in nefarrios quosdam patriae parricidas liberius distringam, quod quandiu sic sum Florentiae, facere non licet: ita omnia pressa video teterrimo iugo servitutis. Qua quidem ipsa de re quia te cras dicturum accipio, cum primum illuxerit, ad vos ibo.

is both in his homeland and free, but also that I might draw the sword of eloquence more openly against certain wicked assassins of their homeland, something I may not do for as long as I remain in Florence — so thoroughly oppressed are we by the dreaded yoke of slavery. Since I understand that you are going to speak on this very point tomorrow, I shall come to you at dawn.

Note on the Text

꒜꒜꒜

Francesco Filelfo's *Commentationes Florentinae de Exilio* has never been printed in its entirety. The only portions previously available in print are a few pages from the first book and a quarter of the third book, selections published over sixty years ago in anthologies edited by Eugenio Garin. Lengthy quotations have also appeared in articles by Aristide Calderini and Gian Mario Cao.*

The text of these selections was taken from a manuscript that is preserved in the Biblioteca Nazionale Centrale in Florence, MS II. II. 70 (F), a carefully produced fifteenth century codex that for a long time had been considered a Filelfo autograph, but which is actually in the hand of Pagano da Rho, a regular copyist for Filelfo, although it does contain some autograph corrections and additions in Filelfo's own hand. All in all, the text has been transmitted in eight manuscripts:

F   Florence, Biblioteca Nazionale Centrale, II. II. 70 (15th
          century)
N   Florence, Biblioteca Nazionale Centrale, II. II. 268 (19th
          century)

---

* Garin, *Cristoforo Landino e Francesco Filelfo*, 43–47, contains the paragraphs 1.8–14 and 1.185b–194. *Prosatori latini del Quattrocento*, also by Garin, 493–517, has a transcription and Italian translation of 3.1–22, 31b–49. Calderini, "Cultura greca di Francesco Filelfo," 204–424, quotes throughout passages that were translated from Greek sources. Cao, "Prehistory of Modern Scepticism," 229–79, has (265–77) paragraphs 3.226–31, 2.95–106, 111–112 and 3.14.23–26, 28–30, 46, facing the Greek quotations from Sextus Empiricus that Filelfo is relying upon in those pages. For a full discussion of the transmission history and an assessment of the relationship between the manuscripts, see De Keyser, "Francesco Filelfo's *Commentationes Florentinae de Exilio*," 7–29.

A	Paris, Bibliothèque de l'Arsenal, 741 (15th century)
P	Paris, Bibliothèque nationale de France, lat. 13040 (16th century)
S	Seville, Biblioteca Capitular y Colombina, MS 5-6-18 (15th century)
O	Vatican City, Biblioteca Apostolica Vaticana, Ottob. lat. 1665 (15th century; books 2-3 only)
V	Vatican City, Biblioteca Apostolica Vaticana, Vat. lat. 3370 (16th century; books 2-3 only)
L	Vatican City, Biblioteca Apostolica Vaticana, Vat. lat. 5913 (15th century)

Of these manuscripts, only L, F, and A are philologically relevant, as O, P, and S have been copied from A, and V from O, while N is a late apograph of F. The hitherto unstudied A is a perfect twin of F: not only is A in the same hand as F—thus adding another item to the long list of manuscripts copied by Pagano da Rho for Filelfo—but it also presents exactly the same textual *facies* and an analogous material appearance, with the same authorized marginal *notabilia*, additions, corrections, and integrations as F. Incidentally, A is also the only codex, with F, to display the totality of the Greek terms in both text and marginalia, and likewise has them in Filelfo's own hand. L, then, is our only witness to the primitive text, that is, a text untouched by Filelfo's editorial intervention as reflected in A and F. However corrupt, L systematically displays the original readings that have sometimes become illegible in A and F after Filelfo's multiple adjustments.

The text in this edition is that of Filelfo's second redaction, that is the text stage α_2 as it emerges from the consensus of A and F, which overall are very sound—and at any rate authoritative, as they contemporarily were commissioned and then corrected by the author, probably as late as the 1460s. It appears that Filelfo kept F,

which apparently generated no offspring during his lifetime, in his private library and sent out *A* to his friends to be read and copied. When the twins diverge, the tie is broken by taking into account *L*, which also is mentioned in the *apparatus criticus* whenever a new reading has been introduced instead of the original one in the original redaction (α_1), for which *L* is our only witness. Apart from these altered readings, where all three *testimonia* have been reported, the apparatus is negative: the mention of a particular error in one of the manuscripts implies therefore that the other two have the correct reading as it is printed in the text. For the reader's convenience, the apparatus also indicates all *loci* where the present text diverges from the edition of the first quarter of Book 3 by Garin.

For the sake of readability, punctuation and capitalization have been modernized, and *u* and *v* have been distinguished, but apart from these generalized interventions, the spelling of the text is the one Filelfo himself advocated. He had indeed very specific, albeit evolving views (which incidentally helps us in dating his manuscripts), and meticulously oversaw the production of the manuscripts containing his writings. Where he deemed it necessary, he did not refrain from micromanaging his copyists and systematically corrected even minor deviations to make the text match his practices. Therefore the twin manuscripts on which this edition is based together offer us a snapshot of Filelfo's orthographic views at a certain point in his career, including the hypercorrect use of aspiration, diphthongs, and doubled consonants, and particular views about word splitting. Hence the sometimes disorienting orthography — from a normalizing, classicizing viewpoint — of, for instance, *fraetus, loetum, oscoene, vaehementer* and *vaendere, dimminuere, nefarrius* and *relligio, flama* and *solertia, consyderare* and *desyderium, iandiu, suiipsius, tibiipsi, veruntamen, honus* (for *onus*), *dehorsum* and *sehorsum*, and even *aesta* (for *exta*).

435

ABBREVIATIONS

ac = ante correctionem	before correction
add. = addidit/addiderunt	text added in one or more manuscripts
codd. = codices	the reading of all manuscripts
exp. = expunxit/expunxerunt	text expunged in one or more manuscripts
expl. = explicit	text ending in this manuscript
mg. = in margine	marginal addition
om. = omittit/omittunt	text missing in one of more manuscripts
pc = post correctionem	after correction
ras = in rasura	text written over an erased original reading
s.l. = supra lineam	interlinear addition
scripsi	the editor's emendation, against the text as transmitted by all manuscripts

Notes to the Text

✼✧✼

1. cognoscerent] nossent L noscerent F^{ac} A^{ac}

2. agnosces] recognosces L F A^{ac}

3. perinde] proinde F^{ras} perinde L A^{pc}

4. continentiam libido] *scripsi* continentia libidinem *codd.*

5. innocentiam avaricia] *scripsi* innocentia avariciam *codd.*

6. perinde] proinde F^{pc} perinde L A^{pc}

7. ac] atque L F A^{ac}

8. imperitaque] inexpertaque L imperitaque F^{ras} A^{ras}

9. itaque] proinde L A itaque F^{ras}

10. novit] noscit L noscens A^{ac} novit F^{ras} A^{ras}

11. secutus] peregit L secutus F^{ras} A^{ras}

12. abundantioris] abundantiores L -is F^{ras} A^{ras}

13. priusque] priusquam L A^{ac}

14. etiam peius] deterius L etiam peius F^{ras} A^{ras}

15. sui] *om.* F

16. a] ac A

17. spuere] *scripsi* [πτύειν *Dio Chrysostomus* 13.24] nubere *codd.*

18. et] *om.* F

19. communem] omnem F

20. perinde] proinde F^{pc} perinde L A^{pc}

21. consueverunt] consuevere L F^{ac} A^{ac}

22. perfectionem] imperfectionem L F^{ac}

23. perinde] proinde F^{pc} perinde L A^{pc}

24. cognosce] nosce L cognosce F^{ras} A^{ras}

25. quare etiam] proinque *L* quare etiam *F^{ras} A^{ras}*

26. habere] se habere *L F^{ac} A^{ac}*

27. humana in mente] humanae menti *L F^{ac} A^{ac}* -a in *F^{ras} A^{ras}*

28. ratiocinatione utens] ratiocinationis indigens *L F A^{ac}*

29. oratio] ratio *A*

30. existimantur] existimabantur *F*

31. etiam te] etiam *L A* etiam te *F^{ras}*

32. itaque] proinde *L* itaque *F^{ras} A^{ras}*

33. durius] deterius *L* durius *F^{ras} A^{ras}*

34. cognosceret] nosceret *L F^{ac} A^{ac}*

35. ullam] illam *A*

36. idem] id *A*

37. propterea] proinde *L* -pterea *F^{ras} A^{ras}*

38. ignorabit] ignorabat *A*

39. paraxida] paraxidem *L* -a *F^{ras} A^{ras}*

40. paraxida] paraxidem *L* -a *F^{ras} A^{ras}*

41. habendae] retinende *L* habedae *A*

42. existimabat] eximabat *F*

43. pientissime] piissime *L F^{ac} A^{ac}*

44. Aemylius] Haemylius *A^{pc}*

45. interficiendo] interficiundo *A*

46. exurrexit] exurgit *L* -rexit *A^{ras} F^{ras}*

47. nova] nova *L om. F add. mg. A^{pc}*

48. et] *om. A*

49. interpolabo] interpellabo *L A^{pc}* interpollabo *A^{ac}* interpolabo *F^{ras}*

50. interpoles] interpelles *L A^{ac}* interpolles *A^{pc}* interpoles *F^{ras}*

51. fidenter] fideliter *L A^{ac}* fidenter *F A^{pc}*

52. quiddam] quidam *L F^{ac}*

53. vellent] vellet A

54. atque] ac L atque F^{ras} A^{ras}

55. quod ex te ipso facile diiudices] *om.* L *add. mg.* F^{pc} A^{pc}

56. Cyclopa] Cyclopem L -a F^{ras} A^{ras}

57. Cyclopa] Cyclopem L -a F^{ras} A^{ras}

58. nonne perpetua epularum illecebra] *om.* L *add. mg.* A^{pc}

59. ducunt] dicunt L F^{ac} A^{ac}

60. Thomyridos] Tomirydis L Thomyridis F^{ac} A^{ac} -dos F^{ras} A^{ras}

61. vel] *om.* L *add.* F^{pc} A^{pc}

62. mercatore] negotiatore L mercatore F^{ras} A^{ras}

63. Thesea] Theseum L -a F^{ras} A^{ras}

64. et] e A

65. tanquam] *om.* L *add. s. l.* F^{pc} *add. mg.* A^{pc}

66. Lampsacenum] Lapsacenum L Lampsaceum A

67. multumque diuque pererrans et mentes] varias iactatus in oras et mores L multumque diuque pererrans et mentes F^{ras} A^{ras}

68. mercator] negotiator L mercator F^{ras} A^{ras}

69. Insubrium ac] *om.* L *add. mg.* F^{pc} A^{pc}

70. Agamemnona] Agamemnonem L -a F^{ras} A^{ras}

71. Volscis] Volsis A

72. imbecilliorisque] imbecillioresque L A^{ac}

73. decere] dicere A

74. Melampoda] Melampodem L -a F^{ras} A^{ras}

75. mercator] negotiator L mercator F^{ras} A^{ras}

76. et] vel A

77. ultroneum] voluntarium L ultroneum F^{ras} A^{ras}

78. pro libera voluntate] pro voluntate A F^{ras} libera *add. s. l.* F^{pc} *add. mg.* A^{pc} Non enim . . . contingant *om.* L

BOOK TWO

1. proinde] perinde L F^{ac} A^{ac} pro- F^{ras} A^{ras}

2. ferant] ferunt L F^{ac} A^{ac}

3. imbecilliore] imbecilliores F

4. pientissimaque] piissimaque L F^{ac} A^{ac}

5. maiestas] maiestas L F^{pc} magestas A

6. Pallas] *om.* F

7. affert] afferet F^{pc}

8. interpolator] interpellator L F^{ac} A

9. maiestas] magestas L maiestas F^{ras} A^{ras}

10. turpius] flagitiosius L turpius F^{ras} A^{ras}

11. flagitiosius] turpius L flagitiosius F^{ras} A^{ras}

12. superque] superque satis L F^{ac} A^{ac} satis *exp.* F^{pc} A^{pc}

13. partum] paratum A

14. censuerint] consuerint L censueverint F^{ac} A censuerint F^{pc}

15. duxerint] ducerent L duxerint F^{ras} A^{ras}

16. temptarit] tentarit L A temptarit F^{ras}

17. omni] *om.* L oî F^{ras}

18. perinde] proinde F^{ras} A^{ac} perinde L A^{pc}

19. fere] *om.* L *add. s. l.* F^{pc} A^{pc}

20. a Germanis] *om.* L *add. s. l.* F^{pc} *add. mg.* A^{pc}

21. Hyagnin] Hyagnim L A -n F^{ras}

22. aut] *om.* A

23. Nicolae] *om.* F

24. ducuntur] dicuntur L A

25. modo morbus quispiam aut membrorum] siquidem quis morbus aut L modo morbus quispiam aut membrorum F^{ras} A^{ras}

26. offensiove] aut cecitas L offensiove F^{ras} A^{ras}

27. maiestatis] magestatis A^{ac} F^{ac} maiestatis L A^{ras} F^{ras}

28. imperitantem rationis vim repraesentans quomodo] rationis incipatum constituens qui se L imperitantem rationis vim repraesentans quomodo F^{ras} A^{ras}

29. modis] om. L add. s. l. F^{pc} add. mg. A^{pc}

30. ista] ipsa L ista F^{ras} A

31. perinde] proinde L F^{ras} perinde A^{ras}

32. ut] atque L F ut A^{ras}

33. cognoscere] noscere L cognoscere F^{pc} A^{pc}

34. uti] veluti L uti F^{ras} A^{ras}

35. antequam] priusquam L antequam F^{ras} A^{ras}

36. obstricta] obnoxia L obstricta F^{ras} A^{ras}

37. esse possit] om. L add. mg. F^{pc} add. mg. et ras. A^{pc}

38. nonnunquam etiam tum potestatem tum virtutem] om. L add. mg. F^{pc} A^{pc}

39. generatione] creatione L generatione F^{ras} A^{ras}

40. inde fit ut] proinde L inde fit ut F^{ras} A^{ras}

41. sit] est L sit F^{ras} A^{ras}

42. ut ita loquar] om. L add. mg. F^{pc} A^{pc}

43. igitur] proinde L igitur F^{ras} A^{ras}

44. siquidam] siquidem L siquidam F^{pc} A^{pc}

45. demus] om. L add. s. l. F^{pc} A^{pc}

46. licet] tametsi L licet F^{ras} A^{ras}

47. in] om. F

48. ipso] ipsa A

49. etiam] et F

50. quod] addidi, om. codd.

51. boni] bona L boni F^{ras} A^{ras}

52. illius] illi L illius F^{pc} A^{pc}

53. id] et id *F*

54. haud] non *L* haud F^{ras} A^{ras}

55. igitur] proinde *L* igitur F^{ras} A^{ras}

56. esse] *om. L add. mg.* F^{pc} A^{pc}

57. sicuti] veluti *L* sicuti F^{ras} A^{ras}

58. obtusiores] obscuriores *L* F^{ac} obtusiores F^{ras} *A*

59. proptereaque] proindeque *L* proptereaque F^{ras} A^{ras}

60. ista] ita *A*

61. ratiocinatione utens] ratiocinationis indigens *L F* ratiocinatione utens A^{pc}

62. inferius] intentus *L* inferius F^{pc} interius *A*

63. ut] et *L* ut *F* A^{ras}

64. ventus] *om. L add. mg.* F^{pc}

65. ancillulam] ancilluluam *A*

66. pientissimum] piissimum *L* pientissimum F^{ras} A^{ras}

67. praesertim] praesertimque *L* F^{ac} A^{ac}

BOOK THREE

1. sis] sit *Garin*

2. Aemylium] Emilium *L* Aemilyum F^{ac} Aemylium F^{pc} A^{ac} Haemylium A^{pc}

3. atque] ac *Garin*

4. universi] universis *Garin*

5. etiam] et *Garin*

6. virtutem] virtutes *Garin*

7. simul] *om. Garin*

8. quare eo] quia vero *Garin*

9. vituperaras] vituperas *Garin*

10. mala] *scripsi* [κακοῦ *Sextus* 11.12] bona *codd.*

11. diiungit] disiungit *L F^{ac}* diungit *F^{pc} A^{ac}* diiungit *A^{pc}*

12. tuum] tum *A*

13. recta mihi] mihi recta *L F A^{ac}* recta mihi *A^{pc}*

14. nec] neque *Garin*

15. at] *scripsi* ac *codd.*

16. gustus] gustum *Garin*

17. de te] te de te *Garin*

18. atque] et *Garin*

19. quodammodo] *om. Garin*

20. turpissimae] turpissima *Garin*

21. eius] *om. Garin*

22. habet] haec *Garin*

23. sapientis] sapienti *Garin*

24. patriam] primam *Garin*

25. Thyestae] Thyestis *Garin*

26. quos] quod *Garin*

27. est] etiam *Garin*

28. necessarias] necessaria *Garin*

29. voluptarias] voluptuarias *L F^{ac} Garin*

30. locutum] locutus *Garin*

31. ingenuis quibusquam] ingenius quibusdam *Garin*

32. qui] cui *Garin*

33. fraudare] fraudari *L F^{ac} A*

34. quid] quod *Garin*

35. hominibus] omnibus *Garin*

36. iis] his *L* usui *Garin*

37. cuiquam] cuique *Garin*

38. ipsa] voluptas *L* ipsa *F*^*ras* *A*^*ras*

39. et] *om. A Garin*

40. gnarus] gravis *L* gnarus *F*^*pc* *A*

41. audeas] ausis *L* -deas *F*^*ras* *A*^*ras*

42. proinde] perinde *L* proinde *F*^*ras* *A*^*ras*

43. Lesbonacta] Lesbonactem *L* -a *F*^*ras* *A*^*ras*

44. Lacedaemona] Lacedaemonem *L* -a *F*^*ras* *A*^*ras*

45. convenientem] communem *F*

46. locum] ordinem *L* locum *F*^*ras* *A*^*ras*

47. subdit] subit *A*

48. definiri] finiri *L* definiri *F*^*pc* *A*^*pc*

49. Nausicaham] Nausicam *A*^*ac* Nausicham *A*^*pc*

50. Phaeacas] Pheaces *L* -as *F*^*ras* *A*^*ras*

51. Phaeacas] Pheaces *L* -as *F*^*ras* *A*^*ras*

52. nummosus] nummatus *L* -osus *F*^*ras* *A*^*ras*

53. sicuti certe est] *om. L add. mg. F*^*pc* *A*^*pc*

54. ubi non Lazarus mendicus sed dives sepultus est] *om. L add. mg.* *F*^*pc* *A*^*pc*

55. mundi] *om. L add. s. l. F*^*pc* *A*^*pc*

56. ille ingratus] *om. L add. mg. F*^*pc* *A*^*pc*

57. Videmus enim non nullos qui scientiae paupertatis nomen atque studium profitentur in cute cum intus sint rapacissimi quidam lupi] *om. L add. mg. F*^*pc* *A*^*pc*

58. divitiae in se] in se divitiae *F*

59. se] sese *A*

60. Nam philosophia quidem] utpote quod philosophia *L* nam philosophia quidem *F*^*ras* *A*^*ras*

61. non invite] voluntaris L non invite F^{ras} A^{ras}

62. optimo] optimum A^{pc}

63. faveat] foveat L F^{ac} A^{ac}

64. omnis] omnes F^{pc} A^{pc}

65. appellemus] appellamus A^{pc}

66. pro] *om. L add. s. l.* F^{pc} A^{pc}

67. oportet] oportet boni ut simus L boni ut simus *exp.* F^{pc} A^{pc}

68. vel] an L vel F^{ras} A^{ras}

69. immobilibus] mobilibus L immobilibus F^{ras} A^{ras}

70. causam] subiectum L causam F^{ras} A^{ras}

71. quam] quod L quam F^{pc} A^{pc}

72. principium] principiis F^{pc}

73. mutetur] mutatur L mutetur F^{pc} A^{pc}

74. mutatur] mutetur L mutatur F^{pc} A^{pc}

75. causa] in causa A^{pc}

76. tris] tres L F^{ac} A^{ac}

77. perinde] utpote quod L proinde F^{pc} perinde A^{pc}

78. id] id est A^{pc}

79. est] sit L est F^{ras} A^{ras}

80. videtur] videatur F^{ac} A^{ac}

81. quoniam] utpote quod L quoniam F^{ras} A^{ras}

82. atque] at L F^{ac} A^{ac}

83. nam spontaneum idem esse quod ultroneum Latinus et litteratus dubitat nemo] *om. L add. mg.* F^{pc} A^{pc}

84. ante] ante F^{ras} A^{ras} (quandoquidem . . . dicendum *om. L*)

85. quod a] quod L quod a F^{ras} A^{ras}

86. Poggi] tu Poggi L F^{ac} A^{ac}

87. eloquenter] *expl. L*

88. Casentino] mon<te> *ante* Casentino *exp.* F^{pc} Casentino F^{ras} A^{ras}

89. alia caena] caena alia F

90. effinxit] finxit F

91. Menalippi] Menelappi A

92. se] sese A

Notes to the Translation

ᚱᛟᚦᛟᚱ

BOOK ONE

1. Plutarch, *Moralia* 176d.

2. Filippo Maria Visconti is styled *Anglus* in the Latin text because of the Visconti claim to be descended from the pseudo-Vergilian hero Anglus, supposedly the grandson of Aeneas; the name is also connected with the Visconti's title as counts of Angleria or Anghera, granted to Giangaleazzo Visconti in 1397.

3. See the Introduction for the original plan of the work in ten books.

4. Filelfo alludes to the Stoic distinction between absolute goods which must be done and *commoda*, or things advantageous, where one may choose.

5. The Florentine magistracy had sentenced Cosimo to exile in September 1433, along with seven other members of his family; in early October Cosimo went first to Padua and then to Venice before his triumphant return to Florence in early September 1434.

6. Giovanni Vitelleschi, one of the famous (or notorious) warrior-prelates of the Renaissance, was made bishop of Macerata and Recanati in 1431, archbishop of Florence and patriarch of Alexandria in 1435, and a cardinal in 1437. Early in his papacy Eugenius IV made Vitelleschi, who had had a military education, commander of the papal armies, in which capacity he became widely hated for his cruelty, ambition, and corrupt practices. Eugenius eventually imprisoned him for conspiracy in the Castel Sant'Angelo in 1440. Filelfo's allusions to his titles and fall from power are thus anachronistic, assuming that the conversations in the dialogue are meant to have taken place in November 1434.

7. For Filelfo's *Oration to the Exiles against Cosimo de' Medici,* see the Introduction.

8. Eugenius IV was lodged in the Dominican convent of Santa Maria Novella during his sojourn in Florence.

9. Plato, *Apology* 21; Diogenes Laertius 2.32.

10. Vergil, *Aeneid* 1.209.

11. Hesiod, *Works and Days* 293–97.

12. This passage (to the end of §33) translates from the Greek text of Dio Chrysostom, 13.16–26.

13. An apparent reference to Naucratis, a city turned over by the pharaohs to Greek traders.

14. A reference to Thyestes, who, by seducing the wife of his brother Atreus, was able to obtain the golden ram, symbol of the kingship of Argos. Atreus, pretending to be reconciled, invited him to a feast at which he served the flesh of Thyestes' own sons; the saga forms the basis of Seneca's extant *Thyestes* (quoted in Book 3, 40).

15. Homer, *Iliad* 2.594–600.

16. I.e., the Persians despised the Greeks for their customs of exercising naked in gymnasiums and spitting in public to ward off the evil eye, spells, or diseases.

17. Aristotle, *Nicomachean Ethics* 1.13, 1102a

18. Aristotle, *Metaphysics* 1022b15.

19. Andronicus of Rhodes, *On the Passions* 1.1.

20. Cicero, *Tusculan Disputations* 4.11.

21. Diogenes Laertius 1.79.

22. Here and in the following paragraphs, Filelfo draws on various Augustinian sources, especially *On the Trinity* books 12 and 13.

23. 1 Corinthians 12:8.

24. Job 28:28.

25. 1 Corinthians 13:12.

26. *Sic* for "Scopas."

27. Plato, *Republic* 511a–e.

28. Euripides, *The Phoenician Women* 357–407 (cf. Plutarch, *Moralia* 605f, 606d–f).

29. Ibid. 442.

30. Vergil, *Aeneid* 1.384–85 and 378–79, respectively.

31. A Peripatetic philosopher, Phormio delivered at Ephesus a lengthy lecture on the duties of a commander and on military affairs in general; the audience included Hannibal, who pronounced the lecturer insane. Cf. Cicero, *On Oratory* 2.75–76.

32. Filelfo draws on a variety of sources for these anecdotes: Aulus Gellius 5.5; Plutarch, *Moralia* 606c; Cicero, *On Divination* 2.52; and Valerius Maximus 3.7 ext. 6.

33. Plato, *Gorgias* 470d–e.

34. Livy 8.21.2–4. Livy does not identify the man from Privernum by name.

35. The sources for the preceding anecdotes, beginning with Diogenes' remark to Philip: Plutarch, *Moralia* 70c–d; Plutarch, *Moralia* 606b; Cicero, *Tusculan Disputations* 5.117, 1.102; and Valerius Maximus 6.2 ext. 3.

36. Plutarch, *Life of Numa* 8.6. Her name is the Latin word for "silent."

37. Valerius Maximus 7.2 ext. 6.

38. [Diogenes], *Letters* 1.

39. Plutarch, *Life of Phocion* 8.3.

40. Suetonius, *Life of Julius Caesar* 49–52.

41. Plutarch, *Life of Phocion* 8.3.

42. Psalms 5:6.

43. Psalms 62:12 (= 63.11).

44. Plutarch, *Moralia* 221c.

45. Aristotle, *Eudemian Ethics* 1219b40.

46. [Diogenes], *Letters* 13.

47. Ibid. 26.

48. Plutarch, *Moralia* 604d.

49. [Diogenes], *Letters* 23.

50. Ibid. 24. Hephaestion was a Macedonian general in the army of Alexander the Great, and rumored to be his lover.

51. Pindar, *Pythian Odes* 2.56–57, where the rarity is, however, at most implied by the predicate "best" (*ariston*).

52. Sappho, fr. 148 Lobel-Page.

53. Matthew 19:21.

54. [Diogenes], *Letters* 16.

55. Plutarch, *Life of Alexander* 14.4.

56. Ibid. 14.5; Plutarch, *Moralia* 605e; Diogenes Laertius 6.32; Cicero, *Tusculan Disputations* 5.92.

57. Homer, *Odyssey* 13.434–38.

58. [Diogenes], *Letters* 7.

59. [Apollonius], *Letters* 48.

60. Ibid. 35.

61. Comic fr. 108–10 Ribbeck², quoted by Aulus Gellius 7.8.5.

62. From Aulus Gellius 4.18.3–12; cf. Valerius Maximus 3.7.1.

63. Callimachus, *Hymns* 1.95–96.

64. Juvenal, *Satires* 3.164–65.

65. Plutarch, *Moralia* 197f.

66. Elsewhere philosophy receives this description; cf. Plato, *Timaeus* 47b ~ Cicero, *Timaeus* 52; Cicero, *On the Laws* 1.58.

67. Valerius Maximus 6.2.3; Plutarch, *Moralia* 201f; Livy 38.55.10–12; Aulus Gellius 4.18.7–12 (Gellius names the tribunes the Petilii; Filelfo combines a gentile name and a praenomen, evidently a misunderstanding). For Socrates see Plato's *Apology*, a work that had been translated by Leonardo Bruni in the 1420s.

68. Cicero, *Letters to Brutus* 25.1 and 11, for this and the previous quotation.

69. Diogenes Laertius 2.79.

70. The reference is to the defeat of Veii and Camillus' successful argument against sending a Roman colony there (Livy 5.19–22 and 51–55).

71. Filelfo appears to confuse P. Clodius, whose legislation prompted Cicero to depart into voluntary exile, with L. Sergius Catilina, whose "conspiracy" Cicero combated as consul; it was the execution of five conspirators without a trial before the people presided over by Cicero on December 5, 63, that gave Clodius a weapon against the former consul. The image of Italy carrying Cicero back from exile on her shoulders comes from *After His Return in the Senate* 39.

72. Livy, *Periochae* 77; Valerius Maximus 2.10.6; Plutarch, *Marius* 39.2; Appian, *Civil War* 1.273–74.

73. Livy, *Periochae* 77 and 80.

74. Plutarch, *Moralia* 175c.

75. Xenophon, *Education of Cyrus* 1.2.8 (a work translated a few decades later by Filelfo).

76. Cicero, *Tusculan Disputations* 5.98; Plutarch, *Life of Lycurgus* 12.7 (where the disappointed monarch is a king of Pontus) and *Moralia* 236f. The same anecdote below at 3.88, where Dionysius and the Persian king are both said to have disapproved.

77. Plutarch, *Moralia* 997e. The point is that according to the doctrine of reincarnation or metempsychosis the soul of a deceased relative could inhabit an animal that might be killed and eaten.

78. "Bambalio" is a Latin nickname, meaning "stammerer." Filelfo borrowed it from Antony's father-in-law, Marcus Fulvius (Cicero, *Philippics* 3.16).

79. Horace, *Epistles* 1.19.6 and 1.19.7–8.

80. Juvenal, *Satires* 1.49–50.

81. Plutarch, *Moralia* 180b.

82. Ennius from an uncertain tragedy (verse 221 Jocelyn) cited by Cicero, *On Duties* 3.62.

83. Hesiod, *Works and Days* 763–64.

84. Vergil, *Aeneid* 4.175.

85. Terence, *Eunuch* 732.

86. Pyrrho of Elis (ca. 365–275 BCE) was the founder of Greek Skepticism; but it was the early Stoics, and still more the Cynics, who were best known for challenging convention.

87. Xenophon, *Constitution of Sparta* 2.5 (a work translated in 1430 by Filelfo).

88. Plutarch, *Moralia* 995b–c.

89. Terence, *Eunuch* 727–29.

90. Homer, *Odyssey* 21.295–302; 9.347–536.

91. Niccolò Niccoli was a copyist and collector of manuscripts and an associate of Cosimo de' Medici and his circle of intellectuals, which included Poggio Bracciolini and Carlo Marsuppini. Though Niccoli attended his lectures, Filelfo developed a strong dislike for the man during his residence in Florence; he allots him no fewer than five pejorative nicknames in his *Satires.*

92. In 1397 Coluccio Salutati, who was then Chancellor of the city, invited Manuel Chrysoloras (1355–1415) to teach Greek in Florence. Filelfo's first wife was Theodora Chrysoloras. At 3.129 he calls her the *neptis* of Manuel, which in the Renaissance can refer to either a granddaughter or a grandniece; the scholarly consensus holds that her father John Chrysoloras, Filelfo's tutor in Greek during his stay in Constantinople, was Manuel's nephew. It is unclear whether Filelfo ever met Manuel, whose memory was revered in Florence for his services to the revival of Greek learning (cf. 3.133).

93. Vergil, *Aeneid* 1.738.

94. Homer, *Iliad* 6.264–65.

95. Horace, *Epistles* 1.19.1–3.

96. Ibid. 1.5.16–20.

97. Juvenal, 1.49–50 (quoted in §143).

98. Plutarch, *Life of Marius* 45.3.

99. A Latin expression meaning "never" (as Greek calendars had no Calends): Suetonius, *Augustus* 87.1.

100. Genesis 4:3–12; Filelfo is confused: Cain's crime was killing his brother, not eating the first fruits.

101. The allusions are to Job 1:13–15; Genesis 25:29–34; 1 Samuel 14:24–46; Numbers 11:4–10; 1 Samuel 2:12–16; 1 Samuel 15:9–35; Genesis 18:20–19.26.

102. Filelfo seems to have in mind the contest between Elijah and the prophets of Baal on Mt. Carmel culminating in the death of the latter: 1 Kings 18:21–40.

103. Genesis 9:20–22; Genesis 19:30–38 (Filelfo confuses Ham and Shem); Luke 16:19–23.

104. An Assyrian monarch, who, on the basis of his alleged epitaph, was for ancient moralists a byword for hedonism. Cf. Aristotle, *Nicomachean Ethics* 1095b19–22; *Eudemian Ethics* 1216a16–19; Cicero, *Tusculan Disputations* 5.101; *On Ends* 2.106.

105. Herodotus 1.211.2.

106. Filelfo appears to have misremembered Herodotus 7.203–38: Leonidas' successes at Thermopylae were due to the narrowness of the pass, which denied the Persians the advantage of their numbers, not their laxity.

107. Filelfo is thinking of Clitus, whom Alexander murdered at a feast. See Seneca, *On Anger* 3.17.1 and 23.1; Plutarch, *Moralia* 458b.

108. Capua's corruption of the Carthaginian invaders: Cicero, *On the Agrarian Law* 2.95; Livy 23.18. The "final massacre" was the Battle of Zama (202).

109. Judith 13:1–10; Judges 4:17–21; Genesis 37:25–30; Matthew 14:1–12 ~ Mark 6:14–29.

110. John 6:27.

111. Plutarch, *Moralia* 87a, 467d, 603d.

112. Vergil, *Aeneid* 7.192–273. According to one version of the legend, when he immigrated to Troy from Samothrace, Dardanus, a son of Zeus, was given part of the kingdom and the hand of his daughter by King Teucer.

113. Filelfo offers a variant of the proverbial phrase "Fortune helps the brave": Livy 8.29.6 and 34.37.5; Pliny, *Letters* 6.16.1.

114. Unidentified tragic fr. 392, quoted by Plutarch, *Moralia* 600f.

115. Cicero, *Tusculan Disputations* 5.108.

116. Cicero, *On the Laws* 1.23.

117. Vergil, *Aeneid* 1.374.

118. Filelfo quotes Plato, *Timaeus* 90a via Plutarch, *Moralia* 600f and includes the latter's exegesis.

119. Ovid, *Metamorphoses* 1.84–86.

120. Isidore of Seville, *Etymologies* 11.1.34.

121. A saying of Bias quoted by Cicero, *Paradoxes of the Stoics* 1.1.8; Valerius Maximus 7.2 ext. 3.

122. This description is usually reserved for the tyrant. Cf. Cicero, *On the Commonwealth* 2.48; *On Duties* 3.32 and 82.

123. Cicero, *Tusculan Disputations* 1.104.

124. Apparently Filelfo's mistake for Eresus.

125. He was actually from Tarsus, though he had lived in Athens prior to his move to Babylon.

126. Plutarch, *Moralia* 603b–c.

127. This (i.e., *Lysios*) is the reading of Plutarch's manuscripts (see next note); editors correct to *Assios* ("of Assos"), his correct ethnicity.

128. The foregoing list of philosophers is mostly based on Plutarch, *Moralia* 605a–b.

129. Homer, *Odyssey* 9.27–28, 1.57–59, and 1–3 respectively.

130. Aristophanes, *Wealth* 1151.

131. Like other scholars of his time, Filelfo does not distinguish the philosopher from the tragic poet.

132. Appian, *Civil War* 2.7, says that the designation (later a regular imperial title) was bestowed on Cicero, on Cato's motion, by vote or accla-

mation of the people; Cicero himself merely claims that it was applied to him by Catulus and/or other senators (*Letters to Atticus* 9.10.3; *Against Piso* 6).

133. Nothing is known of this man.

134. Sophocles, *Ajax* 1252–54.

135. *Medix* (or *meddix*) was the title for mayors or chief magistrates in ancient Oscan cities; the word is attested a number of times in Livy. Humanists in the service of the Medici were accustomed to referring to them as *Cosmus Medices* or *Laurentius Medices* so as to remove the association with the less honorable profession of medicine. The crime of the Medici, the shameful "craft" (*ars*) they engaged in, is presumably usury. It may be noted that the Medici family had been active in the political life of Florence as early as the late thirteenth century; the family held extensive possessions in the Mugello region north of Florence. Filelfo here attempts to portray them as recent arrivals from the countryside, which is certainly a rhetorical distortion, and to suggest their "common" ancestry from physicians (see below, Book Two, n. 18).

136. Cicero, *On Duties* 1.65.

137. Plato, *Apology* 32c–d.

138. Diogenes Laertius 2.35.

139. The following argument (§226–231) derives from Sextus Empiricus, *Against the Professors* 11.43 and 190–94. See the articles by G. M. Cao for an analysis of Filelfo's use of Sextus.

140. Aristotle, *Nicomachean Ethics* 1130a1–2.

141. See Christopher Jones, ed., trans., *The Life of Apollonius of Tyana Books 1–4* (London, 2005), 13–17.

142. Diodorus Siculus, 1.96.1–2.

143. Varro, *On the Latin Language* 5.87; cf. Cicero, *Tusculan Disputations* 2.37.

144. Terence, *Self-Tormentor* 805–6.

145. Livy 1.16; Plutarch, *Life of Romulus* 27.6.

146. As this book closes, Filelfo reminds the reader of the text that formed the basis of the discussion, Polynices' speech about exile from *The Phoenician Women* of Euripides quoted in §57–58 above.

BOOK TWO

1. Plutarch, *Life of Pericles* 31.4.

2. Aeschylus, *Seven Against Thebes* 592; Cicero, *On Duties* 1.65.

3. Filelfo (surely consciously) adapts the cult title of Capitoline Jupiter; cf. also §50 and 3.69.

4. This is the thesis of Cicero, *On Duties* 3.

5. The aristocratic party that opposed Cosimo de' Medici had been traditionally supporters of the Guelf party, and Guelf regimes had dominated Florentine politics for most of the previous century. The papacy was closely identified with the Guelf party, so Rinaldo implies that in siding with Cosimo and the so-called "popular" party in Florence, Eugenius has abandoned his traditional supporters.

6. Gerardo Landriani, Bishop of Lodi from 1419 to 1437, eventually became Bishop of Como in 1437 and later advanced to cardinal in 1439. It is unclear precisely what role he had as an intermediary between Filippo Maria Visconti and the Florentine oligarchs. Landriani corresponded with Leonardo Bruni and in 1421 discovered hitherto unknown works of Cicero at Lodi.

7. A naturally gifted orator, Demades became a leading figure in the pro-Macedonian party, and hence an opponent of Demosthenes, after Athens' defeat at Chaeronea (338); he always spoke extemporaneously (Plutarch, *Demosthenes* 8.7, 10.1) and published no speeches. A pseudonymous speech supposedly by him circulated widely during the Renaissance in what purported to be a Latin translation by Leonardo Bruni.

8. The point was illustrated by the anecdote according to which Demosthenes assigned first, second, and third place to delivery among the factors contributing to success in oratory: Cicero, *Brutus* 142; *Orator* 56; [Plutarch], *Moralia* 845b.

9. The thought comes from Cicero, *On Duties* 3.83.

10. Basic Stoic doctrine, argued for in detail by "Cato" in Cicero, *On Ends* 3.

11. Euripides, *Phoenician Women* 524–25, quoted by Cicero, *On Duties* 3.82.

12. "Endowed with foresight . . . good counsel": a citation of Cicero, *On the Laws* 1.22.

13. C. Verres governed Sicily from 73 to 71 BCE; upon his return to Rome he was prosecuted by Cicero for corrupt administration and went into voluntary exile before the trial was over. M. Licinius Crassus ("the triumvir") is excoriated by Cicero for corruption at *On Duties* 3.73 and in the sixth of the *Paradoxes of the Stoics* ("that only the wise man is wealthy").

14. King Ladislaus of Naples (1376–1414) inherited the kingdom of Naples from his parents, Margaret of Durazzo and Charles III, at the age of nine in 1386 and became titular king of Hungary and Dalmatia in 1390. Successful campaigns in the first decade of the fifteenth century yielded him control of much of central Italy, including the Papal States. His rapid rise moved the republics of Siena and Florence to form an alliance against him. When in 1413 he turned his ambitions north of the Papal States, Florence forestalled war by signing a peace treaty. He died in 1414.

15. See n. 3 above.

16. As a *condottiere* for Florence, Niccolò da Tolentino suffered a major defeat fighting, alongside papal troops supplied by Venice, against Milanese forces at Imola in 1434. He died the following year in Milanese captivity of wounds received in the battle.

17. Vergil, *Aeneid* 4.174–77.

18. *Medici* also means "physicians," a pun; similarly §62.

19. Felice Brancacci was a silk merchant whose marriage in 1431 to Palla Strozzi's daughter Maddalena led to his appointment to major public mandates by the Florentine government. He was instrumental in developing maritime commerce for the city, which kept galleys in the port of Pisa, then part of Florentine territory. Brancacci was among those driven into exile in 1434.

20. Lorenzo de' Medici was Cosimo's brother; the "Averardo" mentioned here was a cousin and close political ally of Cosimo. Cosimo's grandfather, Averardo "detto Bicci" de' Medici, had two sons, Francesco and Giovanni (Cosimo's father). Francesco's son Averardo ran a banking business in partnership with Cosimo's banking establishments and was among the city's wealthier citizens.

21. The names mentioned here of Medici opponents were all among the exiles of 1434; see Dale Kent, *The Rise of the Medici: Faction in Florence, 1426–1434*, Appendix II (Oxford, 1978), 355–57.

22. Physicians: *medici*, a pun on the name.

23. The anecdote is from Dio Chrysostom 1.1–3. Timotheus of Miletus (ca. 450–360 BCE) was a dithyrambic poet; for Hyagnis as the first to play the flute, his son Marsyas, and Olympus as third in the sequence, cf. Plutarch, *Moralia* 1132f.

24. Vergil, *Aeneid* 5.362–484, a boxing match, to which Dares challenges all comers. Entellus at first refuses to fight the younger man but finally relents and, after giving his opponent a relentless pounding, receives the victor's prize from Aeneas.

25. Plutarch, *Moralia* 241a and 242a–b (where it is a son, rather than a brother, who died in battle).

26. Gorgias of Leontini (ca. 485–ca. 380 BCE) was a leading sophist best known for antitheses, assonances, rhymes, etc. ("Gorgianic figures"); it is another sophist, Hippias of Elis, who is associated with the claim to be able to hold forth on any topic.

27. Spartans forbade any talk from their common meals to be repeated in public: Plutarch, *Moralia* 236f, 697e, 714b.

28. Pindar, *Olympian Odes* 7.10.

29. Homer, *Iliad* 7.91; *Odyssey* 9.20; Odysseus is the "wisest man" (*sapientissimus vir*) without ethnic qualifier at Cicero, *On the Orator* 1.196 and *On the Laws* 2.3.

30. Euripides, *Orestes* 1162.

31. For the distinction see Cicero, *On Duties* 1.8 and 3.14–15.

32. Cf. Priscian, *Grammar* 1.13–14 (= p. 11.19–21 Keil).

33. Vergil *Aeneid* 4.188.

34. *facinus*, derived from *facio* ("do"), was originally a term for any deed, whether good or bad, but soon became specialized in the sense "crime."

35. Pyrgopolynices, the antihero of Plautus' *Braggart Soldier*; Terence, *Eunuch*.

36. A citation of the opening of Aristotle's *Metaphysics*.

37. Aristotle, *Rhetoric* 1367b28.

38. Aristotle, *Eudemian Ethics* 1218b35–36.

39. Ibid. 1219b17–18; *Nicomachean Ethics* 1102b6–7.

40. Plato, *Laws* 631c.

41. *Orphic Argonautica* 1–3.

42. Sophocles, *Electra* 989.

43. The next several paragraphs (§95–106) are translated from Sextus Empiricus, *Against the Professors* 11.22–38.

44. Under "compound" Filelfo may have in mind the (probably second-century BCE) philosophers Callipho and Dinomachus, who held that pleasure and moral goodness together constituted the highest good: Cicero, *Lucullus* 131; *On Ends* 2.19, 34–35, and 5.21; *Tusculan Disputations* 5.85; *On Duties* 3.119.

45. Two of Poggio's prose treatises, *On Nobility* and *On the Unhappiness of Princes* (both from 1440), are presented here anachronistically as having already been written.

46. Poggio plays on "to grant to each his own" (*suum cuique tribuere*), a quasiproverbial definition of justice; cf. Cicero, *On Duties* 1.15.

47. Beginning with this sentence the discussion of the human good (§118–123) is based on Albertus Magnus, *Commentary on the Nicomachean Ethics*, 1.2.7, for which see Jörn Müller's edition cited in the bibliography.

48. Aristotle, *On the Soul* 412b18.

49. Plato does not say this in so many words, but the point is implied at *Republic* 517c, where the Idea of the Good is said to be the cause of all

that is right and beautiful; Filelfo is holding the concept of "participation" in reserve for §137ff.

50. In §127–150 Filelfo is paraphrasing and sometimes nearly quoting Albertus Magnus, *Commentary on the Nicomachean Ethics*, 1.2.1–3; §151–54 are more loosely inspired by Albertus, at 1.2.4ff.

51. Augustine, *On Christian Doctrine* 1.75.

52. The first sentence of §144 merely rephrases the last one of §143. Apparently Filelfo was considering two versions of Albertus' *Cum ergo bonum sit in multis non penitus aequivoce existens in illis, necesse est quod sit in uno primo, quod omnium causa sit aliorum in bono* (Müller, 354) but forgot to delete one of the alternatives; or the former version may have been a first draft of the latter.

53. Augustine, *Diverse Questions* 46.2.

54. Cf. 1.53.

55. Psalms 36:9; this paragraph is indebted to [Augustine], *On Spirit and Soul*.

56. Fr. 363 Skutsch, quoted by Cicero, *On Old Age* 10; *On Duties* 1.84, etc.

57. Cicero, *On the Nature of the Gods* 3.25; Isidore, *Differences* 1.421.

58. Cf. §95.

59. Augustine, *City of God* 2.26.5.

60. 2 Corinthians 8:21; 1 Corinthians 10:33; and Philippians 4:8–9. Filelfo may be relying here on Augustine, *On the Good of Widowhood* 27, where the same sources are quoted.

61. Filelfo appears to have in mind Hosea 12:1: "Ephraim feeds on wind and follows after the east wind; he daily increases lies and desolation."

62. Filelfo follows the version of Diodorus 16.93.4–94.6, according to which Pausanias was a lover of King Philip but lost the king's favor to another young man, also named Pausanias. An alternative version at Justin 9.6.4–7.14 makes Pausanias the tool of a group of conspirators against the king.

63. Valerius Maximus 8.14 ext. 4 and 5.

64. Cicero, *Tusculan Disputations* 1.109.

65. Plato, *Republic* 329e–30a; cf. Cicero, *On Old Age* 8, and Plutarch, *Life of Themistocles* 18.3.

66. A reference to the early organization of the Roman army: the *triarii* ("reserves") were the third line of the maniple; the *succenturiatus* ("replacement") was a man called in to fill a vacancy in a *centuria* (a military unit with a notional strength of one hundred soldiers).

67. Cicero, *On Duties* 2.43.

68. Matthew 5:12.

69. Aeschylus, *Seven Against Thebes* 592–94.

70. Here and elsewhere in his writings, Filelfo refers to the so-called Stufa di San Michele Berteldi, a brothel in Florence where Marsuppini, Niccoli, and Poggio allegedly met. See Fiaschi, *Satyrae*, 404 for further references.

BOOK THREE

1. Herodotus describes the rising power of the Lydian kingdom under Croesus (1.26–28), then reports a conversation in which Solon cautions the king that no one should be considered happy until the end of his life (ibid. 29–32).

2. The precept was inscribed at the entrance to Apollo's temple at Delphi; cf. Plato, *Alcibiades* 1 129a and *Charmides* 164d–165a; Cicero, *On the Laws* 1.58, *Tusculan Disputations* 5.70, *On Ends* 5.41; Plutarch, *Moralia* 408e, etc.

3. Similar argument at 2.69.

4. Here Filelfo apparently refers to a brothel in Florence nicknamed the "Medici Monastery." In his *Oration to the Exiles* (Milan, Biblioteca Ambrosiana MS V 10 sup., ff. 24v–25r), he claimed that the Medici family acquired this property in Florence after poisoning its owner, but there is no reason to believe this slanderous charge.

5. Crantor (ca. 335–275 BCE) was an early Academic philosopher and pupil of Xenocrates; the appearance of the various personified goods at a pan-Hellenic assembly was a thought experiment, as Filelfo's source, Sextus Empiricus, *Against the Professors* 11.51–53, makes clear.

6. Aristotle, *Metaphysics*, 981b17–25.

7. That Bruni possessed so large a fortune seems unlikely. He declared an estate valued at 11,800 florins in his tax returns of 1427, and though Florentines notoriously hid their wealth for tax purposes, it would be difficult for a public official to understate his wealth by 80 percent. However, according to the 1427 Catasto, Bruni's net capital left him ranked seventy-second among Florentine fortunes — wealthy by any standard. See Lauro Martines, *The Social World of the Florentine Humanists* (Princeton, 1963), 117–23.

8. An allusion to Cicero, *On the Orator* 2.18.

9. Paragraphs 23 (beginning with "For they say that . . .") through 26 translate from Sextus Empiricus, *Against the Professors* 11.3–17 (with the substitution of the Turks for the Indians). The aside about the translation of *onta* in 23 reflects Bruni's views about literary translation, discussed at length in his treatise *De recta interpretatione*.

10. = fr. 14, p. 80 Iordan, cited by Seneca, *Controversies* 1 pref. 9 and Quintilian, *Education of the Orator* 12.1.1.

11. Boethius, *On Division* (ed. Magee) p. 6 r. 17–26.

12. Leonardo's speech (§29–30) is translated from Sextus Empiricus, *Against the Professors* 11.17–20.

13. A stade (*stadion*) is a Greek measure of distance equivalent to 606 3/4 feet.

14. Timon of Phlius (ca. 320–230 BCE) was a Skeptic and follower of Pyrrho; our verses = *Supplementum Hellenisticum* fr. 842.

15. Juvenal, *Satires* 8.20.

16. Ibid. 8.21–23, 24–26.

17. Seneca, *Thyestes* 923–24; on the form of the name see Book 1 n. 14 above.

18. Sycharbas is an alternative name for the figure known from Vergil as Sychaeus (see n. 42 below); in ancient sources Elissa is an alternative name for Dido (Filelfo uses the names side by side in a letter as well). Demaratus of Corinth settled in the Etruscan town of Tarquinii after the overthrow of Bacchiad rule in his native city (ca. 657 BCE); he was the father of Tarquinius Priscus, founder of the Tarquin dynasty at Rome.

19. Cf. §14 above.

20. Homer, *Odyssey* 14.156–57.

21. Pliny, *Natural History* 18.11; Isidore, *Etymologies* 10.155.

22. On the title "father of his country" (*pater patriae*), see Book 1 n. 132 above.

23. Livy 1.34–35.

24. The anecdote about Crantor (see n. 5 above) is translated from Sextus Empiricus, *Against the Professors* 11.51–58 (Filelfo ignores, however, that in the end it was Courage that took home the first prize).

25. [Diogenes], *Letters* 9.

26. Diogenes Laertius, *Lives of the Philosophers* 9.36.

27. Plutarch, *Moralia* 181e.

28. Aristotle, *Politics* 1259a5–23.

29. [Diogenes], *Letters* 10.

30. Ibid. 11: "priests" renders *Galli*, a reference to the priests of Cybele who underwent self-castration; "effeminates" (*molles*) is Filelfo's euphemistic translation of *kinaidologoi* ("those who speak or write obscene things").

31. For Cyrus' accessibility cf., e.g., Xenophon, *Education of Cyrus* 7.5.46; ibid., 8.7.13 he declares that faithful friends are a monarch's "golden scepter." A strain of ancient theory held that it is better to have few, rather than many friends: Aristotle, *Nicomachean Ethics* 1170b20 ff.; cf. Cicero, *On Friendship* 45.

32. [Crates], *Letters* 2.

33. Filelfo has inferred these relationships from the spurious "letters of Phalaris." The collection includes letters to Epicharmus (61, 98), Stesi-

chorus (78, 92, 94, 104, 145–47), and Pythagoras (23), as well as the tyrant's invitation to Abaris and the latter's insulting refusal (56–57).

34. "Sprinkling poison and brandishing a dagger" comes from the description of Catiline's followers at Cicero, *Catilinarians* 2.23.

35. The phrasing comes from Cicero, *On Behalf of Flaccus* 54 ("by whose tongue the assembly of impoverished men then held was fanned by the fan of sedition").

36. Diogenes Laertius, *Lives of the Philosophers* 2.70.

37. Ibid. 2.69.

38. Baldassare Cossa, Pope John XXIII, who held office from 1410 to 1415 during the Great Schism, was later ruled by the Council of Constance (1414–1418) to have been an antipope. After being convicted of an assortment of crimes at that council, he fled to Germany; returning to Italy in 1418, he died the following year in Florence.

39. Homer, *Odyssey* 6.188–89.

40. Cf. §14; Soderini did not pronounce on the matter, though his fear of poverty and belief that it is an evil might be taken as an endorsement of the view.

41. Thucydides, *Histories* 1.11.1.

42. The brother-in-law of Sycharbas/Sychaeus (see n. 18), Pygmalion, murdered him for his wealth (Vergil, *Aeneid* 1.343–52). Herodotus 1.23–24 narrates how when the wealthy singer Arion of Methymna (ca. 600 BCE) went on a voyage, the sailors plotted to kill him for his treasure; he jumped overboard but was saved by a dolphin.

43. Diogenes Laertius, *Lives of the Philosophers* 2.77.

44. Horace, *Odes* 3.16.9–16. The "Argive augur" is Amphiaraus, whose wife, Eriphyle, received a necklace from Polynices in exchange for persuading her husband to participate in the (ill-fated) expedition against Thebes. "The Macedonian" refers to Philip II, whose bribery undermined the Greek resistance to the Macedonian advance. The reference to "fierce admirals" has been thought to refer to events contemporary with Horace, but the details elude us.

45. Vergil, *Aeneid* 3.56–57.

46. Juvenal, *Satires* 10.22.

47. Cf. §43.

48. Cf. §45.

49. [Apollonius of Tyana], *Letters* 22.

50. Cf. §43.

51. Juvenal, *Satires* 1.74.

52. Ovid, *Ars Amatoria* 2.279–80.

53. [Apollonius of Tyana], *Letters* 62.

54. Ibid. 63.

55. Diogenes Laertius, *Lives of the Philosophers* 2.73.

56. Plutarch, *Moralia* 149a, 191f, 219e.

57. Juvenal, *Satires* 5.99–103.

58. [Crates], *Letters* 14.

59. Ibid. 13.

60. Basil, *Letters* 26.

61. Cicero, *Tusculan Disputations* 5.97; there is a similar story at Plutarch, *Artaxerxes* 12.3.

62. Ibid.

63. Plutarch, *Life of Alexander* 22.7–9.

64. Plutarch, *Moralia* 174a (if named after "friendship" the meals would have been called *philia*). Artaxerxes II Mnemon or Memor ("the Mindful") reigned over Persia from 404 to his death in 359/8 BCE.

65. Cf. the note at 1.140.

66. Euripides, *Hecuba* 375–78a.

67. Literally "giving grass" (*herbam dare*) in token of surrender.

68. Euripides, *Hecuba* 378b.

69. Euripides, *The Phoenician Women* 439.

70. Aulus Gellius 11.2.2 is the source both of the quotation (= Cato, fr. 1, p. 82 Iordan) and of the distinction of two senses of "elegant" (*elegans*).

71. Homer, *Odyssey* 6.

72. Cicero, *Familiar Letters* 7.16.3.

73. Luke 16:9 and 11.

74. Dio Chrysostom 6 is an extended comparison of Diogenes with the king of Persia; here this point is implied but not stated in so many words.

75. Matthew 5:3.

76. Luke 16:19–31.

77. 1 Timothy 6:17.

78. Filelfo means to refer to Paul; cf. 2 Corinthians 6:10.

79. Cf. §39.

80. [Apollonius of Tyana], *Letters* 112.

81. Cf. Cicero, *On Duties* 1.46.

82. Another dig at Poggio's gourmandizing, Palla pretending that Poggio is horrified at the prospect that the time allotted to talk and dining may be equalized (and dining thus receive short shrift).

83. The last third of Book 3, from §107 to 163, is mostly an amalgam of Aristotle's *Eudemian Ethics* with the *Magna Moralia* attributed to Aristotle. The *Eudemian Ethics* was a text new to Latin Christendom, having been brought to the West by Giovanni Aurispa around 1424. Filelfo also adds some appropriate Latin examples. The following footnotes point to the major sources.

84. §107–11 = [Aristotle], *Magna Moralia* 1186b33–1187a34.

85. Manetti was the author of a *Life of Socrates*, completed around 1440.

86. The so-called Socratic paradox that no one commits wrong voluntarily; cf. Plato, *Gorgias* 460b–c and 509e5–7; *Protagoras* 345e.

87. §111–13 = Aristotle, *Eudemian Ethics* 1222b15–37.

88. §114a (through "of generating action?") = [Aristotle], *Magna Moralia* 1187b4–7.

89. §114b–19 = Aristotle, *Eudemian Ethics* 1223a4–b10.

90. §120 = [Aristotle], *Magna Moralia* 1188a13–22.

91. §121–22 = Aristotle, *Eudemian Ethics* 1223b11–29.

92. A mistake in Filelfo's Greek source text: the sense demands "involuntary," not "voluntary."

93. Heraclitus, fr. 85 Diels-Kranz = Plutarch, *Life of Coriolanus* 22.2, and Aristotle, *Eudemian Ethics* 1223b23–24.

94. §123–25 = [Aristotle], *Magna Moralia* 1188a28–b24.

95. For example, by volcanic action and lightning. The passage refers to Aristotle's doctrine in physics, according to which everything in the cosmos has a natural place, and therefore moves naturally to that place; when it does not move naturally to its proper place, the motion is said to be violent.

96. See note on 2.174.

97. I.e., in the Florentine Signoria. Bruni was chancellor of the Signoria from 1427 to 1444, held office as one of the priors in 1443, and served three terms on the Ten of War from 1439 to 1441.

98. Philolaus, fr. 16 Diels-Kranz = Aristotle, *Eudemian Ethics* 1225a33.

99. For Filelfo's family connection to Manuel Chrysoloras, see note on 1.161.

100. Bruni and Palla Strozzi had both been students of Chrysoloras in 1397–1399.

101. Vergil, *Aeneid* 1.76–77 (Aeolus to Juno).

102. §135 = [Aristotle], *Magna Moralia* 1188b25–26 + *Eudemian Ethics* 1225b1–8.

103. Jerome, *Chronicle* under the year of Abraham 1918 = *Patrologia Latina* 27, 425–26.

104. §136 = [Aristotle], *Magna Moralia* 1188b29–38.

105. §137 = Aristotle, *Eudemian Ethics* 1225b8–16.

106. This is high praise coming from Manetti, who translated Aristotle's *Nicomachean* and *Eudemian Ethics* as well as the *Magna Moralia*.

107. Carlo Marsuppini was a Medici client and humanist with whom Filelfo clashed soon after his arrival in Florence. Marsuppini eventually succeeded Leonardo Bruni as Chancellor of Florence, a post he held from 1444 to 1453. Though praised by Medici partisans, Marsuppini failed to leave behind a substantial body of literary work.

108. A damning criticism, since according to rhetorical doctrine writing is the way to perfect one's style; cf. Cicero, *On the Orator* 1.150; Quintilian, *Education of the Orator* 10.3.

109. §145–47 = Aristotle, *Eudemian Ethics* 1225b21–37.

110. Cf. §117.

111. Tydeus was driven out of Aetolia because he accidentally killed a man; he was welcomed to Argos by King Adrastus. In Argos Tydeus also met another exile, Polynices of Thebes, and enrolled as one of the seven heroes aiming to restore him to the Theban throne. In the ensuing battle he is mortally wounded by Menalippus (also spelled Melanippus). Menalippus, however, also falls; one of the besiegers throws Menalippus' head to Tydeus, who, by eating his opponent's brains, forfeits the immortality that had previously been arranged for him. Cf. Statius, *Thebaid* 8.655 ff.

112. §148 = [Aristotle], *Magna Moralia* 1189a7–21.

113. Ganges-dwellers: the *Gangaridae* (or *Gandaridae*; substituted by Filelfo for the general reference to "Indians" in his source) were a people of eastern India first encountered in reports of Alexander's expedition; cf., e.g., Plutarch, *Alexander* 62.3.

114. This sentence = Aristotle, *Eudemian Ethics* 1225b36–37.

115. Ovid, *Metamorphoses* 7.20–21.

116. This chapter (through "we assert choice to be") = Aristotle, *Eudemian Ethics* 1226a6–17; it is somewhat repetitive of §148 because Filelfo is combining two different sources.

117. §154 through the first sentence of §162 (with the exception of parts of §156 and 158; see below) = Aristotle, *Eudemian Ethics* 1226a20–1227a5.

118. The Hyperboreans (substituted by Filelfo for Aristotle's example, the Indians) were a mythic race of Apollo worshippers located in the far north.

119. This sentence through the end of §156 = [Aristotle], *Magna Moralia* 1189b18–25, although Filelfo substitutes "Cicero" for "Archicles" in his source.

120. For this argument through "the place of the matter," cf. Aristotle, *On the Movement of Animals* 700b15–23.

121. I.e., a final cause; one of Aristotle's four causes, the others being material, efficient, and formal.

Bibliography

Adam, Rudolf Georg. "Francesco Filelfo at the Court of Milan (1439–1481): A Contribution to the Study of Humanism in Northern Italy." PhD diss., Oxford University, 1974.

Avesani, R., G. Billanovich, M. Ferrari, and G. Pozzi, eds. *Filelfo nel quinto centenario della morte. Atti del XVII Convegno di Studi Maceratesi (Tolentino, 27–30 settembre 1981)*. Medioevo e umanesimo 58. Padua: Antenore, 1986.

Blanchard, W. Scott. "Patrician Sages and the Humanist Cynic: Francesco Filelfo and the Ethics of World Citizenship." *Renaissance Quarterly* 60.4 (2007): 1107–69.

Calderini, Aristide. "Ricerche intorno alla biblioteca e alla cultura greca di Francesco Filelfo." *Studi italiani di filologia classica* 20 (1913): 204–424.

Cao, Gian Mario. "Tra politica fiorentina e filosofia ellenistica: il dibattito sulla ricchezza nelle *Commentationes* di Francesco Filelfo." *Archivio storico italiano* 45 (1997): 99–126 (extensive bibliography in n. 2).

——— . "The Prehistory of Modern Scepticism: Sextus Empiricus in Fifteenth-Century Italy." *Journal of the Warburg and Courtauld Institutes* 64 (2001): 229–79.

De Keyser, Jeroen. "The Transmission of Francesco Filelfo's *Commentationes Florentinae de Exilio*." *Interpres* 30 (2011): 7–29.

De Keyser, Jeroen, and David Speranzi. "Gli *Epistolographi Graeci* di Francesco Filelfo." *Byzantion* 81 (2011): 177–206.

Errera, Carlo. "Le *Commentationes Florentinae de exilio* di Francesco Filelfo." *Archivio storico italiano* 5.5 (1890): 193–227.

Ferraù, Giacomo. "Le *Commentationes Florentinae de exilio*." In Avesani et al., *Francesco Filelfo nel quinto centenario della morte*, 369–88.

Fiaschi, Silvia. "Deformazioni storiche e propaganda politica negli scritti antimedicei di Francesco Filelfo." In *Il principe e la storia, Atti del Con-*

vegno Scandiano, 18–20 Settembre 2003, Studi Boiardeschi 4, edited by Tina Mattarese and Cristina Montagnani, 415–37. Scandiano: Interlinea, 2005.

Field, Arthur. "Leonardo Bruni, Florentine Traitor?" *Renaissance Quarterly* 51.4 (1998): 1109–50.

Filelfo, Francesco. *Satyrae I (Decadi I–V)*. Edited by Silvia Fiaschi. Rome: Edizioni di Storia e Letteratura, 2005.

Garin, Eugenio. *Prosatori latini del Quattrocento*. Milan: Riccardo Ricciardi, 1952.

———. *Testi inediti e rari di Cristoforo Landino e Francesco Filelfo*. Florence: Fussi Editore, 1949.

Gionta, Daniela. "Per i *Convivia Mediolanensia* di Francesco Filelfo." *Quaderni di filologia medievale e umanistica* 11 (2005): 114–17.

Heitzmann, Christian. "'Non tam Florentia nobis quam nos Florentie desyderio futuri sumus': Exil und Verbannung aus der Sicht italienischer Humanisten." In *Exil, Fremdheit und Ausgrenzung in Mittelalter und früher Neuzeit, Identitäten und Alteritäten 4*, edited by A. Bihrer, S. Limbeck, P. G. Schmidt, 259–74. Würzburg: Ergon, 2000.

McClure, George W. *Sorrow and Consolation in Italian Humanism*. Princeton: Princeton University Press, 1991.

Müller Jörn. "Der Begriff des Guten im zweiten Ethikkommentar des Albertus Magnus: Untersuchung und Edition von *Ethica*, Buch I, Traktat 2." *Recherches de théologie et philosophie médiévales* 69.2 (2002): 318–70

Robin, Diana. *Filelfo in Milan: Writings, 1451–1477*. Princeton: Princeton University Press, 1991.

Rosmini, Carlo de'. *Vita di Francesco Filelfo da Tolentino*. 3 vols. Milan: Luigi Mussi, 1808.

Vasoli, Cesare. "Le *Commentationes de exilio* di Francesco Filelfo." In *Exil et civilisation en Italie (XIIème–XVIème siècles)*, edited by Jacques Heers and Christian Bec, 119–34. Nancy: Presses Universitaires de Nancy, 1990.

Viti, Paolo. "Filelfo, Francesco." In *Dizionario biografico degli italiani*, vol. 47, 613–26. Rome: Istituto dell'Enciclopedia italiana, 1997.

———. "Storia settecentesca di un manoscritto delle *Commentationes Florentinae* di Francesco Filelfo." In Avesani et al., *Francesco Filelfo nel quinto centenario della morte*, 551–75.

Index

Abaris, 353
Abraham, 157
Academics, 251, 321, 325, 333
Academy (Plato's), 149, 323
Achilles, 131
Ada (queen of Caria), 375
Adrastus (king), 133
Aeneas, 17, 47–49, 91, 133
Aeschylus, 153, 305; *Seven Against Thebes*, 456n2, 461n69
Africa, 99
Agamemnon, 23
Agesilaus, 355
Ahala, 177
Albertus Magnus, Saint, x; *Commentary on the Nicomachean Ethics*, 459n47, 460n50
Albizzi, Rinaldo degli, viii, x, xiv–xix, 3, 95–97, 107–9, 159–61, 179, 181, 185, 187–235, 271, 309, 315–37, 387, 403–5, 415
Alcman, 153
Alexander the Great, 69–71, 75, 107, 127, 229, 347, 367, 375
Amphiaraus, 305, 464n44
Anaxagoras, 147–49
Andronicus, 33; *On the Passions*, 448n19
Anghiari, x, xvi
Anglus, 447n2

Antias, Valerius, 83
Antiochus (king), 51–55, 57, 83, 89
Antipater, 149, 367
Antisthenes, 349, 373
Apelles, 37
Apollexis, 67, 75
Apollo, 309
Apollodorus, 37
Apollonius of Tyana, xii, xxii, 77–81, 171, 367, 369–71, 385
[Apollonius of Tyana], *Letters*, 450n59, 465n49, 465n53, 466n80
Appian, *Civil War*, 451n72, 454–55n132
Archedemus, 149
Archelaus (king of Macedonia), 27, 153, 367
Archguelfs, 221
Ardea, 99
Arezzo, xx–xxii
Arion, 363, 464n42
Aristides, 175, 305
Aristippus, 97, 357, 363, 367, 371
Aristo, 149
Aristophanes, 153; *Wealth*, 454n130
Aristotelianism, xiii, xix
Aristotle, 31, 35, 65, 69, 149, 241, 251, 263, 267, 277, 281, 319, 341,

Cicero, Marcus Tullius (*continued*)
  449n35, 450n56, 451n76,
  453n104, 454n115, 454n123,
  455n143, 459n44, 461n64,
  461n2, 465n61
Cimon, 175
Citium, 149
Clazomenae, 147–49
Cleanthes, 149, 153, 253
Clitomachus, 149
Clitus, 453n107
Clodius, P., 451n71
Cnidus, 27
Conon, 27
Constantinople, vii
Copas, 37
Corduba, 153
Coriolanus, 155, 177
Crantor, 319, 341, 343–45, 462n5
Crassus, Marcus, 209
Crassus, M. Licinius, 457n13
Crates, xii, xxii, 67, 147, 313, 347,
  351, 353, 355, 373–75
[Crates], *Letters*, 463n32, 465n58
Cratinus, 121
Critolaus, 149
Croesus (king), xx, 309, 461n1
Curtius Rufus, 456n7
Cyclops, 117
Cynics, xi–xii, xiii, 71, 452n86
Cyrenaics, 105
Cyrus (king of Persia), 127, 295
Cyrus the Elder, 353

Daedalus, 171
Damon, 131
Damonidas, 371–73

Daniel, 125
Dardanus, 133, 453n112
Darius, 375
della Luna, Francesco, 225
della Luna, Niccolò, 181, 193–95,
  227–29, 235–47, 269, 299, 309,
  379
Demades, 197, 456n7
Demaratus, 341, 343, 463n18
Demetrius, 149, 175, 367
Democritus, 171, 313, 347
Demosthenes, xii, 123, 229,
  456nn7–8
Dido, 341, 463n18
Dinomachus, 459n44
Dio Chrysostom, xiii, 448n12,
  458n23, 466n74
Diodorus Siculus, 455n142,
  460n62
Diogenes, xii, xxii, 59, 63, 65–71,
  75–77, 147, 149, 347, 349–53,
  367, 373, 381
[Diogenes], *Letters*, 449n38,
  449n46, 449n49, 450n54,
  450n58, 463n25, 463n29
Diogenes Laertius, 448n9, 448n21,
  450n56, 450n69, 455n138; *Lives
  of the Philosophers*, 463n26,
  464n36, 464n43, 465n55
Dionysius the Elder, 97, 103, 357,
  367, 371, 377
Dionysius the Younger, 3
Diotimus, 79

Egypt, 21, 171
Electra, 247
Empedocles, 103

Publication of this volume has been made possible by

The Myron and Sheila Gilmore Publication Fund at I Tatti
The Robert Lehman Endowment Fund
The Jean-François Malle Scholarly Programs and Publications Fund
The Andrew W. Mellon Scholarly Publications Fund
The Craig and Barbara Smyth Fund
for Scholarly Programs and Publications
The Lila Wallace–Reader's Digest Endowment Fund
The Malcolm Wiener Fund for Scholarly Programs and Publications